2018 SUPPLEMENT TO CASES AND MATERIALS ON

CONSTITUTIONAL LAW

THEMES FOR THE CONSTITUTION'S THIRD CENTURY

Fifth Edition

■ ■ ■

Daniel A. Farber
Sho Sato Professor of Law
University of California, Berkeley

William N. Eskridge Jr.
John A. Garver Professor of Jurisprudence
Yale Law School

Jane S. Schacter
William Nelson Cromwell Professor of Law
Stanford Law School

AMERICAN CASEBOOK SERIES®

WEST
ACADEMIC
PUBLISHING

TABLE OF CONTENTS

TABLE OF CASES

The principal cases are in bold type.

2018 SUPPLEMENT TO
CASES AND MATERIALS ON

CONSTITUTIONAL LAW

THEMES FOR THE CONSTITUTION'S THIRD CENTURY

Fifth Edition

CHAPTER 1

A PROLOGUE ON CONSTITUTIONAL HISTORY

■ ■ ■

SECTION 9. THE MILLENNIAL COURT

Page 64. Insert before the Appendix:

On February 13, 2016, Justice Scalia unexpectedly died during a trip to Texas. He was widely considered the most influential conservative on the Court, and his writings did much to shape constitutional debates on and off the Court. He wrote some important majority opinions, such as the first decision finding the Second Amendment to be a source of enforceable individual rights. But his influence was perhaps more often felt through his concurrences and dissents, along with his extra-judicial writings and speeches. More than most, Scalia's departure from the bench meant the loss of not only a vote, but also a provocative voice that was a flashpoint for both admirers and detractors. To a considerable degree, Scalia's pointed opinions framed the terms of constitutional debate, both on and off the Court.

President Obama nominated Merrick Garland, a widely respected judge on the D.C. Circuit, to replace Scalia. After the nomination was announced in mid-March, Senate Majority Leader Mitch McConnell announced that the Senate would not hold hearings on the nomination. Instead, he said, the Senate would allow the public to have input via the November election, postponing any action until a new President was in office. This left the Supreme Court with only eight Justices for almost all of its October 2016 Term. President Trump nominated Neil Gorsuch to fill the position. Gorsuch was confirmed by the Senate after a rule change to eliminate filibusters on Supreme Court nominees and allow confirmation on a simple majority vote.

Page 67. Add at the end of the last full paragraph:

On June 27, 2018, Justice Kennedy announced that he would retire as of July 31, thus providing President Trump with the opportunity to make his second appointment to the Court (after Neil Gorsuch). Because Kennedy was often the deciding vote in 5–4 cases, his replacement is expected to dramatically shift the Court's center of gravity to the right. On July 9,

President Trump announced the nomination of Brett Kavanaugh, a conservative judge on the D.C. Circuit. His appointment would probably leave Chief Justice Roberts as the swing voter among the five-Justice conservative majority.

Page 68.   Replace the first full paragraph with the following:

Antonin Scalia was, in some ways, a modern, conservative version of Hugo Black. Like Black, he believed in literalism, favored bright-line rules, and abhorred "balancing tests." He also shared Black's penchant for blunt, memorable prose but (very much unlike the genteel Black) tended to lob *ad hominem* barbs at his colleagues when he disagreed with them. Scalia was one of a group of prominent members of the University of Chicago Law School faculty to be appointed to the federal appellate courts. He was nominated along with Rehnquist's appointment to the Chief Justiceship; liberals made a strategic decision to let Scalia sail through while concentrating their fire on Rehnquist. Scalia was the first of Italian ancestry to serve on the Court. He was more interested in legal theory than most of his colleagues on the bench. He was a formidable dissenter, whose blunt and colorful prose was usually aimed over the heads of his colleagues and directed to Federalist Society law professors, bloggers, think tanks, and even political leaders.

Page 71.   Add at the end of the current text:

Neil Gorsuch was born in Denver but graduated from high school in Bethesda, Maryland. His mother briefly headed the Environmental Protection Agency under President Reagan. He graduated from Columbia and then Harvard Law School, before receiving a graduate degree at Oxford. He was a law clerk for Justices White and Kennedy before spending a decade as a litigator in private practice. He then served briefly in the Justice Department. In 2006, he was appointed to the Tenth Circuit. Shortly after President Trump took office, he nominated Gorsuch to fill the position vacated by Justice Scalia's unexpected death. Gorsuch was confirmed near the end of the Supreme Court's Term, but early indications are that he will be a staunch conservative vote.

CHAPTER 3

THE CONSTITUTION AND RACIAL DISCRIMINATION

■ ■ ■

Page 215.   Add before Section 1:

4.   *Race and the Criminal Justice System.* The Court emphasized the uniquely pernicious effects of race in the criminal justice system in two cases in which the defendants were not seeking relief based on the Equal Protection Clause at all. At a time when public questions about race and policing are especially salient, these decisions identify important ideas about racial bias and the legal system, though it remains to be seen whether they will have significance beyond their particular doctrinal contexts.

(a)   In *Pena-Rodriguez v. Colorado*, 137 S.Ct. 759 (2017), the Court ruled that allegations about racially biased statements by a juror during deliberations in a criminal case require an exception to Rule 606(b), which generally precludes impeachment of a jury verdict. The case involved a trial of a Hispanic defendant on charges of attempted sexual assault. After a guilty verdict had been returned, two jurors reported that one of their fellow jurors, H.C., had made a number of racially derogatory statements during deliberations. These included statements that "[H.C.] believed the defendant was guilty because, in [H.C.'s] experience as an ex-law enforcement officer, Mexican men had a bravado that caused them to believe they could do whatever they wanted with women;" that H.C thought the defendant "did it because he's Mexican and Mexican men take whatever they want;' " and that Juror H.C. said that he did not find petitioner's alibi witness credible because, among other things, the witness was " 'an illegal' " (although that witness had testified during trial that he was a legal resident of the United States.) Although the Court had twice before rejected proposed exceptions to the no-impeachment rule, Justice Kennedy, writing for a six-justice majority, said that racial animus was different than one-off irregularities because such bias is:

> a familiar and recurring evil that, if left unaddressed, would risk systemic injury to the administration of justice. This Court's decisions demonstrate that racial bias implicates unique historical, constitutional, and institutional concerns. An effort to address the most grave and serious statements of racial bias is not

an effort to perfect the jury but to ensure that our legal system remains capable of coming ever closer to the promise of equal treatment under the law that is so central to a functioning democracy. * * *

While this language resonates with core themes of the Equal Protection Clause, the case had been litigated under the Sixth Amendment and Kennedy grounded the holding in that Amendment:

> All forms of improper bias pose challenges to the trial process. But there is a sound basis to treat racial bias with added precaution. A constitutional rule that racial bias in the justice system must be addressed—including, in some instances, after the verdict has been entered—is necessary to prevent a systemic loss of confidence in jury verdicts, a confidence that is a central premise of the Sixth Amendment trial right.

Notwithstanding its doctrinal grounding in the Sixth Amendment, the opinion offers broader support for an aggressive judicial approach to racial bias in the criminal justice system:

> It must become the heritage of our Nation to rise above racial classifications that are so inconsistent with our commitment to the equal dignity of all persons. This imperative to purge racial prejudice from the administration of justice was given new force and direction by the ratification of the Civil War Amendments.
>
> "[T]he central purpose of the Fourteenth Amendment was to eliminate racial discrimination emanating from official sources in the States." In the years before and after the ratification of the Fourteenth Amendment, it became clear that racial discrimination in the jury system posed a particular threat both to the promise of the Amendment and to the integrity of the jury trial. "Almost immediately after the Civil War, the South began a practice that would continue for many decades: All-white juries punished black defendants particularly harshly, while simultaneously refusing to punish violence by whites, including Ku Klux Klan members, against blacks and Republicans." Forman, Juries and Race in the Nineteenth Century, 113 Yale L.J. 895, 909–910 (2004). * * * The stark and unapologetic nature of race-motivated outcomes challenged the American belief that "the jury was a bulwark of liberty," and prompted Congress to pass legislation to integrate the jury system and to bar persons from eligibility for jury service if they had conspired to deny the civil rights of African-Americans. Members of Congress stressed that the legislation was necessary to preserve the right to a fair trial and to guarantee the equal protection of the laws.

The duty to confront racial animus in the justice system is not the legislature's alone. Time and again, this Court has been called upon to enforce the Constitution's guarantee against state-sponsored racial discrimination in the jury system. Beginning in 1880, the Court interpreted the Fourteenth Amendment to prohibit the exclusion of jurors on the basis of race. *Strauder v. West Virginia.* The Court has repeatedly struck down laws and practices that systematically exclude racial minorities from juries. To guard against discrimination in jury selection, the Court has ruled that no litigant may exclude a prospective juror on the basis of race. In an effort to ensure that individuals who sit on juries are free of racial bias, the Court has held that the Constitution at times demands that defendants be permitted to ask questions about racial bias during *voir dire.* * * *

The Nation must continue to make strides to overcome race-based discrimination. The progress that has already been made underlies the Court's insistence that blatant racial prejudice is antithetical to the functioning of the jury system and must be confronted in egregious cases like this one despite the general bar of the no-impeachment rule. It is the mark of a maturing legal system that it seeks to understand and to implement the lessons of history. The Court now seeks to strengthen the broader principle that society can and must move forward by achieving the thoughtful, rational dialogue at the foundation of both the jury system and the free society that sustains our Constitution.

(b)   In *Buck v. Davis*, 137 S.Ct. 759 (2017), the Court ruled in favor of a defendant's claim of ineffective assistance of counsel, allowing the defendant to surmount procedural obstacles in pursuit of post-conviction relief. The Court found that the risk of racial bias in the case constituted an "extraordinary circumstance" warranting re-opening the judgment against him under Fed. R. Civ. P. 60(b)(6). In the underlying criminal case, a lawyer representing a black defendant in a capital case put on an expert witness at trial who testified that blacks were statistically more likely to commit crimes. In the relevant testimony in the sentencing phase at trial, the expert concluded that the defendant himself was not likely to be a future danger, but he testified about the portion of his report connecting criminality to race. In his opinion, the Chief Justice emphasized the singularity of race in the context of criminal justice, much as Justice Kennedy had in *Pena-Rodriguez*:

[The expert's] testimony appealed to a powerful racial stereotype—that of black men as "violence prone." In combination with the substance of the jury's inquiry, this created something of a perfect storm. Dr. Quijano's opinion coincided precisely with a particularly noxious strain of racial prejudice, which itself coincided precisely with the central question at sentencing. The effect of this unusual confluence of factors was to provide support for making a decision on life or death on the basis of race.

This effect was heightened due to the source of the testimony. Dr. Quijano took the stand as a medical expert bearing the court's imprimatur. The jury learned at the outset of his testimony that he held a doctorate in clinical psychology, had conducted evaluations in some 70 capital murder cases, and had been appointed by the trial judge (at public expense) to evaluate Buck. Reasonable jurors might well have valued his opinion concerning the central question before them.

For these reasons, we cannot accept the District Court's conclusion that "the introduction of any mention of race" during the penalty phase was *"de minimis."* * * * There were only "two references to race in Dr. Quijano's testimony"—one during direct examination, the other on cross. But when a jury hears expert testimony that expressly makes a defendant's race directly pertinent on the question of life or death, the impact of that evidence cannot be measured simply by how much air time it received at trial or how many pages it occupies in the record. Some toxins can be deadly in small doses. * * *

"Discrimination on the basis of race, odious in all aspects, is especially pernicious in the administration of justice." Relying on race to impose a criminal sanction "poisons public confidence" in the judicial process. It thus injures not just the defendant, but "the law as an institution, . . . the community at large, and . . . the democratic ideal reflected in the processes of our courts."

SECTION 3. THE AFFIRMATIVE ACTION CONTROVERSY: BENIGN RACIAL CLASSIFICATIONS OR REVERSE DISCRIMINATION?

B. THE EVOLUTION OF THE MODERN CASE LAW, 1980–1995

Page 314.   Add before Section C:

In a high profile case involving the meaning of a major federal statute, the Court in *Texas Department of Housing Community Affairs v. Inclusive Communities Project, Inc.,* ___ U.S. ___, 135 S.Ct. 2507 (2015) ruled that plaintiffs have a claim for disparate impact under the Fair Housing Act.

Writing for a 5-member majority, Justice Kennedy reached the result as a matter of statutory interpretation. At several points in the opinion, however, he alluded to the need to narrow disparate impact liability under the Act because of lurking constitutional concerns of the kind flagged in *Ricci*. He noted, for example, that "disparate-impact liability has always been properly limited in key respects that avoid the serious constitutional questions that might arise under the FHA, for instance, if such liability were imposed based solely on a showing of a statistical disparity."

C. REVISITING THE DIVERSITY RATIONALE AND ADMISSION TO STATE UNIVERSITY PROFESSIONAL SCHOOLS

Page 332.   Delete Note 4 and insert the following material at the end of Section 3.C:

In 1996, the Fifth Circuit ruled in *Hopwood v. Texas*, 78 F.3d 932 (5th Cir. 1986) that the University of Texas at Austin's use of race in admissions was unconstitutional. In the wake of *Hopwood*, the University stopped considering race. The state legislature later adopted the Top Ten Percent Law, granting automatic admission to students in the top 10% of their class at a Texas high school. A few years later, the Supreme Court decided *Grutter* and *Gratz*. After those decisions, the University developed a plan to supplement the racial diversity produced by the percentage plan with a policy inspired by the approach upheld in *Grutter*. Abigail Fisher, a white student, applied for admission to the class entering the University of Texas in 2008. She was denied, and then challenged the University's admission policy as violating the equal protection clause. Most of those admitted to the University when Fisher was rejected were in the top 10% of their high school class and admitted on that basis alone. The University admitted the remainder of its class through a holistic set of factors that included race. Fisher was not in the top 10% of her class and did not challenge that aspect of the Texas policy. She argued that the use of race in admitting the remainder of the class was unconstitutional. Citing *Grutter*, the District Court and Fifth Circuit upheld the policy. In 2013, by a 7–1 vote (with Justice Kagan recused and only Justice Ginsburg dissenting), the Supreme Court decided *Fisher I*, holding that the circuit court had misapplied strict scrutiny by deferring excessively to the University. On the narrow-tailoring prong of strict scrutiny, the Court wrote, "the University receives no deference." It remanded, emphasizing that a court should not accept "a school's assertion that its admission process uses race in a permissible way without a court giving close analysis to the evidence of how the process works in practice." After the remand and further proceedings, the Fifth Circuit again upheld the University's policy. The case came back to the

Supreme Court as *Fisher II*, the next case. *Fisher II* was decided by a vote of 4–3. Justice Kagan was again recused. Justice Scalia participated in oral argument in *Fisher II*, but died before the case was decided.

FISHER V. UNIVERSITY OF TEXAS AT AUSTIN
___ U.S. ___, 136 S.Ct. 2198, 195 L.Ed.2d 511 (2016)

JUSTICE KENNEDY delivered the opinion of the Court.

In the wake of *Grutter,* the University embarked upon a year-long study seeking to ascertain whether its admissions policy was allowing it to provide "the educational benefits of a diverse student body . . . to all of the University's undergraduate students." The University concluded that its admissions policy was not providing these benefits. * * *

Although the University's new admissions policy was a direct result of *Grutter,* it is not identical to the policy this Court approved in that case. Instead, consistent with the State's legislative directive, the University continues to fill a significant majority of its class through the Top Ten Percent Plan (or Plan). Today, up to 75 percent of the places in the freshman class are filled through the Plan. As a practical matter, this 75 percent cap, which has now been fixed by statute, means that, while the Plan continues to be referenced as a "Top Ten Percent Plan," a student actually needs to finish in the top seven or eight percent of his or her class in order to be admitted under this category.

The University did adopt an approach similar to the one in *Grutter* for the remaining 25 percent or so of the incoming class. This portion of the class continues to be admitted based on a combination of their [Academic Index, which combines test scores and high school performance and Personal Achievement Index] scores. Now, however, race is given weight as a subfactor within the PAI. The PAI is a number from 1 to 6 (6 is the best) that is based on two primary components. The first component is the average score a reader gives the applicant on two required essays. The second component is a full-file review that results in another 1-to-6 score, the "Personal Achievement Score" or PAS. The PAS is determined by a separate reader, who (1) rereads the applicant's required essays, (2) reviews any supplemental information the applicant submits (letters of recommendation, resumes, an additional optional essay, writing samples, artwork, etc.), and (3) evaluates the applicant's potential contributions to the University's student body based on the applicant's leadership experience, extracurricular activities, awards/honors, community service, and other "special circumstances."

"Special circumstances" include the socioeconomic status of the applicant's family, the socioeconomic status of the applicant's school, the applicant's family responsibilities, whether the applicant lives in a single-parent home, the applicant's SAT score in relation to the average SAT score at the applicant's school, the language spoken at the applicant's home, and, finally, the applicant's race.

Both the essay readers and the full-file readers who assign applicants their PAI undergo extensive training to ensure that they are scoring applicants consistently. The Admissions Office also undertakes regular "reliability analyses" to "measure the frequency of readers scoring within one point of each other." Both the intensive training and the reliability analyses aim to ensure that similarly situated applicants are being treated identically regardless of which admissions officer reads the file.

Once the essay and full-file readers have calculated each applicant's AI and PAI scores, admissions officers from each school within the University set a cutoff PAI/AI score combination for admission, and then admit all of the applicants who are above that cutoff point. In setting the cutoff, those admissions officers only know how many applicants received a given PAI/AI score combination. They do not know what factors went into calculating those applicants' scores. The admissions officers who make the final decision as to whether a particular applicant will be admitted make that decision without knowing the applicant's race. Race enters the admissions process, then, at one stage and one stage only—the calculation of the PAS.

Therefore, although admissions officers can consider race as a positive feature of a minority student's application, there is no dispute that race is but a "factor of a factor of a factor" in the holistic-review calculus. 645 F.Supp.2d 587, 608 (W.D.Tex.2009). Furthermore, consideration of race is contextual and does not operate as a mechanical plus factor for underrepresented minorities. There is also no dispute, however, that race, when considered in conjunction with other aspects of an applicant's background, can alter an applicant's PAS score. Thus, race, in this indirect fashion, considered with all of the other factors that make up an applicant's AI and PAI scores, can make a difference to whether an application is accepted or rejected. * * *

Fisher I set forth three controlling principles relevant to assessing the constitutionality of a public university's affirmative-action program. First, "because racial characteristics so seldom provide a relevant basis for disparate treatment," *Richmond v. J.A. Croson Co.* (1989), "[r]ace may not be considered [by a university] unless the admissions process can withstand strict scrutiny." Strict scrutiny requires the university to demonstrate with clarity that its " 'purpose or interest is both constitutionally permissible and substantial, and that its use of the classification is necessary . . . to the accomplishment of its purpose.' "

Second, *Fisher I* confirmed that "the decision to pursue 'the educational benefits that flow from student body diversity' . . . is, in substantial measure, an academic judgment to which some, but not complete, judicial deference is proper." A university cannot impose a fixed quota or otherwise "define diversity as 'some specified percentage of a particular group merely because of its race or ethnic origin.'" Once, however, a university gives "a reasoned, principled explanation" for its decision, deference must be given "to the University's conclusion, based on its experience and expertise, that a diverse student body would serve its educational goals."

Third, *Fisher I* clarified that no deference is owed when determining whether the use of race is narrowly tailored to achieve the university's permissible goals. A university, *Fisher I* explained, bears the burden of proving a "nonracial approach" would not promote its interest in the educational benefits of diversity "about as well and at tolerable administrative expense." Though "[n]arrow tailoring does not require exhaustion of every conceivable race-neutral alternative" or "require a university to choose between maintaining a reputation for excellence [and] fulfilling a commitment to provide educational opportunities to members of all racial groups," it does impose "on the university the ultimate burden of demonstrating" that "race-neutral alternatives" that are both "available" and "workable" "do not suffice." *Fisher I.*

The University's program is *sui generis*. Unlike other approaches to college admissions considered by this Court, it combines holistic review with a percentage plan. This approach gave rise to an unusual consequence in this case: The component of the University's admissions policy that had the largest impact on petitioner's chances of admission was not the school's consideration of race under its holistic-review process but rather the Top Ten Percent Plan. Because petitioner did not graduate in the top 10 percent of her high school class, she was categorically ineligible for more than three-fourths of the slots in the incoming freshman class. It seems quite plausible, then, to think that petitioner would have had a better chance of being admitted to the University if the school used race-conscious holistic review to select its entire incoming class, as was the case in *Grutter*.

Despite the Top Ten Percent Plan's outsized effect on petitioner's chances of admission, she has not challenged it. For that reason, throughout this litigation, the Top Ten Percent Plan has been taken, somewhat artificially, as a given premise.

Petitioner's acceptance of the Top Ten Percent Plan complicates this Court's review. In particular, it has led to a record that is almost devoid of information about the students who secured admission to the University through the Plan. The Court thus cannot know how students admitted solely based on their class rank differ in their contribution to diversity from students admitted through holistic review.

In an ordinary case, this evidentiary gap perhaps could be filled by a remand to the district court for further factfinding. When petitioner's application was rejected, however, the University's combined percentage-plan/holistic-review approach to admission had been in effect for just three years. While studies undertaken over the eight years since then may be of significant value in determining the constitutionality of the University's current admissions policy, that evidence has little bearing on whether petitioner received equal treatment when her application was rejected in 2008. If the Court were to remand, therefore, further factfinding would be limited to a narrow 3-year sample, review of which might yield little insight. * * *

[T]he University lacks any authority to alter the role of the Top Ten Percent Plan in its admissions process. The Plan was mandated by the Texas Legislature in the wake of [*Hopwood, v. Texas*] so the University, like petitioner in this litigation, has likely taken the Plan as a given since its implementation in 1998. * * *

Under the circumstances of this case, then, a remand would do nothing more than prolong a suit that has already persisted for eight years and cost the parties on both sides significant resources. Petitioner long since has graduated from another college, and the University's policy—and the data on which it first was based—may have evolved or changed in material ways.

The fact that this case has been litigated on a somewhat artificial basis, furthermore, may limit its value for prospective guidance. The Texas Legislature, in enacting the Top Ten Percent Plan, cannot much be criticized, for it was responding to *Hopwood,* which at the time was binding law in the State of Texas. That legislative response, in turn, circumscribed the University's discretion in crafting its admissions policy. These circumstances refute any criticism that the University did not make good-faith efforts to comply with the law.

That does not diminish, however, the University's continuing obligation to satisfy the burden of strict scrutiny in light of changing circumstances. The University engages in periodic reassessment of the constitutionality, and efficacy, of its admissions program. Going forward, that assessment must be undertaken in light of the experience the school has accumulated and the data it has gathered since the adoption of its admissions plan.

As the University examines this data, it should remain mindful that diversity takes many forms. Formalistic racial classifications may sometimes fail to capture diversity in all of its dimensions and, when used in a divisive manner, could undermine the educational benefits the University values. Through regular evaluation of data and consideration of student experience, the University must tailor its approach in light of changing circumstances, ensuring that race plays no greater role than is necessary to meet its compelling interest. The University's examination of the data it has acquired in the years since petitioner's application, for these reasons, must proceed with full respect for the constraints imposed by the Equal Protection Clause. The type of data collected, and the manner in which it is considered, will have a significant bearing on how the University must shape its admissions policy to satisfy strict scrutiny in the years to come. Here, however, the Court is necessarily limited to the narrow question before it: whether, drawing all reasonable inferences in her favor, petitioner has shown by a preponderance of the evidence that she was denied equal treatment at the time her application was rejected.

In seeking to reverse the judgment of the Court of Appeals, petitioner makes four arguments. First, she argues that the University has not articulated its compelling interest with sufficient clarity. According to petitioner, the University must set forth more precisely the level of minority enrollment that would constitute a "critical mass." Without a clearer sense of what the University's ultimate goal is, petitioner argues, a reviewing court cannot assess whether the University's admissions program is narrowly tailored to that goal.

As this Court's cases have made clear, however, the compelling interest that justifies consideration of race in college admissions is not an interest in enrolling a certain number of minority students. Rather, a university may institute a race-conscious admissions program as a means of obtaining "the educational benefits that flow from student body diversity." As this Court has said, enrolling a diverse student body "promotes cross-racial understanding, helps to break down racial stereotypes, and enables students to better understand persons of different races." Equally important, "student body diversity promotes learning outcomes, and better prepares students for an increasingly diverse workforce and society."

Increasing minority enrollment may be instrumental to these educational benefits, but it is not, as petitioner seems to suggest, a goal that can or should be reduced to pure numbers. Indeed, since the University is prohibited from seeking a particular number or quota of minority students, it cannot be faulted for failing to specify the particular level of minority enrollment at which it believes the educational benefits of diversity will be obtained.

On the other hand, asserting an interest in the educational benefits of diversity writ large is insufficient. A university's goals cannot be elusory or amorphous—they must be sufficiently measurable to permit judicial scrutiny of the policies adopted to reach them.

The record reveals that in first setting forth its current admissions policy, the University articulated concrete and precise goals. On the first page of its 2004 "Proposal to Consider Race and Ethnicity in Admissions," the University identifies the educational values it seeks to realize through its admissions process: the destruction of stereotypes, the " 'promot[ion of] cross-racial understanding,' " the preparation of a student body " 'for an increasingly diverse workforce and society,' " and the " 'cultivat[ion of] a set of leaders with legitimacy in the eyes of the citizenry.' " Later in the proposal, the University explains that it strives to provide an "academic environment" that offers a "robust exchange of ideas, exposure to differing cultures, preparation for the challenges of an increasingly diverse workforce, and acquisition of competencies required of future leaders." All of these objectives, as a general matter, mirror the "compelling interest" this Court has approved in its prior cases.

The University has provided in addition a "reasoned, principled explanation" for its decision to pursue these goals. *Fisher I.* The University's 39-page proposal was written following a year-long study, which concluded that "[t]he use of race-neutral policies and programs ha[d] not been successful" in "provid[ing] an educational setting that fosters cross-racial understanding, provid[ing] enlightened discussion and learning, [or] prepar[ing] students to function in an increasingly diverse workforce and society." * * *

Second, petitioner argues that the University has no need to consider race because it had already "achieved critical mass" by 2003 using the Top Ten Percent Plan and race-neutral holistic review. Petitioner is correct that a university bears a heavy burden in showing that it had not obtained the educational benefits of diversity before it turned to a race-conscious plan. The record reveals, however, that, at the time of petitioner's application, the University could not be faulted on this score. * * *

The record itself contains significant evidence, both statistical and anecdotal, in support of the University's position. To start, the demographic data the University has submitted show consistent stagnation in terms of the percentage of minority students enrolling at the University from 1996 to 2002. In 1996, for example, 266 African-American freshmen enrolled, a total that constituted 4.1 percent of the incoming class. In 2003, the year *Grutter* was decided, 267 African-American students enrolled—again, 4.1 percent of the incoming class. The numbers for Hispanic and Asian-American students tell a similar story. Although demographics alone are by no means dispositive, they do have some value as a gauge of the University's ability to enroll students who can offer underrepresented perspectives.

In addition to this broad demographic data, the University put forward evidence that minority students admitted under the *Hopwood* regime experienced feelings of loneliness and isolation. This anecdotal evidence is, in turn, bolstered by further, more nuanced quantitative data. In 2002, 52 percent of undergraduate classes with at least five students had no African-American students enrolled in them, and 27 percent had only one African-

American student. In other words, only 21 percent of undergraduate classes with five or more students in them had more than one African-American student enrolled. Twelve percent of these classes had no Hispanic students, as compared to 10 percent in 1996. Though a college must continually reassess its need for race-conscious review, here that assessment appears to have been done with care, and a reasonable determination was made that the University had not yet attained its goals.

Third, petitioner argues that considering race was not necessary because such consideration has had only a " 'minimal impact' in advancing the [University's] compelling interest." Again, the record does not support this assertion. In 2003, 11 percent of the Texas residents enrolled through holistic review were Hispanic and 3.5 percent were African-American. In 2007, by contrast, 16.9 percent of the Texas holistic-review freshmen were Hispanic and 6.8 percent were African-American. Those increases—of 54 percent and 94 percent, respectively—show that consideration of race has had a meaningful, if still limited, effect on the diversity of the University's freshman class.

In any event, it is not a failure of narrow tailoring for the impact of racial consideration to be minor. The fact that race consciousness played a role in only a small portion of admissions decisions should be a hallmark of narrow tailoring, not evidence of unconstitutionality.

Petitioner's final argument is that "there are numerous other available race-neutral means of achieving" the University's compelling interest. A review of the record reveals, however, that, at the time of petitioner's application, none of her proposed alternatives was a workable means for the University to attain the benefits of diversity it sought. For example, petitioner suggests that the University could intensify its outreach efforts to African-American and Hispanic applicants. But the University submitted extensive evidence of the many ways in which it already had intensified its outreach efforts to those students. The University has created three new scholarship programs, opened new regional admissions centers, increased its recruitment budget by half-a-million dollars, and organized over 1,000 recruitment events. Perhaps more significantly, in the wake of *Hopwood,* the University spent seven years attempting to achieve its compelling interest using race-neutral holistic review. None of these efforts succeeded, and petitioner fails to offer any meaningful way in which the University could have improved upon them at the time of her application.

Petitioner also suggests altering the weight given to academic and socioeconomic factors in the University's admissions calculus. This proposal ignores the fact that the University tried, and failed, to increase diversity through enhanced consideration of socioeconomic and other factors. And it further ignores this Court's precedent making clear that the

Equal Protection Clause does not force universities to choose between a diverse student body and a reputation for academic excellence. *Grutter.*

Petitioner's final suggestion is to uncap the Top Ten Percent Plan, and admit more—if not all—the University's students through a percentage plan. As an initial matter, petitioner overlooks the fact that the Top Ten Percent Plan, though facially neutral, cannot be understood apart from its basic purpose, which is to boost minority enrollment. Percentage plans are "adopted with racially segregated neighborhoods and schools front and center stage." *Fisher I,* 570 U.S., at ___ (GINSBURG, J., dissenting). "It is race consciousness, not blindness to race, that drives such plans." *Ibid.* Consequently, petitioner cannot assert simply that increasing the University's reliance on a percentage plan would make its admissions policy more race neutral.

Even if, as a matter of raw numbers, minority enrollment would increase under such a regime, petitioner would be hard-pressed to find convincing support for the proposition that college admissions would be improved if they were a function of class rank alone. That approach would sacrifice all other aspects of diversity in pursuit of enrolling a higher number of minority students. A system that selected every student through class rank alone would exclude the star athlete or musician whose grades suffered because of daily practices and training. It would exclude a talented young biologist who struggled to maintain above-average grades in humanities classes. And it would exclude a student whose freshman-year grades were poor because of a family crisis but who got herself back on track in her last three years of school, only to find herself just outside of the top decile of her class.

These are but examples of the general problem. Class rank is a single metric, and like any single metric, it will capture certain types of people and miss others. This does not imply that students admitted through holistic review are necessarily more capable or more desirable than those admitted through the Top Ten Percent Plan. It merely reflects the fact that privileging one characteristic above all others does not lead to a diverse student body. Indeed, to compel universities to admit students based on class rank alone is in deep tension with the goal of educational diversity as this Court's cases have defined it. At its center, the Top Ten Percent Plan is a blunt instrument that may well compromise the University's own definition of the diversity it seeks.

In addition to these fundamental problems, an admissions policy that relies exclusively on class rank creates perverse incentives for applicants. Percentage plans "encourage parents to keep their children in low-performing segregated schools, and discourage students from taking challenging classes that might lower their grade point averages." *Gratz,* 539 U.S., at 304, n. 10 (GINSBURG, J., dissenting).

For all these reasons, although it may be true that the Top Ten Percent Plan in some instances may provide a path out of poverty for those who excel at schools lacking in resources, the Plan cannot serve as the admissions solution that petitioner suggests. Wherever the balance between percentage plans and holistic review should rest, an effective admissions policy cannot prescribe, realistically, the exclusive use of a percentage plan.

In short, none of petitioner's suggested alternatives—nor other proposals considered or discussed in the course of this litigation—have been shown to be "available" and "workable" means through which the University could have met its educational goals, as it understood and defined them in 2008. *Fisher I, supra,* at ___. The University has thus met its burden of showing that the admissions policy it used at the time it rejected petitioner's application was narrowly tailored.

A university is in large part defined by those intangible "qualities which are incapable of objective measurement but which make for greatness." *Sweatt v. Painter.* Considerable deference is owed to a university in defining those intangible characteristics, like student body diversity, that are central to its identity and educational mission. But still, it remains an enduring challenge to our Nation's education system to reconcile the pursuit of diversity with the constitutional promise of equal treatment and dignity.

In striking this sensitive balance, public universities, like the States themselves, can serve as "laboratories for experimentation." The University of Texas at Austin has a special opportunity to learn and to teach. The University now has at its disposal valuable data about the manner in which different approaches to admissions may foster diversity or instead dilute it. The University must continue to use this data to scrutinize the fairness of its admissions program; to assess whether changing demographics have undermined the need for a race-conscious policy; and to identify the effects, both positive and negative, of the affirmative-action measures it deems necessary.

The Court's affirmance of the University's admissions policy today does not necessarily mean the University may rely on that same policy without refinement. It is the University's ongoing obligation to engage in constant deliberation and continued reflection regarding its admissions policies.

JUSTICE ALITO, with whom **THE CHIEF JUSTICE** and **JUSTICE THOMAS** join, dissenting.

Something strange has happened since our prior decision in this case. See *Fisher v. University of Tex. at Austin*, 570 U.S. ___ (2013) (*Fisher I*). In that decision, we held that strict scrutiny requires the University of Texas at Austin (UT or University) to show that its use of race and ethnicity in making admissions decisions serves compelling interests and that its plan is narrowly tailored to achieve those ends. Rejecting the argument that we should defer to UT's judgment on those matters, we made it clear that UT was obligated (1) to identify the interests justifying its plan with enough specificity to permit a reviewing court to determine whether the requirements of strict scrutiny were met, and (2) to show that those requirements were in fact satisfied. On remand, UT failed to do what our prior decision demanded. The University has still not identified with any degree of specificity the interests that its use of race and ethnicity is supposed to serve. Its primary argument is that merely invoking 'the educational benefits of diversity' is sufficient and that it need not identify any metric that would allow a court to determine whether its plan is needed to serve, or is actually serving, those interests. This is nothing less than the plea for deference that we emphatically rejected in our prior decision. Today, however, the Court inexplicably grants that request.

To the extent that UT has ever moved beyond a plea for deference and identified the relevant interests in more specific terms, its efforts have been shifting, unpersuasive, and, at times, less than candid. When it adopted its race-based plan, UT said that the plan was needed to promote classroom diversity. It pointed to a study showing that African-American, Hispanic, and Asian-American students were underrepresented in many classes. But UT has never shown that its race-conscious plan actually ameliorates this situation. The University presents no evidence that its admissions officers, in administering the 'holistic' component of its plan, make any effort to determine whether an African-American, Hispanic, or Asian-American student is likely to enroll in classes in which minority students are underrepresented. And although UT's records should permit it to determine without much difficulty whether holistic admittees are any more likely than students admitted through the Top Ten Percent Law, to enroll in the classes lacking racial or ethnic diversity, UT either has not crunched those numbers or has not revealed what they show. Nor has UT explained why the underrepresentation of Asian-American students in many classes justifies its plan, which discriminates *against* those students.

At times, UT has claimed that its plan is needed to achieve a 'critical mass' of African-American and Hispanic students, but it has never explained what this term means. According to UT, a critical mass is neither some absolute number of African-American or Hispanic students nor the percentage of African-Americans or Hispanics in the general population of the State. The term remains undefined, but UT tells us that it will let the courts know when the desired end has been achieved. This is a plea for deference—indeed, for blind deference—the very thing that the Court rejected in *Fisher I.*

UT has also claimed at times that the race-based component of its plan is needed because the Top Ten Percent Plan admits *the wrong kind* of

African-American and Hispanic students, namely, students from poor families who attend schools in which the student body is predominantly African-American or Hispanic. As UT put it in its brief in *Fisher I*, the race-based component of its admissions plan is needed to admit '[t]he African-American or Hispanic child of successful professionals in Dallas.'

After making this argument in its first trip to this Court, UT apparently had second thoughts, and in the latest round of briefing UT has attempted to disavow ever having made the argument. See Brief for Respondents 2 ('Petitioner's argument that UT's interest is favoring 'affluent' minorities is a fabrication'); see also *id.*, at 15. But it did, and the argument turns affirmative action on its head. Affirmative-action programs were created to help *disadvantaged* students.

Although UT now disowns the argument that the Top Ten Percent Plan results in the admission of the wrong kind of African-American and Hispanic students, the Fifth Circuit majority bought a version of that claim. As the panel majority put it, the Top Ten African-American and Hispanic admittees cannot match the holistic African-American and Hispanic admittees when it comes to 'records of personal achievement,' a 'variety of perspectives' and 'life experiences,' and 'unique skills.' All in all, according to the panel majority, the Top Ten Percent students cannot 'enrich the diversity of the student body' in the same way as the holistic admittees. As Judge Garza put it in dissent, the panel majority concluded that the Top Ten Percent admittees are 'somehow more homogenous, less dynamic, and more undesirably stereotypical than those admitted under holistic review.' * * *

It should not have been necessary for us to grant review a second time in this case, and I have no greater desire than the majority to see the case drag on. But that need not happen. When UT decided to adopt its race-conscious plan, it had every reason to know that its plan would have to satisfy strict scrutiny and that this meant that it would be *its burden* to show that the plan was narrowly tailored to serve compelling interests. UT has failed to make that showing. By all rights, judgment should be entered in favor of petitioner.

But if the majority is determined to give UT yet another chance, we should reverse and send this case back to the District Court. What the majority has now done—awarding a victory to UT in an opinion that fails to address the important issues in the case—is simply wrong. * * *

[The dissent then provided an extended analysis of the factual record and challenged the majority's conclusions].

It is important to understand what is and what is not at stake in this case. *What is not at stake* is whether UT or any other university may adopt an admissions plan that results in a student body with a broad representation of students from all racial and ethnic groups. UT previously had a race-neutral plan that it claimed had 'effectively compensated for the loss of affirmative action,' and UT could have taken other steps that would have increased the diversity of its admitted students without taking race or ethnic background into account.

What is at stake is whether university administrators may justify systematic racial discrimination simply by asserting that such discrimination is necessary to achieve 'the educational benefits of diversity,' without explaining—much less proving—why the discrimination is needed or how the discriminatory plan is well crafted to serve its objectives. Even though UT has never provided any coherent explanation for its asserted need to discriminate on the basis of race, and even though UT's position relies on a series of unsupported and noxious racial assumptions, the majority concludes that UT has met its heavy burden. This conclusion is remarkable—and remarkably wrong.

Because UT has failed to satisfy strict scrutiny, I respectfully dissent.

[An additional dissenting opinion by **JUSTICE THOMAS** is omitted.]

NOTES

1.   *Strict Scrutiny?* Did the Court retreat in *Fisher II* from its insistence in *Fisher I* that universities should get no deference on the narrow tailoring prong of strict scrutiny? Or do the majority's repeated cautions about the University's continuing obligation to review and refine its policy indicate that it expects judicial scrutiny to be meaningful and to continue?

2.   *Critical Mass.* The notion of "critical mass" has been notoriously difficult to define in this context. Does *Fisher II* add greater clarity? How does the case define it? Is Justice Alito persuasive in dissent when he says that "[t]he term remains undefined, but UT tells us that it will let the courts know when the desired end has been achieved. This is a plea for deference—indeed, for blind deference—the very thing that the Court rejected in *Fisher I*." Does Justice Kennedy effectively respond when he says that it is unfair to criticize the University for not reducing critical mass to a precise number when doing so would lead to a charge that the University was using a quota?

3.   *Combatting Racial Isolation?* In his opinion, Justice Kennedy noted that the University was aware of "loneliness and isolation" suffered by minority students. When you read *Parents Involved in Community Schools v. Seattle School District No. 1* (Casebook, p. 333), you will notice that Kennedy's influential concurrence identifies a "compelling state interest" in "avoiding racial isolation." Does *Fisher II* suggest this might be an interest distinct from diversity that could justify affirmative action programs?

4.   *Justice Kennedy's Position. Fisher II* reflects the first time that Justice Kennedy voted to uphold an affirmative action plan. What might explain that? Note that his majority opinion calls the circumstances of *Fisher II* "*sui generis*." Given that the case involved only three years in the past, and

that Texas uses the holistic review challenged in this case to supplement the percentage plan, the plan examined in the case is, in fact, unique in important respects. Moreover, the percentage plan is consistent with the sort of facially neutral policy that Kennedy has favored in the past, including the facially race-neutral means of combatting racial isolation that Kennedy endorsed in his *Parents Involved* concurrence. Might Kennedy have been more willing to tolerate race-consciousness in *Fisher II* because it supplemented a race-conscious plan and made race only "a factor of a factor of a factor"? Do these characteristics limit the effect of *Fisher II* going forward? Given that Kennedy provided the fifth vote in this case, his retirement puts very much in question the constitutionality of race-conscious admissions going forward.

5.   *Percentage Plans?* What is the status of percentage plans after *Fisher II?* The majority adopts the view, first expressed by Justice Ginsburg, that such plans are, in fact, race conscious, even if not facially so. Does that mean a percentage plan would trigger strict scrutiny under an *Arlington Heights*-type approach? Or does the fact that the plan does not classify individuals based on race shield it from strict scrutiny? If the Texas percentage plan was challenged by a rejected white applicant to the University of Texas in the future, what do you think a court would and should conclude about the constitutionality of the plan?

6.   *Limits?* What limits does *Fisher II* place on affirmative action plans? The majority says, for example, that "[f]ormalistic racial classifications can sometimes fail to capture diversity in all its dimensions, and when used in a divisive manner, could undermine the educational benefits the University values." What does that mean? How about the majority's statement that the University must "reconcile its pursuit of diversity with the constitutional promise of equal treatment and dignity?"

In between *Fisher I* and *Fisher II*, the Court addressed a different issue concerning affirmative action. The next case tested the constitutionality of a state ballot measure designed to ban affirmative action in a state.

SCHUETTE V. COALITION TO DEFEND AFFIRMATIVE ACTION
572 U.S. 291, 134 S.Ct. 1623, 188 L.Ed.2d 613 (2014)

JUSTICE KENNEDY announced the judgment of the Court and delivered an opinion in which THE CHIEF JUSTICE and JUSTICE ALITO join.

[After the Supreme Court's decisions in the Michigan affirmative action cases (Casebook, p. 314), the voters of Michigan enacted Proposal 2, a measure that amended the state constitution to ban affirmative action. Proposal 2, codified as § 26, provided that the state and its universities "shall not discriminate against, or grant preferential treatment to, any individual or group on the basis of race, sex, color, ethnicity or national origin in the operation of public employment, public education, or public contracting." Sitting *en banc*, the Sixth Circuit struck down the ballot measure as a violation of the Equal Protection Clause. That court relied heavily on cases about unconstitutional restrictions on the political process, especially *Washington v. Seattle School District No. 1* (Casebook, p. 347 and 485) (striking down a ballot measure limiting the use of mandatory busing for school integration) and *Hunter v. Erickson* (Casebook, p. 485) (striking down a ballot measure banning city council passage of non-discrimination ordinances). The Sixth Circuit held that Michigan had created a scheme that subjected only racial minorities to the onerous burden of amending the state constitution to secure favorable policy on university admissions, while other groups could use the ordinary political process to pursue their desired policy].

Before the Court addresses the question presented, it is important to note what this case is not about. It is not about the constitutionality, or the merits, of race-conscious admissions policies in higher education. The consideration of race in admissions presents complex questions, in part addressed last Term in *Fisher.* In *Fisher,* the Court did not disturb the principle that the consideration of race in admissions is permissible, provided that certain conditions are met. In this case, as in *Fisher,* that principle is not challenged. The question here concerns not the permissibility of race-conscious admissions policies under the Constitution but whether, and in what manner, voters in the States may choose to prohibit the consideration of racial preferences in governmental decisions, in particular with respect to school admissions.

This Court has noted that some States have decided to prohibit race-conscious admissions policies. In *Grutter,* the Court noted: "Universities in California, Florida, and Washington State, where racial preferences in admissions are prohibited by state law, are currently engaged in experimenting with a wide variety of alternative approaches. Universities in other States can and should draw on the most promising aspects of these race-neutral alternatives as they develop." In this way, *Grutter* acknowledged the significance of a dialogue regarding this contested and complex policy question among and within States. There was recognition that our federal structure "permits 'innovation and experimentation' " and "enables greater citizen 'involvement in democratic processes.' " While this case arises in Michigan, the decision by the State's voters reflects in part the national dialogue regarding the wisdom and practicality of race-conscious admissions policies in higher education.

In Michigan, the State Constitution invests independent boards of trustees with plenary authority over public universities, including admissions policies. Although the members of the boards are elected, some evidence in the record suggests they delegated authority over admissions policy to the faculty. But whether the boards or the faculty set the specific policy, Michigan's public universities did consider race as a factor in admissions decisions before 2006.

In holding § 26 invalid in the context of student admissions at state universities, the Court of Appeals relied in primary part on *Seattle,* which it deemed to control the case. But that determination extends *Seattle's* holding in a case presenting quite different issues to reach a conclusion that is mistaken here. * * *

Seattle stated that where a government policy "inures primarily to the benefit of the minority" and "minorities . . . consider" the policy to be " 'in their interest,'" then any state action that "place[s] effective decisionmaking authority over" that policy "at a different level of government" must be reviewed under strict scrutiny. In essence, according to the broad reading of *Seattle,* any state action with a "racial focus" that makes it "more difficult for certain racial minorities than for other groups" to "achieve legislation that is in their interest" is subject to strict scrutiny. It is this reading of *Seattle* that the Court of Appeals found to be controlling here. And that reading must be rejected.

* * * The expansive reading of *Seattle* has no principled limitation and raises serious questions of compatibility with the Court's settled equal protection jurisprudence. * * *

In cautioning against "impermissible racial stereotypes," this Court has rejected the assumption that "members of the same racial group— regardless of their age, education, economic status, or the community in which they live—think alike, share the same political interests, and will prefer the same candidates at the polls." It cannot be entertained as a serious proposition that all individuals of the same race think alike. Yet that proposition would be a necessary beginning point were the *Seattle* formulation to control, as the Court of Appeals held it did in this case. And if it were deemed necessary to probe how some races define their own interest in political matters, still another beginning point would be to define individuals according to race. But in a society in which those lines are becoming more blurred, the attempt to define race-based categories also raises serious questions of its own. Government action that classifies individuals on the basis of race is inherently suspect and carries the danger of perpetuating the very racial divisions the polity seeks to transcend. Were courts to embark upon this venture not only would it be undertaken with no clear legal standards or accepted sources to guide judicial decision but also it would result in, or at least impose a high risk of, inquiries and categories dependent upon demeaning stereotypes, classifications of questionable constitutionality on their own terms. * * *

There would be no apparent limiting standards defining what public policies should be included in what *Seattle* called policies that "inur[e] primarily to the benefit of the minority" and that "minorities . . . consider" to be " 'in their interest.' * * * Tax policy, housing subsidies, wage regulations, and even the naming of public schools, highways, and monuments are just a few examples of what could become a list of subjects that some organizations could insist should be beyond the power of voters to decide, or beyond the power of a legislature to decide when enacting limits on the power of local authorities or other governmental entities to address certain subjects. Racial division would be validated, not discouraged, were the *Seattle* formulation, and the reasoning of the Court of Appeals in this case, to remain in force. * * *

Michigan voters exercised their privilege to enact laws as a basic exercise of their democratic power. In the federal system States "respond, through the enactment of positive law, to the initiative of those who seek a voice in shaping the destiny of their own times." Michigan voters used the initiative system to bypass public officials who were deemed not responsive to the concerns of a majority of the voters with respect to a policy of granting race-based preferences that raises difficult and delicate issues.

* * * [F]reedom does not stop with individual rights. Our constitutional system embraces, too, the right of citizens to debate so they can learn and decide and then, through the political process, act in concert to try to shape the course of their own times and the course of a nation that must strive always to make freedom ever greater and more secure. Here Michigan voters acted in concert and statewide to seek consensus and adopt a policy on a difficult subject against a historical background of race in America that has been a source of tragedy and persisting injustice. That history demands that we continue to learn, to listen, and to remain open to new approaches if we are to aspire always to a constitutional order in which all persons are treated with fairness and equal dignity. Were the Court to rule that the question addressed by Michigan voters is too sensitive or complex to be within the grasp of the electorate; or that the policies at issue remain too delicate to be resolved save by university officials or faculties, acting at some remove from immediate public scrutiny and control; or that these matters are so arcane that the electorate's power must be limited because the people cannot prudently exercise that power even after a full debate, that holding would be an unprecedented restriction on the exercise of a fundamental right held not just by one person but by all in common. It is the right to speak and debate and learn and then, as a matter of political will, to act through a lawful electoral process.

The respondents in this case insist that a difficult question of public policy must be taken from the reach of the voters, and thus removed from the realm of public discussion, dialogue, and debate in an election campaign. Quite in addition to the serious First Amendment implications of that position with respect to any particular election, it is inconsistent with the underlying premises of a responsible, functioning democracy. One of those premises is that a democracy has the capacity—and the duty—to learn from its past mistakes; to discover and confront persisting biases; and by respectful, rationale (sic) deliberation to rise above those flaws and injustices. That process is impeded, not advanced, by court decrees based on the proposition that the public cannot have the requisite repose to discuss certain issues. It is demeaning to the democratic process to presume that the voters are not capable of deciding an issue of this sensitivity on decent and rational grounds. * * *

These precepts are not inconsistent with the well-established principle that when hurt or injury is inflicted on racial minorities by the encouragement or command of laws or other state action, the Constitution requires redress by the courts. * * *

For reasons already discussed, [the political process cases] are not precedents that stand for the conclusion that Michigan's voters must be disempowered from acting. Those cases were ones in which the political restriction in question was designed to be used, or was likely to be used, to encourage infliction of injury by reason of race. What is at stake here is not whether injury will be inflicted but whether government can be instructed not to follow a course that entails, first, the definition of racial categories and, second, the grant of favored status to persons in some racial categories and not others. The electorate's instruction to governmental entities not to embark upon the course of race-defined and race-based preferences was adopted, we must assume, because the voters deemed a preference system to be unwise, on account of what voters may deem its latent potential to become itself a source of the very resentments and hostilities based on race that this Nation seeks to put behind it. Whether those adverse results would follow is, and should be, the subject of debate. Voters might likewise consider, after debate and reflection, that programs designed to increase diversity—consistent with the Constitution—are a necessary part of progress to transcend the stigma of past racism.

CHIEF JUSTICE ROBERTS, concurring.

The dissent devotes 11 pages to expounding its own policy preferences in favor of taking race into account in college admissions, while nonetheless concluding that it "do[es] not mean to suggest that the virtues of adopting race-sensitive admissions policies should inform the legal question before the Court." (opinion of SOTOMAYOR, J.). The dissent concedes that the governing boards of the State's various universities could have implemented a policy making it illegal to "discriminate against, or grant preferential treatment to," any individual on the basis of race. On the dissent's view, if the governing boards conclude that drawing racial distinctions in university admissions is undesirable or counterproductive, they are permissibly exercising their policymaking authority. But others who might reach the same conclusion are failing to take race seriously.

The dissent states that "[t]he way to stop discrimination on the basis of race is to speak openly and candidly on the subject of race." And it urges that "[r]ace matters because of the slights, the snickers, the silent judgments that reinforce that most crippling of thoughts: 'I do not belong here.'" But it is not "out of touch with reality" to conclude that racial preferences may themselves have the debilitating effect of reinforcing precisely that doubt, and—if so—that the preferences do more harm than good. To disagree with the dissent's views on the costs and benefits of racial preferences is not to "wish away, rather than confront" racial inequality. People can disagree in good faith on this issue, but it similarly does more harm than good to question the openness and candor of those on either side of the debate.

JUSTICE SCALIA, with whom **JUSTICE THOMAS** joins, concurring in the judgment.

It has come to this. Called upon to explore the jurisprudential twilight zone between two errant lines of precedent, we confront a frighteningly bizarre question: Does the Equal Protection Clause of the Fourteenth Amendment *forbid* what its text plainly *requires*? Needless to say (except that this case obliges us to say it), the question answers itself. * * *

Even taking this Court's sorry line of race-based-admissions cases as a given, I find the question presented only slightly less strange: Does the Equal Protection Clause forbid a State from banning a practice that the Clause barely—and only provisionally—permits? Reacting to those race-based-admissions decisions, some States—whether deterred by the prospect of costly litigation; aware that *Grutter*'s bell may soon toll; or simply opposed in principle to the notion of "benign" racial discrimination—have gotten out of the racial-preferences business altogether. * * *

But the battleground for this case is not the constitutionality of race-based admissions—at least, not quite. Rather, it is the so-called political-process doctrine, derived from this Court's opinions in *Washington v. Seattle School Dist. No. 1* and *Hunter v. Erickson*. I agree with those parts of the plurality opinion that repudiate this doctrine. But I do not agree with its reinterpretation of *Seattle* and *Hunter*, which makes them stand in part for the cloudy and doctrinally anomalous proposition that whenever state action poses "the serious risk . . . of causing specific injuries on account of race," it denies equal protection. I would instead reaffirm that the "ordinary principles of our law [and] of our democratic heritage" require "plaintiffs alleging equal protection violations" stemming from facially neutral acts to "prove intent and causation and not merely the existence of racial disparity." I would further hold that a law directing state actors to provide equal protection is (to say the least) facially neutral, and cannot violate the

Constitution. Section 26 of the Michigan Constitution (formerly Proposal 2) rightly stands. * * *

The dissent trots out the old saw, derived from dictum in a footnote, that legislation motivated by " 'prejudice against discrete and insular minorities' " merits " 'more exacting judicial scrutiny.' " (quoting *United States v. Carolene Products,* 304 U.S. 144, 152–153, n. 4). I say derived from that dictum (expressed by the four-Justice majority of a seven-Justice Court) because the dictum itself merely said *"[n]or need we enquire . . .* whether prejudice against discrete and insular minorities may be a special condition." (emphasis added). The dissent does not argue, of course, that such "prejudice" produced § 26. Nor does it explain why certain racial minorities in Michigan qualify as " 'insular,' " meaning that "other groups will not form coalitions with them—and, critically, not because of lack of common interests but because of 'prejudice.' " Strauss, Is *Carolene Products* Obsolete? 2010 U. Ill. L.Rev. 1251, 1257. Nor does it even make the case that a group's "discreteness" and "insularity" are political *liabilities* rather than political *strengths*—a serious question that alone demonstrates the prudence of the *Carolene Products* dictumizers in leaving the "enquir[y]" for another day. As for the question whether "legislation which restricts those political processes which can ordinarily be expected to bring about repeal of undesirable legislation . . . is to be subjected to more exacting judicial scrutiny," the *Carolene Products* Court found it "unnecessary to consider [that] now." If the dissent thinks that worth considering today, it should explain why the election of a university's governing board is a "political process which can ordinarily be expected to bring about repeal of undesirable legislation," but Michigan voters' ability to amend their Constitution is not. It seems to me quite the opposite. Amending the Constitution requires the approval of only "a majority of the electors voting on the question." Mich. Const., Art. XII, § 2. By contrast, voting in a favorable board (each of which has eight members) at the three major public universities requires electing by majority vote at least 15 different candidates, several of whom would be running during different election cycles. So if Michigan voters, instead of amending their Constitution, had pursued the dissent's preferred path of electing board members promising to "abolish race-sensitive admissions policies," it would have been *harder,* not easier, for racial minorities favoring affirmative action to overturn that decision. But the more important point is that we should not design our jurisprudence to conform to dictum in a footnote in a four-Justice opinion. * * *

I part ways with *Hunter, Seattle,* and (I think) the plurality for an additional reason: Each endorses a version of the proposition that a facially neutral law may deny equal protection solely because it has a disparate racial impact. Few equal-protection theories have been so squarely and soundly rejected. * * *

Notwithstanding our dozens of cases confirming the exceptionless nature of the *Washington v. Davis* rule, the plurality opinion leaves ajar an effects-test escape hatch modeled after *Hunter* and *Seattle*, suggesting that state action denies equal protection when it "ha[s] the *serious risk,* if not purpose, of causing specific injuries on account of race," or is either "designed to be used, or . . . *likely to be used,* to encourage infliction of injury by reason of race." (emphasis added). Since these formulations enable a determination of an equal-protection violation where there is no discriminatory intent, they are inconsistent with the long *Washington v. Davis* line of cases.

JUSTICE BREYER, concurring in the judgment.

I continue to believe that the Constitution permits, though it does not require, the use of the kind of race-conscious programs that are now barred by the Michigan Constitution. The serious educational problems that faced Americans at the time this Court decided *Grutter* endure. And low educational achievement continues to be correlated with income and race. [Justice Breyer then provided citations for these propositions]. * * *

The Constitution allows local, state, and national communities to adopt narrowly tailored race-conscious programs designed to bring about greater inclusion and diversity. But the Constitution foresees the ballot box, not the courts, as the normal instrument for resolving differences and debates about the merits of these programs. * * *

[C]ases such as [*Hunter* and *Seattle*] reflect an important principle, namely, that an individual's ability to participate meaningfully in the political process should be independent of his race. Although racial minorities, like other political minorities, will not always succeed at the polls, they must have the same opportunity as others to secure through the ballot box policies that reflect their preferences. In my view, however, neither *Hunter* nor *Seattle* applies here. * * *

Hunter and *Seattle* involved efforts to manipulate the political process in a way not here at issue. Both cases involved a restructuring of the political process that changed the political level at which policies were enacted. In *Hunter*, decisionmaking was moved from the elected city council to the local electorate at large. And in *Seattle*, decisionmaking by an elected school board was replaced with decisionmaking by the state legislature and electorate at large.

This case, in contrast, does not involve a reordering of the *political* process; it does not in fact involve the movement of decisionmaking from one political level to another. Rather, here, Michigan law delegated broad policymaking authority to elected university boards, but those boards delegated admissions-related decisionmaking authority to unelected university faculty members and administrators. Although the boards unquestionably retained the *power* to set policy regarding race-conscious admissions, see *post,* at 1664–1667 (SOTOMAYOR J., dissenting), in *fact* faculty members and administrators set the race-conscious admissions policies in question. (It is often true that elected bodies—including, for example, school boards, city councils, and state legislatures—have the power to enact policies, but in fact delegate that power to administrators.) Although at limited times the university boards were advised of the content of their race-conscious admissions policies, to my knowledge no board voted to accept or reject any of those policies. Thus, unelected faculty members and administrators, not voters or their elected representatives, adopted the race-conscious admissions programs affected by Michigan's constitutional amendment. The amendment took decisionmaking authority away from these unelected actors and placed it in the hands of the voters.

Why does this matter? For one thing, considered conceptually, the doctrine set forth in *Hunter* and *Seattle* does not easily fit this case. In those cases minorities had participated in the political process and they had won. The majority's subsequent reordering of the political process repealed the minority's successes and made it more difficult for the minority to succeed in the future. The majority thereby diminished the minority's ability to participate meaningfully in the electoral process. But one cannot as easily characterize the movement of the decisionmaking mechanism at issue here—from an administrative process to an electoral process—as diminishing the minority's ability to participate meaningfully in the *political* process. There is no prior electoral process in which the minority participated.

For another thing, to extend the holding of *Hunter* and *Seattle* to reach situations in which decisionmaking authority is moved from an administrative body to a political one would pose significant difficulties. The administrative process encompasses vast numbers of decisionmakers answering numerous policy questions in hosts of different fields. * * *

[M]y discussion here is limited to circumstances in which decisionmaking is moved from an unelected administrative body to a politically responsive one, and in which the targeted race-conscious admissions programs consider race solely in order to obtain the educational benefits of a diverse student body. We need now decide no more than whether the Federal Constitution permits Michigan to apply its constitutional amendment in those circumstances. I would hold that it does.

JUSTICE SOTOMAYOR, with whom **JUSTICE GINSBURG** joins, dissenting.

We are fortunate to live in a democratic society. But without checks, democratically approved legislation can oppress minority groups. For that reason, our Constitution places limits on what a majority of the people may do. This case implicates one such limit: the guarantee of equal protection of the laws. Although that guarantee is traditionally understood to prohibit intentional discrimination under existing laws, equal protection does not end there. Another fundamental strand of our equal protection jurisprudence focuses on process, securing to all citizens the right to participate meaningfully and equally in self-government. That right is the bedrock of our democracy, for it preserves all other rights.

Yet to know the history of our Nation is to understand its long and lamentable record of stymieing the right of racial minorities to participate in the political process. * * *

This case involves [discriminatory political restructuring]: A majority of the Michigan electorate changed the basic rules of the political process in that State in a manner that uniquely disadvantaged racial minorities. Prior to the enactment of the constitutional initiative at issue here, all of the admissions policies of Michigan's public colleges and universities— including race-sensitive admissions policies—were in the hands of each institution's governing board. The members of those boards are nominated by political parties and elected by the citizenry in statewide elections. After over a century of being shut out of Michigan's institutions of higher education, racial minorities in Michigan had succeeded in persuading the elected board representatives to adopt admissions policies that took into account the benefits of racial diversity. And this Court twice blessed such efforts—first in *Regents of Univ. of Cal. v. Bakke* (1978), and again in *Grutter v. Bollinger* (2003), a case that itself concerned a Michigan admissions policy.

In the wake of *Grutter,* some voters in Michigan set out to eliminate the use of race-sensitive admissions policies. Those voters were of course free to pursue this end in any number of ways. For example, they could have persuaded existing board members to change their minds through individual or grassroots lobbying efforts, or through general public awareness campaigns. Or they could have mobilized efforts to vote uncooperative board members out of office, replacing them with members who would share their desire to abolish race-sensitive admissions policies. When this Court holds that the Constitution permits a particular policy, nothing prevents a majority of a State's voters from choosing not to adopt that policy. Our system of government encourages—and indeed, depends on—that type of democratic action.

But instead, the majority of Michigan voters changed the rules in the middle of the game, reconfiguring the existing political process in Michigan in a manner that burdened racial minorities. * * *

As a result of § 26, there are now two very different processes through which a Michigan citizen is permitted to influence the admissions policies of the State's universities: one for persons interested in race-sensitive admissions policies and one for everyone else. A citizen who is a University of Michigan alumnus, for instance, can advocate for an admissions policy that considers an applicant's legacy status by meeting individually with members of the Board of Regents to convince them of her views, by joining with other legacy parents to lobby the Board, or by voting for and supporting Board candidates who share her position. The same options are available to a citizen who wants the Board to adopt admissions policies that consider athleticism, geography, area of study, and so on. The one and only policy a Michigan citizen may not seek through this long-established process is a race-sensitive admissions policy that considers race in an individualized manner when it is clear that race-neutral alternatives are not adequate to achieve diversity. For that policy alone, the citizens of Michigan must undertake the daunting task of amending the State Constitution.

Our precedents do not permit political restructurings that create one process for racial minorities and a separate, less burdensome process for everyone else. * * *

Like the plurality, I have faith that our citizenry will continue to learn from this Nation's regrettable history; that it will strive to move beyond those injustices towards a future of equality. And I, too, believe in the importance of public discourse on matters of public policy. But I part ways with the plurality when it suggests that judicial intervention in this case "impede[s]" rather than "advance[s]" the democratic process and the ultimate hope of equality. I firmly believe that our role as judges includes policing the process of self-government and stepping in when necessary to secure the constitutional guarantee of equal protection. * * *

[The right to participate meaningfully and equally in the process of government] is the bedrock of our democracy, recognized from its very inception. See J. Ely, Democracy and Distrust 87 (1980) (the Constitution "is overwhelmingly concerned, on the one hand, with procedural fairness in the resolution of individual disputes," and on the other, "with ensuring broad participation in the processes and distributions of government"). * * *

[Justice Sotomayor then reviewed *Carolene Products*, footnote 4]. The values identified in *Carolene Products* lie at the heart of the political-process doctrine. Indeed, *Seattle* explicitly relied on *Carolene Products*. These values are central tenets of our equal protection jurisprudence. * * *

My colleagues are of the view that we should leave race out of the picture entirely and let the voters sort it out. We have seen this reasoning before. See *Parents Involved,* 551 U.S., at 748, 127 S.Ct. 2738 ("The way to stop discrimination on the basis of race is to stop discriminating on the basis of race"). It is a sentiment out of touch with reality. * * *

Race matters. Race matters in part because of the long history of racial minorities' being denied access to the political process. * * * And although we have made great strides, "voting discrimination still exists; no one doubts that." *Shelby County*.

Race also matters because of persistent racial inequality in society—inequality that cannot be ignored and that has produced stark socioeconomic disparities. * * *

And race matters for reasons that really are only skin deep, that cannot be discussed any other way, and that cannot be wished away. Race matters to a young man's view of society when he spends his teenage years watching others tense up as he passes, no matter the neighborhood where he grew up. Race matters to a young woman's sense of self when she states her hometown, and then is pressed, "No, where are you *really* from?", regardless of how many generations her family has been in the country. Race matters to a young person addressed by a stranger in a foreign language, which he does not understand because only English was spoken at home. Race matters because of the slights, the snickers, the silent judgments that reinforce that most crippling of thoughts: "I do not belong here."

In my colleagues' view, examining the racial impact of legislation only perpetuates racial discrimination. This refusal to accept the stark reality that race matters is regrettable. The way to stop discrimination on the basis of race is to speak openly and candidly on the subject of race, and to apply the Constitution with eyes open to the unfortunate effects of centuries of racial discrimination. As members of the judiciary tasked with intervening to carry out the guarantee of equal protection, we ought not sit back and wish away, rather than confront, the racial inequality that exists in our society. It is this view that works harm, by perpetuating the facile notion that what makes race matter is acknowledging the simple truth that race *does* matter. * * *

[While acknowledging that the constitutionality of affirmative action was not at issue in this case, Justice Sotomayor noted that, because other justices had suggested that "race-sensitive admissions policies have the 'potential to become . . . the source of the very resentments and hostilities based on race that this Nation seeks to put behind it,'" she would "speak in response." Her dissent went on to offer a lengthy examination of affirmative action in university admissions, including statistics showing reduced minority enrollments in states with measures like Proposal 2, as well as an extended functional defense of diversity]. Colleges and universities must be free to prioritize the goal of diversity. They must be free to immerse their students in a multiracial environment that fosters frequent and meaningful interactions with students of other races, and thereby pushes such students to transcend any assumptions they may hold on the basis of skin color. Without race-sensitive admissions policies, this might well be impossible. The statistics I have described make that fact glaringly obvious. We should not turn a blind eye to something we cannot help but see. * * *

NOTES ON SCHUETTE

1.   *The Political Process Theory.* The *Hunter-Seattle* "political process" theory on which *Schuette* turned has been rarely used by the Supreme Court, and some had questioned the continued vitality of the doctrine. Both the plurality opinion and Justice Breyer's concurrence chose to limit, rather than overrule, that doctrine. How do the formulations in these two opinions differ? Does one leave a more defensible role for the political process doctrine than the other?

2.   *Voter Initiatives and Equal Protection.* While not overruling the political process doctrine, the plurality opinion's praise of voter initiatives left little doubt that it was unwilling to allow the doctrine to become a significant impediment to the use of ballot measures. Was the plurality too sanguine about the deliberative virtues of direct democracy? About the effect of ballot measures on minorities? (As you consider these questions, you might wish to consult the Note on Judicial Review of Popular Initiatives and Referenda, Casebook p. 485.)

3.   *The Intellectual Roots of the Political Process Theory.* While the *Hunter-Seattle* doctrine itself has been of limited significance, it is derived from the broad ideas of representation-reinforcement embedded in *Carolene Products* footnote 4 and the work of Professor Ely. Those ideas have pervaded and critically shaped the jurisprudence of equal protection. Justices Scalia and Sotomayor engage in a rare and extended face-off on footnote 4, which Justice Scalia casts as "an old saw" and a mere "dictum." Who has the better of this debate?

4.   *Justice Sotomayor's Dissent.* Justice Sotomayor's dissent ran to 58 pages, and is the longest of her tenure as a justice. Among its most salient elements is the pointed response to Chief Justice Roberts' much-quoted comment in *Parents Involved* that the "way to stop discrimination on the basis of race is to stop discriminating on the basis of race." (Casebook, p. 342). Justice Sotomayor bluntly calls this sentiment "out of touch with reality" and offers an impassioned argument about how and why "race matters." The Chief Justice characterizes the dissent as "expounding its own policy preferences" and asserts that it "does more harm than good to question the openness and candor of those on either side of the debate." This might be seen as a proxy battle between the forces of realism (championed by Sotomayor) and formalism (championed by Roberts) in approaching questions of race and constitutional equality. Does their debate shed any light on the virtues or vices of the colorblindness ideal?

CHAPTER 4

SEX AND GENDER DISCRIMINATION AND OTHER EQUAL PROTECTION CONCERNS

■ ■ ■

SECTION 2. SEX- AND GENDER-BASED DISCRIMINATION

B. THE JURISPRUDENCE OF EQUAL TREATMENT AND HEIGHTENED SCRUTINY OF SEX-BASED DISTINCTIONS

2. *Deference to Traditional Gender Classifications Based upon "Real Differences"*

Page 432. Insert the following after NOTE ON ROSTKER, NGUYEN, *AND JUDICIAL DEFERENCE TO CERTAIN NATIONAL LEGISLATIVE AND EXECUTIVE POLICIES*:

The Court returned to the issue of gender and immigration law in the next case.

SESSIONS V. MORALES-SANTANA
___ U.S. ___, 137 S.Ct. 1678, 198 L.Ed.2d 150 (2017)

[The Immigration and Nationality Act addresses when a child born outside the United States may acquire U.S. citizenship if only one of the child's parents is a U.S. citizen. Under the provisions in effect at the time relevant to this case, if the parents were married, the citizen-parent must have had ten years' physical presence in the United States before the child's birth, at least five of which were after that parent reached the age of 14. 8 U.S.C. 1401(a)(7) (1958 ed.). If the parents were not married, however, the rules differed based on the gender of the citizen-parent. Under section 1409(a), where the citizen-parent was the father, the same rules that govern married couples applied. But if the citizen-parent was the mother, it was much easier to transmit citizenship. Under section 1409(c), the mother must merely have lived continuously in the United States for one year before the child's birth. These gendered rules were challenged by Luis Ramon Morales-Santana, whom the government sought to deport based on criminal convictions. Morales asserted that he could not be deported because he acquired U.S. citizenship through his citizen-father. Morales' father, however, moved to the Dominican Republic 20 days before he turned 19, thus falling short of the requirement that he have five years physical presence in the United States after the age of 14. Morales challenged the constitutionality of the stricter rule for citizen-fathers than citizen-mothers.]

JUSTICE GINSBURG delivered the opinion of the Court.

Sections 1401 and 1409, we note, date from an era when the lawbooks of our Nation were rife with overbroad generalizations about the way men and women are. Today, laws of this kind are subject to review under the heightened scrutiny that now attends "all gender-based classifications." * * *

The defender of legislation that differentiates on the basis of gender must show "at least that the [challenged] classification serves important governmental objectives and that the discriminatory means employed are substantially related to the achievement of those objectives." Moreover, the classification must substantially serve an important governmental interest *today,* for "in interpreting the [e]qual [p]rotection [guarantee], [we have] recognized that new insights and societal understandings can reveal unjustified inequality . . . that once passed unnoticed and unchallenged." *Obergefell v. Hodges.* Here, the Government has supplied no "exceedingly persuasive justification," *Virginia,* for § 1409(a) and (c)'s "gender-based" and "gender-biased" disparity.

History reveals what lurks behind § 1409. Enacted in the Nationality Act of 1940 (1940 Act), § 1409 ended a century and a half of congressional silence on the citizenship of children born abroad to unwed parents. During this era, two once habitual, but now untenable, assumptions pervaded our Nation's citizenship laws and underpinned judicial and administrative rulings: In marriage, husband is dominant, wife subordinate; unwed mother is the natural and sole guardian of a nonmarital child.

Under the once entrenched principle of male dominance in marriage, the husband controlled both wife and child. "[D]ominance [of] the husband," this Court observed in 1915, "is an ancient principle of our jurisprudence." Through the early 20th century, a male citizen automatically conferred U.S. citizenship on his alien wife. A female citizen, however, was incapable of conferring citizenship on her husband; indeed, she was subject to expatriation if she married an alien. * * *

For unwed parents, the father-controls tradition never held sway. Instead, the mother was regarded as the child's natural and sole guardian. At common law, the mother, and only the mother, was "bound to maintain [a nonmarital child] as its natural guardian." In line with that understanding, in the early 20th century, the State Department sometimes permitted unwed mothers to pass citizenship to their children, despite the absence of any statutory authority for the practice.

In the 1940 Act, Congress discarded the father-controls assumption concerning married parents, but codified the mother-as-sole-guardian perception regarding unmarried parents. The Roosevelt administration, which proposed § 1409, explained: "[T]he mother [of a nonmarital child] stands in the place of the father . . . [,] has a right to the custody and control of such a child as against the putative father, and is bound to maintain it as its natural guardian."

This unwed-mother-as-natural-guardian notion renders § 1409's gender-based residency rules understandable. Fearing that a foreign-born child could turn out "more alien than American in character," the administration believed that a citizen parent with lengthy ties to the United States would counteract the influence of the alien parent. Concern about the attachment of foreign-born children to the United States explains the treatment of unwed citizen fathers, who, according to the familiar stereotype, would care little about, and have scant contact with, their nonmarital children. For unwed citizen mothers, however, there was no need for a prolonged residency prophylactic: The alien father, who might transmit foreign ways, was presumptively out of the picture. * * *

The provision challenged in [*Miller v. Albright*] and *Nguyen* as violative of equal protection requires unwed U.S.-citizen fathers, but not mothers, to formally acknowledge parenthood of their foreign-born children in order to transmit their U.S. citizenship to those children. After *Miller* produced no opinion for the Court, we took up the issue anew in *Nguyen*. There, the Court held that imposing a paternal-acknowledgment requirement on fathers was a justifiable, easily met means of ensuring the existence of a biological parent-child relationship, which the mother establishes by giving birth. Morales-Santana's challenge does not renew the contest over § 1409's paternal-acknowledgment requirement (whether the current version or that in effect in 1970), and the Government does not dispute that Morales-Santana's father, by marrying Morales-Santana's mother, satisfied that requirement.

Unlike the paternal-acknowledgment requirement at issue in *Nguyen* and *Miller,* the physical-presence requirements now before us relate solely to the duration of the parent's prebirth residency in the United States, not to the parent's filial tie to the child. As the Court of Appeals observed in this case, a man needs no more time in the United States than a woman "in order to have assimilated citizenship-related values to transmit to [his] child." And unlike *Nguyen*'s parental-acknowledgment requirement, § 1409(a)'s age-calibrated physical-presence requirements cannot fairly be described as "minimal."

Notwithstanding § 1409(a) and (c)'s provenance in traditional notions of the way women and men are, the Government maintains that the statute serves two important objectives: (1) ensuring a connection between the child to become a citizen and the United States and (2) preventing "statelessness," *i.e.,* a child's possession of no citizenship at all. * * *

An unwed mother, the Government urges, is the child's only "legally recognized" parent at the time of childbirth. An unwed citizen father enters the scene later, as a second parent. A longer physical connection to the United States is warranted for the unwed father, the Government maintains, because of the "competing national influence" of the alien mother. Congress, the Government suggests, designed the statute to bracket an unwed U.S.-citizen mother with a married couple in which both parents are U.S. citizens, and to align an unwed U.S.-citizen father with a married couple, one spouse a citizen, the other, an alien.

Underlying this apparent design is the assumption that the alien father of a nonmarital child born abroad to a U.S.-citizen mother will not accept parental responsibility. For an actual affiliation between alien father and nonmarital child would create the "competing national influence" that, according to the Government, justifies imposing on unwed U.S.-citizen fathers, but not unwed U.S.-citizen mothers, lengthy physical-presence requirements. Hardly gender neutral, that assumption conforms to the long-held view that unwed fathers care little about, indeed are strangers to, their children. Lump characterization of that kind, however, no longer passes equal protection inspection.

Accepting, *arguendo,* that Congress intended the diverse physical-presence prescriptions to serve an interest in ensuring a connection between the foreign-born nonmarital child and the United States, the gender-based means scarcely serve the posited end. The scheme permits the transmission of citizenship to children who have no tie to the United States so long as their mother was a U.S. citizen continuously present in the United States for one year at any point in her life *prior* to the child's birth. The transmission holds even if the mother marries the child's alien father immediately after the child's birth and never returns with the child to the United States. At the same time, the legislation precludes citizenship transmission by a U.S.-citizen father who falls a few days short of meeting § 1401(a)(7)'s longer physical-presence requirements, even if the father acknowledges paternity on the day of the child's birth and raises the child in the United States. One cannot see in this driven-by-gender scheme the close means-end fit required to survive heightened scrutiny.

The Government [also] maintains that Congress established the gender-based residency differential in § 1409(a) and (c) to reduce the risk that a foreign-born child of a U.S. citizen would be born stateless. * * * But there is little reason to believe that a statelessness concern prompted the diverse physical-presence requirements. Nor has the Government shown that the risk of statelessness disproportionately endangered the children of unwed mothers.

As the Court of Appeals pointed out, with one exception, nothing in the congressional hearings and reports on the 1940 and 1952 Acts "refer[s] to the problem of statelessness for children born abroad." * * * It will not do to "hypothesiz[e] or inven[t]" governmental purposes for gender classifications "*post hoc* in response to litigation." *Virginia.*

Infecting the Government's risk-of-statelessness argument is an assumption without foundation. "[F]oreign laws that would put the child of the U.S.-citizen mother at risk of statelessness (by not providing for the child to acquire the father's citizenship at birth)," the Government asserts, "would *protect* the child of the U.S.-citizen father against statelessness by providing that the child would take his mother's citizenship." The Government, however, neglected to expose this supposed "protection" to a reality check. Had it done so, it would have recognized the formidable impediments placed by foreign laws on an unwed mother's transmission of citizenship to her child.

Experts who have studied the issue report that, at the time relevant here, in "at least thirty countries," citizen mothers generally could not transmit their citizenship to nonmarital children born within the mother's country. "[A]s many as forty-five countries," they further report, "did not permit their female citizens to assign nationality to a nonmarital child born outside the subject country with a foreign father." In still other countries, they also observed, there was no legislation in point, leaving the nationality of nonmarital children uncertain. Taking account of the foreign laws actually in force, these experts concluded, "the risk of parenting stateless children abroad was, as of [1940 and 1952], and remains today, substantial for unmarried U.S. fathers, a risk perhaps greater than that for unmarried U.S. mothers." One can hardly characterize as gender neutral a scheme allegedly attending to the risk of statelessness for children of unwed U.S.-citizen mothers while ignoring the same risk for children of unwed U.S.-citizen fathers. * * *

[The Court closed by confronting the issue of remedy.] While the equal protection infirmity in retaining a longer physical-presence requirement for unwed fathers than for unwed mothers is clear, this Court is not equipped to grant the relief Morales-Santana seeks, *i.e.,* extending to his father (and, derivatively, to him) the benefit of the one-year physical-presence term § 1409(c) reserves for unwed mothers.

There are "two remedial alternatives," our decisions instruct, when a statute benefits one class (in this case, unwed mothers and their children), as § 1409(c) does, and excludes another from the benefit (here, unwed fathers and their children). "[A] court may either declare [the statute] a nullity and order that its benefits not extend to the class that the legislature intended to benefit, or it may extend the coverage of the statute to include those who are aggrieved by exclusion." "[W]hen the 'right invoked is that to equal treatment,' the appropriate remedy is a mandate of equal treatment, a result that can be accomplished by withdrawal of benefits from the favored class as well as by extension of benefits to the excluded class." * * *

The choice between these outcomes is governed by the legislature's intent, as revealed by the statute at hand. * * *

Ordinarily, we have reiterated, "extension, rather than nullification, is the proper course." Illustratively, in a series of cases involving federal financial assistance benefits, the Court struck discriminatory exceptions denying benefits to discrete groups, which meant benefits previously denied were extended. Here, however, the discriminatory exception consists of *favorable* treatment for a discrete group (a shorter physical-presence requirement for unwed U.S.-citizen mothers giving birth abroad). Following the same approach as in those benefits cases—striking the discriminatory exception—leads here to extending the general rule of longer physical-presence requirements to cover the previously favored group. * * *

Although extension of benefits is customary in federal benefit cases, all indicators in this case point in the opposite direction. Put to the choice, Congress, we believe, would have abrogated § 1409(c)'s exception, preferring preservation of the general rule. * * *

Going forward, Congress may address the issue and settle on a uniform prescription that neither favors nor disadvantages any person on the basis of gender. In the interim, as the Government suggests, § 1401(a)(7)'s now-five-year requirement should apply, prospectively, to children born to unwed U.S.-citizen mothers.

[In a dissent joined by **JUSTICE ALITO, JUSTICE THOMAS** argued that, given the lack of remedy for Morales-Santana, the Court should not have decided the constitutionality of the provisions in question].

NOTES ON MORALES-SANTANA

1. *Whither* Nguyen? Note that the Court distinguishes *Nguyen*. But does *Morales-Santana* implicitly suggest that *Nguyen* was wrongly decided? Don't both cases involve the same stereotypical assumptions about unmarried mothers and fathers? Setting aside the factual differences, did the Court apply the same version of intermediate scrutiny in *Morales-Santana* as it had in *Nguyen*? Recall that Justice Ginsburg joined Justice O'Connor's dissent in *Nguyen* criticizing the weak form of review applied there.

2. *Obergefell*. The majority imports into its analysis ideas of evolving norms and dignity that it traces to *Obergefell*. Does this signal that these ideas,

and the related "synergy" between equality and liberty emphasized by Justice Kennedy, have taken root in the realm of constitutional sex equality law? What might the implications of that move be for sex equality doctrine going forward?

3.   *Remedy.* The Court leaves the successful plaintiff with no remedy. Was the Court right to level down, rather than levelling up? Was Justice Thomas correct that the absence of a remedy made the constitutional analysis unnecessary?

Page 438.   Insert the following after Problem 4–2:

PROBLEM 4–2.1:
RESTRICTED BATHROOMS

(a)   In 2016, the North Carolina Legislature enacted, as an "emergency" measure, H.B. 2, a law pushing back against Charlotte's new ordinance barring discrimination because of sexual orientation or gender identity. One provision of the law imposed this requirement on public school boards: "Local boards of education shall require every multiple occupancy bathroom or changing facility that is designated for student use to be designated for and used only by students based on their biological sex." N.C. Gen. Stat. § 115C–521.2(b). The law allowed school boards to provide single-occupancy bathrooms, *id.* § 115C–521.2(c), and contained exceptions for custodial, maintenance, medical, and other exceptional purposes. Id. § 115C–521.2(d).

Suppose that, while the law was in effect, a male-to-female transgender high school student, Kim P., asked the school principal for permission to use the girls' restroom in the local North Carolina high school. After consultation with teachers, student groups, and staff, the principal agreed and notified everyone in the school. The local school board vetoed that plan, based upon the new law. The board issued this statement: "We have no discretion to allow access to a school rest room that does not match the student's 'biological sex.'"

If the student sued the school board, claiming a violation of the Equal Protection Clause, how would the District Court evaluate her claim: Is this a "sex discrimination" that triggers the heightened scrutiny of *Craig v. Boren*? If not, does the school board have a "rational basis" for the discrimination? What is the board's best justification? Would it pass *Craig*'s heightened scrutiny?

(b)   In 2017, the North Carolina legislature repealed H.B. 2. But it replaced the bill with H.B. 142, a new law that (1) preempted any state agency, university, local board of education or other political subdivision of the state from regulating access to multiple occupancy restrooms, showers, or changing facilities, except in accordance with an act of the state legislature; and (2) any local government in the state from enacting or amending, before December 2020, any ordinance regulating private employment or public accommodations. The upshot of the replacement bill seems to be that no public entity can regulate to mandate access for transgender students to use the restroom that matches their gender identity unless the state legislature has done so. In addition, no local entity can add new protections against discrimination in employment or public accommodations, including protections based on gender identity, before 2020. If Kim P.'s school board took the same position on restroom access that it took in section (a) above, would the adoption of the new law change the equal protection analysis in Kim's lawsuit? If so, how? As you consider this question, assume (as seems likely) that the state legislature has not enacted any law protecting transgender students' access to restrooms matching their gender identity.

Note: After you have read *Romer v. Evans* (Casebook, p. 474), you may want to revisit the second provision of HB 142, barring the enactment of new local anti-discrimination protections before December 2020.

SECTION 3. WHAT LEVEL OF SCRUTINY FOR OTHER "SUSPICIOUS" CLASSIFICATIONS?

D. SEXUAL ORIENTATION

Page 506.   Insert the following after Problem 4–5:

In 2013, the constitutionality of both California's Proposition 8 (at issue in *Perry v. Brown*, Casebook, p. 494) and Section 3 of the Defense of Marriage Act (addressed in the Holder Letter, Casebook, p. 503) came before the Supreme Court. Both decisions were highly anticipated. In *Hollingsworth v. Perry*, ___ U.S. ___, 133 S.Ct. 2652 (2013), the Court declined to reach the constitutionality of Prop 8. Recall that the ballot measure had been struck down by both District Judge Vaughn Walker in 2010 and by a panel of the Ninth Circuit in 2012. Because none of the California officials named as defendants in the case elected to appeal the district court's judgment, it was the measure's ballot sponsors who had appealed to the Ninth Circuit and then petitioned for certiorari in the case. By a 5–4 vote, the Court found that these ballot sponsors lacked Article III standing to appeal on behalf of the state (see Chapter 9 of this Supplement). The effect of that ruling was to vacate the Ninth Circuit's decision and reinstate Judge Vaughn Walker's opinion invalidating that measure, including the permanent injunction against enforcement of Prop 8. Although there was some debate about the scope of Judge Walker's order, and who precisely was bound by that permanent injunction, same-sex marriages resumed around the state only days after the ruling. Based on their reading of the district court's order, the Governor and Attorney General instructed county clerks to resume issuing marriage licenses to same-sex couples as soon as the Ninth Circuit lifted the stay it had imposed pending Supreme Court resolution, and that stay was lifted quickly. In late June 2013, California became the 13th state to allow same-sex couples to wed.

In the next case, the justices rejected Article III challenges to an appeal from a ruling that sec. 3 of DOMA was unconstitutional (see Chapter 9 of this Supplement), and reached the constitutional question posed in that case.

UNITED STATES V. WINDSOR

570 U.S. 744, 133 S.Ct. 2675, 186 L.Ed.2d 808 (2013)

JUSTICE KENNEDY delivered the opinion of the Court.

In 1996, as some States were beginning to consider the concept of same-sex marriage, and before any State had acted to permit it, Congress enacted the Defense of Marriage Act (DOMA). DOMA contains two operative sections: Section 2, which has not been challenged here, allows States to refuse to recognize same-sex marriages performed under the laws of other States.

Section 3 is at issue here. It amends the Dictionary Act in Title 1, § 7, of the United States Code to provide a federal definition of "marriage" and "spouse." Section 3 of DOMA provides as follows:

> In determining the meaning of any Act of Congress, or of any ruling, regulation, or interpretation of the various administrative bureaus and agencies of the United States, the word 'marriage' means only a legal union between one man and one woman as husband and wife, and the word 'spouse' refers only to a person of the opposite sex who is a husband or a wife.

The definitional provision does not by its terms forbid States from enacting laws permitting same-sex marriages or civil unions or providing state benefits to residents in that status. The enactment's comprehensive definition of marriage for purposes of all federal statutes and other regulations or directives covered by its terms, however, does control over 1,000 federal laws in which marital or spousal status is addressed as a matter of federal law.

Edith Windsor and Thea Spyer met in New York City in 1963 and began a long-term relationship. Windsor and Spyer registered as domestic partners when New York City gave that right to same-sex couples in 1993. Concerned about Spyer's health, the couple made the 2007 trip to Canada for their marriage, but they continued to reside in New York City. The State of New York deems their Ontario marriage to be a valid one.

Spyer died in February 2009, and left her entire estate to Windsor. Because DOMA denies federal recognition to same-sex spouses, Windsor did not qualify for the marital exemption from the federal estate tax, which excludes from taxation "any interest in property which passes or has passed from the decedent to his surviving spouse." Windsor paid $363,053 in estate taxes and sought a refund. The Internal Revenue Service denied the refund, concluding that, under DOMA, Windsor was not a "surviving spouse." Windsor commenced this refund suit, [contending] that DOMA violates the guarantee of equal protection, as applied to the Federal Government through the Fifth Amendment.

While the tax refund suit was pending, the Attorney General of the United States notified the Speaker of the House of Representatives that the Department of Justice would no longer defend the constitutionality of DOMA's § 3. [See Holder Letter, Casebook p. 503] * * *

[The opinion first addressed the jurisdictional question under Article III that the Court had asked the parties to brief. In portions of the opinion excerpted in Chapter 9 of this Supplement, the majority found the case properly before the Court].

It seems fair to conclude that, until recent years, many citizens had not even considered the possibility that two persons of the same sex might aspire to occupy the same status and dignity as that of a man and woman in lawful marriage. For marriage between a man and a woman no doubt had been thought of by most people as essential to the very definition of that term and to its role and function throughout the history of civilization. That belief, for many who long have held it, became even more urgent, more cherished when challenged. For others, however, came the beginnings of a new perspective, a new insight. Accordingly some States concluded that same-sex marriage ought to be given recognition and validity in the law for those same-sex couples who wish to define themselves by their commitment to each other. The limitation of lawful marriage to heterosexual couples, which for centuries had been deemed both necessary and fundamental, came to be seen in New York and certain other States as an unjust exclusion.

Slowly at first and then in rapid course, the laws of New York came to acknowledge the urgency of this issue for same-sex couples who wanted to affirm their commitment to one another before their children, their family, their friends, and their community. And so New York recognized same-sex marriages performed elsewhere; and then it later amended its own marriage laws to permit same-sex marriage. * * *

Against this background of lawful same-sex marriage in some States, the design, purpose, and effect of DOMA should be considered as the beginning point in deciding whether it is valid under the Constitution. * * * [DOMA's] operation is directed to a class of persons that the laws of New York, and of [Massachusetts, Iowa, Vermont, Connecticut, New Hampshire, Washington, Maine, Maryland, Delaware, Rhode Island, and the District of Columbia] have sought to protect. [As reflected in the portions of Justice Kennedy's opinions reproduced in chapter 7 of this Supplement, the Court emphasized the extent to which states, not the federal government, have traditionally defined and regulated marriage].

The States' interest in defining and regulating the marital relation, subject to constitutional guarantees, stems from the understanding that marriage is more than a routine classification for purposes of certain statutory benefits. Private, consensual sexual intimacy between two adult persons of the same sex may not be punished by the State, and it can form "but one element in a personal bond that is more enduring." *Lawrence v. Texas* [Casebook, p. 677]. By its recognition of the validity of same-sex marriages performed in other jurisdictions and then by authorizing same-sex unions and same-sex marriages, New York sought to give further protection and dignity to that bond. For same-sex couples who wished to be married, the State acted to give their lawful conduct a lawful status. This status is a far-reaching legal acknowledgment of the intimate relationship between two people, a relationship deemed by the State worthy of dignity in the community equal with all other marriages. It reflects both the community's considered perspective on the historical roots of the institution of marriage and its evolving understanding of the meaning of equality.

DOMA seeks to injure the very class New York seeks to protect. By doing so it violates basic due process and equal protection principles applicable to the Federal Government [citing the Fifth Amendment]. The Constitution's guarantee of equality "must at the very least mean that a bare congressional desire to harm a politically unpopular group cannot" justify disparate treatment of that group. In determining whether a law is motivated by an improper animus or purpose, " '[d]iscriminations of an unusual character' " especially require careful consideration (quoting *Romer*). DOMA cannot survive under these principles. The responsibility of the States for the regulation of domestic relations is an important indicator of the substantial societal impact the State's classifications have in the daily lives and customs of its people. DOMA's unusual deviation from the usual tradition of recognizing and accepting state definitions of marriage here operates to deprive same-sex couples of the benefits and responsibilities that come with the federal recognition of their marriages. This is strong evidence of a law having the purpose and effect of disapproval of that class. * * *

The history of DOMA's enactment and its own text demonstrate that interference with the equal dignity of same-sex marriages, a dignity conferred by the States in the exercise of their sovereign power, was more than an incidental effect of the federal statute. It was its essence. The House Report announced its conclusion that "it is both appropriate and necessary for Congress to do what it can to defend the institution of traditional heterosexual marriage. . . . H.R. 3396 is appropriately entitled the 'Defense of Marriage Act.' The effort to redefine 'marriage' to extend to homosexual couples is a truly radical proposal that would fundamentally alter the institution of marriage." H.R.Rep. No. 104–664, pp. 12–13 (1996). The House concluded that DOMA expresses "both moral disapproval of homosexuality, and a moral conviction that heterosexuality better comports with traditional (especially Judeo-Christian) morality." * * *

DOMA's operation in practice confirms this purpose. When New York adopted a law to permit same-sex marriage, it sought to eliminate inequality; but DOMA frustrates that objective through a system-wide enactment with no identified connection to any particular area of federal law. DOMA writes inequality into the entire United States Code. The particular case at hand concerns the estate tax, but DOMA is more than a simple determination of what should or should not be allowed as an estate tax refund. Among the over 1,000 statutes and numerous federal regulations that DOMA controls are laws pertaining to Social Security, housing, taxes, criminal sanctions, copyright, and veterans' benefits.

DOMA's principal effect is to identify a subset of state-sanctioned marriages and make them unequal. * * * The differentiation demeans the couple, whose moral and sexual choices the Constitution protects, see *Lawrence*, and whose relationship the State has sought to dignify. And it humiliates tens of thousands of children now being raised by same-sex couples. The law in question makes it even more difficult for the children to understand the integrity and closeness of their own family and its concord with other families in their community and in their daily lives. * * *

DOMA also brings financial harm to children of same-sex couples. It raises the cost of health care for families by taxing health benefits provided by employers to their workers' same-sex spouses. And it denies or reduces benefits allowed to families upon the loss of a spouse and parent, benefits that are an integral part of family security. * * *

The liberty protected by the Fifth Amendment's Due Process Clause contains within it the prohibition against denying to any person the equal protection of the laws. While the Fifth Amendment itself withdraws from Government the power to degrade or demean in the way this law does, the equal protection guarantee of the Fourteenth Amendment makes that Fifth Amendment right all the more specific and all the better understood and preserved. * * *

By seeking to displace [the protection granted by states allowing same-sex marriage] and treating those persons as living in marriages less respected than others, the federal statute is in violation of the Fifth Amendment. This opinion and its holding are confined to those lawful marriages.

CHIEF JUSTICE ROBERTS, dissenting.

The majority [points] out that the Federal Government has generally (though not uniformly) deferred to state definitions of marriage in the past. That is true, of course, but none of those prior state-by-state variations had involved differences over something—as the majority puts it—"thought of by most people as essential to the very definition of [marriage] and to its role and function throughout the history of civilization." That the Federal

Government treated this fundamental question differently than it treated variations over consanguinity or minimum age is hardly surprising—and hardly enough to support a conclusion that the "principal purpose," of the 342 Representatives and 85 Senators who voted for it, and the President who signed it, was a bare desire to harm. Nor do the snippets of legislative history and the banal title of the Act to which the majority points suffice to make such a showing. At least without some more convincing evidence that the Act's principal purpose was to codify malice, and that it furthered *no* legitimate government interests, I would not tar the political branches with the brush of bigotry.

But while I disagree with the result to which the majority's analysis leads it in this case, I think it more important to point out that its analysis leads no further. The Court does not have before it, and the logic of its opinion does not decide, the distinct question whether the States, in the exercise of their "historic and essential authority to define the marital relation," may continue to utilize the traditional definition of marriage. * * *

The dominant theme of the majority opinion is that the Federal Government's intrusion into an area "central to state domestic relations law applicable to its residents and citizens" is sufficiently "unusual" to set off alarm bells. I think the majority goes off course, as I have said, but it is undeniable that its judgment is based on federalism. * * *

JUSTICE SCALIA, with whom JUSTICE THOMAS joins, and with whom THE CHIEF JUSTICE joins as to part I, dissenting. * * *

[II.] [I]f this is meant to be an equal-protection opinion, it is a confusing one. The opinion does not resolve and indeed does not even mention what had been the central question in this litigation: whether, under the Equal Protection Clause, laws restricting marriage to a man and a woman are reviewed for more than mere rationality. That is the issue that divided the parties and the court below. In accord with my previously expressed skepticism about the Court's "tiers of scrutiny" approach, I would review this classification only for its rationality. As nearly as I can tell, the Court agrees with that; its opinion does not apply strict scrutiny, and its central propositions are taken from rational-basis cases like *Moreno*. But the Court certainly does not *apply* anything that resembles that deferential framework.

The majority opinion need not get into the strict-vs.-rational-basis scrutiny question, and need not justify its holding under either, because it says that DOMA is unconstitutional as "a deprivation of the liberty of the person protected by the Fifth Amendment of the Constitution"; that it violates "basic due process" principles; and that it inflicts an "injury and indignity" of a kind that denies "an essential part of the liberty protected by the Fifth Amendment". The majority never utters the dread words "substantive due process," perhaps sensing the disrepute into which that doctrine has fallen, but that is what those statements mean. Yet the opinion does not argue that same-sex marriage is "deeply rooted in this Nation's history and tradition," a claim that would of course be quite absurd. * * *

The penultimate sentence of the majority's opinion is a naked declaration that "[t]his opinion and its holding are confined" to those couples "joined in same-sex marriages made lawful by the State." I have heard such "bald, unreasoned disclaimer[s]" before. When the Court declared a constitutional right to homosexual sodomy, we were assured that the case had nothing, nothing at all to do with "whether the government must give formal recognition to any relationship that homosexual persons seek to enter." (citing *Lawrence*). Now we are told that DOMA is invalid because it "demeans the couple, whose moral and sexual choices the Constitution protects,"—with an accompanying citation of *Lawrence*. It takes real cheek for today's majority to assure us, as it is going out the door, that a constitutional requirement to give formal recognition to same-sex marriage is not at issue here—when what has preceded that assurance is a lecture on how superior the majority's moral judgment in favor of same-sex marriage is to the Congress's hateful moral judgment against it. I promise you this: The only thing that will "confine" the Court's holding is its sense of what it can get away with.

I do not mean to suggest disagreement with THE CHIEF JUSTICE'S view that lower federal courts and state courts can distinguish today's case when the issue before them is state denial of marital status to same-sex couples— or even that this Court could *theoretically* do so. Lord, an opinion with such scatter-shot rationales as this one (federalism noises among them) can be distinguished in many ways. And deserves to be. State and lower federal courts should take the Court at its word and distinguish away.

In my opinion, however, the view that *this* Court will take of state prohibition of same-sex marriage is indicated beyond mistaking by today's opinion. As I have said, the real rationale of today's opinion, whatever disappearing trail of its legalistic argle-bargle one chooses to follow, is that DOMA is motivated by " 'bare . . . desire to harm' " couples in same-sex marriages. How easy it is, indeed how inevitable, to reach the same conclusion with regard to state laws denying same-sex couples marital status. Consider how easy (inevitable) it is to make the following substitutions in a passage from today's opinion: * * *

> "[DOMA] *This state law* tells those couples, and all the world, that their otherwise valid marriages *relationships* are unworthy of federal *state* recognition. This places same-sex couples in an unstable position of being in a second-tier marriage *relationship*.

The differentiation demeans the couple, whose moral and sexual choices the Constitution protects, see *Lawrence,* . . . "

Or this, which does not even require alteration, except as to the invented number:

"And it humiliates ~~tens of~~ thousands of children now being raised by same-sex couples. The law in question makes it even more difficult for the children to understand the integrity and closeness of their own family and its concord with other families in their community and in their daily lives." * * *

Some will rejoice in today's decision, and some will despair at it; that is the nature of a controversy that matters so much to so many. But the Court has cheated both sides, robbing the winners of an honest victory, and the losers of the peace that comes from a fair defeat. We owed both of them better. I dissent.

JUSTICE ALITO, with whom JUSTICE THOMAS joins as to Parts II and III, dissenting.

[III.] Windsor and the United States are really seeking to have the Court resolve a debate between two competing views of marriage.

The first and older view, which I will call the "traditional" or "conjugal" view, sees marriage as an intrinsically opposite-sex institution. * * * [V]irtually every culture, including many not influenced by the Abrahamic religions, has limited marriage to people of the opposite sex. * * * While modern cultural changes have weakened the link between marriage and procreation in the popular mind, there is no doubt that, throughout human history and across many cultures, marriage has been viewed as an exclusively opposite-sex institution and as one inextricably linked to procreation and biological kinship.

The other, newer view is what I will call the "consent-based" vision of marriage, a vision that primarily defines marriage as the solemnization of mutual commitment—marked by strong emotional attachment and sexual attraction—between two persons. At least as it applies to heterosexual couples, this view of marriage now plays a very prominent role in the popular understanding of the institution. Indeed, our popular culture is infused with this understanding of marriage. Proponents of same-sex marriage argue that because gender differentiation is not relevant to this vision, the exclusion of same-sex couples from the institution of marriage is rank discrimination.

The Constitution does not codify either of these views of marriage (although I suspect it would have been hard at the time of the adoption of the Constitution or the Fifth Amendment to find Americans who did not take the traditional view for granted). The silence of the Constitution on this question should be enough to end the matter as far as the judiciary is concerned. * * *

Notes

1.   *The Dissenters' Critiques.* Notice that the dissents level several criticisms against the majority opinion in *Windsor*:

(a)   That the opinion is missing key doctrinal elements, such as the standard of review it is applying, as well as a clear statement of whether the opinion relies on "liberty" as a means of imposing equal protection on the federal government (as suggested by the citations to *Bolling v. Sharpe*, Casebook p. 98) or means to invoke liberty as an independent constitutional norm;

(b)   That the Court ought to leave the question of marriage equality to the political branches and public debate, which have been heavily engaged with the question in recent years;

(c)   That the majority wrongly imputes bias and animus to those who enacted DOMA, rather than a good faith difference of opinion; and

(d)   That, contrary to the disclaimer at the end of the majority opinion, the majority's rationale is unlikely to be limited to DOMA, as opposed to state laws that bar same-sex marriage.

Do you find merit in any of these critiques? Did Justice Kennedy answer them satisfactorily? Could a stronger opinion have been written in support of the result the Court reached? If so, how?

2.   *Dignity.* The majority emphasizes its view that DOMA undermines the dignity of same-sex couples who are married under state law. Indeed, some form of the word "dignity" is used no fewer than ten times in Justice Kennedy's full opinion. What does he mean by dignity? How ought a claim of dignitary harm be demonstrated? Does the idea of dignity merit a special place in 14th Amendment jurisprudence? How might it apply in other contexts, such as disputes over abortion and affirmative action? Note that human dignity is a key concept in some other constitutions, such as Germany's Basic Law. The term is not used in the U.S. Constitution, but is the concept implicit? Will the emphasis on dignity so strongly associated with Kennedy recede with his retirement?

3.   *Connections to* Romer *and* Lawrence. Compare Justice Kennedy's opinion to the opinions he wrote previously in *Romer* (Casebook, p. 474) and *Lawrence* (Casebook, p. 677). Do you notice similarities? Among other things, consider the *Windsor* majority opinion's repeated emphasis on the idea of respect for gay persons (a theme stressed in *Lawrence*) and on the unfair singling out of gay persons alone for a broadly-drawn legal disability (a theme stressed in *Romer*).

Two years to the day after *Windsor*, in an opinion once again authored by Justice Kennedy, the Court returned to the issue of same-sex marriage in the landmark case of *Obergefell v. Hodges*, ___ U.S. ___, 135 S.Ct. 2584 (2015). *Obergefell* declared a broad right of marriage equality applicable in every state. The Court placed principal emphasis not on equal protection, but on the fundamental right to marry. For that reason, the case appears in Chapter 5 of this Supplement. While the opinion focuses on due process, you will note that the majority invokes the equal protection clause as part of its analysis. After you read *Obergefell* in the next chapter, consider the following Problem.

PROBLEM 4–6:
A BAN ON LESBIAN, GAY OR TRANSGENDER
GRADE SCHOOL TEACHERS

Suppose a state enacts a law banning gay or lesbian persons from becoming public school teachers in kindergarten through fifth grade classes. The state cites as its justification its desire to shield young children for as long as possible from the complex issues of sexual orientation and gender identity. Gay, lesbian and transgender teachers challenge the law as a violation of equal protection. Consider the following questions.

(a)   What tier of scrutiny will be applied to this policy? Would a court distinguish the restriction on gay and lesbian teachers from the restriction on transgender teachers? Should it?

(b)   With respect to the ban on gay and lesbian teachers, review the argument for heightened scrutiny in the context of sexual orientation-based discrimination made in the Holder Letter on the federal Defense of Marriage Act (Casebook, pp. 503–505). What, if anything, does the *Obergefell* majority add on the issue of heightened scrutiny? Is it significant that Justice Kennedy's opinion in that case twice characterizes sexual orientation as immutable? That he begins his opinion by reviewing in detail the history of how American law has regarded homosexuality? Do you find anything else in the opinion that might bear on the tier of scrutiny a court would use?

(c)   How might the language about equal protection in the *Obergefell* majority bear on whether the ban on gay or lesbian teachers would pass muster under equal protection? How would this law fare if strict or intermediate scrutiny is used? If neither form of heightened scrutiny is used, do you think the law would survive equal protection challenge? You will note that there is no mention in *Obergefell* of the idea of "animus" that was employed in *Romer* and *Windsor*. Will the absence of that term in *Obergefell* affect subsequent equal protection challenges to laws discriminating on the basis of sexual orientation? Or is *Obergefell* best seen as limited to state marriage laws?

(d)   With respect to the ban on transgender teachers, review Problem 4–2.1 in this Supplement and consider whether it sheds any light. How would this part of the policy on teachers fare under the constitutional standard for sex discrimination? To the extent that discrimination on gender identity is not considered a form of sex discrimination, is there an independent basis to argue for heightened scrutiny of gender identity classifications under the criteria invoked in the Holder letter? If not, how would an animus argument fare? For arguments about the level of scrutiny for gender identity discrimination, see Kevin M. Barry, Brian Farrell, Jennifer L. Levi and Neelima Vanguri, *A Bare Desire to Harm: Transgender People and the Equal Protection Clause*, 57 B.C. L. REV. 507 (2016).

CHAPTER 5

PROTECTING FUNDAMENTAL RIGHTS

■ ■ ■

SECTION 2. PROTECTING ECONOMIC LIBERTY AND PROPERTY

C. THE TAKINGS CLAUSE

Page 569. Insert before Section 3:

———————

In *Horne v. Department of Agriculture*, ___ U.S. ___, 135 S.Ct. 2419 (2015), a 5–4 majority of the Court held that the Takings Clause applies to personal property, just as it applies to real property. The case involved a challenge by raisin growers to a federal agricultural subsidy program that required them to set aside a percentage of their annual crop. The purpose of the program is to limit supply as a way to stabilize prices. Pursuant to the program, the government physically takes possession of the raisins mandated to be set aside. Chief Justice Roberts wrote that "the Government has a categorical duty to pay just compensation when it takes your car, just as when it takes your home." Language in *Lucas* suggesting a different approach to *regulatory takings* of personal versus real property is irrelevant, the Court said, to takings involving the physical appropriation of property.

On the other hand, the Court handed property right advocates a defeat in Murr v. Wisconsin, ___ U.S. ___, 137 S.Ct. 1933 (2017). *Murr* involved the denominator problem raised by the *Lucas* total taking doctrine. The case involved two pieces of adjoining property on the banks of the St. Croix River, both owned by the same people. Because of the small size of the lots, the owners were only allowed to develop them together. Since neither lot could be developed separately, the claim was that this was a total taking of each lot.

The majority by Justice Kennedy and the dissent by Chief Justice Roberts rejected the owners' claim of a total taking, but on different grounds. The majority said that the "parcel" should be defined as both lots put together, based on a multi-factored test. Since the combined lot continued to have a lot of value, there was not a total taking. The dissenters said that each lot was a separate piece of property, but still concluded that there was no total taking. While the dissent wasn't willing to be flexible in defining the relevant parcel for determining a total taking, it was flexible in considering whether a total taking of that parcel took place. The reason was that each lot retained considerable usefulness, since it could be combined with the adjoining lot in a very profitable construction project. While joining the main dissent, Justice Thomas also suggested that it was time to reopen the question of the original meaning of the Constitution and the extent to which it supported current doctrine.

Both the Kennedy and Roberts opinions stressed the flexibility needed to apply the takings clause. By doing so, they seem to deemphasize the strict categorical rules favored by Justice Scalia without rejecting them outright.

SECTION 3. EQUAL PROTECTION AND "FUNDAMENTAL INTERESTS"

A. VOTING

Page 580. Insert after *PROBLEM 5–1: POLITICAL GERRYMANDERING*:

One mechanism some states have used to control political gerrymandering is the creation of independent commissions to handle redistricting. The voters in Arizona pursued this course in 2000 by passing a state constitutional amendment that reallocated authority from the state legislature to the Arizona Independent Redistricting Commission. The state legislature challenged this measure as a violation of the Elections Clause, Art. I, § 4, cl. 1, which provides that the "Times, Places and Manner of holding Elections for Senators and Representatives shall be prescribed in each State by the *Legislature* thereof." (emphasis added). In *Arizona State Legislature v. Arizona Independent Redistricting Comm'n*, ___ U.S. ___, 135 S.Ct. 2652 (2015), the Court by a 5–4 majority rejected this challenge. The case turned on how to interpret the word "legislature" in the Clause. Justice Ginsburg's opinion for the Court reasoned that when the legislative power of a state is given by state constitution to the people, acting through the initiative process, they constitute the "legislature" for purposes of the Elections Clause. The opinion emphasized the norm of self-government (noting that direct democracy is consistent with the idea of popular sovereignty that underlies the Constitution's creation of republican government) and the policy consequences that would flow from a contrary ruling (noting that many election-related laws passed directly by voters around the country would be jeopardized). In dissent, Chief Justice Roberts argued that Senators were chosen by state legislatures, not popular vote, under the original Constitution. If judges could legitimately read the word legislature in the Elections Clause to include the people acting in a legislative capacity, he suggested, there would have been no need for the Seventeenth Amendment because even a change as consequential as popular election of Senators could have been accomplished by an act of simple judicial interpretation.

The Court decided two cases in its most recent Term that gave the justices the opportunity to determine whether political gerrymandering is subject to meaningful judicial review and, if it is, to identify the governing standard. In neither case did the Court do so. Instead, both cases were decided on procedural questions. *Gill v. Whitford*, ___ U.S. ___, 138 S.Ct. 1916 (2018) (remanding for determination whether plaintiffs have standing under the principles identified in opinion); *Benisek v. Lamone*, ___ U.S. ___, 138 S.Ct. 1942 (2018) (affirming lower court ruling that had declined to preliminarily enjoin the disputed map). In light of these rulings, uncertainty about the constitutionality of partisan gerrymandering remains.

SECTION 4. FUNDAMENTAL PRIVACY RIGHTS

B. ABORTION

Page 674.   Insert after *NOTE ON* GONZALES V. CARHART:

WHOLE WOMAN'S HEALTH V. HELLERSTEDT
___ U.S. ___, 136 S.Ct. 2292, 195 L.Ed.2d 665 (2016)

JUSTICE BREYER delivered the opinion of the Court.

In *Planned Parenthood of Southeastern Pa. v. Casey*, a plurality of the Court concluded that there "exists" an "undue burden" on a woman's right to decide to have an abortion, and consequently a provision of law is constitutionally invalid, if the "*purpose or effect*" of the provision "*is to place a substantial obstacle* in the path of a woman seeking an abortion before the fetus attains viability." (Emphasis added.) The plurality added that "[u]nnecessary health regulations that have the purpose or effect of presenting a substantial obstacle to a woman seeking an abortion impose an undue burden on the right."

We must here decide whether two provisions of Texas' House Bill 2 violate the Federal Constitution as interpreted in *Casey*. The first provision, which we shall call the "*admitting-privileges requirement,*" says that

> "[a] physician performing or inducing an abortion . . . must, on the date the abortion is performed or induced, have active admitting privileges at a hospital that . . . is located not further than 30 miles from the location at which the abortion is performed or induced." Tex. Health & Safety Code Ann. § 171.0031(a) (West Cum. Supp. 2015).

This provision amended Texas law that had previously required an abortion facility to maintain a written protocol "for managing medical emergencies and the transfer of patients requiring further emergency care to a hospital." 38 Tex. Reg. 6546 (2013).

The second provision, which we shall call the *"surgical-center requirement,"* says that

> "the minimum standards for an abortion facility must be equivalent to the minimum standards adopted under [the Texas Health and Safety Code section] for ambulatory surgical centers." Tex. Health & Safety Code Ann. § 245.010(a).

We conclude that neither of these provisions confers medical benefits sufficient to justify the burdens upon access that each imposes. Each places a substantial obstacle in the path of women seeking a previability abortion, each constitutes an undue burden on abortion access, and each violates the Federal Constitution.

[The Court reviewed the procedural history of the Texas legislation. The admitting privileges requirement was first challenged in court in 2013. The District Court enjoined the measure, but the Fifth Circuit upheld it. After that ruling, a group of abortion providers, some of whom had participated in the first lawsuit, filed a new challenge and pointed to changed circumstances since the first lawsuit was filed. This second lawsuit challenged the admitting privileges requirement as applied to physicians at two abortion facilities, and added new claims challenging the surgical center requirement. The District Court held a bench trial to determine the constitutionality of the requirements.] On the basis of the stipulations, depositions, and testimony, [the District Court] reached the following conclusions:

1. Of Texas' population of more than 25 million people, "approximately 5.4 million" are "women" of "reproductive age," living within a geographical area of "nearly 280,000 square miles."

2. "In recent years, the number of abortions reported in Texas has stayed fairly consistent at approximately 15–16% of the reported pregnancy rate, for a total number of approximately 60,000–72,000 legal abortions performed annually."

3. Prior to the enactment of H.B. 2, there were more than 40 licensed abortion facilities in Texas, which "number dropped by almost half leading up to and in the wake of enforcement of the admitting-privileges requirement that went into effect in late-October 2013."

4. If the surgical-center provision were allowed to take effect, the number of abortion facilities, after September 1, 2014, would be reduced further, so that "only seven facilities and a potential eighth will exist in Texas."

5. Abortion facilities "will remain only in Houston, Austin, San Antonio, and the Dallas/Fort Worth metropolitan region." These include "one facility in Austin, two in Dallas, one in Fort Worth, two in Houston, and either one or two in San Antonio."

6.   "Based on historical data pertaining to Texas's average number of abortions, and assuming perfectly equal distribution among the remaining seven or eight providers, this would result in each facility serving between 7,500 and 10,000 patients per year. Accounting for the seasonal variations in pregnancy rates and a slightly unequal distribution of patients at each clinic, it is foreseeable that over 1,200 women per month could be vying for counseling, appointments, and follow-up visits at some of these facilities."

7.   The suggestion "that these seven or eight providers could meet the demand of the entire state stretches credulity."

8.   "Between November 1, 2012 and May 1, 2014," that is, before and after enforcement of the admitting-privileges requirement, "the decrease in geographical distribution of abortion facilities" has meant that the number of women of reproductive age living more than 50 miles from a clinic has doubled (from 800,000 to over 1.6 million); those living more than 100 miles has increased by 150% (from 400,000 to 1 million); those living more than 150 miles has increased by more than 350% (from 86,000 to 400,000); and those living more than 200 miles has increased by about 2,800% (from 10,000 to 290,000). After September 2014, should the surgical-center requirement go into effect, the number of women of reproductive age living significant distances from an abortion provider will increase as follows: 2 million women of reproductive age will live more than 50 miles from an abortion provider; 1.3 million will live more than 100 miles from an abortion provider; 900,000 will live more than 150 miles from an abortion provider; and 750,000 more than 200 miles from an abortion provider.

9.   The "two requirements erect a particularly high barrier for poor, rural, or disadvantaged women."

10.   "The great weight of evidence demonstrates that, before the act's passage, abortion in Texas was extremely safe with particularly low rates of serious complications and virtually no deaths occurring on account of the procedure."

11.   "Abortion, as regulated by the State before the enactment of House Bill 2, has been shown to be much safer, in terms of minor and serious complications, than many common medical procedures not subject to such intense regulation and scrutiny." App. 223–224 (describing risks in colonoscopies), 254 (discussing risks in vasectomy and endometrial biopsy, among others), 275–277 (discussing complication rate in plastic surgery).

12.   "Additionally, risks are not appreciably lowered for patients who undergo abortions at ambulatory surgical centers as compared to nonsurgical-center facilities."

13. "[W]omen will not obtain better care or experience more frequent positive outcomes at an ambulatory surgical center as compared to a previously licensed facility."

14. "[T]here are 433 licensed ambulatory surgical centers in Texas," of which "336 . . . are apparently either 'grandfathered' or enjo[y] the benefit of a waiver of some or all" of the surgical-center "requirements."

15. The "cost of coming into compliance" with the surgical-center requirement "for existing clinics is significant," "undisputedly approach[ing] 1 million dollars," and "most likely exceed[ing] 1.5 million dollars," with "[s]ome . . . clinics" unable to "comply due to physical size limitations of their sites." The "cost of acquiring land and constructing a new compliant clinic will likely exceed three million dollars." * * *

[The Court reviewed and rejected the state's argument that that petitioners' constitutional claims were barred by principles of res judicata. It then turned to the merits]. * * *

We begin with the standard, as described in *Casey*. We recognize that the "State has a legitimate interest in seeing to it that abortion, like any other medical procedure, is performed under circumstances that insure maximum safety for the patient." But, we added, "a statute which, while furthering [a] valid state interest, has the effect of placing a substantial obstacle in the path of a woman's choice cannot be considered a permissible means of serving its legitimate ends." Moreover, "[u]nnecessary health regulations that have the purpose or effect of presenting a substantial obstacle to a woman seeking an abortion impose an undue burden on the right."

The Court of Appeals wrote that a state law is "constitutional if: (1) it does not have the purpose or effect of placing a substantial obstacle in the path of a woman seeking an abortion of a nonviable fetus; and (2) it is reasonably related to (or designed to further) a legitimate state interest." The Court of Appeals went on to hold that "the district court erred by substituting its own judgment for that of the legislature" when it conducted its "undue burden inquiry," in part because "medical uncertainty underlying a statute is for resolution by legislatures, not the courts." *Id.,* at 587 (citing *Gonzales v. Carhart*).

The Court of Appeals' articulation of the relevant standard is incorrect. The first part of the Court of Appeals' test may be read to imply that a district court should not consider the existence or nonexistence of medical benefits when considering whether a regulation of abortion constitutes an undue burden. The rule announced in *Casey,* however, requires that courts consider the burdens a law imposes on abortion access together with the benefits those laws confer. See 505 U.S., at 887–898 (opinion of the Court) (performing this balancing with respect to a spousal notification provision); *id.,* at 899–901 (joint opinion of O'Connor, KENNEDY, and Souter, JJ.)

(same balancing with respect to a parental notification provision). And the second part of the test is wrong to equate the judicial review applicable to the regulation of a constitutionally protected personal liberty with the less strict review applicable where, for example, economic legislation is at issue. See, *e.g., Williamson v. Lee Optical of Okla., Inc.* The Court of Appeals' approach simply does not match the standard that this Court laid out in *Casey,* which asks courts to consider whether any burden imposed on abortion access is "undue."

The statement that legislatures, and not courts, must resolve questions of medical uncertainty is also inconsistent with this Court's case law. Instead, the Court, when determining the constitutionality of laws regulating abortion procedures, has placed considerable weight upon evidence and argument presented in judicial proceedings. In *Casey,* for example, we relied heavily on the District Court's factual findings and the research-based submissions of *amici* in declaring a portion of the law at issue unconstitutional. 505 U.S., at 888–894 (opinion of the Court) (discussing evidence related to the prevalence of spousal abuse in determining that a spousal notification provision erected an undue burden to abortion access). And, in *Gonzales* the Court, while pointing out that we must review legislative "factfinding under a deferential standard," added that we must not "place dispositive weight" on those "findings." *Gonzales* went on to point out that the *"Court retains an independent constitutional duty to review factual findings where constitutional rights are at stake." Ibid.* (emphasis added). Although there we upheld a statute regulating abortion, we did not do so solely on the basis of legislative findings explicitly set forth in the statute, noting that "evidence presented in the District Courts contradicts" some of the legislative findings. In these circumstances, we said, "[u]ncritical deference to Congress' factual findings . . . is inappropriate."

Unlike in *Gonzales,* the relevant statute here does not set forth any legislative findings. Rather, one is left to infer that the legislature sought to further a constitutionally acceptable objective (namely, protecting women's health). For a district court to give significant weight to evidence in the judicial record in these circumstances is consistent with this Court's case law. As we shall describe, the District Court did so here. It did not simply substitute its own judgment for that of the legislature. It considered the evidence in the record—including expert evidence, presented in stipulations, depositions, and testimony. It then weighed the asserted benefits against the burdens. We hold that, in so doing, the District Court applied the correct legal standard.

Turning to the lower courts' evaluation of the evidence, we first consider the admitting-privileges requirement. Before the enactment of H.B. 2, doctors who provided abortions were required to "have admitting privileges *or* have a working arrangement with a physician(s) who has admitting privileges at a local hospital in order to ensure the necessary back up for medical complications." (emphasis added). The new law changed this requirement by requiring that a "physician performing or inducing an abortion . . . must, on the date the abortion is performed or induced, have active admitting privileges at a hospital that . . . is located not further than 30 miles from the location at which the abortion is performed or induced." * * *

The purpose of the admitting-privileges requirement is to help ensure that women have easy access to a hospital should complications arise during an abortion procedure. But the District Court found that it brought about no such health-related benefit. The court found that "[t]he great weight of evidence demonstrates that, before the act's passage, abortion in Texas was extremely safe with particularly low rates of serious complications and virtually no deaths occurring on account of the procedure." Thus, there was no significant health-related problem that the new law helped to cure.

The evidence upon which the court based this conclusion included, among other things:

- A collection of at least five peer-reviewed studies on abortion complications in the first trimester, showing that the highest rate of major complications—including those complications requiring hospital admission—was less than one-quarter of 1%.

- Figures in three peer-reviewed studies showing that the highest complication rate found for the much rarer second trimester abortion was less than one-half of 1% (0.45% or about 1 out of about 200).

- Expert testimony to the effect that complications rarely require hospital admission, much less immediate transfer to a hospital from an outpatient clinic. * * *

- Expert testimony stating that "it is extremely unlikely that a patient will experience a serious complication at the clinic that requires emergent hospitalization" and "in the rare case in which [one does], the quality of care that the patient receives is not affected by whether the abortion provider has admitting privileges at the hospital."

- Expert testimony stating that in respect to surgical abortion patients who do suffer complications requiring hospitalization, most of these complications occur in the days after the abortion, not on the spot.

- Expert testimony stating that a delay before the onset of complications is also expected for medical abortions, as "abortifacient drugs take time to exert their effects, and thus the abortion itself almost always occurs after the patient has left the abortion facility."

- Some experts added that, if a patient needs a hospital in the day or week following her abortion, she will likely seek medical attention at the hospital nearest her home.

We have found nothing in Texas' record evidence that shows that, compared to prior law (which required a "working arrangement" with a doctor with admitting privileges), the new law advanced Texas' legitimate interest in protecting women's health.

We add that, when directly asked at oral argument whether Texas knew of a single instance in which the new requirement would have helped even one woman obtain better treatment, Texas admitted that there was no evidence in the record of such a case. See Tr. of Oral Arg. 47. This answer is consistent with the findings of the other Federal District Courts that have considered the health benefits of other States' similar admitting-privileges laws.

At the same time, the record evidence indicates that the admitting-privileges requirement places a "substantial obstacle in the path of a woman's choice." *Casey* (plurality opinion). The District Court found, as of the time the admitting-privileges requirement began to be enforced, the number of facilities providing abortions dropped in half, from about 40 to about 20. Eight abortion clinics closed in the months leading up to the requirement's effective date. Eleven more closed on the day the admitting-privileges requirement took effect.

Other evidence helps to explain why the new requirement led to the closure of clinics. We read that other evidence in light of a brief filed in this Court by the Society of Hospital Medicine. That brief describes the undisputed general fact that "hospitals often condition admitting privileges on reaching a certain number of admissions per year." Returning to the District Court record, we note that, in direct testimony, the president of Nova Health Systems, implicitly relying on this general fact, pointed out that it would be difficult for doctors regularly performing abortions at the El Paso clinic to obtain admitting privileges at nearby hospitals because "[d]uring the past 10 years, over 17,000 abortion procedures were performed at the El Paso clinic [and n]ot a single one of those patients had to be transferred to a hospital for emergency treatment, much less admitted to the hospital." In a word, doctors would be unable to maintain admitting privileges or obtain those privileges for the future, because the fact that abortions are so safe meant that providers were unlikely to have any patients to admit. * * *

In our view, the record contains sufficient evidence that the admitting-privileges requirement led to the closure of half of Texas' clinics, or thereabouts. Those closures meant fewer doctors, longer waiting times, and increased crowding. Record evidence also supports the finding that after the admitting-privileges provision went into effect, the "number of women of reproductive age living in a county ... more than 150 miles from a provider increased from approximately 86,000 to 400,000 ... and the number of women living in a county more than 200 miles from a provider from approximately 10,000 to 290,000." We recognize that increased driving distances do not always constitute an "undue burden." See *Casey* (joint opinion of O'Connor, KENNEDY, and Souter, JJ.). But here, those increases are but one additional burden, which, when taken together with others that the closings brought about, and when viewed in light of the virtual absence of any health benefit, lead us to conclude that the record adequately supports the District Court's "undue burden" conclusion. * * *

The second challenged provision of Texas' new law sets forth the surgical-center requirement. Prior to enactment of the new requirement, Texas law required abortion facilities to meet a host of health and safety requirements. * * * These requirements are policed by random and announced inspections, at least annually, as well as administrative penalties, injunctions, civil penalties, and criminal penalties for certain violations.

H.B. 2 added the requirement that an "abortion facility" meet the "minimum standards . . . for ambulatory surgical centers" under Texas law. The surgical-center regulations include, among other things, detailed specifications relating to the size of the nursing staff, building dimensions, and other building requirements. The nursing staff must comprise at least "an adequate number of [registered nurses] on duty to meet the following minimum staff requirements: director of the department (or designee), and supervisory and staff personnel for each service area to assure the immediate availability of [a registered nurse] for emergency care or for any patient when needed," as well as "a second individual on duty on the premises who is trained and currently certified in basic cardiac life support until all patients have been discharged from the facility" for facilities that provide moderate sedation, such as most abortion facilities. Facilities must include a full surgical suite with an operating room that has "a clear floor area of at least 240 square feet" in which "[t]he minimum clear dimension between built-in cabinets, counters, and shelves shall be 14 feet." There must be a preoperative patient holding room and a postoperative recovery suite. The former "shall be provided and arranged in a one-way traffic pattern so that patients entering from outside the surgical suite can change, gown, and move directly into the restricted corridor of the surgical suite," and the latter "shall be arranged to provide a one-way traffic pattern from the restricted surgical corridor to the postoperative recovery suite, and then to the extended observation rooms or discharge." Surgical centers must meet numerous other spatial requirements, including specific corridor widths. Surgical centers must also have an advanced heating, ventilation, and air conditioning system, and must satisfy particular piping system and plumbing requirements. Dozens of other sections list additional requirements that apply to surgical centers.

There is considerable evidence in the record supporting the District Court's findings indicating that the statutory provision requiring all abortion facilities to meet all surgical-center standards does not benefit patients and is not necessary. The District Court found that "risks are not appreciably lowered for patients who undergo abortions at ambulatory surgical centers as compared to nonsurgical-center facilities." The court added that women "will not obtain better care or experience more frequent positive outcomes at an ambulatory surgical center as compared to a previously licensed facility." And these findings are well supported.

The record makes clear that the surgical-center requirement provides no benefit when complications arise in the context of an abortion produced through medication. That is because, in such a case, complications would almost always arise only after the patient has left the facility. The record also contains evidence indicating that abortions taking place in an abortion facility are safe—indeed, safer than numerous procedures that take place outside hospitals and to which Texas does not apply its surgical-center requirements. * * *

Moreover, many surgical-center requirements are inappropriate as applied to surgical abortions. [The opinion described extensive requirements designed to prevent infection]. But abortions typically involve either the administration of medicines or procedures performed through the natural opening of the birth canal, which is itself not sterile. Nor do provisions designed to safeguard heavily sedated patients (unable to help themselves) during fire emergencies provide any help to abortion patients, as abortion facilities do not use general anesthesia or deep sedation. Further, since the few instances in which serious complications do arise following an abortion almost always require hospitalization, not treatment at a surgical center, surgical-center standards will not help in those instances either.

The upshot is that this record evidence, along with the absence of any evidence to the contrary, provides ample support for the District Court's conclusion that "[m]any of the building standards mandated by the act and its implementing rules have such a tangential relationship to patient safety in the context of abortion as to be nearly arbitrary." * * * The record evidence thus supports the ultimate legal conclusion that the surgical-center requirement is not necessary.

At the same time, the record provides adequate evidentiary support for the District Court's conclusion that the surgical-center requirement places a substantial obstacle in the path of women seeking an abortion. The parties stipulated that the requirement would further reduce the number of abortion facilities available to seven or eight facilities, located in Houston, Austin, San Antonio, and Dallas/Fort Worth. In the District Court's view, the proposition that these "seven or eight providers could meet the demand of the entire State stretches credulity." We take this statement as a finding that these few facilities could not "meet" that "demand." * * *

More fundamentally, in the face of no threat to women's health, Texas seeks to force women to travel long distances to get abortions in crammed-to-capacity superfacilities. Patients seeking these services are less likely to get the kind of individualized attention, serious conversation, and emotional support that doctors at less taxed facilities may have offered. Healthcare facilities and medical professionals are not fungible commodities. Surgical centers attempting to accommodate sudden, vastly increased demand, may find that quality of care declines. Another commonsense inference that the District Court made is that these effects would be harmful to, not supportive of, women's health. * * *

We agree with the District Court that the surgical-center requirement, like the admitting-privileges requirement, provides few, if any, health benefits for women, poses a substantial obstacle to women seeking abortions, and constitutes an "undue burden" on their constitutional right to do so. * * *

JUSTICE GINSBURG, concurring.

Many medical procedures, including childbirth, are far more dangerous to patients, yet are not subject to ambulatory-surgical-center or hospital admitting-privileges requirements. Given those realities, it is beyond rational belief that H.B. 2 could genuinely protect the health of women, and certain that the law "would simply make it more difficult for them to obtain abortions." When a State severely limits access to safe and legal procedures, women in desperate circumstances may resort to unlicensed rogue practitioners, *faute de mieux,* at great risk to their health and safety. So long as this Court adheres to *Roe v. Wade* and *Planned Parenthood of Southeastern Pa. v. Casey*, Targeted Regulation of Abortion Providers laws like H.B. 2 that "do little or nothing for health, but rather strew impediments to abortion," cannot survive judicial inspection.

JUSTICE THOMAS, dissenting.

I remain fundamentally opposed to the Court's abortion jurisprudence. Even taking *Casey* as the baseline, however, the majority radically rewrites the undue-burden test. * * *

First, the majority's free-form balancing test is contrary to *Casey*. * * * *Casey* did not balance the benefits and burdens of Pennsylvania's spousal and parental notification provisions, either. Pennsylvania's spousal notification requirement, the plurality said, imposed an undue burden because findings established that the requirement would "likely . . . prevent a significant number of women from obtaining an abortion"—not because these burdens outweighed its benefits. * * *

Second, by rejecting the notion that "legislatures, and not courts, must resolve questions of medical uncertainty," the majority discards another core element of the *Casey* framework. Before today, this Court had "given state and federal legislatures wide discretion to pass legislation in areas where there is medical and scientific uncertainty." This Court emphasized that this "traditional rule" of deference "is consistent with *Casey*." This Court underscored that legislatures should not be hamstrung "if some part of the medical community were disinclined to follow the proscription." And this Court concluded that "[c]onsiderations of marginal safety, including the balance of risks, are within the legislative competence when the regulation is rational and in pursuit of legitimate ends." This Court could not have been clearer: Whenever medical justifications for an abortion restriction are debatable, that "provides a sufficient basis to conclude in [a] facial attack that the [law] does not impose an undue burden." *Gonzales*. Otherwise, legislatures would face "too exacting" a standard.

Finally, the majority overrules another central aspect of *Casey* by requiring laws to have more than a rational basis even if they do not substantially impede access to abortion. "Where [the State] *has a rational basis to act* and it does not impose an undue burden," this Court previously held, "the State may use its regulatory power" to impose regulations "in furtherance of its legitimate interests in regulating the medical profession in order to promote respect for life, including life of the unborn." *Gonzales*. No longer. Though the majority declines to say how substantial a State's interest must be, one thing is clear: The State's burden has been ratcheted to a level that has not applied for a quarter century. * * *

The majority's undue-burden test looks far less like our post-*Casey* precedents and far more like the strict-scrutiny standard that *Casey* rejected, under which only the most compelling rationales justified restrictions on abortion. One searches the majority opinion in vain for any acknowledgment of the "premise central" to *Casey*'s rejection of strict scrutiny: "that the government has a legitimate and substantial interest in preserving and promoting fetal life" from conception, not just in regulating medical procedures. Meanwhile, the majority's undue-burden balancing approach risks ruling out even minor, previously valid infringements on access to abortion. * * *

The majority's furtive reconfiguration of the standard of scrutiny applicable to abortion restrictions also points to a deeper problem. The undue-burden standard is just one variant of the Court's tiers-of-scrutiny approach to constitutional adjudication. And the label the Court affixes to its level of scrutiny in assessing whether the government can restrict a given right—be it "rational basis," intermediate, strict, or something else—is increasingly a meaningless formalism. As the Court applies whatever standard it likes to any given case, nothing but empty words separates our constitutional decisions from judicial fiat.

Though the tiers of scrutiny have become a ubiquitous feature of constitutional law, they are of recent vintage. Only in the 1960's did the Court begin in earnest to speak of "strict scrutiny" versus reviewing legislation for mere rationality, and to develop the contours of these tests. See Fallon, Strict Judicial Scrutiny, 54 UCLA L. Rev. 1267, 1274, 1284–1285 (2007). * * *

The illegitimacy of using "made-up tests" to "displace longstanding national traditions as the primary determinant of what the Constitution means" has long been apparent. The Constitution does not prescribe tiers of scrutiny. The three basic tiers—"rational basis," intermediate, and strict scrutiny—"are no more scientific than their names suggest, and a further element of randomness is added by the fact that it is largely up to us which test will be applied in each case."

But the problem now goes beyond that. If our recent cases illustrate anything, it is how easily the Court tinkers with levels of scrutiny to achieve its desired result. This Term, it is easier for a State to survive strict scrutiny despite discriminating on the basis of race in college admissions than it is for the same State to regulate how abortion doctors and clinics operate under the putatively less stringent undue-burden test. * * *

Today's decision will prompt some to claim victory, just as it will stiffen opponents' will to object. But the entire Nation has lost something essential. The majority's embrace of a jurisprudence of rights-specific exceptions and balancing tests is "a regrettable concession of defeat—an acknowledgement that we have passed the point where 'law,' properly speaking, has any further application." Scalia, The Rule of Law as a Law of Rules, 56 U. Chi. L. Rev. 1175, 1182 (1989). I respectfully dissent.

[**JUSTICE ALITO**, joined by **JUSTICE THOMAS** and the **CHIEF JUSTICE**, wrote a dissent that focused on the res judicata issue and then contested the factual sufficiency of the case against the both Texas requirements].

NOTES

1. *Whole Woman's Health* was decided nearly 25 years after *Casey*. During those years, state legislatures skeptical about abortion had passed scores of so-called Targeted Regulation of Abortion Provider (TRAP) laws all over the country. Notice the fact-intensive nature of Justice Breyer's majority opinion. What limits has this case placed on TRAP laws? Does the Court's approach suggest that trial courts will play a particularly significant role? That expert witnesses will be important?

2.　On the state's factual basis for regulating abortion, compare Justice Breyer's approach in this case to Justice Kennedy's in *Gonzales v. Carhart* (Casebook, p. 665), the Court's last major opinion on abortion. On the subject of women coming to regret abortions, Kennedy said in *Gonzales* that "[w]hile we find no reliable data to measure the phenomenon, it seems unexceptionable to conclude that some women come to regret their choice to abort the infant life they once created and sustained" (citing an amicus brief). Does Justice Breyer's detailed approach to the evidence suggest that states will now have to be more data-driven if they seek to justify abortion regulation as a way to protect women's interests?

3.　Consider the debate between Justices Breyer and Thomas as to whether or not the "undue burden" test imposed by *Casey* requires courts to consider the benefits of an abortion regulation to women or just the burdens the law imposes. In light of your reading of *Casey*, who has the better of this argument? Does the word "undue" itself suggest that a court must consider the justification for a law in order to determine whether its burden is unlawfully imposed or not? To the extent that *Casey* had not clearly resolved the question, do you think Justice Breyer's approach makes sense?

4.　Perhaps the most doctrinally significant aspect of the case was how it resolved questions about the standard of review courts should use in assessing the necessity for an abortion regulation. The Court rejected the argument—pressed by the state and the Fifth Circuit—that courts should separate their review of medical necessity from the question of undue burden, and should consider the necessity issue under the forgiving standard of rationality. What standard did the Court substitute in place of rational basis? In this aspect of the analysis, did the Court depart from the approach to legislative beliefs about medical facts that was employed in *Gonzales v. Carhart*? What do you make of Justice Thomas' argument that the Court functionally reinstated the strict scrutiny of *Roe* or something close to it? Had the Court given the clear endorsement of rational-basis review for medical necessity that Justice Thomas favored, would it have functionally overruled *Roe* in its entirety?

5.　Justice Ginsburg's dissent was brief and pointed. Although not all of it is reproduced here, it consisted of only one long paragraph. Is her dissent suggesting that the very purpose of TRAP laws is to create an obstacle to abortion? Recall that *Casey* says a law creates an undue burden if it has the purpose *or* effect of creating an obstacle to abortion. Would the majority have been justified in focusing less on effects and concluding, instead, that the purpose of the Texas requirements was to reduce access to abortion? For an illustration of this more aggressive approach, see Judge Richard Posner's conclusion about a similar admitting privilege requirement imposed in Wisconsin. *Planned Parenthood of Wis., Inc. v. Schimel*, 806 F.3d 908, 921 (7th Cir. 2015) ("Opponents of abortion reveal their true objectives when they procure legislation limited to a medical procedure—abortion—that rarely produces a medical emergency").

6.   In light of Justice Kennedy's pivotal role in *Casey*, and his vote with the majority in *Whole Women's Health*, his retirement occasioned extended commentary about what his departure might mean for *Roe v. Wade* and abortion rights. Note that overruling *Roe*—and *Casey*—would by no means be the only way to further restrict abortion rights. As Justice Thomas' dissent in *Whole Woman's Health* suggests, the "undue burden" test could be interpreted and applied so as to permit greater state regulation that substantially reduces access to abortion.

D. THE RIGHT TO MARRY

Page 691.   Delete *NOTE ON THE CONSTITUTIONAL RIGHT TO MARRY* and insert the following material at the end of Section 4:

In a highly anticipated ruling near the end of the Term, the Supreme Court decided what seems destined to become one of the most significant cases in a generation or more. It inspired a heated debate among the justices about the appropriate role of courts.

OBERGEFELL V. HODGES
___ U.S. ___, 135 S.Ct. 2584, 192 L.Ed.2d 609 (2015)

[Voters in Michigan, Kentucky, Ohio and Tennessee enacted state constitutional amendments defining marriage as a union between one man and one woman. Same-sex couples challenged the denial of their right to marry and to have out-of-state marriages that were valid where performed recognized in any of these states. The Sixth Circuit upheld the bans in 2014. That decision conflicted with decisions of several federal appellate courts in favor of marriage equality. Two Terms after it had struck down the federal Defense of Marriage Act as unconstitutional in *United States v. Windsor* (Chapter Four of this Supplement), the Supreme Court granted review to decide whether the Fourteenth Amendment requires states to license a marriage between two people of the same-sex and/or to recognize a same-sex marriage licensed in another state.]

JUSTICE KENNEDY delivered the opinion of the Court.

[II.] From their beginning to their most recent page, the annals of human history reveal the transcendent importance of marriage. The lifelong union of a man and a woman always has promised nobility and dignity to all persons, without regard to their station in life. Marriage is sacred to those who live by their religions and offers unique fulfillment to those who find meaning in the secular realm. Its dynamic allows two people to find a life that could not be found alone, for a marriage becomes greater than just the two persons. Rising from the most basic human needs, marriage is essential to our most profound hopes and aspirations.

The centrality of marriage to the human condition makes it unsurprising that the institution has existed for millennia and across civilizations. Since the dawn of history, marriage has transformed strangers into relatives, binding families and societies together. * * *

The petitioners acknowledge this history but contend that these cases cannot end there. * * * Far from seeking to devalue marriage, the petitioners seek it for themselves because of their respect—and need—for its privileges and responsibilities. And their immutable nature dictates that same-sex marriage is their only real path to this profound commitment.

Recounting the circumstances of three of these cases illustrates the urgency of the petitioners' cause from their perspective. Petitioner James Obergefell, a plaintiff in the Ohio case, met John Arthur over two decades ago. They fell in love and started a life together, establishing a lasting, committed relation. In 2011, however, Arthur was diagnosed with amyotrophic lateral sclerosis, or ALS. This debilitating disease is progressive, with no known cure. Two years ago, Obergefell and Arthur decided to commit to one another, resolving to marry before Arthur died. To fulfill their mutual promise, they traveled from Ohio to Maryland, where same-sex marriage was legal. It was difficult for Arthur to move, and so the couple were wed inside a medical transport plane as it remained on the tarmac in Baltimore. Three months later, Arthur died. Ohio law does not permit Obergefell to be listed as the surviving spouse on Arthur's death certificate. By statute, they must remain strangers even in death, a state-imposed separation Obergefell deems "hurtful for the rest of time." He brought suit to be shown as the surviving spouse on Arthur's death certificate.

April DeBoer and Jayne Rowse are co-plaintiffs in the case from Michigan. They celebrated a commitment ceremony to honor their permanent relation in 2007. They both work as nurses, DeBoer in a neonatal unit and Rowse in an emergency unit. In 2009, DeBoer and Rowse fostered and then adopted a baby boy. Later that same year, they welcomed another son into their family. The new baby, born prematurely and abandoned by his biological mother, required around-the-clock care. The next year, a baby girl with special needs joined their family. Michigan, however, permits only opposite-sex married couples or single individuals to adopt, so each child can have only one woman as his or her legal parent. If an emergency were to arise, schools and hospitals may treat the three children as if they had only one parent. And, were tragedy to befall either DeBoer or Rowse, the other would have no legal rights over the children she had not been permitted to adopt. This couple seeks relief from the continuing uncertainty their unmarried status creates in their lives.

Army Reserve Sergeant First Class Ijpe DeKoe and his partner Thomas Kostura, co-plaintiffs in the Tennessee case, fell in love. In 2011, DeKoe received orders to deploy to Afghanistan. Before leaving, he and Kostura married in New York. A week later, DeKoe began his deployment, which lasted for almost a year. When he returned, the two settled in Tennessee, where DeKoe works full-time for the Army Reserve. Their lawful marriage is stripped from them whenever they reside in Tennessee, returning and disappearing as they travel across state lines. DeKoe, who served this Nation to preserve the freedom the Constitution protects, must endure a substantial burden. * * *

The ancient origins of marriage confirm its centrality, but it has not stood in isolation from developments in law and society. The history of marriage is one of both continuity and change. That institution—even as confined to opposite-sex relations—has evolved over time.

For example, marriage was once viewed as an arrangement by the couple's parents based on political, religious, and financial concerns; but by the time of the Nation's founding it was understood to be a voluntary contract between a man and a woman. As the role and status of women changed, the institution further evolved. Under the centuries-old doctrine of coverture, a married man and woman were treated by the State as a single, male-dominated legal entity. As women gained legal, political, and property rights, and as society began to understand that women have their own equal dignity, the law of coverture was abandoned. These and other developments in the institution of marriage over the past centuries were not mere superficial changes. Rather, they worked deep transformations in its structure, affecting aspects of marriage long viewed by many as essential. * * *

These new insights have strengthened, not weakened, the institution of marriage. Indeed, changed understandings of marriage are characteristic of a Nation where new dimensions of freedom become apparent to new generations, often through perspectives that begin in pleas or protests and then are considered in the political sphere and the judicial process.

This dynamic can be seen in the Nation's experiences with the rights of gays and lesbians. Until the mid-20th century, same-sex intimacy long had been condemned as immoral by the state itself in most Western nations, a belief often embodied in the criminal law. For this reason, among others, many persons did not deem homosexuals to have dignity in their own distinct identity. A truthful declaration by same-sex couples of what was in their hearts had to remain unspoken. Even when a greater awareness of the humanity and integrity of homosexual persons came in the period after World War II, the argument that gays and lesbians had a just claim to dignity was in conflict with both law and widespread social conventions. Same-sex intimacy remained a crime in many States. Gays and lesbians were prohibited from most government employment, barred from military service, excluded under immigration laws, targeted by police, and burdened in their rights to associate.

For much of the 20th century, moreover, homosexuality was treated as an illness. When the American Psychiatric Association published the first Diagnostic and Statistical Manual of Mental Disorders in 1952, homosexuality was classified as a mental disorder, a position adhered to until 1973. Only in more recent years have psychiatrists and others recognized that sexual orientation is both a normal expression of human sexuality and immutable.

In the late 20th century, following substantial cultural and political developments, same-sex couples began to lead more open and public lives and to establish families. This development was followed by a quite extensive discussion of the issue in both governmental and private sectors and by a shift in public attitudes toward greater tolerance. As a result, questions about the rights of gays and lesbians soon reached the courts, where the issue could be discussed in the formal discourse of the law.

[Justice Kennedy first recounted the history of the Court's cases addressing "the legal status of homosexuals" in *Bowers v. Hardwick*, [Casebook, p. 675], *Romer v. Evans* [Casebook, p. 474], and *Lawrence v. Texas* [Casebook, p. 677]. He then reviewed the history of the same-sex marriage debate, highlighting the Hawaii Supreme Court's decision in *Baehr v. Lewin* [Casebook p. 507], which began the contemporary debate; the Massachusetts Supreme Judicial Court's decision in *Goodridge v. Department of Public Health* [Casebook, p. 487] finding for the first time that a state constitution protected the right of same-sex couples to wed; the Court's own 2013 decision in *United States v. Windsor*, invalidating DOMA to the extent it barred the Federal Government from treating a same-sex marriage as valid even when it was lawful in the State where it was licensed; and the many cases addressing marriage equality in federal appellate and district courts, as well as state supreme courts.] After years of litigation, legislation, referenda, and the discussions that attended these public acts, the States are now divided on the issue of same-sex marriage.

[III.] Under the Due Process Clause of the Fourteenth Amendment, no State shall "deprive any person of life, liberty, or property, without due process of law." The fundamental liberties protected by this Clause include most of the rights enumerated in the Bill of Rights. In addition these liberties extend to certain personal choices central to individual dignity and autonomy, including intimate choices that define personal identity and beliefs. The identification and protection of fundamental rights is an enduring part of the judicial duty to interpret the Constitution. That responsibility, however, "has not been reduced to any formula." *Poe v.*

Ullman (Harlan, J., dissenting) [Casebook, p. 613]. Rather, it requires courts to exercise reasoned judgment in identifying interests of the person so fundamental that the State must accord them its respect. That process is guided by many of the same considerations relevant to analysis of other constitutional provisions that set forth broad principles rather than specific requirements. History and tradition guide and discipline this inquiry but do not set its outer boundaries. See *Lawrence*. That method respects our history and learns from it without allowing the past alone to rule the present.

The nature of injustice is that we may not always see it in our own times. The generations that wrote and ratified the Bill of Rights and the Fourteenth Amendment did not presume to know the extent of freedom in all of its dimensions, and so they entrusted to future generations a charter protecting the right of all persons to enjoy liberty as we learn its meaning. When new insight reveals discord between the Constitution's central protections and a received legal stricture, a claim to liberty must be addressed.

Applying these established tenets, the Court has long held the right to marry is protected by the Constitution. In *Loving v. Virginia* [Casebook, p. 216], which invalidated bans on interracial unions, a unanimous Court held marriage is "one of the vital personal rights essential to the orderly pursuit of happiness by free men." The Court reaffirmed that holding in *Zablocki v. Redhail* [Casebook, p. 687], which held the right to marry was burdened by a law prohibiting fathers who were behind on child support from marrying. The Court again applied this principle in *Turner v. Safley* [Casebook, p. 688], which held the right to marry was abridged by regulations limiting the privilege of prison inmates to marry. Over time and in other contexts, the Court has reiterated that the right to marry is fundamental under the Due Process Clause. * * *

The four principles and traditions to be discussed demonstrate that the reasons marriage is fundamental under the Constitution apply with equal force to same-sex couples.

A first premise of the Court's relevant precedents is that the right to personal choice regarding marriage is inherent in the concept of individual autonomy. This abiding connection between marriage and liberty is why *Loving* invalidated interracial marriage bans under the Due Process Clause. Like choices concerning contraception, family relationships, procreation, and childrearing, all of which are protected by the Constitution, decisions concerning marriage are among the most intimate that an individual can make. * * *

A second principle in this Court's jurisprudence is that the right to marry is fundamental because it supports a two-person union unlike any other in its importance to the committed individuals. This point was central to *Griswold v. Connecticut,* which held the Constitution protects the right of married couples to use contraception. * * *

The right to marry thus dignifies couples who "wish to define themselves by their commitment to each other." *Windsor.* Marriage responds to the universal fear that a lonely person might call out only to find no one there. It offers the hope of companionship and understanding and assurance that while both still live there will be someone to care for the other. * * *

Lawrence confirmed a dimension of freedom that allows individuals to engage in intimate association without criminal liability [but], it does not follow that freedom stops there. Outlaw to outcast may be a step forward, but it does not achieve the full promise of liberty.

A third basis for protecting the right to marry is that it safeguards children and families and thus draws meaning from related rights of childrearing, procreation, and education. See *Pierce v. Society of Sisters; Meyer v. Nebraska* [Casebook, pp. 609–611]. * * *

As all parties agree, many same-sex couples provide loving and nurturing homes to their children, whether biological or adopted. And hundreds of thousands of children are presently being raised by such couples. Most States have allowed gays and lesbians to adopt, either as individuals or as couples, and many adopted and foster children have same-sex parents. This provides powerful confirmation from the law itself that gays and lesbians can create loving, supportive families.

Excluding same-sex couples from marriage thus conflicts with a central premise of the right to marry. Without the recognition, stability, and predictability marriage offers, their children suffer the stigma of knowing their families are somehow lesser. They also suffer the significant material costs of being raised by unmarried parents, relegated through no fault of their own to a more difficult and uncertain family life. The marriage laws at issue here thus harm and humiliate the children of same-sex couples.

That is not to say the right to marry is less meaningful for those who do not or cannot have children. An ability, desire, or promise to procreate is not and has not been a prerequisite for a valid marriage in any State. In light of precedent protecting the right of a married couple not to procreate, it cannot be said the Court or the States have conditioned the right to marry on the capacity or commitment to procreate. The constitutional marriage right has many aspects, of which childbearing is only one.

Fourth and finally, this Court's cases and the Nation's traditions make clear that marriage is a keystone of our social order. * * *

[J]ust as a couple vows to support each other, so does society pledge to support the couple, offering symbolic recognition and material benefits to protect and nourish the union. Indeed, while the States are in general free to vary the benefits they confer on all married couples, they have throughout our history made marriage the basis for an expanding list of governmental rights, benefits, and responsibilities. These aspects of marital status include: taxation; inheritance and property rights; rules of intestate succession; spousal privilege in the law of evidence; hospital access; medical decisionmaking authority; adoption rights; the rights and benefits of survivors; birth and death certificates; professional ethics rules; campaign finance restrictions; workers' compensation benefits; health insurance; and child custody, support, and visitation rules. Valid marriage under state law is also a significant status for over a thousand provisions of federal law. See *Windsor*. The States have contributed to the fundamental character of the marriage right by placing that institution at the center of so many facets of the legal and social order.

There is no difference between same- and opposite-sex couples with respect to this principle. Yet by virtue of their exclusion from that institution, same-sex couples are denied the constellation of benefits that the States have linked to marriage. This harm results in more than just material burdens. * * * It demeans gays and lesbians for the State to lock them out of a central institution of the Nation's society. Same-sex couples, too, may aspire to the transcendent purposes of marriage and seek fulfillment in its highest meaning.

Objecting that this does not reflect an appropriate framing of the issue, the respondents refer to *Washington v. Glucksberg,* [Casebook, p. 692], which called for a " 'careful description' " of fundamental rights. They assert the petitioners do not seek to exercise the right to marry but rather a new and nonexistent "right to same-sex marriage." *Glucksberg* did insist that liberty under the Due Process Clause must be defined in a most circumscribed manner, with central reference to specific historical practices. Yet while that approach may have been appropriate for the asserted right there involved (physician-assisted suicide), it is inconsistent with the approach this Court has used in discussing other fundamental rights, including marriage and intimacy. *Loving* did not ask about a "right to interracial marriage"; *Turner* did not ask about a "right of inmates to marry"; and *Zablocki* did not ask about a "right of fathers with unpaid child support duties to marry." Rather, each case inquired about the right to marry in its comprehensive sense, asking if there was a sufficient justification for excluding the relevant class from the right.

That principle applies here. If rights were defined by who exercised them in the past, then received practices could serve as their own continued justification and new groups could not invoke rights once denied. This Court has rejected that approach, both with respect to the right to marry and the rights of gays and lesbians. See *Loving*; *Lawrence*. * * *

The right of same-sex couples to marry that is part of the liberty promised by the Fourteenth Amendment is derived, too, from that Amendment's guarantee of the equal protection of the laws. The Due Process Clause and the Equal Protection Clause are connected in a profound way, though they set forth independent principles. Rights implicit in liberty and rights secured by equal protection may rest on different precepts and are not always co-extensive, yet in some instances each may be instructive as to the meaning and reach of the other. In any particular case one Clause may be thought to capture the essence of the right in a more accurate and comprehensive way, even as the two Clauses may converge in the identification and definition of the right. This interrelation of the two principles furthers our understanding of what freedom is and must become.

The Court's cases touching upon the right to marry reflect this dynamic. In *Loving* the Court invalidated a prohibition on interracial marriage under both the Equal Protection Clause and the Due Process Clause. The Court first declared the prohibition invalid because of its unequal treatment of interracial couples. It stated: "There can be no doubt that restricting the freedom to marry solely because of racial classifications violates the central meaning of the Equal Protection Clause." With this link to equal protection the Court proceeded to hold the prohibition offended central precepts of liberty: "To deny this fundamental freedom on so unsupportable a basis as the racial classifications embodied in these statutes, classifications so directly subversive of the principle of equality at the heart of the Fourteenth Amendment, is surely to deprive all the State's citizens of liberty without due process of law." The reasons why marriage is a fundamental right became more clear and compelling from a full awareness and understanding of the hurt that resulted from laws barring interracial unions.

The synergy between the two protections is illustrated further in *Zablocki*. There the Court invoked the Equal Protection Clause as its basis for invalidating the challenged law, which, as already noted, barred fathers who were behind on child-support payments from marrying without judicial approval. The equal protection analysis depended in central part on the Court's holding that the law burdened a right "of fundamental importance." It was the essential nature of the marriage right, discussed at length in *Zablocki* that made apparent the law's incompatibility with requirements of equality. Each concept—liberty and equal protection—leads to a stronger understanding of the other.

Indeed, in interpreting the Equal Protection Clause, the Court has recognized that new insights and societal understandings can reveal unjustified inequality within our most fundamental institutions that once passed unnoticed and unchallenged. To take but one period, this occurred with respect to marriage in the 1970's and 1980's. Notwithstanding the gradual erosion of the doctrine of coverture, invidious sex-based classifications in marriage remained common through the mid-20th century. These classifications denied the equal dignity of men and women. One State's law, for example, provided in 1971 that "the husband is the head of the family and the wife is subject to him; her legal civil existence is merged in the husband, except so far as the law recognizes her separately, either for her own protection, or for her benefit." Responding to a new awareness, the Court invoked equal protection principles to invalidate laws imposing sex-based inequality on marriage. [Justice Kennedy collected here a set of gender discrimination cases decided in the 1970s and 1980s]. * * *

[*Lawrence* also] drew upon principles of liberty and equality to define and protect the rights of gays and lesbians, holding the State "cannot demean their existence or control their destiny by making their private sexual conduct a crime." * * *

Here the marriage laws enforced by the respondents are in essence unequal: same-sex couples are denied all the benefits afforded to opposite-sex couples and are barred from exercising a fundamental right. Especially against a long history of disapproval of their relationships, this denial to same-sex couples of the right to marry works a grave and continuing harm. * * *

These considerations lead to the conclusion that the right to marry is a fundamental right inherent in the liberty of the person, and under the Due Process and Equal Protection Clauses of the Fourteenth Amendment couples of the same-sex may not be deprived of that right and that liberty. The Court now holds that same-sex couples may exercise the fundamental right to marry. No longer may this liberty be denied to them. * * *

[IV]. There may be an initial inclination in these cases to proceed with caution—to await further legislation, litigation, and debate. The respondents warn there has been insufficient democratic discourse before deciding an issue so basic as the definition of marriage. In its ruling on the cases now before this Court, the majority opinion for the Court of Appeals made a cogent argument that it would be appropriate for the respondents' States to await further public discussion and political measures before licensing same-sex marriages. Yet there has been far more deliberation than this argument acknowledges. [The majority noted here the many "referenda, legislative debates, and grassroots campaigns, studies, as well as countless studies, papers, books, and other popular and scholarly writings," and the scores of amicus briefs filed in *Obergefell* itself. Justice Kennedy also attached to the opinion two appendices that listed state and federal litigation addressing, and state legislation legalizing, same-sex marriage.]

Of course, the Constitution contemplates that democracy is the appropriate process for change, so long as that process does not abridge fundamental rights. Last Term, a plurality of this Court reaffirmed the importance of the democratic principle in *Schuette v. BAMN*, noting the "right of citizens to debate so they can learn and decide and then, through the political process, act in concert to try to shape the course of their own times." Indeed, it is most often through democracy that liberty is preserved and protected in our lives. But as *Schuette* also said, "[t]he freedom secured by the Constitution consists, in one of its essential dimensions, of the right of the individual not to be injured by the unlawful exercise of governmental power." * * *

The idea of the Constitution "was to withdraw certain subjects from the vicissitudes of political controversy, to place them beyond the reach of majorities and officials and to establish them as legal principles to be applied by the courts." This is why "fundamental rights may not be submitted to a vote; they depend on the outcome of no elections." It is of no moment whether advocates of same-sex marriage now enjoy or lack momentum in the democratic process. * * *

The petitioners' stories make clear the urgency of the issue they present to the Court. * * *

The respondents also argue allowing same-sex couples to wed will harm marriage as an institution by leading to fewer opposite-sex marriages. This may occur, the respondents contend, because licensing same-sex marriage severs the connection between natural procreation and marriage. That argument, however, rests on a counterintuitive view of opposite-sex couple's decisionmaking processes regarding marriage and parenthood. Decisions about whether to marry and raise children are based on many personal, romantic, and practical considerations; and it is unrealistic to conclude that an opposite-sex couple would choose not to marry simply because same-sex couples may do so. * * * Indeed, with respect to this asserted basis for excluding same-sex couples from the right to marry, it is appropriate to observe these cases involve only the rights of two consenting adults whose marriages would pose no risk of harm to themselves or third parties.

Finally, it must be emphasized that religions, and those who adhere to religious doctrines, may continue to advocate with utmost, sincere conviction that, by divine precepts, same-sex marriage should not be condoned. The First Amendment ensures that religious organizations and persons are given proper protection as they seek to teach the principles that are so fulfilling and so central to their lives and faiths, and to their own deep aspirations to continue the family structure they have long revered. The same is true of those who oppose same-sex marriage for other reasons. In turn, those who believe allowing same-sex marriage is proper or indeed essential, whether as a matter of religious conviction or secular belief, may engage those who disagree with their view in an open and searching debate. The Constitution, however, does not permit the State to bar same-sex couples from marriage on the same terms as accorded to couples of the opposite sex.

[V. The Court then held that the same reasons cited for affording same-sex couples the right to marry also affords them the right to have an out-of-state marriage recognized.] * * *

It would misunderstand [the plaintiffs] to say they disrespect the idea of marriage. Their plea is that they do respect it, respect it so deeply that they seek to find its fulfillment for themselves. Their hope is not to be condemned to live in loneliness, excluded from one of civilization's oldest institutions. They ask for equal dignity in the eyes of the law. The Constitution grants them that right.

CHIEF JUSTICE ROBERTS, with whom **JUSTICE SCALIA** and **JUSTICE THOMAS** join, dissenting.

Petitioners make strong arguments rooted in social policy and considerations of fairness. They contend that same-sex couples should be allowed to affirm their love and commitment through marriage, just like opposite-sex couples. That position has undeniable appeal; over the past six years, voters and legislators in eleven States and the District of Columbia have revised their laws to allow marriage between two people of the same sex.

But this Court is not a legislature. Whether same-sex marriage is a good idea should be of no concern to us. Under the Constitution, judges have power to say what the law is, not what it should be. The people who ratified the Constitution authorized courts to exercise "neither force nor will but merely judgment." The Federalist No. 78, p. 465

Although the policy arguments for extending marriage to same-sex couples may be compelling, the legal arguments for requiring such an extension are not. The fundamental right to marry does not include a right to make a State change its definition of marriage. * * *

Today, however, the Court takes the extraordinary step of ordering every State to license and recognize same-sex marriage. Many people will rejoice at this decision, and I begrudge none their celebration. But for those who believe in a government of laws, not of men, the majority's approach is deeply disheartening. Supporters of same-sex marriage have achieved considerable success persuading their fellow citizens—through the democratic process—to adopt their view. That ends today. Five lawyers have closed the debate and enacted their own vision of marriage as a matter of constitutional law. Stealing this issue from the people will for many cast a cloud over same-sex marriage, making a dramatic social change that much more difficult to accept.

The majority's decision is an act of will, not legal judgment. The right it announces has no basis in the Constitution or this Court's precedent. The majority expressly disclaims judicial "caution" and omits even a pretense of humility, openly relying on its desire to remake society according to its own "new insight" into the "nature of injustice." As a result, the Court invalidates the marriage laws of more than half the States and orders the transformation of a social institution that has formed the basis of human society for millennia, for the Kalahari Bushmen and the Han Chinese, the Carthaginians and the Aztecs. Just who do we think we are? * * *

[I.] [The] universal definition of marriage as the union of a man and a woman is no historical coincidence. Marriage did not come about as a result of a political movement, discovery, disease, war, religious doctrine, or any other moving force of world history—and certainly not as a result of a prehistoric decision to exclude gays and lesbians. It arose in the nature of things to meet a vital need: ensuring that children are conceived by a mother and father committed to raising them in the stable conditions of a lifelong relationship. * * *

The human race must procreate to survive. Procreation occurs through sexual relations between a man and a woman. When sexual relations result in the conception of a child, that child's prospects are generally better if the mother and father stay together rather than going their separate ways. Therefore, for the good of children and society, sexual relations that can lead to procreation should occur only between a man and a woman committed to a lasting bond.

Society has recognized that bond as marriage. And by bestowing a respected status and material benefits on married couples, society encourages men and women to conduct sexual relations within marriage rather than without. * * *

There is no dispute that every State at the founding—and every State throughout our history until a dozen years ago—defined marriage in the traditional, biologically rooted way. * * *

[II.] Petitioners' "fundamental right" claim falls into the most sensitive category of constitutional adjudication. Petitioners do not contend that their States' marriage laws violate an *enumerated* constitutional right, such as the freedom of speech protected by the First Amendment. There is, after all, no "Companionship and Understanding" or "Nobility and Dignity" Clause in the Constitution. They argue instead that the laws violate a right *implied* by the Fourteenth Amendment's requirement that "liberty" may not be deprived without "due process of law." * * *

Allowing unelected federal judges to select which unenumerated rights rank as "fundamental"—and to strike down state laws on the basis of that determination—raises obvious concerns about the judicial role. Our precedents have accordingly insisted that judges "exercise the utmost care" in identifying implied fundamental rights, "lest the liberty protected by the Due Process Clause be subtly transformed into the policy preferences of the Members of this Court." *Washington v. Glucksberg.*

The need for restraint in administering the strong medicine of substantive due process is a lesson this Court has learned the hard way. The Court first applied substantive due process to strike down a statute in *Dred Scott.* There the Court invalidated the Missouri Compromise on the ground that legislation restricting the institution of slavery violated the implied rights of slaveholders. The Court relied on its own conception of liberty and property in doing so. * * *

Dred Scott's holding was overruled on the battlefields of the Civil War and by constitutional amendment after Appomattox, but its approach to the Due Process Clause reappeared. In a series of early 20th-century cases, most prominently *Lochner v. New York,* this Court invalidated state statutes that presented "meddlesome interferences with the rights of the individual," and "undue interference with liberty of person and freedom of contract." In *Lochner* itself, the Court struck down a New York law setting maximum hours for bakery employees, because there was "in our judgment, no reasonable foundation for holding this to be necessary or appropriate as a health law."

The dissenting Justices in *Lochner* explained that the New York law could be viewed as a reasonable response to legislative concern about the health of bakery employees, an issue on which there was at least "room for debate and for an honest difference of opinion." (opinion of Harlan, J.). The majority's contrary conclusion required adopting as constitutional law "an economic theory which a large part of the country does not entertain." (opinion of Holmes, J.). As Justice Holmes memorably put it, "The Fourteenth Amendment does not enact Mr. Herbert Spencer's Social Statics," a leading work on the philosophy of Social Darwinism. The Constitution "is not intended to embody a particular economic theory. . . . It is made for people of fundamentally differing views, and the accident of our finding certain opinions natural and familiar or novel and even shocking ought not to conclude our judgment upon the question whether statutes embodying them conflict with the Constitution."

In the decades after *Lochner,* the Court struck down nearly 200 laws as violations of individual liberty, often over strong dissents contending that "[t]he criterion of constitutionality is not whether we believe the law to be for the public good." * * *

Eventually, the Court recognized its error and vowed not to repeat it. * * * [I]t has become an accepted rule that the Court will not hold laws unconstitutional simply because we find them "unwise, improvident, or out of harmony with a particular school of thought." *Williamson v. Lee Optical of Okla., Inc.* [Casebook, p. 550]. * * *

None of the laws at issue in [the cases cited by the majority finding a fundamental right to marry] purported to change the core definition of marriage as the union of a man and a woman. * * * The laws challenged in *Zablocki* and *Turner* did not define marriage as "the union of a man and a woman, *where neither party owes child support or is in prison.*" Nor did the interracial marriage ban at issue in *Loving* define marriage as "the union of a man and a woman *of the same race.*" Removing racial barriers to marriage therefore did not change what a marriage was any more than integrating schools changed what a school was. As the majority admits, the institution of "marriage" discussed in every one of these cases "presumed a relationship involving opposite-sex partners." * * *

Neither *Lawrence* nor any other precedent in the privacy line of cases supports the right that petitioners assert here. Unlike criminal laws banning contraceptives and sodomy, the marriage laws at issue here involve no government intrusion. They create no crime and impose no punishment. * * *

Perhaps recognizing how little support it can derive from precedent, the majority goes out of its way to jettison the "careful" approach to implied fundamental rights taken by this Court in *Glucksberg*. It is revealing that the majority's position requires it to effectively overrule *Glucksberg,* the leading modern case setting the bounds of substantive due process. At least this part of the majority opinion has the virtue of candor. Nobody could rightly accuse the majority of taking a careful approach. * * *

One immediate question invited by the majority's position is whether States may retain the definition of marriage as a union of two people. Although the majority randomly inserts the adjective "two" in various places, it offers no reason at all why the two-person element of the core definition of marriage may be preserved while the man-woman element may not. Indeed, from the standpoint of history and tradition, a leap from opposite-sex marriage to same-sex marriage is much greater than one from a two-person union to plural unions, which have deep roots in some cultures around the world. If the majority is willing to take the big leap, it is hard to see how it can say no to the shorter one.

It is striking how much of the majority's reasoning would apply with equal force to the claim of a fundamental right to plural marriage. If "[t]here is dignity in the bond between two men or two women who seek to marry and in their autonomy to make such profound choices," why would there be any less dignity in the bond between three people who, in exercising their autonomy, seek to make the profound choice to marry? If a same-sex couple has the constitutional right to marry because their children would otherwise "suffer the stigma of knowing their families are somehow lesser," why wouldn't the same reasoning apply to a family of three or more persons raising children? If not having the opportunity to marry "serves to disrespect and subordinate" gay and lesbian couples, why wouldn't the same "imposition of this disability," serve to disrespect and subordinate people who find fulfillment in polyamorous relationships? * * *

Near the end of its opinion, the majority offers perhaps the clearest insight into its decision. Expanding marriage to include same-sex couples, the majority insists, would "pose no risk of harm to themselves or third parties." * * *

Then and now, this assertion of the "harm principle" sounds more in philosophy than law. The elevation of the fullest individual self-realization over the constraints that society has expressed in law may or may not be attractive moral philosophy. But a Justice's commission does not confer any special moral, philosophical, or social insight sufficient to justify imposing those perceptions on fellow citizens under the pretense of "due process." There is indeed a process due the people on issues of this sort—the democratic process. Respecting that understanding requires the Court to be guided by law, not any particular school of social thought. As Judge Henry Friendly once put it, echoing Justice Holmes's dissent in *Lochner,* the Fourteenth Amendment does not enact John Stuart Mill's On Liberty any more than it enacts Herbert Spencer's Social Statics. And it certainly does not enact any one concept of marriage. * * *

[III.] In addition to their due process argument, petitioners contend that the Equal Protection Clause requires their States to license and recognize same-sex marriages. The majority does not seriously engage with this claim. Its discussion is, quite frankly, difficult to follow. The central point seems to be that there is a "synergy between" the Equal Protection Clause and the Due Process Clause, and that some precedents relying on one Clause have also relied on the other. Absent from this portion of the opinion, however, is anything resembling our usual framework for deciding equal protection cases. It is casebook doctrine that the "modern Supreme Court's treatment of equal protection claims has used a means-ends methodology in which judges ask whether the classification the government is using is sufficiently related to the goals it is pursuing." * * *

Those who founded our country would not recognize the majority's conception of the judicial role. They after all risked their lives and fortunes for the precious right to govern themselves. They would never have imagined yielding that right on a question of social policy to unaccountable and unelected judges. * * * In our democracy, debate about the content of the law is not an exhaustion requirement to be checked off before courts can impose their will. * * *

By deciding this question under the Constitution, the Court removes it from the realm of democratic decision. There will be consequences to shutting down the political process on an issue of such profound public significance. Closing debate tends to close minds. People denied a voice are less likely to accept the ruling of a court on an issue that does not seem to be the sort of thing courts usually decide. As a thoughtful commentator observed about another issue, "The political process was moving . . . , not swiftly enough for advocates of quick, complete change, but majoritarian institutions were listening and acting. Heavy-handed judicial intervention was difficult to justify and appears to have provoked, not resolved, conflict." Ginsburg, Some Thoughts on Autonomy and Equality in Relation to *Roe* v. *Wade*, 63 N.C.L.Rev. 375, 385–386 (1985) (footnote omitted). Indeed, however heartened the proponents of same-sex marriage might be on this day, it is worth acknowledging what they have lost, and lost forever: the opportunity to win the true acceptance that comes from persuading their fellow citizens of the justice of their cause. And they lose this just when the winds of change were freshening at their backs. * * *

Respect for sincere religious conviction has led voters and legislators in every State that has adopted same-sex marriage democratically to include accommodations for religious practice. The majority's decision imposing same-sex marriage cannot, of course, create any such accommodations. The majority graciously suggests that religious believers may continue to "advocate" and "teach" their views of marriage. The First Amendment guarantees, however, the freedom to "*exercise*" religion. Ominously, that is not a word the majority uses. * * *

If you are among the many Americans—of whatever sexual orientation—who favor expanding same-sex marriage, by all means celebrate today's decision. Celebrate the achievement of a desired goal. Celebrate the opportunity for a new expression of commitment to a partner. Celebrate the availability of new benefits. But do not celebrate the Constitution. It had nothing to do with it.

JUSTICE SCALIA, with whom **JUSTICE THOMAS** joins, dissenting.

When the Fourteenth Amendment was ratified in 1868, every State limited marriage to one man and one woman, and no one doubted the constitutionality of doing so. That resolves these cases. When it comes to determining the meaning of a vague constitutional provision—such as "due process of law" or "equal protection of the laws"—it is unquestionable that the People who ratified that provision did not understand it to prohibit a practice that remained both universal and uncontroversial in the years after ratification. We have no basis for striking down a practice that is not expressly prohibited by the Fourteenth Amendment's text, and that bears the endorsement of a long tradition of open, widespread, and unchallenged use dating back to the Amendment's ratification. Since there is no doubt whatever that the People never decided to prohibit the limitation of marriage to opposite-sex couples, the public debate over same-sex marriage must be allowed to continue. * * *

Judges are selected precisely for their skill as lawyers; whether they reflect the policy views of a particular constituency is not (or should not be) relevant. Not surprisingly then, the Federal Judiciary is hardly a cross-section of America. Take, for example, this Court, which consists of only nine men and women, all of them successful lawyers who studied at Harvard or Yale Law School. Four of the nine are natives of New York City. Eight of them grew up in east- and west-coast States. Only one hails from the vast expanse in-between. Not a single Southwesterner or even, to tell the truth, a genuine Westerner (California does not count). Not a single evangelical Christian (a group that comprises about one quarter of Americans), or even a Protestant of any denomination. The strikingly unrepresentative character of the body voting on today's social upheaval would be irrelevant if they were functioning as *judges,* answering the legal question whether the American people had ever ratified a constitutional provision that was understood to proscribe the traditional definition of marriage. But of course the Justices in today's majority are not voting on that basis; *they say they are not.* And to allow the policy question of same-sex marriage to be considered and resolved by a select, patrician, highly unrepresentative panel of nine is to violate a principle even more fundamental than no taxation without representation: no social transformation without representation.

[II.] But what really astounds is the hubris reflected in today's judicial Putsch. The five Justices who compose today's majority are entirely comfortable concluding that every State violated the Constitution for all of the 135 years between the Fourteenth Amendment's ratification and Massachusetts' permitting of same-sex marriages in 2003. They have discovered in the Fourteenth Amendment a "fundamental right" overlooked by every person alive at the time of ratification, and almost everyone else in the time since. * * *

JUSTICE THOMAS, with whom JUSTICE SCALIA joins, dissenting.

As used in the Due Process Clauses, "liberty" most likely refers to "the power of locomotion, of changing situation, or removing one's person to whatsoever place one's own inclination may direct; without imprisonment or restraint, unless by due course of law." 1 W. Blackstone, Commentaries on the Laws of England 130 (1769) (Blackstone). That definition is drawn from the historical roots of the Clauses and is consistent with our Constitution's text and structure. * * *

Even assuming that the "liberty" in those Clauses encompasses something more than freedom from physical restraint, it would not include the types of rights claimed by the majority. In the American legal tradition, liberty has long been understood as individual freedom *from* governmental action, not as a right *to* a particular governmental entitlement.

The founding-era understanding of liberty was heavily influenced by John Locke, whose writings "on natural rights and on the social and governmental contract" were cited "[i]n pamphlet after pamphlet" by American writers. * * * Because [the] state of nature left men insecure in their persons and property, they entered civil society, trading a portion of their natural liberty for an increase in their security. Upon consenting to that order, men obtained civil liberty, or the freedom "to be under no other legislative power but that established by consent in the commonwealth; nor under the dominion of any will or restraint of any law, but what that legislative shall enact according to the trust put in it." * * *

Petitioners cannot claim, under the most plausible definition of "liberty," that they have been imprisoned or physically restrained by the States for participating in same-sex relationships. To the contrary, they have been able to cohabitate and raise their children in peace. They have been able to hold civil marriage ceremonies in States that recognize same-sex marriages and private religious ceremonies in all States. They have been able to travel freely around the country, making their homes where they please. Far from being incarcerated or physically restrained, petitioners have been left alone to order their lives as they see fit. * * *

Instead, the States have refused to grant them governmental entitlements. Petitioners claim that as a matter of "liberty," they are entitled to access privileges and benefits that exist solely *because of* the government. They want, for example, to receive the State's *imprimatur* on their marriages—on state issued marriage licenses, death certificates, or other official forms. And they want to receive various monetary benefits, including reduced inheritance taxes upon the death of a spouse, compensation if a spouse dies as a result of a work-related injury, or loss of consortium damages in tort suits. But receiving governmental recognition and benefits has nothing to do with any understanding of "liberty" that the Framers would have recognized. * * *

Petitioners' misconception of liberty carries over into their discussion of our precedents identifying a right to marry, not one of which has expanded the concept of "liberty" beyond the concept of negative liberty. Those precedents all involved absolute prohibitions on private actions associated with marriage. *Loving v. Virginia,* for example, involved a couple who was criminally prosecuted for marrying in the District of Columbia and cohabiting in Virginia. They were each sentenced to a year of imprisonment, suspended for a term of 25 years on the condition that they not reenter the Commonwealth together during that time. In a similar vein, *Zablocki v. Redhail* involved a man who was prohibited, on pain of criminal penalty, from "marry[ing] in Wisconsin or elsewhere" because of his outstanding child-support obligations. And *Turner v. Safley* involved state inmates who were prohibited from entering marriages without the permission of the superintendent of the prison, permission that could not be granted absent compelling reasons. In *none* of those cases were individuals denied solely governmental recognition and benefits associated with marriage. * * *

[IV.] Human dignity has long been understood in this country to be innate. When the Framers proclaimed in the Declaration of Independence that "all men are created equal" and "endowed by their Creator with certain unalienable Rights," they referred to a vision of mankind in which all humans are created in the image of God and therefore of inherent worth. That vision is the foundation upon which this Nation was built.

The corollary of that principle is that human dignity cannot be taken away by the government. Slaves did not lose their dignity (any more than they lost their humanity) because the government allowed them to be enslaved. Those held in internment camps did not lose their dignity because the government confined them. And those denied governmental benefits certainly do not lose their dignity because the government denies them those benefits. The government cannot bestow dignity, and it cannot take it away. * * *

JUSTICE ALITO, with whom JUSTICE SCALIA and JUSTICE THOMAS join, dissenting.

Today's decision usurps the constitutional right of the people to decide whether to keep or alter the traditional understanding of marriage. The decision will also have other important consequences.

It will be used to vilify Americans who are unwilling to assent to the new orthodoxy. In the course of its opinion, the majority compares traditional marriage laws to laws that denied equal treatment for African-Americans and women. The implications of this analogy will be exploited by those who are determined to stamp out every vestige of dissent.

Perhaps recognizing how its reasoning may be used, the majority attempts, toward the end of its opinion, to reassure those who oppose same-sex marriage that their rights of conscience will be protected. We will soon see whether this proves to be true. I assume that those who cling to old beliefs will be able to whisper their thoughts in the recesses of their homes, but if they repeat those views in public, they will risk being labeled as bigots and treated as such by governments, employers, and schools.

The system of federalism established by our Constitution provides a way for people with different beliefs to live together in a single nation. If the issue of same-sex marriage had been left to the people of the States, it is likely that some States would recognize same-sex marriage and others would not. It is also possible that some States would tie recognition to protection for conscience rights. The majority today makes that impossible. By imposing its own views on the entire country, the majority facilitates the marginalization of the many Americans who have traditional ideas. Recalling the harsh treatment of gays and lesbians in the past, some may think that turnabout is fair play. But if that sentiment prevails, the Nation will experience bitter and lasting wounds. * * *

NOTES

1. *Possible Rationales.* The parties and amici in *Obergefell* presented the Court with several ways to find bans on same-sex marriage unconstitutional under the Fourteenth Amendment. The principal theories argued that the bans:

- Violated the fundamental right to marry grounded in the due process clause;

- Violated the fundamental right to marry (or interest in marriage) grounded in the equal protection clause;

- Violated the equal protection clause by discriminating against same-sex couples based on their sexual orientation; and

- Violated the equal protection clause by discriminating against same-sex couples based on gender.

The first of these alternatives plainly forms a core part of the opinion, which says explicitly that same-sex couples have a fundamental right to marry as part of the liberty protected by the due process clause. Given Justice Kennedy's invocation of equal protection, as well, do you read the opinion to bring in any of the other rationales? Do you think Justice Kennedy chose the strongest framing for the right vindicated in the case?

2. *Strict Scrutiny?* As you consider the fundamental right to marry identified in the opinion, recall that under established doctrine, a finding that a right is fundamental triggers strict scrutiny. Strict scrutiny, in turn, requires the reviewing court to determine whether the state has a compelling interest and has used the least restrictive alternative in the challenged policy. Puzzlingly, there is no explicit application of strict scrutiny in the opinion. Note that the opinion, in section IV, does discuss what might be seen as three state interests: the interest in allowing a state's democratic process to define marriage; the interest in linking marriage to procreation as a way to channel birth parents into marriage; and the interest in protecting the religious liberties of those opposing same-sex marriage. Is the first of these three—letting majorities decide—a cognizable state "interest" at all? As to all three, does the majority's rejection of them serve as a version of strict, or at least heightened, scrutiny? If so, does it matter that the relevant doctrinal language

about compelling interests and narrow tailoring is never used? What should lower courts take away from this approach? Is this what heightened scrutiny in the realm of due process now looks like? Recall that *Lawrence* and *Windsor* were also doctrinally idiosyncratic, although *Obergefell* is clearer than they were in saying unambiguously that a fundamental right is involved.

3. *Synergy Between Liberty and Equality*. What does Justice Kennedy mean when he links due process and equal protection in the opinion and speaks of a "synergy" between them? This is not a new idea, as his discussion of *Loving* and *Lawrence*, among others, suggests. For scholarly elaborations of this idea, see Rebecca L. Brown, *Liberty, the New Equality*, 77 N.Y.U. L. REV. 1491 (2002); Cary Franklin, *Marrying Liberty and Equality: The New Jurisprudence of Gay Rights*, 100 VA. L. REV. 817 (2014); Reva B. Siegel, *Dignity and the Politics of Protection: Abortion Restrictions Under Casey/Carhart*, 117 YALE L.J. 1694 (2008); Laurence H. Tribe, *Lawrence v. Texas: The "Fundamental Right" that Dare Not Speak Its Name*, 117 HARV. L. REV. 1893 (2004); Kenji Yoshino, *The New Equal Protection*, 124 HARV. L. REV. 747 (2011). How, if at all, does Justice Kennedy's use of equal protection language change the due process holding in this case? Does it suggest that the Court has now embraced a new understanding of liberty itself? Does the liberty-equality synergy implicate any of the other rationales listed in note 1 above?

4. *Role of Justice Kennedy*. It is both striking and unusual that Justice Kennedy wrote all four of the major LGBT rights opinions decided by the Supreme Court since *Romer*, in 1996. *Obergefell* contains some of the hallmarks of the jurisprudence he created through *Romer, Lawrence, Windsor*, especially his focus on rejecting laws that demean gays and lesbians and protecting the dignity of this group. From the institutional perspective of the Court, would it be preferable for more than one justice to write major opinions in a highly salient and controversial area like this one?

5. *Praise of Marriage*. Justice Kennedy is lavish in his praise of marriage as an institution, calling it, for example, of "transcendent importance," "sacred," "offer[ing] unique fulfillment," "essential to our most profound hopes and aspirations," and a "keystone of our social order." Does he go too far? Is he overreaching when he twice casts marriage as the antidote to "loneliness?" Does the rhetoric in the opinion stigmatize those who are not married?

6. *Bitterness on the Court*. After *Obergefell* was decided, various observers, including former Solicitor Generals from both parties, noted that some of the dissents contained particularly bitter language. See Nina Totenberg, Liberal Minority Won Over Conservatives in Historic Supreme Court Term, July 6, 2015, http://www.npr.org/sections/itsallpolitics/2015/07/06/420289254/liberal-minority-won-over-conservatives-in-historic-supreme-court-term (quoting Charles Fried, who served in the Reagan Administration and Walter Dellinger, who served in the Clinton Administration). In addition to what is in the excerpts above, the dissents by Chief Justice Roberts and Justice Scalia both called the majority opinion "pretentious," and Scalia said

he would "hide [his] head in a bag" before joining any opinion with such language. Former Solicitor General Fried suggested that Justice Kennedy might have helped to provoke that reaction by aiming more for poetry than precedent laid out in a straightforward way. Does the heated rhetoric suggest that not much is left to the norm of civility on the Court, at least on the part of some Justices? Or is the problem merely a reflection of growing polarization in society as a whole? Or, perhaps, an indication that Justices may be directing parts of their opinions at a public (rather than professional) audience? And is the problem merely an issue of etiquette or something that may affect the Court's institutional functioning and legitimacy?

7. *Links to* Roe. Given the Chief Justice's emphasis on the perils of "Lochnerizing," is it surprising that he did he not invoke *Roe v. Wade* as an example of this danger? *Roe*, after all, has been the most controversial of the modern Court's substantive due process cases. (And, indeed, a year later, Justice Thomas alluded to *Lochner* in a portion of his dissent from *Whole Woman's Health* that is not reproduced above). The closest the Chief comes is citing an article by Justice Ginsburg suggesting how the Court could have avoided some of the controversy generated by *Roe*. How do you think Justice Ginsburg might respond to the parallel Roberts draws here? Do you think *Obergefell* will be controversial in the way *Roe* has been? Is it relevant to consider the rapid recent shift of public opinion in favor of marriage equality, and, especially the strong generational tilt in favor? See Chris Cillizza, *How Unbelievably Quickly Public Opinion Changed on Gay Marriage, in 5 Charts*, Washington Post, June 26, 2015 (http://www.washingtonpost.com/blogs/the-fix/wp/2015/06/26/how-unbelievably-quickly-public-opinion-changed-on-gay-marriage-in-6-charts/).

8. *Theories of Interpretation.* The opinions in the case offer a rich basis for exploring theories of constitutional interpretation. The justices divide along familiar jurisprudential lines; the majority espouses the virtues of living constitutionalism, while the dissents counter with arguments grounded in originalism and excoriate what they see as illegitimate judicial activism. Two of us have examined how the marriage debate can be understood in terms of a range of constitutional theories. For an argument that there is an unappreciated originalist case *in favor of* marriage equality, see William N. Eskridge, Jr., The Nineteenth Annual Frankel Lecture, *Original Meaning and Marriage Equality*, 52 HOUSTON L. REV. 1067 (2015); see also Steven G. Calabresi and Hannah Begley, *Originalism and Same-Sex Marriage*, http://papers.ssrn.com/sol3/papers.cfm?abstract_id=2509443. For an argument about the interlocking roles of popular and living constitutionalism in the debate, see Jane S. Schacter, Commentary, *What Marriage Equality Can Tell Us About Popular Constitutionalism (and Vice-Versa)*, 52 HOUSTON L. REV. 1147 (2015).

9. *Glucksberg.* Note the focus on *Washington v. Glucksberg* (Casebook, p. 692), the next major case in this unit. *Glucksberg* emphasizes the normative weight of history and tradition in substantive due process analysis. The *Obergefell* majority says that "history and tradition guide and discipline this

inquiry but do not set its outer boundaries." What will that mean? As you read *Glucksberg*, consider what remains of it in the wake of *Obergefell*.

10. *Same-Sex Marriage After* Obergefell.

(a) On the last day of the October 2016 Term, the Supreme Court issued a surprise *per curiam* opinion in *Pavan v. Smith*, 2017 WL 2722472 (2017). Two married same-sex couples had challenged an Arkansas statute that allowed the state to list only the birth mother on a child's birth certificate, while excluding her female spouse, the child's other parent. The plaintiff couples conceived through donor insemination. As the Arkansas Supreme Court interpreted state law, the *husband* of a woman who conceived through donor insemination was required to be listed on the birth certificate, but a similarly-situated *same-sex spouse* could be excluded. Without briefing or argument, the Court reversed and remanded, holding that *Obergefell* "proscribes such disparate treatment" because it mandates that married same-sex couples have access to the full "constellation of benefits" that a state links to marriage. In a dissent, newly-seated Justice Gorsuch, joined by Justices Thomas and Alito, argued that *Obergefell* did not speak at all to the question whether a state may create "rules designed to ensure that the biological parents of a child are listed on the child's birth certificate." Was this an odd characterization of the Arkansas policy, given that the husband of a woman inseminated by donor sperm is not a biological parent? The dissent also objected to using the "strong medicine of summary reversal" in the case and thus suggested that it did not see the scope of *Obergefell* as settled law.

Only days after the Supreme Court's decision in *Pavan*, the Texas Supreme Court issued a ruling very narrowly interpreting *Obergefell*. In *Pidgeon v. Turner*, 538 S.W.3d 73 (Tex. 2017), the state court unanimously held that while *Obergefell* requires Texas to provide marriage licenses to same-sex couples and to recognize as valid same-sex marriages contracted in other states, it does not necessarily require the city of Houston to provide equal benefits to married same-sex couples. The court said it is for the trial court to determine on remand whether the city must do so, but the state justices signaled their embrace of limiting *Obergefell*'s meaning. Given *Pavan*'s plain statement that *Obergefell* entitles married same-sex couples to the full "constellation of benefits" afforded married heterosexuals, it is unclear how the *Pidgeon* ruling can survive *Pavan*. On this point, the Texas Supreme Court said that *Obergefell*'s reach has yet to be determined. If nothing else, it seems clear that opponents of *Obergefell* will litigate vigorously to limit its effect.

(b) In *Masterpiece Cakeshop v. Colorado Civil Rights Comm'n*, ___ U.S. ___, 138 S.Ct. 1719 (2018), the Court ruled in favor of a baker who, citing his rights to free speech and free exercise of religion, declined to bake a wedding cake for a same-sex couple. The baker had been found by the Colorado courts to have discriminated against the couple in violation of state civil rights law. The opinion, written by Justice Kennedy, appears in chapter 6 of this Supplement. As reflected in the notes following the case, the Court's ruling relied on free exercise and not free speech, and was narrower than it might have been because it relied so heavily on findings that the case was adjudicated by the Colorado Civil Rights Commission with particular bias against religion. The majority opinion also included extensive language affirming the importance of anti-discrimination laws. The Court may have another chance soon to revisit the scope of its holding. Shortly after deciding *Masterpiece*, the Court remanded a case in which a florist had, like the Colorado baker, declined to provide flowers for a same-sex wedding. *Arlene's Flowers, Inc. v. Washington*, ___ U.S.___, ___ S.Ct. ___, 2018 WL 3096308 (June 25, 2018). She lost in the state supreme court, and the Supreme Court instructed that court to reconsider its ruling in light of *Masterpiece*. Because there do not appear to be facts in the record to build a case of the kind of anti-religious bias found by the Court in *Masterpiece*, the florist's case may give the justices an opportunity to revisit soon the scope of a merchant's right to decline to serve same-sex couples. This is yet another area in which Justice Kennedy's departure may prove consequential.

PROBLEM 5–4(a):
PLURAL MARRIAGE

In 1878, the Supreme Court rejected a challenge to a federal ban on bigamy. In *Reynolds v. United States*, 98 U.S. 145 (1879), the Court ruled that this ban did not violate the free exercise rights of Mormon men who, at the time, wished to have multiple wives. Chief Justice Roberts's *Obergefell* dissent argues that the logic of Justice Kennedy's majority opinion entails constitutional protection under the Fourteenth Amendment for plural marriage. The dissent cited a newspaper story about three lesbians who consider themselves married, and who plan to raise together the baby carried by one of them. See *Married Lesbian "Throuple" Expecting First Child*, N.Y. Post, Apr. 23, 2014. Two of the women were legally married in Massachusetts, but the three cohabitate, divide household labor, are supported by the wages of one, and intend to co-parent. Suppose these three women seek to be recognized as married to one another, and challenge as unconstitutional Massachusetts law permitting only two persons to be recognized as legal spouses. What arguments will each side make under *Obergefell*, and how do you think a court would and should rule? After you set out your arguments, you may wish to consult recent scholarly analysis of this question. See *Symposium: Polygamous Unions? Charting the Contours of Marriage Law's Frontier*, 64 Emory L.J. 1669 et seq. (2015). The Roberts dissent cited an article from this collection: Otter, *Three May Not Be a Crowd: The Case for a Constitutional Right to Plural Marriage*, 64 Emory L.J.1977 (2015).

SECTION 6. PROCEDURAL DUE PROCESS

C. DEFINING "WHAT PROCESS IS DUE"

Page 726.   Insert after NOTES ON CAPERTON *AND THE RIGHT TO AN* IMPARTIAL TRIBUNAL**:**

WILLIAMS V. PENNSYLVANIA
___ U.S. ___, 136 S.Ct. 1899, 195 L.Ed.2d 132 (2016)

JUSTICE KENNEDY delivered the opinion of the Court.

In this case, the Supreme Court of Pennsylvania vacated the decision of a postconviction court, which had granted relief to a prisoner convicted of first-degree murder and sentenced to death. One of the justices on the State Supreme Court [Chief Justice Castille] had been the district attorney who gave his official approval to seek the death penalty in the prisoner's case. The justice in question denied the prisoner's motion for recusal and participated in the decision to deny relief. The question presented is whether the justice's denial of the recusal motion and his subsequent judicial participation violated the Due Process Clause of the Fourteenth Amendment. [Williams, the prisoner, alleged that the prosecution had concealed favorable evidence and had deliberately presented false testimony. The lower state court, the Pennsylvania Post Conviction Relief Act court (PCRA court), ruled in his favor. The state supreme court unanimously rejected this claim, with Chief Justice Castille writing a concurrence decrying what he described as obstructive tactics by death penalty opponents.]

This Court's precedents set forth an objective standard that requires recusal when the likelihood of bias on the part of the judge " 'is too high to be constitutionally tolerable.' " [*Caperton*] Applying this standard, the Court concludes that due process compelled the justice's recusal.

Williams contends that Chief Justice Castille's decision as district attorney to seek a death sentence against him barred the chief justice from later adjudicating Williams's petition to overturn that sentence. Chief Justice Castille, Williams argues, violated the Due Process Clause of the Fourteenth Amendment by acting as both accuser and judge in his case.

The Court's due process precedents do not set forth a specific test governing recusal when, as here, a judge had prior involvement in a case as a prosecutor. For the reasons explained below, however, the principles on which these precedents rest dictate the rule that must control in the circumstances here. The Court now holds that under the Due Process Clause there is an impermissible risk of actual bias when a judge earlier had significant, personal involvement as a prosecutor in a critical decision regarding the defendant's case.

Due process guarantees "an absence of actual bias" on the part of a judge. *In re Murchison*, 349 U.S. 133 (1955). Bias is easy to attribute to others and difficult to discern in oneself. To establish an enforceable and workable framework, the Court's precedents apply an objective standard that, in the usual case, avoids having to determine whether actual bias is present. The Court asks not whether a judge harbors an actual, subjective bias, but instead whether, as an objective matter, "the average judge in his position is 'likely' to be neutral, or whether there is an unconstitutional 'potential for bias.' " [*Caperton*] Of particular relevance to the instant case, the Court has determined that an unconstitutional potential for bias exists when the same person serves as both accuser and adjudicator in a case. This objective risk of bias is reflected in the due process maxim that "no man can be a judge in his own case and no man is permitted to try cases where he has an interest in the outcome."

The due process guarantee that "no man can be a judge in his own case" would have little substance if it did not disqualify a former prosecutor from sitting in judgment of a prosecution in which he or she had made a critical decision. This conclusion follows from the Court's analysis in *In re Murchison*. That case involved a "one-man judge-grand jury" proceeding, conducted pursuant to state law, in which the judge called witnesses to testify about suspected crimes. During the course of the examinations, the judge became convinced that two witnesses were obstructing the proceeding. He charged one witness with perjury and then, a few weeks later, tried and convicted him in open court. The judge charged the other witness with contempt and, a few days later, tried and convicted him as well. This Court overturned the convictions on the ground that the judge's dual position as accuser and decisionmaker in the contempt trials violated due process: "Having been a part of [the accusatory] process a judge cannot be, in the very nature of things, wholly disinterested in the conviction or acquittal of those accused."

No attorney is more integral to the accusatory process than a prosecutor who participates in a major adversary decision. When a judge has served as an advocate for the State in the very case the court is now asked to adjudicate, a serious question arises as to whether the judge, even with the most diligent effort, could set aside any personal interest in the outcome. There is, furthermore, a risk that the judge "would be so psychologically wedded" to his or her previous position as a prosecutor that the judge "would consciously or unconsciously avoid the appearance of having erred or changed position." In addition, the judge's "own personal knowledge and impression" of the case, acquired through his or her role in the prosecution, may carry far more weight with the judge than the parties' arguments to the court.

Pennsylvania argues that *Murchison* does not lead to the rule that due process requires disqualification of a judge who, in an earlier role as a prosecutor, had significant involvement in making a critical decision in the case. The facts of *Murchison,* it should be acknowledged, differ in many respects from a case like this one. In *Murchison,* over the course of several weeks, a single official (the so-called judge-grand jury) conducted an investigation into suspected crimes; made the decision to charge witnesses for obstruction of that investigation; heard evidence on the charges he had lodged; issued judgments of conviction; and imposed sentence. By contrast, a judge who had an earlier involvement in a prosecution might have been just one of several prosecutors working on the case at each stage of the proceedings; the prosecutor's immediate role might have been limited to a particular aspect of the prosecution; and decades might have passed before the former prosecutor, now a judge, is called upon to adjudicate a claim in the case.

These factual differences notwithstanding, the constitutional principles explained in *Murchison* are fully applicable where a judge had a direct, personal role in the defendant's prosecution. The involvement of other actors and the passage of time are consequences of a complex criminal justice system, in which a single case may be litigated through multiple proceedings taking place over a period of years. This context only heightens the need for objective rules preventing the operation of bias that otherwise might be obscured. Within a large, impersonal system, an individual prosecutor might still have an influence that, while not so visible as the one-man grand jury in *Murchison,* is nevertheless significant. A prosecutor may bear responsibility for any number of critical decisions, including what charges to bring, whether to extend a plea bargain, and which witnesses to call. Even if decades intervene before the former prosecutor revisits the matter as a jurist, the case may implicate the effects and continuing force of his or her original decision. In these circumstances, there remains a serious risk that a judge would be influenced by an improper, if inadvertent, motive to validate and preserve the result obtained through the adversary process. The involvement of multiple actors and the passage of time do not relieve the former prosecutor of the duty to withdraw in order to ensure the neutrality of the judicial process in determining the consequences that his or her own earlier, critical decision may have set in motion.

This leads to the question whether Chief Justice Castille's authorization to seek the death penalty against Williams amounts to significant, personal involvement in a critical trial decision. The Court now concludes that it was a significant, personal involvement; and, as a result, Chief Justice Castille's failure to recuse from Williams's case presented an unconstitutional risk of bias.

As an initial matter, there can be no doubt that the decision to pursue the death penalty is a critical choice in the adversary process. Indeed, after a defendant is charged with a death-eligible crime, whether to ask a jury to end the defendant's life is one of the most serious discretionary decisions a prosecutor can be called upon to make.

Nor is there any doubt that Chief Justice Castille had a significant role in this decision. Without his express authorization, the Commonwealth would not have been able to pursue a death sentence against Williams. The importance of this decision and the profound consequences it carries make it evident that a responsible prosecutor would deem it to be a most significant exercise of his or her official discretion and professional judgment.

Pennsylvania nonetheless contends that Chief Justice Castille in fact did not have significant involvement in the decision to seek a death sentence against Williams. The chief justice, the Commonwealth points out, was the head of a large district attorney's office in a city that saw many capital murder trials. According to Pennsylvania, his approval of the trial prosecutor's request to pursue capital punishment in Williams's case amounted to a brief administrative act limited to "the time it takes to read a one-and-a-half-page memo." In this Court's view, that characterization cannot be credited. The Court will not assume that then-District Attorney Castille treated so major a decision as a perfunctory task requiring little time, judgment, or reflection on his part.

Chief Justice Castille's own comments while running for judicial office refute the Commonwealth's claim that he played a mere ministerial role in capital sentencing decisions. During the chief justice's election campaign, multiple news outlets reported his statement that he "sent 45 people to death rows" as district attorney. Chief Justice Castille's willingness to take personal responsibility for the death sentences obtained during his tenure as district attorney indicate that, in his own view, he played a meaningful role in those sentencing decisions and considered his involvement to be an important duty of his office.

Although not necessary to the disposition of this case, the [lower state court' court's ruling underscores the risk of permitting a former prosecutor to be a judge in what had been his or her own case. The PCRA court determined that the trial prosecutor—Chief Justice Castille's former subordinate in the district attorney's office—had engaged in multiple, intentional *Brady* violations during Williams's prosecution. While there is no indication that Chief Justice Castille was aware of the alleged prosecutorial misconduct, it would be difficult for a judge in his position not to view the PCRA court's findings as a criticism of his former office and, to some extent, of his own leadership and supervision as district attorney.

The potential conflict of interest posed by the PCRA court's findings illustrates the utility of statutes and professional codes of conduct that "provide more protection than due process requires." Most questions of recusal are addressed by more stringent and detailed ethical rules, which in many jurisdictions already require disqualification under the circumstances of this case. At the time Williams filed his recusal motion with the Pennsylvania Supreme Court, for example, Pennsylvania's Code of Judicial Conduct disqualified judges from any proceeding in which "they served as a lawyer in the matter in controversy, or a lawyer with whom they previously practiced law served during such association as a lawyer concerning the matter. . . ." The fact that most jurisdictions have these rules in place suggests that today's decision will not occasion a significant change in recusal practice.

Chief Justice Castille's significant, personal involvement in a critical decision in Williams's case gave rise to an unacceptable risk of actual bias. This risk so endangered the appearance of neutrality that his participation in the case "must be forbidden if the guarantee of due process is to be adequately implemented."

Having determined that Chief Justice Castille's participation violated due process, the Court must resolve whether Williams is entitled to relief. In past cases, the Court has not had to decide the question whether a due process violation arising from a jurist's failure to recuse amounts to harmless error if the jurist is on a multimember court and the jurist's vote was not decisive. For the reasons discussed below, the Court holds that an unconstitutional failure to recuse constitutes structural error even if the judge in question did not cast a deciding vote.

The Court has little trouble concluding that a due process violation arising from the participation of an interested judge is a defect "not amenable" to harmless-error review, regardless of whether the judge's vote was dispositive. The deliberations of an appellate panel, as a general rule, are confidential. As a result, it is neither possible nor productive to inquire whether the jurist in question might have influenced the views of his or her colleagues during the decisionmaking process. Indeed, one purpose of judicial confidentiality is to assure jurists that they can reexamine old ideas and suggest new ones, while both seeking to persuade and being open to persuasion by their colleagues. As Justice Brennan wrote in his *Lavoie* concurrence,

> "The description of an opinion as being 'for the court' connotes more than merely that the opinion has been joined by a majority of the participating judges. It reflects the fact that these judges have exchanged ideas and arguments in deciding the case. It reflects the collective process of deliberation which shapes the court's perceptions of which issues must be addressed and, more importantly, how they must be addressed. And, while the influence of any single participant in this process can never be measured with precision, experience teaches us that each

member's involvement plays a part in shaping the court's ultimate disposition." * * *

Where a judge has had an earlier significant, personal involvement as a prosecutor in a critical decision in the defendant's case, the risk of actual bias in the judicial proceeding rises to an unconstitutional level. Due process entitles Terrance Williams to "a proceeding in which he may present his case with assurance" that no member of the court is "predisposed to find against him."

The judgment of the Supreme Court of Pennsylvania is vacated, and the case is remanded for further proceedings not inconsistent with this opinion.

CHIEF JUSTICE ROBERTS, with whom JUSTICE ALITO joins, dissenting.

The majority opinion rests on proverb rather than precedent. This Court has held that there is "a presumption of honesty and integrity in those serving as adjudicators." To overcome that presumption, the majority relies on *In re Murchison*. We concluded there that the Due Process Clause is violated when a judge adjudicates the same question—based on the same facts—that he had already considered as a grand juror in the same case. Here, however, Williams does not allege that Chief Justice Castille had *any* previous knowledge of the contested facts at issue in the habeas petition, or that he had previously made *any* decision on the questions raised by that petition. I would accordingly hold that the Due Process Clause did not require Chief Justice Castille's recusal.

JUSTICE THOMAS, dissenting.

The Court concludes that it violates the Due Process Clause for the chief justice of the Supreme Court of Pennsylvania, a former district attorney who was not the trial prosecutor in petitioner Terrance Williams' case, to review Williams' fourth petition for state postconviction review. That conclusion is flawed. The specter of bias alone in a judicial proceeding is not a deprivation of due process. Rather than constitutionalize every judicial disqualification rule, the Court has left such rules to legislatures, bar associations, and the judgment of individual adjudicators. Williams, moreover, is not a criminal defendant. His complaint is instead that the due process protections in his state postconviction proceedings—an altogether new civil matter, not a continuation of his criminal trial—were lacking. Ruling in Williams' favor, the Court ignores this posture and our precedents commanding less of state postconviction proceedings than of criminal prosecutions involving defendants whose convictions are not yet final. I respectfully dissent.

NOTES ON WILLIAMS V. PENNSYLVANIA

1. *Judicial Elections and the Presumption of Impartiality.* The dissenters in both *Caperton* and *Williams* correctly observe that those two opinions go well beyond prior precedents in applying due process analysis to judicial recusal. Both opinions make a point of mentioning judicial campaigns—*Caperton* in terms of campaign expenditures and *Williams* in terms of the judge's campaign platform. Could the shift in the Court's stance be related to growing concerns about how the increased politicization of state judicial elections might impair judicial objectivity? Is that a realistic concern for the Court to consider?

2. *Recusal Boundaries.* Is the Court in the process of constitutionalizing the judicial ethical code? Would this be an undesirable development? Or perhaps the Court is in the process of evolving its own common law of judicial bias—a process that could leave judges up in the air for a considerable time about constitutional recusal requirements.

NELSON V. COLORADO
___ U.S. ___, 137 S.Ct. 1249, 197 L.Ed.2d 611 (2017)

JUSTICE GINSBURG delivered the opinion of the Court.

When a criminal conviction is invalidated by a reviewing court and no retrial will occur, is the State obliged to refund fees, court costs, and restitution exacted from the defendant upon, and as a consequence of, the conviction? Our answer is yes. Absent conviction of a crime, one is presumed innocent. Under the Colorado law before us in these cases, however, the State retains conviction-related assessments unless and until the prevailing defendant institutes a discrete civil proceeding and proves her innocence by clear and convincing evidence. This scheme, we hold, offends the Fourteenth Amendment's guarantee of due process. * * *

The familiar procedural due process inspection instructed by *Mathews v. Eldridge,* 424 U.S. 319, 96 S.Ct. 893, 47 L.Ed.2d 18 (1976), governs these cases. Colorado argues that we should instead apply the standard from *Medina v. California,* 505 U.S. 437, 445, 112 S.Ct. 2572, 120 L.Ed.2d 353 (1992), and inquire whether Nelson and Madden were exposed to a procedure offensive to a fundamental principle of justice. *Medina* "provide[s] the appropriate framework for assessing the validity of state procedural rules" that "are part of the criminal process." Such rules concern, for example, the allocation of burdens of proof and the type of evidence qualifying as admissible. These cases, in contrast, concern the continuing deprivation of property after a conviction has been reversed or vacated, with no prospect of reprosecution. Because no further criminal process is implicated, *Mathews* "provides the relevant inquiry." * * *

Under the *Mathews* balancing test, a court evaluates (A) the private interest affected; (B) the risk of erroneous deprivation of that interest through the procedures used; and (C) the governmental interest at stake. All three considerations weigh decisively against Colorado's scheme.

Nelson and Madden have an obvious interest in regaining the money they paid to Colorado. Colorado urges, however, that the funds belong to the State because Nelson's and Madden's convictions were in place when the funds were taken. But once those convictions were erased, the presumption of their innocence was restored. "[A]xiomatic and elementary," the presumption of innocence "lies at the foundation of our criminal law." Colorado may not retain funds taken from Nelson and Madden solely because of their now-invalidated convictions, for Colorado may not presume a person, adjudged guilty of no crime, nonetheless guilty *enough* for monetary exactions.

That petitioners prevailed on subsequent review rather than in the first instance, moreover, should be inconsequential. Suppose a trial judge grants a motion to set aside a guilty verdict for want of sufficient evidence. In that event, the defendant pays no costs, fees, or restitution. Now suppose the trial court enters judgment on a guilty verdict, ordering cost, fee, and restitution payments by reason of the conviction, but the appeals court upsets the conviction for evidentiary insufficiency. By what right does the State retain the amount paid out by the defendant? "[I]t should make no difference that the *reviewing* court, rather than the trial court, determined the evidence to be insufficient." The vulnerability of the State's argument that it can keep the amounts exacted so long as it prevailed in the court of first instance is more apparent still if we assume a case in which the sole penalty is a fine. On Colorado's reasoning, an appeal would leave the defendant emptyhanded; regardless of the outcome of an appeal, the State would have no refund obligation.

Is there a risk of erroneous deprivation of defendants' interest in return of their funds if, as Colorado urges, the Exoneration Act is the exclusive remedy? Indeed yes, for the Act conditions refund on defendants' proof of innocence by clear and convincing evidence. But to get their money back, defendants should not be saddled with any proof burden. Instead, as explained *supra,* they are entitled to be presumed innocent.

Furthermore, as Justice Hood noted in dissent, the Act provides no remedy at all for any assessments tied to invalid misdemeanor convictions. (Nelson had three). And when amounts a defendant seeks to recoup are not large, as is true in Nelson's and Madden's cases, the cost of mounting a claim under the Exoneration Act and retaining a lawyer to pursue it would be prohibitive.

Colorado argued on brief that if the Exoneration Act provides sufficient process to compensate a defendant for the loss of her liberty, the Act should also suffice "when a defendant seeks compensation for the less significant deprivation of monetary assessments paid pursuant to a conviction that is later overturned." The comparison is inapt. Nelson and Madden seek restoration of funds they paid to the State, not compensation for temporary deprivation of those funds. Petitioners seek only their money back, not interest on those funds for the period the funds were in the State's custody. Just as the restoration of liberty on reversal of a conviction is not compensation, neither is the return of money taken by the State on account of the conviction. * * *

Colorado has no interest in withholding from Nelson and Madden money to which the State currently has zero claim of right. "Equitable [c]onsiderations," Colorado suggests, may bear on whether a State may withhold funds from criminal defendants after their convictions are overturned. Colorado, however, has identified no such consideration relevant to petitioners' cases, nor has the State indicated any way in which the Exoneration Act embodies "equitable considerations."

Colorado's scheme fails due process measurement because defendants' interest in regaining their funds is high, the risk of erroneous deprivation of those funds under the Exoneration Act is unacceptable, and the State has shown no countervailing interests in retaining the amounts in question. To comport with due process, a State may not impose anything more than minimal procedures on the refund of exactions dependent upon a conviction subsequently invalidated.

[Justice Gorsuch took no part in the consideration or decision of these cases. Justice Alito concurred in the judgment, arguing that the proper test was *Medina* but that the Colorado law was invalid under that test to the extent it involved repayment of fines. He did not view the issue of amounts paid for victim restitution as properly before the Court, but argued that the Colorado law should be considered valid in that context. Justice Thomas dissenting, arguing that once the funds became the property of the state or of a victim who had received restitution, the only right to recover the payments was that granted by state law, which was conditional on compliance with the state's statutory requirements and procedures.]

NOTES ON NELSON *AND DUE PROCESS*

1. *Criminal Procedure and Due Process. Matthews* is a pragmatic cost-benefit analysis of procedures, whereas *Medina* is phrased in terms of fundamental injustice, seemingly a much higher standard. Thus, it appears, a state may not use a procedure to deprive a person of property in a civil context when the risks of erroneous results outweigh the benefits of the procedure. But it can do so in the criminal context, unless the higher threshold of fundamental injustice is reached—and in fact, can even do so where not just property but liberty (and even life) are at stake. Does this hands-off attitude toward the criminal process make sense? If so, why?

2.   *Procedural Versus Substantive Due Process?* Justice Thomas takes the majority to task for failing to inquire into the source of the defendant's right to restoration of funds after a conviction is reversed or vacated on collateral appeal. The majority brushes the question aside, finding it obvious that once the presumption of innocence is restored, the defendant is entitled to a refund. Thomas's argument seems especially strong when a conviction is upheld on appeal and is later vacated in collateral attack (especially on grounds unrelated to guilt or innocence). Why does the Constitution require a state to refund money to which it received title under a final judgment? Is that really a procedural issue, or is it a question of substantive injustice?

CHAPTER 6

THE FIRST AMENDMENT

■ ■ ■

Page 728.   Insert before Section 1:

The Court further refined the test for content neutrality in the following case. Unlike the preceding cases, which dealt with controversial actions like flag burning, this one involved the far more mundane issue of location signs for public events.

REED V. TOWN OF GILBERT
___ U.S. ___, 135 S.Ct. 2218, 192 L.Ed.2d 236 (2015)

JUSTICE THOMAS delivered the opinion of the Court.

The town of Gilbert, Arizona (or Town), has adopted a comprehensive code governing the manner in which people may display outdoor signs. The Sign Code identifies various categories of signs based on the type of information they convey, then subjects each category to different restrictions. One of the categories is "Temporary Directional Signs Relating to a Qualifying Event," loosely defined as signs directing the public to a meeting of a nonprofit group. The Code imposes more stringent restrictions on these signs than it does on signs conveying other messages. We hold that these provisions are content-based regulations of speech that cannot survive strict scrutiny.

The Sign Code prohibits the display of outdoor signs anywhere within the Town without a permit, but it then exempts 23 categories of signs from that requirement. These exemptions include everything from bazaar signs to flying banners. Three categories of exempt signs are particularly relevant here.

The first is "Ideological Sign[s]." This category includes any "sign communicating a message or ideas for noncommercial purposes that is not a Construction Sign, Directional Sign, Temporary Directional Sign Relating to a Qualifying Event, Political Sign, Garage Sale Sign, or a sign owned or required by a governmental agency." Of the three categories discussed here, the Code treats ideological signs most favorably, allowing them to be up to 20 square feet in area and to be placed in all "zoning districts" without time limits.

The second category is "Political Sign[s]." This includes any "temporary sign designed to influence the outcome of an election called by a public body." The Code treats these signs less favorably than ideological signs. The Code allows the placement of political signs up to 16 square feet on residential property and up to 32 square feet on nonresidential property, undeveloped municipal property, and "rights-of-way." These signs may be displayed up to 60 days before a primary election and up to 15 days following a general election.

The third category is "Temporary Directional Signs Relating to a Qualifying Event." * * * The Code treats temporary directional signs even less favorably than political signs. Temporary directional signs may be no larger than six square feet. They may be placed on private property or on a public right-of-way, but no more than four signs may be placed on a single property at any time. And, they may be displayed no more than 12 hours before the "qualifying event" and no more than 1 hour afterward. * * *

Government regulation of speech is content based if a law applies to particular speech because of the topic discussed or the idea or message expressed. This commonsense meaning of the phrase "content based" requires a court to consider whether a regulation of speech "on its face" draws distinctions based on the message a speaker conveys. Some facial distinctions based on a message are obvious, defining regulated speech by particular subject matter, and others are more subtle, defining regulated speech by its function or purpose. Both are distinctions drawn based on the message a speaker conveys, and, therefore, are subject to strict scrutiny.

Our precedents have also recognized a separate and additional category of laws that, though facially content neutral, will be considered content-based regulations of speech: laws that cannot be " 'justified without reference to the content of the regulated speech,' " or that were adopted by the government "because of disagreement with the message [the speech] conveys." Those laws, like those that are content based on their face, must also satisfy strict scrutiny.

The Town's Sign Code is content based on its face. It defines "Temporary Directional Signs" on the basis of whether a sign conveys the message of directing the public to church or some other "qualifying event." It defines "Political Signs" on the basis of whether a sign's message is "designed to influence the outcome of an election." And it defines "Ideological Signs" on the basis of whether a sign "communicat[es] a message or ideas" that do not fit within the Code's other categories. It then subjects each of these categories to different restrictions.

The restrictions in the Sign Code that apply to any given sign thus depend entirely on the communicative content of the sign. * * * On its face, the Sign Code is a content-based regulation of speech. We thus have no need to consider the government's justifications or purposes for enacting the Code to determine whether it is subject to strict scrutiny.

Because the Town's Sign Code imposes content-based restrictions on speech, those provisions can stand only if they survive strict scrutiny * * * . Thus, it is the Town's burden to demonstrate that the Code's differentiation between temporary directional signs and other types of signs, such as political signs and ideological signs, furthers a compelling governmental interest and is narrowly tailored to that end.

The Town cannot do so. It has offered only two governmental interests in support of the distinctions the Sign Code draws: preserving the Town's aesthetic appeal and traffic safety. Assuming for the sake of argument that those are compelling governmental interests, the Code's distinctions fail as hopelessly underinclusive. * * *

We acknowledge that a city might reasonably view the general regulation of signs as necessary because signs "take up space and may obstruct views, distract motorists, displace alternative uses for land, and pose other problems that legitimately call for regulation." At the same time, the presence of certain signs may be essential, both for vehicles and pedestrians, to guide traffic or to identify hazards and ensure safety. A sign ordinance narrowly tailored to the challenges of protecting the safety of pedestrians, drivers, and passengers—such as warning signs marking hazards on private property, signs directing traffic, or street numbers associated with private houses—well might survive strict scrutiny. The signs at issue in this case, including political and ideological signs and signs for events, are far removed from those purposes. As discussed above, they are facially content based and are neither justified by traditional safety concerns nor narrowly tailored.

JUSTICE BREYER, concurring in the judgment.

The better approach is to generally treat content discrimination as a strong reason weighing against the constitutionality of a rule where a traditional public forum, or where viewpoint discrimination, is threatened, but elsewhere treat it as a rule of thumb, finding it a helpful, but not determinative legal tool, in an appropriate case, to determine the strength of a justification. I would use content discrimination as a supplement to a more basic analysis, which, tracking most of our First Amendment cases, asks whether the regulation at issue works harm to First Amendment interests that is disproportionate in light of the relevant regulatory objectives. Answering this question requires examining the seriousness of the harm to speech, the importance of the countervailing objectives, the extent to which the law will achieve those objectives, and whether there are other, less restrictive ways of doing so. But it does permit the government to regulate speech in numerous instances where the voters have authorized the government to regulate and where courts should hesitate to substitute judicial judgment for that of administrators.

Here, regulation of signage along the roadside, for purposes of safety and beautification is at issue. There is no traditional public forum nor do I find any general effort to censor a particular viewpoint. Consequently, the specific regulation at issue does not warrant "strict scrutiny."

JUSTICE KAGAN, joined by **JUSTICE GINSBURG** and **JUSTICE BREYER**, concurring in the judgment.

Countless cities and towns across America have adopted ordinances regulating the posting of signs, while exempting certain categories of signs based on their subject matter. For example, some municipalities generally prohibit illuminated signs in residential neighborhoods, but lift that ban for signs that identify the address of a home or the name of its owner or occupant. In other municipalities, safety signs such as "Blind Pedestrian Crossing" and "Hidden Driveway" can be posted without a permit, even as other permanent signs require one. Elsewhere, historic site markers—for example, "George Washington Slept Here"—are also exempt from general regulations. And similarly, the federal Highway Beautification Act limits signs along interstate highways unless, for instance, they direct travelers to "scenic and historical attractions" or advertise free coffee.

Given the Court's analysis, many sign ordinances of that kind are now in jeopardy. * * * The consequence—unless courts water down strict scrutiny to something unrecognizable—is that our communities will find themselves in an unenviable bind: They will have to either repeal the exemptions that allow for helpful signs on streets and sidewalks, or else lift their sign restrictions altogether and resign themselves to the resulting clutter.

Although the majority insists that applying strict scrutiny to all such ordinances is "essential" to protecting First Amendment freedoms, I find it challenging to understand why that is so. * * *

* * * Subject-matter regulation, in other words, may have the intent or effect of favoring some ideas over others. When that is realistically possible—when the restriction "raises the specter that the Government may effectively drive certain ideas or viewpoints from the marketplace"— we insist that the law pass the most demanding constitutional test

But when that is not realistically possible, we may do well to relax our guard so that "entirely reasonable" laws imperiled by strict scrutiny can survive. * * * To do its intended work, of course, the category of content-based regulation triggering strict scrutiny must sweep more broadly than the actual harm; that category exists to create a buffer zone guaranteeing that the government cannot favor or disfavor certain viewpoints. But that buffer zone need not extend forever. We can administer our content-regulation doctrine with a dose of common sense, so as to leave standing laws that in no way implicate its intended function. * * *

NOTES ON REED

1. *Defining Content Neutrality.* The majority defines content neutrality very narrowly. To be content neutral, a law must neither (a) draw any distinctions based on communicative content, nor (b) have a purpose related to communicative content. Any other regulation of private speech is subject to strict scrutiny. Absent a compelling interest, if the state allows any category of messages, it must allow all categories of messages equally, even if there seems to be a commonsense justification for treating some messages (such as address signs) differently.

2. *Why Not Allow Commonsense Distinctions?* Consider a law that allows owners to illuminate their house numbers but not other kinds of signs. Why should that be subject to strict scrutiny? Is the reason that there might be some discriminatory intent behind theses seemingly innocuous distinctions that would be difficult to establish more directly? (Perhaps the city wanted to prevent illumination of some other particular kind of sign in drawing this distinction?) Or is the reason that cities are likely to want to allow addresses to be illuminated and that an anti-discrimination rule will then provide an opportunity for other signs to be illuminated, increasing the possibilities for communication? (Notice that these reasons are quite different: one is an effort to prevent hidden harms while the other one is an effort to open up broader channels of communication.) Or is the reason that there is something intrinsically unjust about distinctions based on communicative message, no matter how trivial they may seem? Or, finally, do we not trust judges to decide when a particular type of content distinction poses no threat to public discourse?

PACKINGHAM V. NORTH CAROLINA
___ U.S. ___, 137 S.Ct. 1730, 198 L.Ed.2d 273 (2017)

JUSTICE KENNEDY delivered the opinion of the Court.

[North Carolina law makes it a felony for a registered sex offender "to access a commercial social networking Web site where the sex offender knows that the site permits minor children to become members or to create or maintain personal Web pages." § 14–202.5 The statute exempts websites that "[p]rovid[e] only one of the following discrete services: photo-sharing, electronic mail, instant messenger, or chat room or message board platform." The law also exempts websites that have as their "primary purpose the facilitation of commercial transactions involving goods or services between [their] members or visitors." The statute applies to about 20,000 people in North Carolina and the State has prosecuted over 1,000 people for violating it.]

A fundamental principle of the First Amendment is that all persons have access to places where they can speak and listen, and then, after reflection, speak and listen once more. The Court has sought to protect the right to speak in this spatial context. A basic rule, for example, is that a street or a park is a quintessential forum for the exercise of First Amendment rights. See Ward v. Rock Against Racism, 491 U.S. 781, 796, 109 S.Ct. 2746, 105 L.Ed.2d 661 (1989). Even in the modern era, these places are still essential venues for public gatherings to celebrate some views, to protest others, or simply to learn and inquire.

While in the past there may have been difficulty in identifying the most important places (in a spatial sense) for the exchange of views, today the answer is clear. It is cyberspace—the "vast democratic forums of the Internet" in general, and social media in particular. Seven in ten American adults use at least one Internet social networking service. One of the most popular of these sites is Facebook, the site used by petitioner leading to his conviction in this case. According to sources cited to the Court in this case, Facebook has 1.79 billion active users. This is about three times the population of North America.

Social media offers "relatively unlimited, low-cost capacity for communication of all kinds." On Facebook, for example, users can debate religion and politics with their friends and neighbors or share vacation photos. On LinkedIn, users can look for work, advertise for employees, or review tips on entrepreneurship. And on Twitter, users can petition their elected representatives and otherwise engage with them in a direct manner. Indeed, Governors in all 50 States and almost every Member of Congress have set up accounts for this purpose. In short, social media users employ these websites to engage in a wide array of protected First Amendment activity on topics "as diverse as human thought."

The nature of a revolution in thought can be that, in its early stages, even its participants may be unaware of it. And when awareness comes, they still may be unable to know or foresee where its changes lead. So too here. While we now may be coming to the realization that the Cyber Age is a revolution of historic proportions, we cannot appreciate yet its full dimensions and vast potential to alter how we think, express ourselves, and define who we want to be. The forces and directions of the Internet are so new, so protean, and so far reaching that courts must be conscious that what they say today might be obsolete tomorrow.

This case is one of the first this Court has taken to address the relationship between the First Amendment and the modern Internet. As a result, the Court must exercise extreme caution before suggesting that the First Amendment provides scant protection for access to vast networks in that medium.

This background informs the analysis of the North Carolina statute at issue. Even making the assumption that the statute is content neutral and thus subject to intermediate scrutiny, the provision cannot stand. In order to survive intermediate scrutiny, a law must be "narrowly tailored to serve a significant governmental interest." In other words, the law must not "burden substantially more speech than is necessary to further the government's legitimate interests." For centuries now, inventions heralded as advances in human progress have been exploited by the criminal mind. New technologies, all too soon, can become instruments used to commit serious crimes. * * * So it will be with the Internet and social media.

There is also no doubt that, as this Court has recognized, "[t]he sexual abuse of a child is a most serious crime and an act repugnant to the moral instincts of a decent people." And it is clear that a legislature "may pass valid laws to protect children" and other victims of sexual assault "from abuse." The government, of course, need not simply stand by and allow these evils to occur. But the assertion of a valid governmental interest "cannot, in every context, be insulated from all constitutional protections."

It is necessary to make two assumptions to resolve this case. First, given the broad wording of the North Carolina statute at issue, it might well bar access not only to commonplace social media websites but also to websites as varied as Amazon.com, Washingtonpost.com, and Webmd.com. The Court need not decide the precise scope of the statute. It is enough to assume that the law applies (as the State concedes it does) to social networking sites "as commonly understood"—that is, websites like Facebook, LinkedIn, and Twitter.

Second, this opinion should not be interpreted as barring a State from enacting more specific laws than the one at issue. Specific criminal acts are not protected speech even if speech is the means for their commission. Though the issue is not before the Court, it can be assumed that the First Amendment permits a State to enact specific, narrowly tailored laws that prohibit a sex offender from engaging in conduct that often presages a sexual crime, like contacting a minor or using a website to gather information about a minor. Specific laws of that type must be the State's first resort to ward off the serious harm that sexual crimes inflict. (Of importance, the troubling fact that the law imposes severe restrictions on persons who already have served their sentence and are no longer subject to the supervision of the criminal justice system is also not an issue before the Court.)

Even with these assumptions about the scope of the law and the State's interest, the statute here enacts a prohibition unprecedented in the scope of First Amendment speech it burdens. Social media allows users to gain access to information and communicate with one another about it on any subject that might come to mind. By prohibiting sex offenders from using those websites, North Carolina with one broad stroke bars access to what for many are the principal sources for knowing current events, checking ads for employment, speaking and listening in the modern public square, and otherwise exploring the vast realms of human thought and knowledge. These websites can provide perhaps the most powerful mechanisms available to a private citizen to make his or her voice heard. They allow a person with an Internet connection to "become a town crier with a voice that resonates farther than it could from any soapbox."

In sum, to foreclose access to social media altogether is to prevent the user from engaging in the legitimate exercise of First Amendment rights. It is unsettling to suggest that only a limited set of websites can be used even by persons who have completed their sentences. Even convicted criminals—and in some instances especially convicted criminals—might receive legitimate benefits from these means for access to the world of ideas, in particular if they seek to reform and to pursue lawful and rewarding lives.

The primary response from the State is that the law must be this broad to serve its preventative purpose of keeping convicted sex offenders away from vulnerable victims. The State has not, however, met its burden to show that this sweeping law is necessary or legitimate to serve that purpose.

* * *

It is well established that, as a general rule, the Government "may not suppress lawful speech as the means to suppress unlawful speech." That is what North Carolina has done here. Its law must be held invalid.

JUSTICE GORSUCH took no part in the consideration or decision of this case.

JUSTICE ALITO, with whom the CHIEF JUSTICE and JUSTICE THOMAS join, concurring in the judgment.

The North Carolina statute at issue in this case was enacted to serve an interest of "surpassing importance."—but it has a staggering reach. It makes it a felony for a registered sex offender simply to visit a vast array of websites, including many that appear to provide no realistic opportunity for communications that could facilitate the abuse of children. Because of the law's extraordinary breadth, I agree with the Court that it violates the Free Speech Clause of the First Amendment.

I cannot join the opinion of the Court, however, because of its undisciplined dicta. The Court is unable to resist musings that seem to equate the entirety of the internet with public streets and parks. And this language is bound to be interpreted by some to mean that the States are largely powerless to restrict even the most dangerous sexual predators from visiting any internet sites, including, for example, teenage dating sites and sites designed to permit minors to discuss personal problems with their peers. I am troubled by the implications of the Court's unnecessary rhetoric. [In the remainder of his concurrence, Justice Alito concluded that, although the statute served a compelling interest, it was not narrowly tailored and therefore failed strict scrutiny.]

NOTES ON PACKINGHAM AND INTERNET REGULATION

1. *Application of Content Neutrality.* The state law limits access by sex offenders to particular websites, not speech with particular content. But obviously the state's purpose is deeply intertwined with concerns about the possible content of the speech by these individuals. Since the Court finds that the law is too sweeping to withstand scrutiny even under the standard for content neutral regulations, it does not need to determine whether the law is content neutral. How would you resolve that question?

2. *Drafting Problem.* Both the majority opinion and the concurrence fault the statute for sweeping too many websites within its reach. Try to draft a narrower statute that protects minors from sex offenders without impeding legitimate Internet use.

3. *The Analogy to Physical Public Spaces.* The Court analogizes the Internet to traditional public spaces such as parks and streets, which have traditionally been open to a broad range of communicative activities. As we will see later in discussing public forum doctrine, the First Amendment imposes special limits on government control of communication in those places. Note, however, that these spaces are owned and controlled by the government. The same is not true of the Internet. Although the government originally created and operated the Internet, control was transferred to private hands in 1997. Today the Internet is operated by a combination of website (governmental and private), Internet Service Providers (ISPs) (generally private), and internet backbone operators (private). The U.S. government has relinquished control of domain names, a fundamental aspect of internet governance, to a nonprofit, the Internet Corporation for Assigned Names and Numbers (ICANN). See Kal Raustiala, *Governing the Internet*, 110 AM. J. INT'L L. 491 (2016). Thus, unlike streets and parks, the Internet is not a governmental facility. Moreover, all of the websites named by the Court are privately owned and operated. So the analogy between the Internet and traditional public forums (streets, parks, etc.) is imperfect. Yet, the Court is surely right in its appraisal of the crucial role of the Internet, and social media of all kinds, in today's society.

4. *Confronting Novel Technologies.* Some uses of the Internet seem functionally similar to older forms of communication: email to postal letters, on-line stores to mail order catalogues, blogs to newspapers and newsletters. Justice Kennedy's analogy to public spaces is suggestive, because plazas, streets and parks do provide places for people to meet, hear speeches and concerts, receive printed handouts, and express their own views, much like portions of the Internet. But the Internet also has unique features—unlike

public spaces, the Internet is structured in ways that are often invisible to users by firms like Facebook and is prone to hacking and other forms of manipulation that can warp communication. Dealing with the challenges posed by new and rapidly changing technologies is likely to become a central focus of First Amendment law.

The Supreme Court has continued to make aggressive use of the doctrine of content neutrality, brushing aside arguable exceptions. Consider the following case.

NATIONAL INSTITUTE OF FAMILY AND LIFE ADVOCATES [NIFLA] V. BECERRA
___ U.S. ___, 138 S.Ct. 2361, ___ L.Ed.2d ___ (2018)

[The California Reproductive Freedom, Accountability, Comprehensive Care, and Transparency Act (FACT Act) was enacted to regulate crisis pregnancy centers—pro-life centers that offer pregnancy-related services. The FACT Act required clinics that primarily serve pregnant women to provide certain notices. Clinics that are licensed must notify women that California provides free or low-cost services, including abortions, and give them a phone number to call. Its stated purpose was to make sure that state residents know their rights and what health care services are available to them. Unlicensed clinics must notify women that California has not licensed the clinics to provide medical services.]

JUSTICE THOMAS delivered the opinion of the Court.

The California Reproductive Freedom, Accountability, Comprehensive Care, and Transparency Act (FACT Act) requires clinics that primarily serve pregnant women to provide certain notices. Cal. Health & Safety Code Ann. § 123470 et seq. (West 2018). Licensed clinics must notify women that California provides free or low-cost services, including abortions, and give them a phone number to call. Unlicensed clinics must notify women that California has not licensed the clinics to provide medical services. The question in this case is whether these notice requirements violate the First Amendment. We first address the licensed notice.[2]

The licensed notice is a content-based regulation of speech. By compelling individuals to speak a particular message, such notices "alte[r] the content of [their] speech." Here, for example, licensed clinics must provide a government-drafted script about the availability of state-sponsored services, as well as contact information for how to obtain them. One of those services is abortion—the very practice that petitioners are devoted to opposing. By requiring petitioners to inform women how they can obtain state-subsidized abortions—at the same time petitioners try to

---

[2] Petitioners raise serious concerns that both the licensed and unlicensed notices discriminate based on viewpoint. Because the notices are unconstitutional either way, as explained below, we need not reach that issue.

dissuade women from choosing that option—the licensed notice plainly "alters the content" of petitioners' speech.

Although the licensed notice is content based, the Ninth Circuit did not apply strict scrutiny because it concluded that the notice regulates "professional speech." Some Courts of Appeals have recognized "professional speech" as a separate category of speech that is subject to different rules. So defined, these courts except professional speech from the rule that content-based regulations of speech are subject to strict scrutiny.

But this Court has not recognized "professional speech" as a separate category of speech. Speech is not unprotected merely because it is uttered by "professionals." This Court has "been reluctant to mark off new categories of speech for diminished constitutional protection." This Court's precedents do not permit governments to impose content-based restrictions on speech without " 'persuasive evidence . . . of a long (if heretofore unrecognized) tradition' " to that effect.

This Court's precedents do not recognize such a tradition for a category called "professional speech." This Court has afforded less protection for professional speech in two circumstances—neither of which turned on the fact that professionals were speaking. First, our precedents have applied more deferential review to some laws that require professionals to disclose factual, noncontroversial information in their "commercial speech." Second, under our precedents, States may regulate professional conduct, even though that conduct incidentally involves speech. But neither line of precedents is implicated here.

This Court's precedents have applied a lower level of scrutiny to laws that compel disclosures in certain contexts. In Zauderer [v. Office of Disciplinary Counsel of Supreme Court of Ohio, 471 U.S. 626, 651, 105 S.Ct. 2265, 85 L.Ed.2d 652 (1985)], for example, this Court upheld a rule requiring lawyers who advertised their services on a contingency-fee basis to disclose that clients might be required to pay some fees and costs. Noting that the disclosure requirement governed only "commercial advertising" and required the disclosure of "purely factual and uncontroversial information about the terms under which . . . services will be available," the Court explained that such requirements should be upheld unless they are "unjustified or unduly burdensome."

The *Zauderer* standard does not apply here. Most obviously, the licensed notice is not limited to "purely factual and uncontroversial information about the terms under which . . . services will be available." The notice in no way relates to the services that licensed clinics provide. Instead, it requires these clinics to disclose information about state-sponsored services—including abortion, anything but an "uncontroversial" topic. Accordingly, *Zauderer* has no application here.

In addition to disclosure requirements under *Zauderer*, this Court has upheld regulations of professional conduct that incidentally burden speech. "[T]he First Amendment does not prevent restrictions directed at commerce or conduct from imposing incidental burdens on speech," and professionals are no exception to this rule,. Longstanding torts for professional malpractice, for example, "fall within the traditional purview of state regulation of professional conduct." While drawing the line between speech and conduct can be difficult, this Court's precedents have long drawn it.

In *Planned Parenthood of Southeastern Pa. v. Casey*, for example, this Court upheld a law requiring physicians to obtain informed consent before they could perform an abortion. Pennsylvania law required physicians to inform their patients of "the nature of the procedure, the health risks of the abortion and childbirth, and the 'probable gestational age of the unborn child.'" The law also required physicians to inform patients of the availability of printed materials from the State, which provided information about the child and various forms of assistance.

The joint opinion in *Casey* rejected a free-speech challenge to this informed-consent requirement. It described the Pennsylvania law as "a requirement that a doctor give a woman certain information as part of obtaining her consent to an abortion," which "for constitutional purposes, [was] no different from a requirement that a doctor give certain specific information about any medical procedure." The joint opinion explained that the law regulated speech only "as part of the practice of medicine, subject to reasonable licensing and regulation by the State." Indeed, the requirement that a doctor obtain informed consent to perform an operation is "firmly entrenched in American tort law."

The licensed notice at issue here is not an informed-consent requirement or any other regulation of professional conduct. The notice does not facilitate informed consent to a medical procedure. In fact, it is not tied to a procedure at all. It applies to all interactions between a covered facility and its clients, regardless of whether a medical procedure is ever sought, offered, or performed. If a covered facility does provide medical procedures, the notice provides no information about the risks or benefits of those procedures. Tellingly, many facilities that provide the exact same services as covered facilities—such as general practice clinics, see § 123471(a)—are not required to provide the licensed notice. The licensed notice regulates speech as speech.

Outside of the two contexts discussed above—disclosures under *Zauderer* and professional conduct—this Court's precedents have long protected the First Amendment rights of professionals. For example, this Court has applied strict scrutiny to content-based laws that regulate the noncommercial speech of lawyers. And the Court emphasized that the lawyer's statements in *Zauderer* would have been "fully protected" if they were made in a context other than advertising. Moreover, this Court has stressed the danger of content-based regulations "in the fields of medicine and public health, where information can save lives."

The dangers associated with content-based regulations of speech are also present in the context of professional speech. As with other kinds of speech, regulating the content of professionals' speech "pose[s] the inherent risk that the Government seeks not to advance a legitimate regulatory goal, but to suppress unpopular ideas or information." Take medicine, for example. * * * Throughout history, governments have "manipulat[ed] the content of doctor-patient discourse" to increase state power and suppress minorities.

In sum, neither California nor the Ninth Circuit has identified a persuasive reason for treating professional speech as a unique category that is exempt from ordinary First Amendment principles. We do not foreclose the possibility that some such reason exists. We need not do so because the licensed notice cannot survive even intermediate scrutiny. [The Court argued that the notice was a poor fit with its asserted goal of providing low-income women with information about state-sponsored services. Assuming that this is a substantial state interest, the licensed notice is not sufficiently drawn to achieve it, since it included only family planning and pregnancy-related services and excluded federal clinics. Moreover, California could achieve its goal in less intrusive ways, such as advertising about free medical services.]

We next address the unlicensed notice. The parties dispute whether the unlicensed notice is subject to deferential review under Zauderer. We need not decide whether the *Zauderer* standard applies to the unlicensed notice. Even under *Zauderer,* a disclosure requirement cannot be "unjustified or unduly burdensome." Our precedents require disclosures to remedy a harm that is "potentially real not purely hypothetical," and to extend "no broader than reasonably necessary." Otherwise, they risk "chilling" protected speech." Importantly, California has the burden to prove that the unlicensed notice is neither unjustified nor unduly burdensome. It has not met its burden. [The Court concluded that "California has not demonstrated any justification for the unlicensed notice that is more than "purely hypothetical." The state's only asserted justification was informing women when they are getting care from licensed professionals, but there was no evidence to show that women were unaware of that fact.]

Even if California had presented a nonhypothetical justification for the unlicensed notice, the FACT Act unduly burdens protected speech. The unlicensed notice imposes a government-scripted, speaker-based disclosure requirement that is wholly disconnected from California's informational interest. It requires covered facilities to post California's precise notice, no matter what the facilities say on site or in their advertisements. And it covers a curiously narrow subset of speakers. While the licensed notice applies to facilities that provide "family planning" services and "contraception or contraceptive methods," the California Legislature dropped these triggering conditions for the unlicensed notice. The unlicensed notice applies only to facilities that primarily provide "pregnancy-related" services. Thus, a facility that advertises and provides pregnancy tests is covered by the unlicensed notice, but a facility across the street that advertises and provides nonprescription contraceptives is excluded—even though the latter is no less likely to make women think it is licensed. This Court's precedents are deeply skeptical of laws that "distinguis[h] among different speakers, allowing speech by some but not others." Speaker-based laws run the risk that "the State has left unburdened those speakers whose messages are in accord with its own views."

The application of the unlicensed notice to advertisements demonstrates just how burdensome it is. The notice applies to all "print and digital advertising materials" by an unlicensed covered facility. These materials must include a government-drafted statement that "[t]his facility is not licensed as a medical facility by the State of California and has no licensed medical provider who provides or directly supervises the provision of services." An unlicensed facility must call attention to the notice, instead of its own message, by some method such as larger text or contrasting type or color. This scripted language must be posted in English and as many other languages as California chooses to require. As California conceded at oral argument, a billboard for an unlicensed facility that says "Choose Life" would have to surround that two-word statement with a 29-word statement from the government, in as many as 13 different languages. In this way, the unlicensed notice drowns out the facility's own message. More likely, the "detail required" by the unlicensed notice "effectively rules out" the possibility of having such a billboard in the first place.

For all these reasons, the unlicensed notice does not satisfy Zauderer, assuming that standard applies. California has offered no justification that the notice plausibly furthers. It targets speakers, not speech, and imposes an unduly burdensome disclosure requirement that will chill their protected speech. Taking all these circumstances together, we conclude that the unlicensed notice is unjustified and unduly burdensome under Zauderer. We express no view on the legality of a similar disclosure requirement that is better supported or less burdensome.

[A concurring opinion by Justice Kennedy, joined by Chief Justice Robert and Justices Alito and Gorsuch, flagged the risk that the law was viewpoint based because it focused on anti-abortion groups.]

JUSTICE BREYER, joined by JUSTICES GINSBURG, SOTOMAYOR, and KAGAN, dissenting.

Before turning to the specific law before us, I focus upon the general interpretation of the First Amendment that the majority says it applies. It applies heightened scrutiny to the Act because the Act, in its view, is "content based." "By compelling individuals to speak a particular message," it adds, "such notices 'alte[r] the content of [their] speech.'" "As a general matter," the majority concludes, such laws are "presumptively unconstitutional" and are subject to "stringent" review.

The majority recognizes exceptions to this general rule: It excepts laws that "require professionals to disclose factual, noncontroversial information in their 'commercial speech,'" provided that the disclosure "relates to the services that [the regulated entities] provide." It also excepts laws that "regulate professional conduct" and only "incidentally burden speech."

This constitutional approach threatens to create serious problems. Because much, perhaps most, human behavior takes place through speech and because much, perhaps most, law regulates that speech in terms of its content, the majority's approach at the least threatens considerable litigation over the constitutional validity of much, perhaps most, government regulation. Virtually every disclosure law could be considered "content based," for virtually every disclosure law requires individuals "to speak a particular message." Thus, the majority's view, if taken literally, could radically change prior law, perhaps placing much securities law or consumer protection law at constitutional risk, depending on how broadly its exceptions are interpreted. * * *

Precedent does not require a test such as the majority's. Rather, in saying the Act is not a longstanding health and safety law, the Court substitutes its own approach—without a defining standard—for an approach that was reasonably clear. Historically, the Court has been wary of claims that regulation of business activity, particularly health-related activity, violates the Constitution. Ever since this Court departed from the approach it set forth in Lochner v. New York, 198 U.S. 45, 25 S.Ct. 539, 49 L.Ed. 937 (1905), ordinary economic and social legislation has been thought to raise little constitutional concern. As Justice Brandeis wrote, typically this Court's function in such cases "is only to determine the reasonableness of the Legislature's belief in the existence of evils and in the effectiveness of the remedy provided." * * *

Even during the Lochner era, when this Court struck down numerous economic regulations concerning industry, this Court was careful to defer to state legislative judgments concerning the medical profession. The Court took the view that a State may condition the practice of medicine on any number of requirements, and physicians, in exchange for following those reasonable requirements, could receive a license to practice medicine from the State. Medical professionals do not, generally speaking, have a right to use the Constitution as a weapon allowing them rigorously to control the content of those reasonable conditions. In the name of the First Amendment, the majority today treads into territory where the pre-New Deal, as well as the post-New Deal, Court refused to go.

The Court, in justification, refers to widely accepted First Amendment goals, such as the need to protect the Nation from laws that " 'suppress unpopular ideas or information' " or inhibit the " 'marketplace of ideas in which truth will ultimately prevail.' " The concurrence highlights similar First Amendment interests. I, too, value this role that the First Amendment plays—in an appropriate case. But here, the majority enunciates a general test that reaches far beyond the area where this Court has examined laws closely in the service of those goals. And, in suggesting that heightened scrutiny applies to much economic and social legislation, the majority pays those First Amendment goals a serious disservice through dilution. Using the First Amendment to strike down economic and social laws that legislatures long would have thought themselves free to enact will, for the American public, obscure, not clarify, the true value of protecting freedom of speech.

The majority tries to distinguish *Casey* as concerning a regulation of professional conduct that only incidentally burdened speech. * * * *Casey*, in its view, applies only when obtaining "informed consent" to a medical procedure is directly at issue.

This distinction, however, lacks moral, practical, and legal force. The individuals at issue here are all medical personnel engaging in activities that directly affect a woman's health—not significantly different from the doctors at issue in Casey. After all, the statute here applies only to "primary care clinics," which provide "services for the care and treatment of patients for whom the clinic accepts responsibility." And the persons responsible for patients at those clinics are all persons "licensed, certified or registered to provide" pregnancy-related medical services. The petitioners have not, either here or in the District Court, provided any example of a covered clinic that is not operated by licensed doctors or what the statute specifies are equivalent professionals.

The Act requires these medical professionals to disclose information about the possibility of abortion (including potential financial help) that is as likely helpful to granting "informed consent" as is information about the possibility of adoption and childbirth (including potential financial help). That is why I find it impossible to drive any meaningful legal wedge between the law, as interpreted in *Casey*, and the law as it should be applied in this case. If the law in *Casey* regulated speech "only 'as part of the practice of medicine,' " so too here.

The majority contends that the disclosure here is unrelated to a "medical procedure," unlike that in Casey, and so the State has no reason to inform a woman about alternatives to childbirth (or, presumably, the health risks of childbirth). Really? No one doubts that choosing an abortion is a medical procedure that involves certain health risks. But the same is true of carrying a child to term and giving birth. That is why prenatal care often involves testing for anemia, infections, measles, chicken pox, genetic disorders, diabetes, pneumonia, urinary tract infections, preeclampsia, and hosts of other medical conditions. Childbirth itself, directly or through pain management, risks harms of various kinds, some connected with caesarean or surgery-related deliveries, some related to more ordinary methods of delivery. Indeed, nationwide "childbirth is 14 times more likely than abortion to result in" the woman's death. Health considerations do not favor disclosure of alternatives and risks associated with the latter but not those associated with the former.

In any case, informed consent principles apply more broadly than only to discrete "medical procedures." Prescription drug labels warn patients of risks even though taking prescription drugs may not be considered a "medical procedure." In California, clinics that screen for breast cancer must post a sign in their offices notifying patients that, if they are diagnosed with breast cancer, their doctor must provide "a written summary of alternative efficacious methods of treatment," a notification that does not relate to the screening procedure at issue. If even these disclosures fall outside the majority's cramped view of Casey and informed consent, it undoubtedly would invalidate the many other disclosures that are routine in the medical context as well.

The majority also finds it "[t]ellin[g]" that general practice clinics—i.e., paid clinics—are not required to provide the licensed notice. But the lack-of-information problem that the statute seeks to ameliorate is a problem that the State explains is commonly found among low-income women. That those with low income might lack the time to become fully informed and that this circumstance might prove disproportionately correlated with income is not intuitively surprising. Nor is it surprising that those with low income, whatever they choose in respect to pregnancy, might find information about financial assistance particularly useful. There is "nothing inherently suspect" about this distinction, which is not "based on the content of [the advocacy] each group offers," but upon the patients the group generally serves and the needs of that population.

Separately, finding no First Amendment infirmity in the licensed notice is consistent with earlier Court rulings. For instance, in *Zauderer* we upheld a requirement that attorneys disclose in their advertisements that clients might be liable for significant litigation costs even if their lawsuits were unsuccessful. We refused to apply heightened scrutiny, instead asking whether the disclosure requirements were "reasonably related to the State's interest in preventing deception of consumers.".

The majority concludes that *Zauderer* does not apply because the disclosure "in no way relates to the services that licensed clinics provide." But information about state resources for family planning, prenatal care, and abortion is related to the services that licensed clinics provide. These clinics provide counseling about contraception (which is a family-planning service), ultrasounds or pregnancy testing (which is prenatal care), or abortion. The required disclosure is related to the clinic's services because it provides information about state resources for the very same services. A patient who knows that she can receive free prenatal care from the State may well prefer to forgo the prenatal care offered at one of the clinics here. And for those interested in family planning and abortion services, information about such alternatives is relevant information to patients offered prenatal care, just as *Casey* considered information about adoption to be relevant to the abortion decision.

* * *

Of course, one might take the majority's decision to mean that speech about abortion is special, that it involves in this case not only professional medical matters, but also views based on deeply held religious and moral beliefs about the nature of the practice. To that extent, arguably, the speech here is different from that at issue in *Zauderer*. But assuming that is so, the law's insistence upon treating like cases alike should lead us to reject the petitioners' arguments that I have discussed. This insistence, the need for evenhandedness, should prove particularly weighty in a case involving abortion rights. That is because Americans hold strong, and differing, views about the matter. Some Americans believe that abortion involves the death of a live and innocent human being. Others believe that the ability to choose an abortion is "central to personal dignity and autonomy," [*Casey*] and note that the failure to allow women to choose an abortion involves the deaths of innocent women. We have previously noted that we cannot try to adjudicate who is right and who is wrong in this moral debate. But we can do our best to interpret American constitutional law so that it applies fairly within a Nation whose citizens strongly hold these different points of view. That is one reason why it is particularly important to interpret the First Amendment so that it applies evenhandedly as between those who disagree so strongly. For this reason too a Constitution that allows States to insist that medical providers tell women about the possibility of adoption should also allow States similarly to insist that medical providers tell women about the possibility of abortion.

NOTES ON *NIFLA V. BECERRA*

1. *Is the Majority Opinion Content Neutral?* The dissent accuses the majority of favoring anti-abortion requirements over those designed to increase access to abortions. Suppose the state requirement had been set up differently, so as to require all medical personnel offering pregnancy-related services to inform patients at the time of the service about the availability of abortion. Would such a requirement be valid under the majority's approach?

2. Lochner *and the First Amendment.* First Amendment doctrine requires more rigorous scrutiny than is typically applied to economic regulations today. But as the scope of First Amendment coverage expands, there is correspondingly less room for states to engage in regulation of subjects that they traditionally regulated. A striking example is provided by the next case.

Janus v. American Federation of State, County, and Municipal Employees, ___ U.S. ___, 138 S.Ct. 2448, ___ L.Ed.2d ___ (2018). Under Illinois law, when a majority of public employees vote to form a union, that union becomes the exclusive bargaining agent for all employees, including nonmembers. Nonmembers are required to pay a fee for the union's collective bargaining and related activities. The Court upheld a similar law in *Abood v. Detroit Bd. of Ed.*, 431 U.S. 209, 97 S.Ct. 1782, 52 L.Ed.2d 261 (1977). **Justice Alito** wrote for the conservative majority, overruling *Abood*. He stressed that, in addition to the values involved generally in restrictions on free speech, compelled speech places at risk additional values:

> When speech is compelled, however, additional damage is done. In that situation, individuals are coerced into betraying their convictions. Forcing free and independent individuals to endorse ideas they find objectionable is always demeaning, and for this reason, one of our landmark free speech cases said that a law commanding "involuntary affirmation" of objected-to beliefs would require "even more immediate and urgent grounds" than a law demanding silence.

Because Illinois law required non-union members to pay for speech by the union in collective bargaining with which they disagreed, it was subject to strict scrutiny. The *Abood* Court had found such laws to be constitutional based on the state's interest in "labor peace," but the Court concluded that collective bargaining by unions could function well without requiring non-members' financial support. The Court also rejected an alternative justification, holding that the state's interest in preventing non-members from free riding on the union's activities on their behalf was not compelling.

JUSTICE KAGAN's dissent on behalf of the four liberal Justices stressed stare decisis:

> Rarely if ever has the Court overruled a decision—let alone one of this import—with so little regard for the usual principles of *stare decisis*. There are no special justifications for reversing *Abood*. It has

proved workable. No recent developments have eroded its underpinnings. And it is deeply entrenched, in both the law and the real world. More than 20 States have statutory schemes built on the decision. Those laws underpin thousands of ongoing contracts involving millions of employees. Reliance interests do not come any stronger than those surrounding *Abood*. And likewise, judicial disruption does not get any greater than what the Court does today.

The dissent closed by tying *Janus* to *NIFLA v. Becerra*:

And maybe most alarming, the majority has chosen the winners by turning the First Amendment into a sword, and using it against workaday economic and regulatory policy. Today is not the first time the Court has wielded the First Amendment in such an aggressive way. [Citing *NIFLA v. Becerra* and other cases.] And it threatens not to be the last. Speech is everywhere—a part of every human activity (employment, health care, securities trading, you name it). For that reason, almost all economic and regulatory policy affects or touches speech. So the majority's road runs long. And at every stop are black-robed rulers overriding citizens' choices. The First Amendment was meant for better things. It was meant not to undermine but to protect democratic governance—including over the role of public-sector unions.

SECTION 2. REGULATION OF POLITICAL EXPRESSION

C. CAMPAIGN EXPENDITURES

Page 777.   Insert before Section 3:

McCutcheon v. Federal Election Commission, 572 U.S. ___, 134 S.Ct. 1434 (2014). *Buckley* upheld a limit on the total contributions that an individual can make to federal candidates during an election cycle, as well the limits on contributions to individual candidates. In *McCutcheon*, the Court struck down the aggregate limit. Chief Justice Roberts' plurality opinion (joined by Scalia, Kennedy and Alito) focused on whether the aggregate limit was necessary to prevent quid pro quo corruption, which it considered the only valid purpose for campaign regulation. The plurality concluded that the risk of quid pro quo corruption was adequately addressed by the limit on contributions to each individual candidate. Because of anti-circumvention regulations adopted since *Buckley* was decided, the plurality dismissed the government's argument that the aggregate limit was necessary to prevent schemes evading the individual candidate limit. Justice Thomas concurred in the judgment, arguing that *Buckley* should be overruled outright. In dissent, Justice Breyer (joined by

Justices Ginsburg, Sotomayor, and Kagan), argued as in *Citizens United* that corruption included broader forms of influence peddling than simple bribery, and that the aggregate limit was in fact required to prevent circumvention of the individual limits. Breyer also chided the majority for deciding factual issues about the potential for circumvention without any evidentiary hearing in the lower court, while Roberts responded that the parties had not pressed for a remand on this basis.

The following case was a departure from the strong trend of invalidating campaign finance regulations under the Roberts Court.

WILLIAMS-YULEE V. FLORIDA BAR
___ U.S. ___, 135 S.Ct. 1656, 191 L.Ed.2d 570 (2015)

CHIEF JUSTICE ROBERTS delivered the opinion of the Court, except as to Part II.

Our Founders vested authority to appoint federal judges in the President, with the advice and consent of the Senate, and entrusted those judges to hold their offices during good behavior. The Constitution permits States to make a different choice, and most of them have done so. In 39 States, voters elect trial or appellate judges at the polls. In an effort to preserve public confidence in the integrity of their judiciaries, many of those States prohibit judges and judicial candidates from personally soliciting funds for their campaigns. We must decide whether the First Amendment permits such restrictions on speech.

We hold that it does. Judges are not politicians, even when they come to the bench by way of the ballot. And a State's decision to elect its judiciary does not compel it to treat judicial candidates like campaigners for political office. A State may assure its people that judges will apply the law without fear or favor—and without having personally asked anyone for money. We affirm the judgment of the Florida Supreme Court.

[Part I provides background on judicial elections in Florida, including a corruption scandal. Williams-Yulee decided to run for a seat on the county court and then sent out a fundraising letter. She lost the primary and then was subject to an ethics proceeding by the Florida Bar for violating Canon 7C(1), which prohibits direct requests for campaign contributions by candidates for judicial office. Part II of the opinion, which was joined by only three Justices, reaffirmed that restrictions on the speech of judicial candidates are subject to strict scrutiny. Justice Breyer and Ginsburg argued for allowing greater latitude to states for regulation in the context of judicial elections. The following portions of the opinion were joined by five Justices, however.]

The Florida Bar faces a demanding task in defending Canon 7C(1) against Yulee's First Amendment challenge. We have emphasized that "it is the rare case" in which a State demonstrates that a speech restriction is narrowly tailored to serve a compelling interest. Here, Canon 7C(1) advances the State's compelling interest in preserving public confidence in the integrity of the judiciary, and it does so through means narrowly tailored to avoid unnecessarily abridging speech. This is therefore one of the rare cases in which a speech restriction withstands strict scrutiny.

The Florida Supreme Court adopted Canon 7C(1) to promote the State's interests in "protecting the integrity of the judiciary" and "maintaining the public's confidence in an impartial judiciary." The way the Canon advances those interests is intuitive: Judges, charged with exercising strict neutrality and independence, cannot supplicate campaign donors without diminishing public confidence in judicial integrity. This principle dates back at least eight centuries to Magna Carta, which proclaimed, "To no one will we sell, to no one will we refuse or delay, right or justice." The same concept underlies the common law judicial oath, which binds a judge to "do right to all manner of people . . . without fear or favour, affection or ill-will," and the oath that each of us took to "administer justice without respect to persons, and do equal right to the poor and to the rich." Simply put, Florida and most other States have concluded that the public may lack confidence in a judge's ability to administer justice without fear or favor if he comes to office by asking for favors.

The interest served by Canon 7C(1) has firm support in our precedents. We have recognized the "vital state interest" in safeguarding "public confidence in the fairness and integrity of the nation's elected judges." * * *

The parties devote considerable attention to our cases analyzing campaign finance restrictions in political elections. But a State's interest in preserving public confidence in the integrity of its judiciary extends beyond its interest in preventing the appearance of corruption in legislative and executive elections. As we explained in *White,* States may regulate judicial elections differently than they regulate political elections, because the role of judges differs from the role of politicians. Politicians are expected to be appropriately responsive to the preferences of their supporters. Indeed, such "responsiveness is key to the very concept of self-governance through elected officials." The same is not true of judges. In deciding cases, a judge is not to follow the preferences of his supporters, or provide any special consideration to his campaign donors. A judge instead must "observe the utmost fairness," striving to be "perfectly and completely independent, with nothing to influence or controul him but God and his conscience." * * *

The vast majority of elected judges in States that allow personal solicitation serve with fairness and honor. But "[e]ven if judges were able to refrain from favoring donors, the mere possibility that judges' decisions may be motivated by the desire to repay campaign contributions is likely to undermine the public's confidence in the judiciary." In the eyes of the public, a judge's personal solicitation could result (even unknowingly) in "a possible temptation . . . which might lead him not to hold the balance nice, clear and true." That risk is especially pronounced because most donors are lawyers and litigants who may appear before the judge they are supporting.

The concept of public confidence in judicial integrity does not easily reduce to precise definition, nor does it lend itself to proof by documentary record. But no one denies that it is genuine and compelling. In short, it is the regrettable but unavoidable appearance that judges who personally ask for money may diminish their integrity that prompted the Supreme Court of Florida and most other States to sever the direct link between judicial candidates and campaign contributors. As the Supreme Court of Oregon explained, "the spectacle of lawyers or potential litigants directly handing over money to judicial candidates should be avoided if the public is to have faith in the impartiality of its judiciary." * * *

Yulee acknowledges the State's compelling interest in judicial integrity. She argues, however, that the Canon's failure to restrict other speech equally damaging to judicial integrity and its appearance undercuts the Bar's position. In particular, she notes that Canon 7C(1) allows a judge's campaign committee to solicit money, which arguably reduces public confidence in the integrity of the judiciary just as much as a judge's personal solicitation. Yulee also points out that Florida permits judicial candidates to write thank you notes to campaign donors, which ensures that candidates know who contributes and who does not. [The Court did not find that these aspects of the law were fatal flaws, because the state had focused on the category of judicial speech posing the greatest appearance of impropriety.]

* * * Yulee argues that the Canon cannot constitutionally be applied to her chosen form of solicitation: a letter posted online and distributed via mass mailing. No one, she contends, will lose confidence in the integrity of the judiciary based on personal solicitation to such a broad audience.

This argument misperceives the breadth of the compelling interest that underlies Canon 7C(1). Florida has reasonably determined that personal appeals for money by a judicial candidate inherently create an appearance of impropriety that may cause the public to lose confidence in the integrity of the judiciary. That interest may be implicated to varying degrees in particular contexts, but the interest remains whenever the public perceives the judge personally asking for money.

Moreover, the lines Yulee asks us to draw are unworkable. Even under her theory of the case, a mass mailing would create an appearance of impropriety if addressed to a list of all lawyers and litigants with pending cases. So would a speech soliciting contributions from the 100 most frequently appearing attorneys in the jurisdiction. Yulee says she might accept a ban on one-to-one solicitation, but is the public impression really any different if a judicial candidate tries to buttonhole not one prospective donor but two at a time? Ten? Yulee also agrees that in person solicitation creates a problem. But would the public's concern recede if the request for money came in a phone call or a text message?

We decline to wade into this swamp. The First Amendment requires that Canon 7C(1) be narrowly tailored, not that it be "perfectly tailored."

JUSTICE SCALIA, joined by **JUSTICE THOMAS**, dissenting.

Because Canon 7C(1) restricts fully protected speech on the basis of content, it presumptively violates the First Amendment. We may uphold it only if the State meets its burden of showing that the Canon survives strict scrutiny—that is to say, only if it shows that the Canon is narrowly tailored to serve a compelling interest. I do not for a moment question the Court's conclusion that States have different compelling interests when regulating judicial elections than when regulating political ones. Unlike a legislator, a judge must be impartial—without bias for or against any party or attorney who comes before him. I accept for the sake of argument that States have a compelling interest in ensuring that its judges are *seen* to be impartial. I will likewise assume that a judicial candidate's request to a litigant or attorney presents a danger of coercion that a political candidate's request to a constituent does not. But Canon 7C(1) does not narrowly target concerns about impartiality or its appearance; it applies even when the person asked for a financial contribution has no chance of ever appearing in the candidate's court. And Florida does not invoke concerns about coercion, presumably because the Canon bans solicitations regardless of whether their object is a lawyer, litigant, or other person vulnerable to judicial pressure. So Canon 7C(1) fails exacting scrutiny and infringes the First Amendment. This case should have been just that straightforward. * * *

This Court has not been shy to enforce the First Amendment in recent Terms—even in cases that do not involve election speech. It has accorded robust protection to depictions of animal torture, sale of violent video games to children, and lies about having won military medals. Who would have thought that the same Court would today exert such heroic efforts to save so plain an abridgement of the freedom of speech? It is no great mystery what is going on here. The judges of this Court, like the judges of the Supreme Court of Florida who promulgated Canon 7C(1), evidently consider the preservation of public respect for the courts a policy objective of the highest order. So it is—but so too are preventing animal torture, protecting the innocence of children, and honoring valiant soldiers. The Court did not relax the Constitution's guarantee of freedom of speech when legislatures pursued those goals; it should not relax the guarantee when the Supreme Court of Florida pursues this one. The First Amendment is not abridged for the benefit of the Brotherhood of the Robe.

JUSTICE KENNEDY, dissenting.

The dissenting opinion by Justice Scalia gives a full and complete explanation of the reasons why the Court's opinion contradicts settled First Amendment principles. This separate dissent is written to underscore the irony in the Court's having concluded that the very First Amendment protections judges must enforce should be lessened when a judicial candidate's own speech is at issue. It is written to underscore, too, the irony in the Court's having weakened the rigors of the First Amendment in a case concerning elections, a paradigmatic forum for speech and a process intended to protect freedom in so many other manifestations.

First Amendment protections are both personal and structural. Free speech begins with the right of each person to think and then to express his or her own ideas. Protecting this personal sphere of intellect and conscience, in turn, creates structural safeguards for many of the processes that define a free society. The individual speech here is political speech. The process is a fair election. These realms ought to be the last place, not the first, for the * * *

With all due respect for the Court, it seems fair and necessary to say its decision rests on two premises, neither one correct. One premise is that in certain elections—here an election to choose the best qualified judge—the public lacks the necessary judgment to make an informed choice. Instead, the State must protect voters by altering the usual dynamics of free speech. The other premise is that since judges should be accorded special respect and dignity, their election can be subject to certain content-based rules that would be unacceptable in other elections. In my respectful view neither premise can justify the speech restriction at issue here. Although States have a compelling interest in seeking to ensure the appearance and the reality of an impartial judiciary, it does not follow that the State may alter basic First Amendment principles in pursuing that goal.

While any number of troubling consequences will follow from the Court's ruling, a simple example can suffice to illustrate the dead weight its decision now ties to public debate. Assume a judge retires, and two honest lawyers, Doe and Roe, seek the vacant position. Doe is a respected, prominent lawyer who has been active in the community and is well known to business and civic leaders. Roe, a lawyer of extraordinary ability and high ethical standards, keeps a low profile. As soon as Doe announces his or her candidacy, a campaign committee organizes of its own accord and begins raising funds. But few know or hear about Roe's potential candidacy, and no one with resources or connections is available to assist in raising the funds necessary for even a modest plan to speak to the electorate. Today the Court says the State can censor Roe's speech, imposing a gag on his or her request for funds, no matter how close Roe is to the potential benefactor or donor. The result is that Roe's personal freedom, the right of speech, is cut off by the State.

The First Amendment consequences of the Court's ruling do not end with its denial of the individual's right to speak. For the very purpose of the candidate's fundraising was to facilitate a larger speech process: an election campaign. By cutting off one candidate's personal freedom to speak, the broader campaign debate that might have followed—a debate that might have been informed by new ideas and insights from both candidates—now is silenced.

JUSTICE ALITO, dissenting.

I largely agree with what I view as the essential elements of the dissents filed by Justices Scalia and Kennedy. The Florida rule before us regulates speech that is part of the process of selecting those who wield the power of the State. Such speech lies at the heart of the protection provided by the First Amendment. The Florida rule regulates that speech based on content and must therefore satisfy strict scrutiny. This means that it must be narrowly tailored to further a compelling state interest. Florida has a compelling interest in making sure that its courts decide cases impartially and in accordance with the law and that its citizens have no good reason to lack confidence that its courts are performing their proper role. But the Florida rule is not narrowly tailored to serve that interest.

Indeed, this rule is about as narrowly tailored as a burlap bag. It applies to all solicitations made in the name of a candidate for judicial office—including, as was the case here, a mass mailing. It even applies to an ad in a newspaper. It applies to requests for contributions in any amount, and it applies even if the person solicited is not a lawyer, has never had any interest at stake in any case in the court in question, and has no prospect of ever having any interest at stake in any litigation in that court. If this rule can be characterized as narrowly tailored, then narrow tailoring has no meaning, and strict scrutiny, which is essential to the protection of free speech, is seriously impaired.

When petitioner sent out a form letter requesting campaign contributions, she was well within her First Amendment rights. The Florida Supreme Court violated the Constitution when it imposed a financial penalty and stained her record with a finding that she had engaged in unethical conduct. I would reverse the judgment of the Florida Supreme Court.

NOTES ON WILLIAMS-YULEE AND JUDICIAL ELECTIONS

1.   *Narrow Tailoring.* The dissent seems right that the majority does not seem to be demanding as much precision in the fit between ends and means as

in some other cases of strict scrutiny. On the other hand, once avoiding the appearance of partiality is accepted as a compelling state interest, is it possible to draw rules as precise as those that the dissenters demand?

2.   *The Paradox of Judicial Elections.* Due process requires impartial decision-makers. Judicial elections inevitably create some risk that judicial decisions will be warped by the desire to appeal to potential supporters, whether newspapers or others. If judicial candidates are dependent on campaign contributions, it is hard to see how they can be completely impartial in considering the interests of major contributors, whether they receive the contributions personally or not. As an extreme case, consider the *Caperton* case [Casebook p. 722], where the majority ruled that this appearance of special influence was grave enough to violate due process.

The dissenters seem sanguine about the possibility that judges might become as responsive to contributors as other office-holders. To the extent that the governmental interest is public confidence in the institutions of government, isn't the dissent right that this interest is neither more nor less important as applied to judges as to others? On the other hand, could the majority argue that there is a special interest in giving litigants (as opposed to the general public) confidence that there cases are being decided impartially?

SECTION 4. SPEECH WITH A GOVERNMENT NEXUS

A. PUBLIC FORUM DOCTRINE

Page 807.   Insert after *Hill*:

McCULLEN V. COAKLEY
573 U.S. ___, 134 S.Ct. 2518, 189 L.Ed.2d 502 (2014)

CHIEF JUSTICE ROBERTS delivered the opinion of the Court.

A Massachusetts statute makes it a crime to knowingly stand on a "public way or sidewalk" within 35 feet of an entrance or driveway to any place, other than a hospital, where abortions are performed. Petitioners are individuals who approach and talk to women outside such facilities, attempting to dissuade them from having abortions. The statute prevents petitioners from doing so near the facilities' entrances. The question presented is whether the statute violates the First Amendment. * * *

The Act exempts four classes of individuals: (1) "persons entering or leaving such facility"; (2) "employees or agents of such facility acting within the scope of their employment"; (3) "law enforcement, ambulance, firefighting, construction, utilities, public works and other municipal agents acting within the scope of their employment"; and (4) "persons using the public sidewalk or street right-of-way adjacent to such facility solely for the purpose of reaching a destination other than such facility." The legislature also retained the separate provision from the 2000 version that proscribes the knowing obstruction of access to a facility. * * *

Petitioners at all three clinics claim that the buffer zones have considerably hampered their counseling efforts. Although they have managed to conduct some counseling and to distribute some literature outside the buffer zones—particularly at the Boston clinic—they say they have had many fewer conversations and distributed many fewer leaflets since the zones went into effect.

The second statutory exemption allows clinic employees and agents acting within the scope of their employment to enter the buffer zones. Relying on this exemption, the Boston clinic uses "escorts" to greet women as they approach the clinic, accompanying them through the zones to the clinic entrance. Petitioners claim that the escorts sometimes thwart petitioners' attempts to communicate with patients by blocking petitioners from handing literature to patients, telling patients not to "pay any attention" or "listen to" petitioners, and disparaging petitioners as "crazy." * * *

By its very terms, the Massachusetts Act regulates access to "public way[s]" and "sidewalk[s]." Such areas occupy a "special position in terms of First Amendment protection" because of their historic role as sites for discussion and debate. It is no accident that public streets and sidewalks have developed as venues for the exchange of ideas. Even today, they remain one of the few places where a speaker can be confident that he is not simply preaching to the choir. With respect to other means of communication, an individual confronted with an uncomfortable message can always turn the page, change the channel, or leave the Web site. Not so on public streets and sidewalks. There, a listener often encounters speech he might otherwise tune out. In light of the First Amendment's purpose "to preserve an uninhibited marketplace of ideas in which truth will ultimately prevail," this aspect of traditional public fora is a virtue, not a vice.

In short, traditional public fora are areas that have historically been open to the public for speech activities. Thus, even though the Act says nothing about speech on its face, there is no doubt—and respondents do not dispute—that it restricts access to traditional public fora and is therefore subject to First Amendment scrutiny. See Brief for Respondents 26 (although "[b]y its terms, the Act regulates only conduct," it "incidentally regulates the place and time of protected speech"). * * *

Petitioners contend that the Act is not content neutral for two independent reasons: First, they argue that it discriminates against abortion-related speech because it establishes buffer zones only at clinics that perform abortions. Second, petitioners contend that the Act, by exempting clinic employees and agents, favors one viewpoint about abortion over the other. If either of these arguments is correct, then the Act must satisfy strict scrutiny—that is, it must be the least restrictive means of achieving a compelling state interest. Respondents do not argue that the Act can survive this exacting standard. * * *

The Act applies only at a "reproductive health care facility," defined as "a place, other than within or upon the grounds of a hospital, where abortions are offered or performed." Given this definition, petitioners argue, "virtually all speech affected by the Act is speech concerning abortion," thus rendering the Act content based.

We disagree. To begin, the Act does not draw content-based distinctions on its face. The Act would be content based if it required "enforcement authorities" to "examine the content of the message that is conveyed to determine whether" a violation has occurred. But it does not. Whether petitioners violate the Act "depends" not "on what they say," but simply on where they say it. Indeed, petitioners can violate the Act merely by standing in a buffer zone, without displaying a sign or uttering a word.

It is true, of course, that by limiting the buffer zones to abortion clinics, the Act has the "inevitable effect" of restricting abortion-related speech more than speech on other subjects. But a facially neutral law does not become content based simply because it may disproportionately affect speech on certain topics. On the contrary, "[a] regulation that serves purposes unrelated to the content of expression is deemed neutral, even if it has an incidental effect on some speakers or messages but not others." The question in such a case is whether the law is " 'justified without reference to the content of the regulated speech.' "

The Massachusetts Act is. Its stated purpose is to "increase forthwith public safety at reproductive health care facilities." Respondents have articulated similar purposes before this Court—namely, "public safety, patient access to healthcare, and the unobstructed use of public sidewalks and roadways." It is not the case that "[e]very objective indication shows that the provision's primary purpose is to restrict speech that opposes abortion."

We have previously deemed the foregoing concerns to be content neutral. Obstructed access and congested sidewalks are problems no matter what caused them. A group of individuals can obstruct clinic access and clog sidewalks just as much when they loiter as when they protest abortion or counsel patients.

To be clear, the Act would not be content neutral if it were concerned with undesirable effects that arise from "the direct impact of speech on its audience" or "[l]isteners' reactions to speech." If, for example, the speech outside Massachusetts abortion clinics caused offense or made listeners uncomfortable, such offense or discomfort would not give the Commonwealth a content-neutral justification to restrict the speech. All of the problems identified by the Commonwealth here, however, arise irrespective of any listener's reactions. Whether or not a single person reacts to abortion protestors' chants or petitioners' counseling, large crowds outside abortion clinics can still compromise public safety, impede access, and obstruct sidewalks.

Petitioners do not really dispute that the Commonwealth's interests in ensuring safety and preventing obstruction are, as a general matter, content neutral. But petitioners note that these interests "apply outside every building in the State that hosts any activity that might occasion protest or comment," not just abortion clinics. By choosing to pursue these interests only at abortion clinics, petitioners argue, the Massachusetts Legislature evinced a purpose to "single[ ] out for regulation speech about one particular topic: abortion."

We cannot infer such a purpose from the Act's limited scope. The broad reach of a statute can help confirm that it was not enacted to burden a narrower category of disfavored speech. At the same time, however, "States adopt laws to address the problems that confront them. The First Amendment does not require States to regulate for problems that do not exist." The Massachusetts Legislature amended the Act in 2007 in response to a problem that was, in its experience, limited to abortion clinics. There was a record of crowding, obstruction, and even violence outside such clinics. There were apparently no similar recurring problems associated with other kinds of healthcare facilities, let alone with "every building in the State that hosts any activity that might occasion protest or comment." In light of the limited nature of the problem, it was reasonable for the Massachusetts Legislature to enact a limited solution. When selecting among various options for combating a particular problem, legislatures should be encouraged to choose the one that restricts less speech, not more. * * *

Petitioners also argue that the Act is content based because it exempts four classes of individuals, one of which comprises "employees or agents of [a reproductive healthcare] facility acting within the scope of their employment." This exemption, petitioners say, favors one side in the abortion debate and thus constitutes viewpoint discrimination—an "egregious form of content discrimination." In particular, petitioners argue that the exemption allows clinic employees and agents—including the volunteers who "escort" patients arriving at the Boston clinic—to speak inside the buffer zones. [But the Court concluded that there is "nothing inherently suspect about providing some kind of exemption to allow individuals who work at the clinics to enter or remain within the buffer zones." However, "[i]t would be a very different question if it turned out that a clinic authorized escorts to speak about abortion inside the buffer zones." In that case, the statute would be invalid as applied because of viewpoint discrimination. No such showing was made.]

Even though the Act is content neutral, it still must be "narrowly tailored to serve a significant governmental interest." The tailoring requirement does not simply guard against an impermissible desire to censor. The government may attempt to suppress speech not only because it disagrees with the message being expressed, but also for mere convenience. Where certain speech is associated with particular problems, silencing the speech is sometimes the path of least resistance. But by demanding a close fit between ends and means, the tailoring requirement prevents the government from too readily "sacrific[ing] speech for efficiency."

For a content-neutral time, place, or manner regulation to be narrowly tailored, it must not "burden substantially more speech than is necessary to further the government's legitimate interests." Such a regulation, unlike a content-based restriction of speech, "need not be the least restrictive or least intrusive means of" serving the government's interests. But the government still "may not regulate expression in such a manner that a substantial portion of the burden on speech does not serve to advance its goals."

As noted, respondents claim that the Act promotes "public safety, patient access to healthcare, and the unobstructed use of public sidewalks and roadways." Petitioners do not dispute the significance of these interests. We have, moreover, previously recognized the legitimacy of the government's interests in "ensuring public safety and order, promoting the free flow of traffic on streets and sidewalks, protecting property rights, and protecting a woman's freedom to seek pregnancy-related services." The buffer zones clearly serve these interests.

At the same time, the buffer zones impose serious burdens on petitioners' speech. At each of the three Planned Parenthood clinics where petitioners attempt to counsel patients, the zones carve out a significant portion of the adjacent public sidewalks, pushing petitioners well back from the clinics' entrances and driveways. The zones thereby compromise petitioners' ability to initiate the close, personal conversations that they view as essential to "sidewalk counseling." * * *

Respondents also emphasize that the Act does not prevent petitioners from engaging in various forms of "protest"—such as chanting slogans and displaying signs—outside the buffer zones. That misses the point. Petitioners are not protestors. They seek not merely to express their opposition to abortion, but to inform women of various alternatives and to provide help in pursuing them. Petitioners believe that they can accomplish this objective only through personal, caring, consensual conversations. * * * It is thus no answer to say that petitioners can still be "seen and heard" by women within the buffer zones. If all that the women can see and hear are vociferous opponents of abortion, then the buffer zones have effectively stifled petitioners' message. * * *

The buffer zones burden substantially more speech than necessary to achieve the Commonwealth's asserted interests. At the outset, we note that the Act is truly exceptional: Respondents and their *amici* identify no other State with a law that creates fixed buffer zones around abortion clinics. That of course does not mean that the law is invalid. It does, however, raise concern that the Commonwealth has too readily forgone options that could serve its interests just as well, without substantially burdening the kind of speech in which petitioners wish to engage.

That is the case here. The Commonwealth's interests include ensuring public safety outside abortion clinics, preventing harassment and intimidation of patients and clinic staff, and combating deliberate obstruction of clinic entrances. The Act itself contains a separate provision, subsection (e)—unchallenged by petitioners—that prohibits much of this conduct. That provision subjects to criminal punishment "[a]ny person who knowingly obstructs, detains, hinders, impedes or blocks another person's entry to or exit from a reproductive health care facility." If Massachusetts determines that broader prohibitions along the same lines are necessary, it could enact legislation similar to the federal Freedom of Access to Clinic Entrances Act of 1994 (FACE Act), 18 U.S.C. § 248(a)(1), which subjects to both criminal and civil penalties anyone who "by force or threat of force or by physical obstruction, intentionally injures, intimidates or interferes with or attempts to injure, intimidate or interfere with any person because that person is or has been, or in order to intimidate such person or any other person or any class of persons from, obtaining or providing reproductive health services." Some dozen other States have done so. If the Commonwealth is particularly concerned about harassment, it could also consider an ordinance such as the one adopted in New York City that not only prohibits obstructing access to a clinic, but also makes it a crime "to follow and harass another person within 15 feet of the premises of a reproductive health care facility." * * *

In addition, subsection (e) of the Act, the FACE Act, and the New York City anti-harassment ordinance are all enforceable not only through criminal prosecutions but also through public and private civil actions for injunctions and other equitable relief. We have previously noted the First Amendment virtues of targeted injunctions as alternatives to broad, prophylactic measures. Such an injunction "regulates the activities, and perhaps the speech, of a group," but only "because of the group's past *actions* in the context of a specific dispute between real parties." Moreover, given the equitable nature of injunctive relief, courts can tailor a remedy to ensure that it restricts no more speech than necessary. In short, injunctive relief focuses on the precise individuals and the precise conduct causing a particular problem. The Act, by contrast, categorically excludes non-exempt individuals from the buffer zones, unnecessarily sweeping in innocent individuals and their speech. * * *

The point is not that Massachusetts must enact all or even any of the proposed measures discussed above. The point is instead that the Commonwealth has available to it a variety of approaches that appear capable of serving its interests, without excluding individuals from areas historically open for speech and debate.

JUSTICE SCALIA, with whom **JUSTICE KENNEDY** and **JUSTICE THOMAS** join, concurring in the judgment.

The majority points only to the statute's stated purpose of increasing " 'public safety' " at abortion clinics, and to the additional aims articulated by respondents before this Court—namely, protecting " 'patient access to healthcare . . . and the unobstructed use of public sidewalks and roadways.' " Really? Does a statute become "justified without reference to the content of the regulated speech" simply because the statute itself and those defending it in court *say* that it is? Every objective indication shows that the provision's primary purpose is to restrict speech that opposes abortion. [Justice Scalia stressed that the law covered all abortion clinics in the state, although only the Boston clinic had faced serious problems in maintaining order and access. He argued that this undermined the credibility of the state's claimed interest.]

Is there any serious doubt that *abortion-clinic employees or agents* "acting within the scope of their employment" near clinic entrances may— indeed, often will—speak in favor of abortion ("You are doing the right thing")? Or speak in opposition to the message of abortion opponents— saying, for example, that "this is a safe facility" to rebut the statement that it is not? The Court's contrary assumption is simply incredible. And the majority makes no attempt to establish the further necessary proposition that abortion-clinic employees and agents do not engage in nonspeech activities directed to the suppression of antiabortion speech by hampering the efforts of counselors to speak to prospective clients. Are we to believe that a clinic employee sent out to "escort" prospective clients into the building would not seek to prevent a counselor like Eleanor McCullen from communicating with them? He could pull a woman away from an approaching counselor, cover her ears, or make loud noises to drown out the counselor's pleas. * * *

There is not a shadow of a doubt that the assigned or foreseeable conduct of a clinic employee or agent can include both speaking in favor of abortion rights and countering the speech of people like petitioners. * * *

In sum, the Act should be reviewed under the strict-scrutiny standard applicable to content-based legislation. That standard requires that a regulation represent "the least restrictive means" of furthering "a compelling Government interest." Respondents do not even attempt to argue that subsection (b) survives this test. "Suffice it to say that if protecting people from unwelcome communications"—the actual purpose of the provision—"is a compelling state interest, the First Amendment is a dead letter."

Having determined that the Act is content based and does not withstand strict scrutiny, I need not pursue the inquiry [into whether the statute is narrowly tailored.] I suppose I *could* do so, * * * and if I did, I suspect I would agree with the majority that the legislation is not narrowly tailored to advance the interests asserted by respondents. But I prefer not to take part in the assembling of an apparent but specious unanimity. I leave both the plainly unnecessary and erroneous half and the arguably correct half of the Court's analysis to the majority.

[**JUSTICE ALITO** concurred in the judgment on the ground that the exemption for clinic employees constituted viewpoint discrimination, but agreed with the majority that in any event the statute was not narrowly tailored.]

NOTES ON MCCULLEN

1. *Realism and Judicial Review.* Whose version of the statute's purpose and effect seems most plausible—the majority's or Justice Scalia's? Note that neither side offers direct evidence about the intentions of the legislatures. Both purport to infer purpose from the face of the statute and the context, but with an important difference: the majority takes the statute as it is written, while Justice Scalia is willing to make inferences about the political dynamics. Which approach is preferable?

2. *Harassment or Outreach?* A traditional argument for protecting speech involves the ability to speakers to reach willing listeners without government interference. But the Court valorizes public forums for the ability of speakers to reach listeners who would prefer to be left alone. Should there be a constitutional right to avoid unwanted communications?

3. *Sauce for the Goose Versus Sauce for the Gander?* There is a large buffer zone excluding from the Supreme Court's grounds, including the plaza in front of the building, the following activities: "demonstrations, picketing, speechmaking, marching, holding vigils or religious services and all other like forms of conduct that involve the communication or expression of views or grievances, engaged in by one or more persons, the conduct of which is reasonably likely to draw a crowd of onlookers." Is this buffer zone constitutional?

Page 811. Insert the following before Section B:

Note that a public forum is an actual or metaphorical space that the government provides for the use of private speakers. This must be distinguished from speech by the government itself. In many cases, the nature of government speech is obvious. But as the following case shows, it can sometimes be difficult to determine whether the government is offering its own message or providing space for the messages of others.

WALKER V. TEXAS DIVISION, SONS OF CONFEDERATE VETERANS
___ U.S. ___, 135 S.Ct. 2239, 192 L.Ed.2d 274 (2015)

JUSTICE BREYER delivered the opinion of the Court. Texas offers automobile owners a choice between ordinary and specialty license plates. Those who want the State to issue a particular specialty plate may propose a plate design, comprising a slogan, a graphic, or (most commonly) both. If the Texas Department of Motor Vehicles Board approves the design, the State will make it available for display on vehicles registered in Texas.

In this case, the Texas Division of the Sons of Confederate Veterans proposed a specialty license plate design featuring a Confederate battle flag. The Board rejected the proposal. We must decide whether that rejection violated the Constitution's free speech guarantees. We conclude that it did not. * * *

When government speaks, it is not barred by the Free Speech Clause from determining the content of what it says. *Pleasant Grove City v. Summum,* 555 U.S. 460, 467–468, 129 S.Ct. 1125, 172 L.Ed.2d 853 (2009). That freedom in part reflects the fact that it is the democratic electoral process that first and foremost provides a check on government speech.

In our view, specialty license plates issued pursuant to Texas's statutory scheme convey government speech. Our reasoning rests primarily on our analysis in *Summum,* a recent case that presented a similar problem. We conclude here, as we did there, that our precedents regarding government speech (and not our precedents regarding forums for private speech) provide the appropriate framework through which to approach the case.

In *Summum,* we considered a religious organization's request to erect in a 2.5-acre city park a monument setting forth the organization's religious tenets. In the park were 15 other permanent displays. At least 11 of these—including a wishing well, a September 11 monument, a historic granary, the city's first fire station, and a Ten Commandments monument—had been donated to the city by private entities. The religious organization argued that the Free Speech Clause required the city to display the organization's proposed monument because, by accepting a broad range of permanent exhibitions at the park, the city had created a forum for private speech in the form of monuments.

This Court rejected the organization's argument. We held that the city had not "provid[ed] a forum for private speech" with respect to monuments. Rather, the city, even when "accepting a privately donated monument and placing it on city property," had "engage[d] in expressive conduct." The speech at issue, this Court decided, was "best viewed as a form of government speech" and "therefore [was] not subject to scrutiny under the Free Speech Clause." * * *

Our analysis in *Summum* leads us to the conclusion that here, too, government speech is at issue. First, the history of license plates shows that, insofar as license plates have conveyed more than state names and vehicle identification numbers, they long have communicated messages from the States. In 1917, Arizona became the first State to display a graphic on its plates. The State presented a depiction of the head of a Hereford steer. In the years since, New Hampshire plates have featured the profile of the "Old Man of the Mountain," Massachusetts plates have included a representation of the Commonwealth's famous codfish, and Wyoming plates have displayed a rider atop a bucking bronco.

In 1928, Idaho became the first State to include a slogan on its plates. The 1928 Idaho plate proclaimed "Idaho Potatoes" and featured an illustration of a brown potato, onto which the license plate number was superimposed in green. *Id.,* at 61. The brown potato did not catch on, but slogans on license plates did. Over the years, state plates have included the phrases "North to the Future" (Alaska), "Keep Florida Green" (Florida), "Hoosier Hospitality" (Indiana), "The Iodine Products State" (South Carolina), "Green Mountains" (Vermont), and "America's Dairyland" (Wisconsin). States have used license plate slogans to urge action, to promote tourism, and to tout local industries. * * *

Second, Texas license plate designs "are often closely identified in the public mind with the [State]." Each Texas license plate is a government article serving the governmental purposes of vehicle registration and identification. The governmental nature of the plates is clear from their faces: The State places the name "TEXAS" in large letters at the top of every plate. Moreover, the State requires Texas vehicle owners to display license plates, and every Texas license plate is issued by the State. Texas also owns the designs on its license plates, including the designs that Texas adopts on the basis of proposals made by private individuals and organizations. Texas dictates the manner in which drivers may dispose of unused plates.

* * *

Indeed, a person who displays a message on a Texas license plate likely intends to convey to the public that the State has endorsed that message. If not, the individual could simply display the message in question in larger letters on a bumper sticker right next to the plate. But the individual prefers a license plate design to the purely private speech expressed through bumper stickers. That may well be because Texas's license plate designs convey government agreement with the message displayed.

Third, Texas maintains direct control over the messages conveyed on its specialty plates. Texas law provides that the State "has sole control over the design, typeface, color, and alphanumeric pattern for all license plates." The Board must approve every specialty plate design proposal before the design can appear on a Texas plate. And the Board and its predecessor have actively exercised this authority. Texas asserts, and SCV concedes, that the State has rejected at least a dozen proposed designs. * * *

SCV believes that Texas's specialty license plate designs are not government speech, at least with respect to the designs (comprising slogans and graphics) that were initially proposed by private parties. According to SCV, the State does not engage in expressive activity through such slogans and graphics, but rather provides a forum for private speech by making license plates available to display the private parties' designs. We cannot agree.

We have previously used what we have called "forum analysis" to evaluate government restrictions on purely private speech that occurs on government property. But forum analysis is misplaced here. Because the State is speaking on its own behalf, the First Amendment strictures that attend the various types of government-established forums do not apply. * * *

The fact that private parties take part in the design and propagation of a message does not extinguish the governmental nature of the message or transform the government's role into that of a mere forum-provider. In *Summum,* private entities "financed and donated monuments that the government accept[ed] and display[ed] to the public." Here, similarly, private parties propose designs that Texas may accept and display on its license plates. In this case, as in *Summum,* the "government entity may exercise [its] freedom to express its views" even "when it receives assistance from private sources for the purpose of delivering a government-controlled message." And in this case, as in *Summum,* forum analysis is inapposite. * * *

Our determination that Texas's specialty license plate designs are government speech does not mean that the designs do not also implicate the free speech rights of private persons. We have acknowledged that drivers who display a State's selected license plate designs convey the messages communicated through those designs. And we have recognized that the First Amendment stringently limits a State's authority to compel a private party to express a view with which the private party disagrees. But here, compelled private speech is not at issue. And just as Texas cannot require SCV to convey "the State's ideological message,", SCV cannot force Texas to include a Confederate battle flag on its specialty license plates.

JUSTICE ALITO, joined by CHIEF JUSTICE ROBERTS, JUSTICE SCALIA, and JUSTICE KENNEDY, dissenting.

Here is a test. Suppose you sat by the side of a Texas highway and studied the license plates on the vehicles passing by. You would see, in addition to the standard Texas plates, an impressive array of specialty plates. (There are now more than 350 varieties.) You would likely observe plates that honor numerous colleges and universities. You might see plates bearing the name of a high school, a fraternity or sorority, the Masons, the Knights of Columbus, the Daughters of the American Revolution, a realty company, a favorite soft drink, a favorite burger restaurant, and a favorite NASCAR driver.

As you sat there watching these plates speed by, would you really think that the sentiments reflected in these specialty plates are the views of the State of Texas and not those of the owners of the cars? If a car with a plate that says "Rather Be Golfing" passed by at 8:30 am on a Monday morning, would you think: "This is the official policy of the State—better to golf than to work?" * * * And when a car zipped by with a plate that reads "NASCAR—24 Jeff Gordon," would you think that Gordon (born in California, raised in Indiana, resides in North Carolina) is the official favorite of the State government?

This capacious understanding of government speech takes a large and painful bite out of the First Amendment. Specialty plates may seem innocuous. They make motorists happy, and they put money in a State's coffers. But the precedent this case sets is dangerous. While all license plates unquestionably contain *some* government speech (*e.g.,* the name of the State and the numbers and/or letters identifying the vehicle), the State of Texas has converted the remaining space on its specialty plates into little mobile billboards on which motorists can display their own messages. And what Texas did here was to reject one of the messages that members of a private group wanted to post on some of these little billboards because the State thought that many of its citizens would find the message offensive. That is blatant viewpoint discrimination. * * *

I begin with history. As we said in *Summum,* governments have used monuments since time immemorial to express important government messages, and there is no history of governments giving equal space to those wishing to express dissenting views, and members of the public understand this.

The history of messages on license plates is quite different. After the beginning of motor vehicle registration in 1917, more than 70 years passed before the proliferation of specialty plates in Texas. It was not until the 1990's that motorists were allowed to choose from among 10 messages, such as "Read to Succeed" and "Keep Texas Beautiful."

Up to this point, the words on the Texas plates can be considered government speech. The messages were created by the State, and they plausibly promoted state programs. But when, at some point within the last 20 years or so, the State began to allow private entities to secure plates conveying their own messages, Texas crossed the line.

The contrast between the history of public monuments, which have been used to convey government messages for centuries, and the Texas license plate program could not be starker. * * *

What Texas has done by selling space on its license plates is to create what we have called a limited public forum. It has allowed state property (*i.e.,* motor vehicle license plates) to be used by private speakers according to rules that the State prescribes. Under the First Amendment, however, those rules cannot discriminate on the basis of viewpoint. But that is exactly what Texas did here. The Board rejected Texas SCV's design, "specifically the confederate flag portion of the design, because public comments have shown that many members of the general public find the design offensive, and because such comments are reasonable." These statements indisputably demonstrate that the Board denied Texas SCV's design because of its viewpoint.

NOTES ON WALKER AND GOVERNMENT SPEECH

1. *Category Confusion?* It seems clear that Texas could not ban bumper stickers portraying the Confederate flag. It seems equally clear that Texas is not compelled to use the flag as an insignia on state vehicles. Thus, the question is whether the license plate is more like a bumper sticker or a state insignia. That question divides the Court 5–4. One might wonder, however, whether this categorizing effort is really the best way to decide whether rejection of the CVS license plate design is consistent with First Amendment values. The structure of current doctrine, however, seems to make it difficult for the Court to approach cases in such functional terms.

2. *Some Historical Context.* The Court's decision was released on June 18, 2015. The night before, a white man entered a Bible study session at a black church in Charleston, South Carolina. He opened fire, and killed eighteen people, killing nine of them. Richard Fuasset, John Eligon, Jason Horowitz and Frances Roblesa, *Hectic Day at Charleston Church, and Then a Hellish Visitor*, N.Y. Times (June 30, 2015). The killer's White Supremacist background sparked a debate about racism, and about the Confederate flag in particular. Within five days, the state had decided to take down the Confederate flag that had flown outside South Carolina's capitol for decades. Michael Barbaro and Jonathan Martin, *5 Days That Left a Confederate Flag Wavering, and Likely to Fall*, N.Y. Times (June 28, 2015). All of those events took place too late to have impacted the Court's decision, but they may help place it in historic context. Note that Justice Thomas was the fifth vote in the case; his

understanding of the meaning of the Confederate flag may well have been shaped by his experience of growing up as an African-American in the South.

3. *The First Amendment and the Commercial State.* It appears that the state's purpose is neither to provide a communication for private parties nor to convey its own messages, but simply to make money. This blurring of the line between governance and private enterprise presents challenges for traditional constitutional analysis. In that sense, the license plates might be analogized to the T-shirts that might be on sale in a gift shop in a public building. A private shop owner would certainly be selective in its choices of T-shirts, based on factors such as how popular the images on a shirt would be with buyers, whether controversial shirts would fit the store's image, etc. Would a state-owned gift shop be entitled to make similar choices? How would the *Walker* majority and dissent analyze the problem?

MATAL V. TAM
___ U.S. ___, 137 S.Ct. 1744, 198 L.Ed.2d 366 (2017)

JUSTICE ALITO announced the judgment of the Court and delivered the opinion of the Court with respect to Parts I, II, and III-A, and an opinion with respect to Parts III-B, III-C, and IV, in which the **CHIEF JUSTICE**, **JUSTICE THOMAS**, and **JUSTICE BREYER** join.

This case concerns a dance-rock band's application for federal trademark registration of the band's name, "The Slants." "Slants" is a derogatory term for persons of Asian descent, and members of the band are Asian-Americans. But the band members believe that by taking that slur as the name of their group, they will help to "reclaim" the term and drain its denigrating force.

The Patent and Trademark Office (PTO) denied the application based on a provision of federal law prohibiting the registration of trademarks that may "disparage . . . or bring . . . into contemp[t] or disrepute" any "persons, living or dead." 15 U.S.C. § 1052(a). We now hold that this provision violates the Free Speech Clause of the First Amendment. It offends a bedrock First Amendment principle: Speech may not be banned on the ground that it expresses ideas that offend. * * *

[Part I of the opinion reviews federal trademark law and the facts of the case. Part II rejects a statutory argument against applying § 1052(a) to trademarks that disparage racial or ethnic groups.]

III

Because the disparagement clause applies to marks that disparage the members of a racial or ethnic group, we must decide whether the clause violates the Free Speech Clause of the First Amendment. And at the outset, we must consider three arguments that would either eliminate any First Amendment protection or result in highly permissive rational-basis review.

Specifically, the Government contends (1) that trademarks are government speech, not private speech, (2) that trademarks are a form of government subsidy, and (3) that the constitutionality of the disparagement clause should be tested under a new "government-program" doctrine. We address each of these arguments below.

A [for the Court]

The First Amendment prohibits Congress and other government entities and actors from "abridging the freedom of speech"; the First Amendment does not say that Congress and other government entities must abridge their own ability to speak freely. And our cases recognize that "[t]he Free Speech Clause . . . does not regulate government speech." As we have said, "it is not easy to imagine how government could function" if it were subject to the restrictions that the First Amendment imposes on private speech. " '[T]he First Amendment forbids the government to regulate speech in ways that favor some viewpoints or ideas at the expense of others," but imposing a requirement of viewpoint-neutrality on government speech would be paralyzing. When a government entity embarks on a course of action, it necessarily takes a particular viewpoint and rejects others. The Free Speech Clause does not require government to maintain viewpoint neutrality when its officers and employees speak about that venture.

Here is a simple example. During the Second World War, the Federal Government produced and distributed millions of posters to promote the war effort. There were posters urging enlistment, the purchase of war bonds, and the conservation of scarce resources. These posters expressed a viewpoint, but the First Amendment did not demand that the Government balance the message of these posters by producing and distributing posters encouraging Americans to refrain from engaging in these activities. But while the government-speech doctrine is important—indeed, essential—it is a doctrine that is susceptible to dangerous misuse. If private speech could be passed off as government speech by simply affixing a government seal of approval, government could silence or muffle the expression of disfavored viewpoints. For this reason, we must exercise great caution before extending our government-speech precedents.

At issue here is the content of trademarks that are registered by the PTO, an arm of the Federal Government. The Federal Government does not dream up these marks, and it does not edit marks submitted for registration. Except as required by the statute involved here, an examiner may not reject a mark based on the viewpoint that it appears to express. Thus, unless that section is thought to apply, an examiner does not inquire whether any viewpoint conveyed by a mark is consistent with Government policy or whether any such viewpoint is consistent with that expressed by other marks already on the principal register. Instead, if the mark meets the Lanham Act's viewpoint-neutral requirements, registration is mandatory. *Ibid.* (requiring that "[n]o trademark . . . shall be refused registration on the principal register on account of its nature unless" it falls within an enumerated statutory exception). And if an examiner finds that a mark is eligible for placement on the principal register, that decision is not reviewed by any higher official unless the registration is challenged. Moreover, once a mark is registered, the PTO is not authorized to remove it from the register unless a party moves for cancellation, the registration expires, or the Federal Trade Commission initiates proceedings based on certain grounds.

In light of all this, it is far-fetched to suggest that the content of a registered mark is government speech. If the federal registration of a trademark makes the mark government speech, the Federal Government is babbling prodigiously and incoherently. It is saying many unseemly things. It is expressing contradictory views. It is unashamedly endorsing a vast array of commercial products and services. And it is providing Delphic advice to the consuming public.

For example, if trademarks represent government speech, what does the Government have in mind when it advises Americans to "make.believe" (Sony), "Think different" (Apple), "Just do it" (Nike), or "Have it your way" (Burger King)? Was the Government warning about a coming disaster when it registered the mark "EndTime Ministries"? * * *

This brings us to the case on which the Government relies most heavily, *Walker,* which likely marks the outer bounds of the government-speech doctrine. Holding that the messages on Texas specialty license plates are government speech, the *Walker* Court cited three factors * * * . First, license plates have long been used by the States to convey state messages. Second, license plates "are often closely identified in the public mind" with the State, since they are manufactured and owned by the State, generally designed by the State, and serve as a form of "government ID." Third, Texas "maintain[ed] direct control over the messages conveyed on its specialty plates." As explained above, none of these factors are present in this case. * * *

[In Part III(B) of his opinion, Justice Alito argued for a plurality that the Court's prior cases dealing with government subsidies were distinguishable because "all involved cash subsidies or their equivalent." In Part III(C), he rejected the government's request that the Court recognize a new doctrine for "government programs," merging government speech cases and subsidy cases.]

IV [for the Court]

[The parties disputed whether trademarks are commercial speech, but the Court found it unnecessary to resolve that dispute because it found that the disparagement clause did not survive even under the standards applying to commercial speech.] Under *Central Hudson,* a restriction of speech must serve "a substantial interest," and it must be "narrowly drawn." This means, among other things, that "[t]he regulatory technique may extend only as far as the interest it serves." The disparagement clause fails this requirement.

It is claimed that the disparagement clause serves two interests. The first is phrased in a variety of ways in the briefs. Echoing language in one of the opinions below, the Government asserts an interest in preventing "underrepresented groups" from being "bombarded with demeaning messages in commercial advertising." An *amicus* supporting the Government refers to "encouraging racial tolerance and protecting the privacy and welfare of individuals." But no matter how the point is phrased, its unmistakable thrust is this: The Government has an interest in preventing speech expressing ideas that offend. And, as we have explained, that idea strikes at the heart of the First Amendment. Speech that demeans on the basis of race, ethnicity, gender, religion, age, disability, or any other similar ground is hateful; but the proudest boast of our free speech jurisprudence is that we protect the freedom to express "the thought that we hate."

The second interest asserted is protecting the orderly flow of commerce. Commerce, we are told, is disrupted by trademarks that "involv[e] disparagement of race, gender, ethnicity, national origin, religion, sexual orientation, and similar demographic classification." Such trademarks are analogized to discriminatory conduct, which has been recognized to have an adverse effect on commerce. A simple answer to this argument is that the disparagement clause is not "narrowly drawn" to drive out trademarks that support invidious discrimination. The clause reaches any trademark that disparages *any person, group, or institution.* It applies to trademarks like the following: "Down with racists," "Down with sexists," "Down with homophobes." It is not an anti-discrimination clause; it is a happy-talk clause. In this way, it goes much further than is necessary to serve the interest asserted.

The clause is far too broad in other ways as well. The clause protects every person living or dead as well as every institution. Is it conceivable that commerce would be disrupted by a trademark saying: "James Buchanan was a disastrous president" or "Slavery is an evil institution"?

There is also a deeper problem with the argument that commercial speech may be cleansed of any expression likely to cause offense. The commercial market is well stocked with merchandise that disparages prominent figures and groups, and the line between commercial and non-commercial speech is not always clear, as this case illustrates. If affixing the commercial label permits the suppression of any speech that may lead to political or social "volatility," free speech would be endangered.

JUSTICE GORSUCH took no part in the consideration or decision of this case.

JUSTICES KENNEDY, with whom JUSTICE GINSBURG, JUSTICE SOTOMAYOR, and JUSTICE KAGAN join, concurring in part and concurring in the judgment.

As the Court is correct to hold, § 1052(a) constitutes viewpoint discrimination—a form of speech suppression so potent that it must be subject to rigorous constitutional scrutiny. The Government's action and the statute on which it is based cannot survive this scrutiny.

The Court is correct in its judgment, and I join Parts I, II, and III-A of its opinion. This separate writing explains in greater detail why the First Amendment's protections against viewpoint discrimination apply to the trademark here. It submits further that the viewpoint discrimination rationale renders unnecessary any extended treatment of other questions raised by the parties. * * *

At its most basic, the test for viewpoint discrimination is whether—within the relevant subject category—the government has singled out a subset of messages for disfavor based on the views expressed. In the instant case, the disparagement clause the Government now seeks to implement and enforce identifies the relevant subject as "persons, living or dead, institutions, beliefs, or national symbols." Within that category, an applicant may register a positive or benign mark but not a derogatory one. The law thus reflects the Government's disapproval of a subset of messages it finds offensive. This is the essence of viewpoint discrimination.

The Government disputes this conclusion. It argues, to begin with, that the law is viewpoint neutral because it applies in equal measure to any trademark that demeans or offends. This misses the point. A subject that is first defined by content and then regulated or censored by mandating only one sort of comment is not viewpoint neutral. To prohibit all sides from criticizing their opponents makes a law more viewpoint based, not less so. The logic of the Government's rule is that a law would be viewpoint neutral even if it provided that public officials could be praised but not condemned. The First Amendment's viewpoint neutrality principle protects more than the right to identify with a particular side. It protects the right to create and present arguments for particular positions in particular ways, as the speaker chooses. By mandating positivity, the law here might silence dissent and distort the marketplace of ideas.

The Government next suggests that the statute is viewpoint neutral because the disparagement clause applies to trademarks regardless of the applicant's personal views or reasons for using the mark. Instead, registration is denied based on the expected reaction of the applicant's audience. In this way, the argument goes, it cannot be said that Government is acting with hostility toward a particular point of view. For example, the Government does not dispute that respondent seeks to use his mark in a positive way. Indeed, respondent endeavors to use The Slants to supplant a racial epithet, using new insights, musical talents, and wry humor to make it a badge of pride. Respondent's application was denied not because the Government thought his object was to demean or offend but because the Government thought his trademark would have that effect on at least some Asian-Americans.

The Government may not insulate a law from charges of viewpoint discrimination by tying censorship to the reaction of the speaker's audience. The Court has suggested that viewpoint discrimination occurs when the government intends to suppress a speaker's beliefs, but viewpoint discrimination need not take that form in every instance. The danger of viewpoint discrimination is that the government is attempting to remove certain ideas or perspectives from a broader debate. That danger is all the greater if the ideas or perspectives are ones a particular audience might think offensive, at least at first hearing. An initial reaction may prompt further reflection, leading to a more reasoned, more tolerant position.

Indeed, a speech burden based on audience reactions is simply government hostility and intervention in a different guise. The speech is targeted, after all, based on the government's disapproval of the speaker's choice of message. And it is the government itself that is attempting in this case to decide whether the relevant audience would find the speech offensive. For reasons like these, the Court's cases have long prohibited the government from justifying a First Amendment burden by pointing to the offensiveness of the speech to be suppressed.

The Government's argument in defense of the statute assumes that respondent's mark is a negative comment. In addressing that argument on its own terms, this opinion is not intended to imply that the Government's interpretation is accurate. From respondent's submissions, it is evident he would disagree that his mark means what the Government says it does. The trademark will have the effect, respondent urges, of reclaiming an offensive term for the positive purpose of celebrating all that Asian-Americans can and do contribute to our diverse Nation. While thoughtful persons can agree or disagree with this approach, the dissonance between the trademark's potential to teach and the Government's insistence on its own, opposite, and negative interpretation confirms the constitutional vice of the statute. * * *

A law that can be directed against speech found offensive to some portion of the public can be turned against minority and dissenting views to the detriment of all. The First Amendment does not entrust that power to the government's benevolence. Instead, our reliance must be on the substantial safeguards of free and open discussion in a democratic society.

[Justice Gorsuch did not take part in the decision. Justice Thomas declined to join the statutory portion of Alito's opinion because he did not believe the argument was properly before the Court.]

NOTES ON THE IMPLICATIONS OF MATAL

1. *Limiting* Walker *to Its Facts?* Note that the Court sets on outer boundary on the government speech cases by calling the case the "outer limit" of the government speech doctrine. This is generally a sign that a case is no longer to be considered a precedent for other rulings, which suggests that the Court has doubts about its validity without going so far as to overrule it. It is a bit surprising to see such a recent precedent given such short shrift, suggesting that perhaps some of the Justices who joined it may be having second thoughts.

2. *How Strong is the Prohibition on Viewpoint Discrimination?* Although we have called Alito's the "plurality opinion" for convenience in this sections where he did not have a majority, in fact the Court was equally divided on those sections given that Gorsuch did not participate. The division seems to represent a division on the Court regarding the degree to which viewpoint discrimination is forbidden across the board, including areas like commercial speech where regulations are generally subject to lower scrutiny. The group led by Justice Alito seems unwilling to take that step, whereas the group led by Justice Kennedy seems unwilling to allow regulation on this basis (including the offensiveness of speech) in any context other than government speech.

3. *Campus Restrictions on Hate Speech and Micro Aggressions.* The government's asserted interests in preventing disparagement of racial groups in trademarks involved the impact of this type of speech on minorities. How broad are the implications of the opinion for other types of efforts to protect minorities from similar impacts? The Kennedy opinion seems to imply that any restriction on speech based on the effect of speech on its audience could be at risk of being considered viewpoint discrimination and hence impermissible unless government speech is involved. The Alito opinion does not seem to rule out government consideration of audience effect in commercial speech and perhaps other areas where speech is subject to reduced protection. Neither opinion expresses any strong endorsement of the government's purposes. Lower courts will be left with the problem of sorting out the implications for regulation of speech in campus settings.

B. GOVERNMENT-SUPPORTED SPEECH

Page 812. Insert at the end of the *NOTE ON PUBLIC EMPLOYEE SPEECH***:**

A related issue relating to employee speech is whether public employees can be required to pay union dues. In *Abood v. Detroit Bd. of Education*, 431 U.S. 209 (1977), the Court upheld state laws that require nonmember employees to pay an "agency fee" for the union's collective bargaining services, since they benefit from the collective bargaining agreement. In *Harris v. Quinn*, 134 S.Ct. 2618 (2014), the Court said that given what it considered the shaky foundation of *Abood*, it would not extend the *Abood* holding to quasi-public workers such as home care workers paid by Medicaid but chosen by the patient. The dissenters defended *Abood* and argued for its extension.

The continued vitality of *Abood* is unclear after *Harris*, and some public employee unions are concerned that their own viability could be threatened if *Abood* were to be overruled. Note, however, that even if *Abood* was overruled, the state could avoid any First Amendment problem by agreeing to pay service fee for all workers directly to the union, so that the union's fee for its members would include only non-bargaining expenses. Assuming this approach was allowed by state law, it would raise no First Amendment problem since the money would no longer be part of the non-member's salary. Because government funds not linked to any individual worker would be used, workers could not complain about compelled speech even though economically the outcome is indistinguishable from an agency fee.

Pages 816–819. Replace *Velazquez* and the Notes after the opinion with the following:

AGENCY FOR INTERNATIONAL DEVELOPMENT V. ALLIANCE FOR OPEN SOCIETY INT'L, INC.
570 U.S. 205, 133 S.Ct. 2321, 186 L.Ed.2d 398 (2013)

CHIEF JUSTICE ROBERTS delivered the opinion of the Court.

The United States Leadership Against HIV/AIDS, Tuberculosis, and Malaria Act of 2003 (Leadership Act), 22 U.S.C. § 7601 et seq., outlined a comprehensive strategy to combat the spread of HIV/AIDS around the world. As part of that strategy, Congress authorized the appropriation of billions of dollars to fund efforts by nongovernmental organizations to assist in the fight. The Act imposes two related conditions on that funding: First, no funds made available by the Act "may be used to promote or advocate the legalization or practice of prostitution or sex trafficking." § 7631(e). And second, no funds may be used by an organization "that does not have a policy explicitly opposing prostitution and sex trafficking." § 7631(f). This case concerns the second of these conditions, referred to as the Policy Requirement. The question is whether that funding condition violates a recipient's First Amendment rights. * * *

Respondents are a group of domestic organizations engaged in combating HIV/AIDS overseas. In addition to substantial private funding, they receive billions annually in financial assistance from the United States, including under the Leadership Act. Their work includes programs aimed at limiting injection drug use in Uzbekistan, Tajikistan, and Kyrgyzstan, preventing mother-to-child HIV transmission in Kenya, and promoting safer sex practices in India. Respondents fear that adopting a policy explicitly opposing prostitution may alienate certain host governments, and may diminish the effectiveness of some of their programs by making it more difficult to work with prostitutes in the fight against HIV/AIDS. They are also concerned that the Policy Requirement may require them to censor their privately funded discussions in publications, at conferences, and in other forums about how best to prevent the spread of HIV/AIDS among prostitutes. * * *

The Policy Requirement mandates that recipients of Leadership Act funds explicitly agree with the Government's policy to oppose prostitution and sex trafficking. It is, however, a basic First Amendment principle that "freedom of speech prohibits the government from telling people what they must say." *Rumsfeld v. Forum for Academic and Institutional Rights, Inc.*, 547 U.S. 47 (2006) (citing *West Virginia Bd. of Ed. v. Barnette*, 319 U.S. 624 (1943), and *Wooley v. Maynard*, 430 U.S. 705 (1977)). "At the heart of the First Amendment lies the principle that each person should decide for himself or herself the ideas and beliefs deserving of expression, consideration, and adherence." *Turner Broadcasting System, Inc. v. FCC*, 512 U.S. 622 (1994). Were it enacted as a direct regulation of speech, the Policy Requirement would plainly violate the First Amendment. The question is whether the Government may nonetheless impose that requirement as a condition on the receipt of federal funds. * * *

As a general matter, if a party objects to a condition on the receipt of federal funding, its recourse is to decline the funds. This remains true when the objection is that a condition may affect the recipient's exercise of its First Amendment rights. See, e.g., *United States v. American Library Assn., Inc.*, 539 U.S. 194 (2003) (plurality opinion) (rejecting a claim by public libraries that conditioning funds for Internet access on the libraries' installing filtering software violated their First Amendment rights, explaining that "[t]o the extent that libraries wish to offer unfiltered access, they are free to do so without federal assistance"); *Regan v. Taxation With Representation of Wash.*, 461 U.S. 540, 546 (1983) (dismissing "the notion that First Amendment rights are somehow not fully realized unless they are subsidized by the State" (internal quotation marks omitted)).

At the same time, however, we have held that the Government " 'may not deny a benefit to a person on a basis that infringes his constitutionally protected . . . freedom of speech even if he has no entitlement to that benefit.' " In some cases, a funding condition can result in an unconstitutional burden on First Amendment rights.

The dissent thinks that can only be true when the condition is not relevant to the objectives of the program (although it has its doubts about that), or when the condition is actually coercive, in the sense of an offer that cannot be refused. See post (opinion of SCALIA, J.). Our precedents, however, are not so limited. In the present context, the relevant distinction that has emerged from our cases is between conditions that define the limits of the government spending program—those that specify the activities Congress wants to subsidize—and conditions that seek to leverage funding to regulate speech outside the contours of the program itself. The line is hardly clear, in part because the definition of a particular program can always be manipulated to subsume the challenged condition. We have held, however, that "Congress cannot recast a condition on funding as a mere definition of its program in every case, lest the First Amendment be reduced to a simple semantic exercise." *Legal Services Corporation v. Velazquez*, 531 U.S. 533, 547 (2001).

A comparison of two cases helps illustrate the distinction: In *Regan v. Taxation With Representation of Washington*, the Court upheld a requirement that nonprofit organizations seeking tax-exempt status under 26 U.S.C. § 501(c)(3) not engage in substantial efforts to influence legislation. The tax-exempt status, we explained, "ha[d] much the same effect as a cash grant to the organization." And by limiting § 501(c)(3) status to organizations that did not attempt to influence legislation, Congress had merely "chose[n] not to subsidize lobbying." In rejecting the nonprofit's First Amendment claim, the Court highlighted * * * the fact that the condition did not prohibit that organization from lobbying Congress altogether. By returning to a "dual structure" it had used in the past—separately incorporating as a § 501(c)(3) organization and § 501(c)(4) organization—the nonprofit could continue to claim § 501(c)(3) status for its nonlobbying activities, while attempting to influence legislation in its § 501(c)(4) capacity with separate funds. Ibid. Maintaining such a structure, the Court noted, was not "unduly burdensome." The condition thus did not deny the organization a government benefit "on account of its intention to lobby."

In *FCC v. League of Women Voters of California,* by contrast, the Court struck down a condition on federal financial assistance to noncommercial broadcast television and radio stations that prohibited all editorializing, including with private funds. Even a station receiving only one percent of its overall budget from the Federal Government, the Court explained, was "barred absolutely from all editorializing." Unlike the situation in *Regan,* the law provided no way for a station to limit its use of federal funds to non-editorializing activities, while using private funds "to make known its views on matters of public importance." The prohibition thus went beyond ensuring that federal funds not be used to subsidize "public broadcasting station editorials," and instead leveraged the federal funding to regulate the stations' speech outside the scope of the program.

Our decision in *Rust v. Sullivan* elaborated on the approach reflected in *Regan* and *League of Women Voters*. In *Rust*, we considered Title X of the Public Health Service Act, a Spending Clause program that issued grants to nonprofit health-care organizations "to assist in the establishment and operation of voluntary family planning projects [to] offer a broad range of acceptable and effective family planning methods and services." The organizations received funds from a variety of sources other than the Federal Government for a variety of purposes. The Act, however, prohibited the Title X federal funds from being "used in programs where abortion is a method of family planning." Ibid. (internal quotation marks omitted). To enforce this provision, HHS regulations barred Title X projects from advocating abortion as a method of family planning, and required grantees to ensure that their Title X projects were " 'physically and financially separate' " from their other projects that engaged in the prohibited activities—group of Title X funding recipients brought suit, claiming the regulations imposed an unconstitutional condition on their First Amendment rights. We rejected their claim.

We explained that Congress can, without offending the Constitution, selectively fund certain programs to address an issue of public concern, without funding alternative ways of addressing the same problem. In Title X, Congress had defined the federal program to encourage only particular family planning methods. The challenged regulations were simply "designed to ensure that the limits of the federal program are observed," and "that public funds [are] spent for the purposes for which they were authorized."

In making this determination, the Court stressed that "Title X expressly distinguishes between a Title X grantee and a Title X project." The regulations governed only the scope of the grantee's Title X projects, leaving it "unfettered in its other activities." I "The Title X grantee can continue to . . . engage in abortion advocacy; it simply is required to conduct those activities through programs that are separate and independent from the project that receives Title X funds." Because the regulations did not "prohibit[ ] the recipient from engaging in the protected conduct outside the scope of the federally funded program," they did not run afoul of the First Amendment.

As noted, the distinction drawn in these cases—between conditions that define the federal program and those that reach outside it—is not always self-evident. As Justice Cardozo put it in a related context, "Definition more precise must abide the wisdom of the future." *Steward Machine Co. v. Davis*, 301 U.S. 548, 591 (1937). Here, however, we are confident that the Policy Requirement falls on the unconstitutional side of the line.

To begin, it is important to recall that the Leadership Act has two conditions relevant here. The first—unchallenged in this litigation— prohibits Leadership Act funds from being used "to promote or advocate the legalization or practice of prostitution or sex trafficking." 22 U.S.C.

§ 7631(e). The Government concedes that § 7631(e) by itself ensures that federal funds will not be used for the prohibited purposes

The Policy Requirement therefore must be doing something more— and it is. The dissent views the Requirement as simply a selection criterion by which the Government identifies organizations "who believe in its ideas to carry them to fruition." As an initial matter, whatever purpose the Policy Requirement serves in selecting funding recipients, its effects go beyond selection. The Policy Requirement is an ongoing condition on recipients' speech and activities, a ground for terminating a grant after selection is complete. In any event, as the Government acknowledges, it is not simply seeking organizations that oppose prostitution. Rather, it explains, "Congress has expressed its purpose 'to eradicate' prostitution and sex trafficking, 22 U.S.C. § 7601(23), and it wants recipients to adopt a similar stance." This case is not about the Government's ability to enlist the assistance of those with whom it already agrees. It is about compelling a grant recipient to adopt a particular belief as a condition of funding.

By demanding that funding recipients adopt—as their own—the Government's view on an issue of public concern, the condition by its very nature affects "protected conduct outside the scope of the federally funded program." A recipient cannot avow the belief dictated by the Policy Requirement when spending Leadership Act funds, and then turn around and assert a contrary belief, or claim neutrality, when participating in activities on its own time and dime. By requiring recipients to profess a specific belief, the Policy Requirement goes beyond defining the limits of the federally funded program to defining the recipient.

The Government contends that the affiliate guidelines, established while this litigation was pending, save the program. Under those guidelines, funding recipients are permitted to work with affiliated organizations that do not abide by the condition, as long as the recipients retain "objective integrity and independence" from the unfettered affiliates. The Government suggests the guidelines alleviate any unconstitutional burden on the respondents' First Amendment rights by allowing them to either: (1) accept Leadership Act funding and comply with Policy Requirement, but establish affiliates to communicate contrary views on prostitution; or (2) decline funding themselves (thus remaining free to express their own views or remain neutral), while creating affiliates whose sole purpose is to receive and administer Leadership Act funds, thereby "cabin[ing] the effects" of the Policy Requirement within the scope of the federal program.

Neither approach is sufficient. When we have noted the importance of affiliates in this context, it has been because they allow an organization bound by a funding condition to exercise its First Amendment rights outside the scope of the federal program. Affiliates cannot serve that purpose when the condition is that a funding recipient espouse a specific belief as its own. If the affiliate is distinct from the recipient, the arrangement does not afford a means for the recipient to express its beliefs. If the affiliate is more clearly identified with the recipient, the recipient can express those beliefs only at the price of evident hypocrisy. The guidelines themselves make that clear.

The Government suggests that the Policy Requirement is necessary because, without it, the grant of federal funds could free a recipient's private funds "to be used to promote prostitution or sex trafficking." That argument assumes that federal funding will simply supplant private funding, rather than pay for new programs or expand existing ones. The Government offers no support for that assumption as a general matter, or any reason to believe it is true here. And if the Government's argument were correct, *League of Women Voters* would have come out differently, and much of the reasoning of *Regan* and *Rust* would have been beside the point.
* * *

Pressing its argument further, the Government contends that "if organizations awarded federal funds to implement Leadership Act programs could at the same time promote or affirmatively condone prostitution or sex trafficking, whether using public or private funds, it would undermine the government's program and confuse its message opposing prostitution and sex trafficking." But the Policy Requirement goes beyond preventing recipients from using private funds in a way that would undermine the federal program. It requires them to pledge allegiance to the Government's policy of eradicating prostitution. As to that, we cannot improve upon what Justice Jackson wrote for the Court 70 years ago: "If there is any fixed star in our constitutional constellation, it is that no official, high or petty, can prescribe what shall be orthodox in politics, nationalism, religion, or other matters of opinion or force citizens to confess by word or act their faith therein."

The Policy Requirement compels as a condition of federal funding the affirmation of a belief that by its nature cannot be confined within the scope of the Government program. In so doing, it violates the First Amendment and cannot be sustained.

KAGAN, J., took no part in the consideration or decision of this case.

JUSTICE SCALIA, with whom **JUSTICE THOMAS** joins dissenting.

The Leadership Act provides that "any group or organization that does not have a policy explicitly opposing prostitution and sex trafficking" may not receive funds appropriated under the Act. 22 U.S.C. § 7631(f). This Policy Requirement is nothing more than a means of selecting suitable agents to implement the Government's chosen strategy to eradicate HIV/AIDS. That is perfectly permissible under the Constitution.

The First Amendment does not mandate a viewpoint-neutral government. Government must choose between rival ideas and adopt some as its own: competition over cartels, solar energy over coal, weapon development over disarmament, and so forth. Moreover, the government may enlist the assistance of those who believe in its ideas to carry them to fruition; and it need not enlist for that purpose those who oppose or do not support the ideas. That seems to me a matter of the most common sense. For example: One of the purposes of America's foreign-aid programs is the fostering of good will towards this country. If the organization Hamas—reputed to have an efficient system for delivering welfare—were excluded from a program for the distribution of U.S. food assistance, no one could reasonably object. And that would remain true if Hamas were an organization of United States citizens entitled to the protection of the Constitution. So long as the unfunded organization remains free to engage in its activities (including anti-American propaganda) "without federal assistance," refusing to make use of its assistance for an enterprise to which it is opposed does not abridge its speech. And the same is true when the rejected organization is not affirmatively opposed to, but merely unsupportive of, the object of the federal program, which appears to be the case here. (Respondents do not promote prostitution, but neither do they wish to oppose it.) A federal program to encourage healthy eating habits need not be administered by the American Gourmet Society, which has nothing against healthy food but does not insist upon it.

The argument is that this commonsense principle will enable the government to discriminate against, and injure, points of view to which it is opposed. * * * The constitutional prohibition at issue here is not a prohibition against discriminating against or injuring opposing points of view, but the First Amendment's prohibition against the coercing of speech. I am frankly dubious that a condition for eligibility to participate in a minor federal program such as this one runs afoul of that prohibition even when the condition is irrelevant to the goals of the program. Not every disadvantage is a coercion.

But that is not the issue before us here. Here the views that the Government demands an applicant forswear—or that the Government insists an applicant favor—are relevant to the program in question. The program is valid only if the Government is entitled to disfavor the opposing view (here, advocacy of or toleration of prostitution). And if the program can disfavor it, so can the selection of those who are to administer the program. There is no risk that this principle will enable the Government to discriminate arbitrarily against positions it disfavors. It would not, for example, permit the Government to exclude from bidding on defense contracts anyone who refuses to abjure prostitution. But here a central part of the Government's HIV/AIDS strategy is the suppression of prostitution, by which HIV is transmitted. It is entirely reasonable to admit to participation in the program only those who believe in that goal. * * *

Of course the most obvious manner in which the admission to a program of an ideological opponent can frustrate the purpose of the program is by freeing up the opponent's funds for use in its ideological opposition. To use the Hamas example again: Subsidizing that organization's provision of social services enables the money that it would otherwise use for that purpose to be used, instead, for anti-American propaganda. Perhaps that problem does not exist in this case since the respondents do not affirmatively promote prostitution. But the Court's analysis categorically rejects that justification for ideological requirements in all cases, demanding "record indica[tion]" that "federal funding will simply supplant private funding, rather than pay for new programs." Ante, at 14. This seems to me quite naive. Money is fungible. The economic reality is that when NGOs can conduct their AIDS work on the Government's dime, they can expend greater resources on policies that undercut the Leadership Act. The Government need not establish by record evidence that this will happen. To make it a valid consideration in determining participation in federal programs, it suffices that this is a real and obvious risk. * * *

The Court's opinion contains stirring quotations * * * . They serve only to distract attention from the elephant in the room: that the Government is not forcing anyone to say anything. What Congress has done here—requiring an ideological commitment relevant to the Government task at hand—is approved by the Constitution itself. Americans need not support the Constitution; they may be Communists or anarchists. But "[t]he Senators and Representatives . . . , and the Members of the several State Legislatures, and all executive and judicial Officers, both of the United States and of the several States, shall be bound by Oath or Affirmation, to support [the] Constitution." U.S. Const., Art. VI, cl. 3. The Framers saw the wisdom of imposing affirmative ideological commitments prerequisite to assisting in the government's work. And so should we.

NOTES

1. *A Unified Test.* In *AID*, the Court finally seems to have settled on a First Amendment test for funding conditions relating to speech. The downside is that, as Chief Justice Roberts concedes, applying the test may not always be difficult. We've already seen a similar problem before, where we saw that subject matter limits in defining a limited public forum are fine, but subject matter carve-outs from the forum are not. Yet, the distinction between the two situations can be elusive. But at least the Court has now provided a framework in which to conduct the argument.

2. *Should Coercion Be the Test?* Justice Scalia argues that, at least when the condition is relevant to the goal of a government program, the text should

be coercion. But he does not explain why as a general matter coercion should be the test for funding conditions. After all, the word "coercion" does not appear in the First Amendment. Instead, it forbids abridging the freedom of speech. Is it implausible to say that a person's freedom of speech has been "abridged" if they are required express a view or refrain from expressing a view in order to participate in a government program?

3. *The Oath of Office as an Analogy.* How good an analogy is the oath of office? Employees have a duty of loyalty toward their employers, and this is especially true for the employers' officers and directors. But this isn't true of independent contractors. Also, doesn't the new regulation allowing the use of affiliates underlie this argument? After all, this mechanism is designed to allow grants to go to recipients who actually do not share the government's purpose but are willing to go through a charade to meet the law's requirements. So the regulation seems ill-suited to test for genuine enthusiasm about the abortion funding restriction.

SECTION 7. THE RELIGION CLAUSES

A. FREE EXERCISE

Page 849. Insert after the *NOTES ON* HOSANNA-TABOR:

Recall that in the aftermath of *Smith*, Congress passed the Religious Freedom Restoration Act, which the Court then declared unconstitutional as applied to the states. RFRA does, however, remain in effect with regard to the federal government. In Burwell v. Hobby Lobby Stores, ___ U.S. ___, 134 S.Ct. 2751 (2014), a five-Justice majority held that RFRA immunized a closely held corporation from being required to provide contraception coverage to female employees. The majority concluded that RFRA protected the religious scruples of the owners, who sincerely objected to providing insurance for actions by employees that violated their religious views. The majority found that the government had a less restrictive alternative: extending to for-profit corporations an optional mechanism already provided to non-profit religious organizations. Justice Kennedy concurred to emphasize the narrowness of the decision in applying only to contraception (indeed, on the facts, only to forms of contraception that operate after intercourse has already occurred). He also stressed the existence of the off-the-rack accommodation already devised by the government. The four dissenters expressed concern that the Court had opened the door for corporations to object to coverage for a wide range of medical procedures and to claim religious exemptions from anti-discrimination and other laws. They also suggested that publicly held corporations might well try to take advantage of the ruling.

Burwell makes it clear that, as a practical matter, *Smith* has no significance as applied to the federal government, given the existence of RCRA. State governments, however, may retain more discretion regarding religious exemptions. But this does not mean they are entitled to excluded religious groups from programs unrelated to religion, as the following case indicates.

Trinity Lutheran Church of Columbia, Inc. v. Comer, 137 S.Ct. 2012. A Lutheran childcare center, which had merged with a church, applied for funding as part of a state program to install safer surfaces made of recycled tires at playgrounds at nonprofits. The government rejected the ground because of its strict policy against providing any funding to churches. In an opinion by **Chief Justice Roberts**, the Court held that this government policy was unconstitutional. According to the Court, because the policy "expressly discriminates against otherwise eligible recipients by disqualifying them from a public benefit solely because of their religious character," it was subject to "the most exacting scrutiny." The opinion concluded:

> The Missouri Department of Natural Resources has not subjected anyone to chains or torture on account of religion. And the result of the State's policy is nothing so dramatic as the denial of political office. The consequence is, in all likelihood, a few extra scraped knees. But the exclusion of Trinity Lutheran from a public benefit for which it is otherwise qualified, solely because it is a church, is odious to our Constitution all the same, and cannot stand.

Footnote 3 of the opinion, which was joined only by the Roberts, Kennedy, Alito, and Kagan, limited the scope of the opinion: "This case involves express discrimination based on religious identity with respect to playground resurfacing. We do not address religious uses of funding or other forms of discrimination." **Justices Thomas** and **Justice Gorsuch** wrote separately to express disapproval of this footnote. Justice Breyer, concurring in the judgement, emphasized the health and safety nature of the benefit in the case.

In dissent, **Justice Sotomayor** (joined by **Justice Ginsberg**), argued that the decision represented an important breach in the separation of church and state:

> To hear the Court tell it, this is a simple case about recycling tires to resurface a playground. The stakes are higher. This case is about nothing less than the relationship between religious institutions and the civil government—that is, between church and state. The Court today profoundly changes that relationship by holding, for the first time, that the Constitution requires the government to provide public funds directly to a church. Its decision slights both our precedents and our history, and its reasoning weakens this country's longstanding commitment to a separation of church and state beneficial to both.

The biggest immediate question posed by *Trinity Lutheran* relates to school voucher programs. The Court had previously held that it is constitutional to include religious schools in such programs. After *Trinity Lutheran*, is it constitutional to *exclude* religious schools from such programs?

In the following case, the Court returned to the issue of anti-religious animus, perhaps opening the door to widespread challenges to the enforcement of anti-discrimination laws against members of religious groups.

MASTERPIECE CAKESHOP V. COLORADO CIVIL RIGHTS COMM'N

___ U.S. ___, 138 S.Ct. 1719, ___ L.Ed.2d ___ (2018)

JUSTICE KENNEDY delivered the opinion of the Court.

In 2012 a same-sex couple visited Masterpiece Cakeshop, a bakery in Colorado, to make inquiries about ordering a cake for their wedding reception. The shop's owner told the couple that he would not create a cake for their wedding because of his religious opposition to same-sex marriages—marriages the State of Colorado itself did not recognize at that time. The couple filed a charge with the Colorado Civil Rights Commission alleging discrimination on the basis of sexual orientation in violation of the Colorado Anti-Discrimination Act.

The Commission determined that the shop's actions violated the Act and ruled in the couple's favor. The Colorado state courts affirmed the ruling and its enforcement order, and this Court now must decide whether the Commission's order violated the Constitution.

The case presents difficult questions as to the proper reconciliation of at least two principles. The first is the authority of a State and its governmental entities to protect the rights and dignity of gay persons who are, or wish to be, married but who face discrimination when they seek goods or services. The second is the right of all persons to exercise fundamental freedoms under the First Amendment, as applied to the States through the Fourteenth Amendment.

The freedoms asserted here are both the freedom of speech and the free exercise of religion. The free speech aspect of this case is difficult, for few persons who have seen a beautiful wedding cake might have thought of its creation as an exercise of protected speech. This is an instructive example, however, of the proposition that the application of constitutional freedoms in new contexts can deepen our understanding of their meaning.

One of the difficulties in this case is that the parties disagree as to the extent of the baker's refusal to provide service. If a baker refused to design a special cake with words or images celebrating the marriage—for instance, a cake showing words with religious meaning—that might be different from a refusal to sell any cake at all. In defining whether a baker's creation can be protected, these details might make a difference.

The same difficulties arise in determining whether a baker has a valid free exercise claim. A baker's refusal to attend the wedding to ensure that the cake is cut the right way, or a refusal to put certain religious words or decorations on the cake, or even a refusal to sell a cake that has been baked for the public generally but includes certain religious words or symbols on it are just three examples of possibilities that seem all but endless.

Whatever the confluence of speech and free exercise principles might be in some cases, the Colorado Civil Rights Commission's consideration of this case was inconsistent with the State's obligation of religious neutrality. The reason and motive for the baker's refusal were based on his sincere religious beliefs and convictions. The Court's precedents make clear that the baker, in his capacity as the owner of a business serving the public, might have his right to the free exercise of religion limited by generally applicable laws. Still, the delicate question of when the free exercise of his religion must yield to an otherwise valid exercise of state power needed to be determined in an adjudication in which religious hostility on the part of the State itself would not be a factor in the balance the State sought to reach. That requirement, however, was not met here. When the Colorado Civil Rights Commission considered this case, it did not do so with the religious neutrality that the Constitution requires. * * *

The neutral and respectful consideration to which Phillips was entitled was compromised here, however. The Civil Rights Commission's treatment of his case has some elements of a clear and impermissible hostility toward the sincere religious beliefs that motivated his objection.

That hostility surfaced at the Commission's formal, public hearings, as shown by the record. On May 30, 2014, the seven-member Commission convened publicly to consider Phillips' case. At several points during its meeting, commissioners endorsed the view that religious beliefs cannot legitimately be carried into the public sphere or commercial domain, implying that religious beliefs and persons are less than fully welcome in Colorado's business community. One commissioner suggested that Phillips can believe "what he wants to believe," but cannot act on his religious beliefs "if he decides to do business in the state." A few moments later, the commissioner restated the same position: "[I]f a businessman wants to do business in the state and he's got an issue with the—the law's impacting his personal belief system, he needs to look at being able to compromise." Standing alone, these statements are susceptible of different interpretations. On the one hand, they might mean simply that a business cannot refuse to provide services based on sexual orientation, regardless of the proprietor's personal views. On the other hand, they might be seen as inappropriate and dismissive comments showing lack of due consideration for Phillips' free exercise rights and the dilemma he faced. In view of the comments that followed, the latter seems the more likely.

On July 25, 2014, the Commission met again. This meeting, too, was conducted in public and on the record. On this occasion another commissioner made specific reference to the previous meeting's discussion but said far more to disparage Phillips' beliefs. The commissioner stated:

> "I would also like to reiterate what we said in the hearing or the last meeting. Freedom of religion and religion has been used to justify all kinds of discrimination throughout history, whether it be slavery, whether it be the holocaust, whether it be—I mean, we—we can list hundreds of situations where freedom of religion has been used to justify discrimination. And to me it is one of the most despicable pieces of rhetoric that people can use to—to use their religion to hurt others."

To describe a man's faith as "one of the most despicable pieces of rhetoric that people can use" is to disparage his religion in at least two distinct ways: by describing it as despicable, and also by characterizing it as merely rhetorical—something insubstantial and even insincere. The commissioner even went so far as to compare Phillips' invocation of his sincerely held religious beliefs to defenses of slavery and the Holocaust. This sentiment is inappropriate for a Commission charged with the solemn responsibility of fair and neutral enforcement of Colorado's antidiscrimination law—a law that protects discrimination on the basis of religion as well as sexual orientation.

The record shows no objection to these comments from other commissioners. And the later state-court ruling reviewing the Commission's decision did not mention those comments, much less express concern with their content. Nor were the comments by the commissioners disavowed in the briefs filed in this Court. For these reasons, the Court cannot avoid the conclusion that these statements cast doubt on the fairness and impartiality of the Commission's adjudication of Phillips' case. Members of the Court have disagreed on the question whether statements made by lawmakers may properly be taken into account in determining whether a law intentionally discriminates on the basis of religion. In this case, however, the remarks were made in a very different context—by an adjudicatory body deciding a particular case.

Another indication of hostility is the difference in treatment between Phillips' case and the cases of other bakers who objected to a requested cake on the basis of conscience and prevailed before the Commission.

As noted above, on at least three other occasions the Civil Rights Division considered the refusal of bakers to create cakes with images that conveyed disapproval of same-sex marriage, along with religious text. Each time, the Division found that the baker acted lawfully in refusing service. It made these determinations because, in the words of the Division, the requested cake included "wording and images [the baker] deemed derogatory."

The treatment of the conscience-based objections at issue in these three cases contrasts with the Commission's treatment of Phillips' objection. The Commission ruled against Phillips in part on the theory that any message the requested wedding cake would carry would be attributed to the customer, not to the baker. Yet the Division did not address this point in any of the other cases with respect to the cakes depicting anti-gay marriage symbolism. Additionally, the Division found no violation of CADA in the other cases in part because each bakery was willing to sell other products, including those depicting Christian themes, to the prospective customers. But the Commission dismissed Phillips' willingness to sell "birthday cakes, shower cakes, [and] cookies and brownies," to gay and lesbian customers as irrelevant. The treatment of the other cases and Phillips' case could reasonably be interpreted as being inconsistent as to the question of whether speech is involved, quite apart from whether the cases should ultimately be distinguished. In short, the Commission's consideration of Phillips' religious objection did not accord with its treatment of these other objections.

Before the Colorado Court of Appeals, Phillips protested that this disparity in treatment reflected hostility on the part of the Commission toward his beliefs. He argued that the Commission had treated the other bakers' conscience-based objections as legitimate, but treated his as illegitimate—thus sitting in judgment of his religious beliefs themselves. The Court of Appeals addressed the disparity only in passing and relegated its complete analysis of the issue to a footnote. There, the court stated that "[t]his case is distinguishable from the Colorado Civil Rights Division's recent findings that [the other bakeries] in Denver did not discriminate against a Christian patron on the basis of his creed" when they refused to create the requested cakes. In those cases, the court continued, there was no impermissible discrimination because "the Division found that the bakeries ... refuse[d] the patron's request ... because of the offensive nature of the requested message."

A principled rationale for the difference in treatment of these two instances cannot be based on the government's own assessment of offensiveness. Just as "no official, high or petty, can prescribe what shall be orthodox in politics, nationalism, religion, or other matters of opinion," it is not, as the Court has repeatedly held, the role of the State or its officials to prescribe what shall be offensive. The Colorado court's attempt to account for the difference in treatment elevates one view of what is offensive over another and itself sends a signal of official disapproval of Phillips' religious beliefs. The court's footnote does not, therefore, answer the baker's concern that the State's practice was to disfavor the religious basis of his objection.

NOTES

1. *Compelled Speech.* Phillips's primary claim was that the wedding cake was expressive conduct on his part. Perhaps the Court avoided this question because of the difficulty of line-drawing: if a wedding cake is covered, how about the flowers or the wedding photos? Or wedding-specific clothing like a bridal gown?

2. *Evidence of Intent.* How persuasive is the evidence that the decision was tainted by religious prejudice? The four dissenters argued that the state had drawn reasonable distinctions between cakes with verbal messages and wedding cakes. This seems to come back to the free speech issue: are wedding cakes inherently expressive in a way that distinguishes them from other goods. Suppose stores sell plain white T-shirts but offers customers the opportunity to have slogans printed on them. Would it be legitimate for the state to distinguish between a store owner who refused to sell a plain white T-shirt to a gay customer and one who refused to print a slogan that the owner found offensive?

3. *Narrow Ruling.* The Court's rationale explicitly left for another day the larger question whether wedding vendors or businesses can decline service to same-sex couples where the record does not contain any hostile comments about religious objections or claims that religious objectors are singled out for especially harsh treatment. But several passages in the majority opinion suggest resistance to any broad, religiously based exemption for merchants. The opinion emphasized that American "society has come to the recognition that gay persons and gay couples cannot be treated as social outcasts or as inferior in dignity or worth," such that "the exercise of their freedom on terms equal to others must be given great weight by the courts." It also said that while "religious and philosophical objections are protected, it is a general rule that such objections do not allow business owners to deny protected persons equal access to goods and service under a neutral and generally applicable public accommodations law." And it said that any principle favoring bakers like Phillips would have to be "sufficiently constrained, lest all purveyors of goods and services who object to gay marriages for moral and religious reasons in effect be allowed to put up signs saying 'no goods or services will be sold if they will be used for gay marriages,' something that would impose a serious stigma on gay persons." With Justice Kennedy retiring shortly after this decision was released, the import of these words is less clear than it might have been had he stayed on the Court.

B. THE ESTABLISHMENT CLAUSE

2. *Government Endorsement of Religion*

Page 864.   Insert at the end of the NOTE ON ALLEGHANY COUNTY AND THE *LEMON* DEBATE:

Although the Court was willing to inquire into legislative purpose in order to ensure religious neutrality in *Alleghany County*, it severely limited its inquiry into presidential purpose in *Trump v. Hawaii*, 138 S. Ct. 2392 (2018). This case involved the third effort by President Trump to ban travel from certain countries, the first two having been struck down by the lower courts. Because it found immigration matters to be a "fundamental sovereign attribute exercised by the Government's political departments largely immune from judicial control," the Court applied only what it called a truncated form of judicial review. Prior statements by President Trump provided at least strong suggestions of anti-Muslim animus. The majority said that it would consider this evidence but would "uphold the policy so long as it can reasonably be understood to result from a justification independent of unconstitutional grounds." It found "persuasive evidence that the entry suspension has a legitimate grounding in national security concerns, quite apart from any religious hostility." In dissent, Justice Sotomayor accused the majority of "ignoring the facts, misconstruing our legal precedent, and turning a blind eye to the pain and suffering the Proclamation inflicts upon countless families and individuals, many of whom are United States citizens." *Trump v. Hawaii* seems to carve out an area of minimal constitutional scrutiny cases involving government support of the borders, but probably does not affect Establishment Clause analysis more generally. The separation of powers aspects of the case, and the degree to which it frees the President from normal constitutional scrutiny, are discussed in detail in Chapter 8.

Page 865.   Insert at end of Note 3:

The Court has continued to find line drawing difficult in considering arguable governmental endorsements of religion. In Town of Greece, N.Y. v. Galloway, ___ U.S. ___, 134 S.Ct. 1811 (2014), the town board began public meetings with prayers by local ministers, some of which were sectarian. Given the long tradition of legislative prayers, the plurality opinion (by Justice Kennedy) did not find problematic the city's failure to broaden the roster of invitees to include more non-Christians or by the sectarian nature of the prayers. Concurring, Justice Scalia and Thomas found that the prayers were not comparable to coercive state establishments of the Founding era, even assuming that the Establishment Clause was incorporated into the Fourteenth Amendment. The dissenting Justices pointed out that citizens were required to attend board meetings on occasion in order to obtain zoning variances or other actions, and that non-Christians in the audience would undoubtedly perceive a message of exclusion from the succession of Christian ministers.

CHAPTER 7

FEDERALISM: CONGRESSIONAL POWER AND STATE AUTHORITY

■ ■ ■

SECTION 3. CONGRESSIONAL AUTHORITY TO PROMOTE CIVIL RIGHTS

C. CONGRESSIONAL POWER TO RESPOND TO DISCRIMINATION AGAINST WOMEN AND TO PROTECT FUNDAMENTAL RIGHTS

Page 1015. Insert the following Case and Notes at the end of Section 3, right after Problem 7–6:

SHELBY COUNTY, ALABAMA V. HOLDER
570 U.S. 529, 133 S.Ct. 2612, 186 L.Ed.2d 651 (2013)

CHIEF JUSTICE ROBERTS delivered the opinion of the Court.

[As illustrated in the *Katzenbach* Cases and *City of Rome* in the Casebook (pp. 952–66), § 5 of the Voting Rights Act of 1965 imposed preclearance requirements on jurisdictions defined in § 4(b) as those states or political subdivisions that on November 1, 1964 maintained a test or device that limited voting *and* had voting levels lower than 50% of the eligible voters in the 1964 election. Congress reauthorized the Act with minimal changes to the § 4(b) coverage formula in 1970 and 1975 (notably, to include language barriers to the definition of tests or devices limiting voting opportunities, which added Texas, Arizona, and Alaska to the roster of covered jurisdictions), and with no changes to the formula in 1982, and 2006. In 2006, Congress significantly expanded the § 5 preclearance restrictions. Shelby County fell under the coverage formula of § 4(b) but objected to preclearance on the ground that this portion of the Voting Rights Act was unconstitutional.]

Nearly 50 years later, [the § 5 preclearance requirements for covered jurisdictions] are still in effect; indeed, they have been made more stringent, and are now scheduled to last until 2031. There is no denying, however, that the conditions that originally justified these measures no longer characterize voting in the covered jurisdictions. By 2009, "the racial gap in voter registration and turnout [was] lower in the States originally

163

covered by § 5 than it [was] nationwide." *Northwest Austin Municipal Util. Dist. No. One* v. *Holder*, 557 U.S. 193, 203–204 (2009) (Casebook, p. 1014).[1] Since that time, Census Bureau data indicate that African-American voter turnout has come to exceed white voter turnout in five of the six States originally covered by § 5, with a gap in the sixth State of less than one half of one percent. See Dept. of Commerce, Census Bureau, Reported Voting and Registration, by Sex, Race and Hispanic Origin, for States (Nov. 2012) (Table 4b). * * *

[II.] In *Northwest Austin*, we stated that "the Act imposes current burdens and must be justified by current needs." And we concluded that "a departure from the fundamental principle of equal sovereignty requires a showing that a statute's disparate geographic coverage is sufficiently related to the problem that it targets." *Ibid.* These basic principles guide our review of the question before us. [The Chief Justice set forth the well-established federalist structure of government and the substantial "autonomy" the states have in structuring their electoral processes, especially in state elections.]

Not only do States retain sovereignty under the Constitution, there is also a "fundamental principle of *equal* sovereignty" among the States. *Northwest Austin* (emphasis added). Over a hundred years ago, this Court explained that our Nation "was and is a union of States, equal in power, dignity and authority." *Coyle* v. *Smith*, 221 U.S. 559, 567 (1911). Indeed, "the constitutional equality of the States is essential to the harmonious operation of the scheme upon which the Republic was organized." *Id.,* at 580. *Coyle* concerned the admission of new States, and *Katzenbach* rejected the notion that the principle operated as a *bar* on differential treatment outside that context. At the same time, as we made clear in *Northwest Austin*, the fundamental principle of equal sovereignty remains highly pertinent in assessing subsequent disparate treatment of States.

The Voting Rights Act sharply departs from these basic principles. It suspends "*all* changes to state election law—however innocuous—until they have been precleared by federal authorities in Washington, D.C." States must beseech the Federal Government for permission to implement laws that they would otherwise have the right to enact and execute on their own, subject of course to any injunction in a § 2 action. The Attorney General has 60 days to object to a preclearance request, longer if he requests more information. See 28 CFR §§ 51.9, 51.37. If a State seeks preclearance from a three judge court, the process can take years.

---

[1]   [Eds.] In *Northwest Austin*, the Court faced a "serious" constitutional challenge to §§ 4–5 but declined to address it, because there was a statutory ground for giving relief to a local government objecting to preclearance. To avoid the serious constitutional problems with §§ 4(b) and 5, the Court interpreted the "bailout" provision in § 4(a) broadly. Shelby County did not seek bailout under § 4(a), and so its challenge did not offer the Court a statutory solution.

And despite the tradition of equal sovereignty, the Act applies to only nine States (and several additional counties). While one State waits months or years and expends funds to implement a validly enacted law, its neighbor can typically put the same law into effect immediately, through the normal legislative process. [Invoking these background principles, the Chief Justice explained that *Katzbenbach's* willingness to uphold the extraordinary requirements in §§ 4–5 was premised upon their temporary remedial features.]

Nearly 50 years later, things have changed dramatically. Shelby County contends that the preclearance requirement, even without regard to its disparate coverage, is now unconstitutional. Its arguments have a good deal of force. In the covered jurisdictions, "[v]oter turnout and registration rates now approach parity. Blatantly discriminatory evasions of federal decrees are rare. And minority candidates hold office at unprecedented levels." *Northwest Austin.* The tests and devices that blocked access to the ballot have been forbidden nationwide for over 40 years. See § 6, 84 Stat. 315; § 102, 89 Stat. 400. [The Chief Justice summed up the progress by reference to data on voting turn-out, by race, that was compiled by the House and Senate Judiciary Committees for the 2006 reauthorization:]

	1965			2004		
	White	Black	Gap	White	Black	Gap
Alabama	69.2	19.3	49.9	73.8	72.9	0.9
Georgia	62.[6]	27.4	35.2	63.5	64.2	− 0.7
Louisiana	80.5	31.6	48.9	75.1	71.1	4.0
Mississippi	69.9	6.7	63.2	72.3	76.1	− 3.8
South Carolina	75.7	37.3	38.4	74.4	71.1	3.3
Virginia	61.1	38.3	22.8	68.2	57.4	10.8

See S. Rep. No. 109–295, p. 11 (2006); H. R. Rep. No. 109–478, at 12.

[In light of these data, the Chief Justice found Congress's reauthorization of the Voting Rights Act, with no change in the coverage formula, in 1982 and 2006 astonishing. In Part III of his opinion, the Chief Justice explained that applying the old 1965 formula to impose preclearance obligations on states, like Alabama, that had not used voting tests since 1965 and that now had virtually complete parity in racial voting levels over several election cycles, was constitutionally unsustainable. The Fifteenth Amendment was intended to ensure voting rights now and in the future, not to punish jurisdictions for past discriminations.]

[The government argued that Congress compiled an extensive record of continuing evasions by the covered jurisdictions.] The court below and the parties have debated what that record shows * * * . Regardless of how to look at the record, however, no one can fairly say that it shows anything approaching the "pervasive," "flagrant," "widespread," and "rampant" discrimination that faced Congress in 1965, and that clearly distinguished the covered jurisdictions from the rest of the Nation at that time. *Katzenbach*; *Northwest Austin*.

But a more fundamental problem remains: Congress did not use the record it compiled to shape a coverage formula grounded in current conditions. It instead reenacted a formula based on 40-year-old facts having no logical relation to the present day. The dissent relies on "second generation barriers," which are not impediments to the casting of ballots, but rather electoral arrangements that affect the weight of minority votes. That does not cure the problem. Viewing the preclearance requirements as targeting such efforts simply highlights the irrationality of continued reliance on the § 4 coverage formula, which is based on voting tests and access to the ballot, not vote dilution. We cannot pretend that we are reviewing an updated statute, or try our hand at updating the statute ourselves, based on the new record compiled by Congress. Contrary to the dissent's contention, we are not ignoring the record; we are simply recognizing that it played no role in shaping the statutory formula before us today. * * *

[The Chief Justice concluded with an invitation to Congress to reconsider the coverage formula and enact one that remedies current rather than historical impediments to exercise of the franchise by racial minorities.]

[**JUSTICE THOMAS** wrote a concurring opinion agreeing with the Chief Justice that the coverage formula in § 4 goes beyond Congress's Fifteenth Amendment authority, but also arguing that the preclearance requirements of § 5 are unconstitutional as well. The "extraordinary" burdens imposed by § 5 would be unconstitutional even if § 4 could be more narrowly tailored, Justice Thomas concluded.]

JUSTICE GINSBURG, with whom **JUSTICE BREYER, JUSTICE SOTOMAYOR,** and **JUSTICE KAGAN** join, dissenting.

In the Court's view, the very success of § 5 of the Voting Rights Act demands its dormancy. Congress was of another mind. Recognizing that large progress has been made, Congress determined, based on a voluminous record, that the scourge of discrimination was not yet extirpated. The question this case presents is who decides whether, as currently operative, § 5 remains justifiable, this Court, or a Congress charged with the obligation to enforce the post-Civil War Amendments "by appropriate legislation." [XV Am., § 2.] With overwhelming support in both

Houses, Congress concluded that, for two prime reasons, § 5 should continue in force, unabated. First, continuance would facilitate completion of the impressive gains thus far made; and second, continuance would guard against backsliding. Those assessments were well within Congress' province to make and should elicit this Court's unstinting approbation. * * *

After considering the full legislative record, Congress made the following findings: The VRA has directly caused significant progress in eliminating first-generation barriers to ballot access, leading to a marked increase in minority voter registration and turnout and the number of minority elected officials. 2006 Reauthorization § 2(b)(1). But despite this progress, "second generation barriers constructed to prevent minority voters from fully participating in the electoral process" continued to exist, as well as racially polarized voting in the covered jurisdictions, which increased the political vulnerability of racial and language minorities in those jurisdictions. §§ 2(b)(2)–(3). Extensive "[e]vidence of continued discrimination," Congress concluded, "clearly show[ed] the continued need for Federal oversight" in covered jurisdictions. §§ 2(b)(4)–(5). The overall record demonstrated to the federal lawmakers that, "without the continuation of the Voting Rights Act of 1965 protections, racial and language minority citizens will be deprived of the opportunity to exercise their right to vote, or will have their votes diluted, undermining the significant gains made by minorities in the last 40 years." § 2(b)(9).

Based on these findings, Congress reauthorized preclearance for another 25 years, while also undertaking to reconsider the extension after 15 years to ensure that the provision was still necessary and effective. [These findings, supported by exhaustive legislative hearings and factual materials assembled for Congress, are entitled to the Court's deference, argued Justice Ginsburg. This is particularly true where Congress is implementing the Fifteenth Amendment, whose text borrows the expansive language of § 2. Cf. *McCulloch* (an example of liberal construction for Congress's discretion in implementing core constitutional grants of authority).]

I begin with the evidence on which Congress based its decision to continue the preclearance remedy. The surest way to evaluate whether that remedy remains in order is to see if preclearance is still effectively preventing discriminatory changes to voting laws. See *City of Rome* (identifying "information on the number and types of submissions made by covered jurisdictions and the number and nature of objections interposed by the Attorney General" as a primary basis for upholding the 1975 reauthorization). On that score, the record before Congress was huge. In fact, Congress found there were *more* DOJ objections between 1982 and 2004 (626) than there were between 1965 and the 1982 reauthorization (490). 1 Voting Rights Act: Evidence of Continued Need, Hearing before the

Subcommittee on the Constitution of the House Committee on the Judiciary, 109th Cong., 2d Sess., p. 172 (2006) (hereinafter Evidence of Continued Need).

All told, between 1982 and 2006, DOJ objections blocked over 700 voting changes based on a determination that the changes were discriminatory. H.R. Rep. No. 109–478, at 21. Congress found that the majority of DOJ objections included findings of discriminatory intent, and that the changes blocked by preclearance were "calculated decisions to keep minority voters from fully participating in the political process." H.R. Rep. 109–478, at 21. On top of that, over the same time period the DOJ and private plaintiffs succeeded in more than 100 actions to enforce the § 5 preclearance requirements. 1 Evidence of Continued Need 186, 250.

In addition to blocking proposed changes through preclearing, DOJ may request more information from a jurisdiction proposing a change. In turn, the jurisdiction may modify or withdraw the proposed change. The number of such modifications or withdrawals provides an indication of how many discriminatory proposals are deterred without need for formal objection. Congress received evidence that more than 800 proposed changes were altered or withdrawn since the last reauthorization in 1982. H.R. Rep. No. 109–478, at 40–41. Congress also received empirical studies finding that DOJ's requests for more information had a significant effect on the degree to which covered jurisdictions "compl[ied] with their obligatio[n]" to protect minority voting rights. 2 Evidence of Continued Need 2555. * * *

The number of discriminatory changes blocked or deterred by the preclearance requirement suggests that the state of voting rights in the covered jurisdictions would have been significantly different absent this remedy. Surveying the type of changes stopped by the preclearance procedure conveys a sense of the extent to which § 5 continues to protect minority voting rights. Set out below are characteristic examples of changes blocked in the years leading up to the 2006 reauthorization:

- In 1995, Mississippi sought to reenact a dual voter registration system, "which was initially enacted in 1892 to disenfranchise Black voters," and for that reason, was struck down by a federal court in 1987. H.R. Rep. No. 109–478, at 39. * * *

- In 2006, this Court found that Texas' attempt to redraw a congressional district to reduce the strength of Latino voters bore "the mark of intentional discrimination that could give rise to an equal protection violation," and ordered the district redrawn in compliance with the VRA. *League of United Latin American Citizens* v. *Perry*, 548 U.S. 399, 440 (2006). In response, Texas sought to undermine this Court's order by curtailing early voting in the district, but was blocked by an action to enforce the § 5 preclearance requirement. See Order in *League of United Latin American Citizens* v. *Texas*, No. 06-cv-1046 (WD Tex.), Doc. 8.

- In 2003, after African-Americans won a majority of the seats on the school board for the first time in history, Charleston County, South Carolina, proposed an at-large voting mechanism for the board. The proposal, made without consulting any of the African-American members of the school board, was found to be an " 'exact replica' " of an earlier voting scheme that, a federal court had determined, violated the VRA. 811 F.Supp.2d 424, 483 (DDC 2011). See also S. Rep. No. 109–295, at 309. DOJ invoked § 5 to block the proposal. * * *

[These examples, and others invoked by Justice Ginsburg, were only the "tip of the iceberg," as Congress received and credited ample evidence that covered jurisdictions evaded the VRA through subtle as well as blatant measures. Justice Ginsburg then considered evidence that § 4(b)'s coverage formula still addressed current and not just historical needs for remedy.]

There is no question, moreover, that the covered jurisdictions have a unique history of problems with racial discrimination in voting. Consideration of this long history, still in living memory, was altogether appropriate. The Court criticizes Congress for failing to recognize that "history did not end in 1965." But the Court ignores that "what's past is prologue." W. Shakespeare, The Tempest, act 2, sc. 1. And "[t]hose who cannot remember the past are condemned to repeat it." 1 G. Santayana, The Life of Reason 284 (1905). Congress was especially mindful of the need to reinforce the gains already made and to prevent backsliding. 2006 Reauthorization § 2(b)(9).

Of particular importance, even after 40 years and thousands of discriminatory changes blocked by preclearance, conditions in the covered jurisdictions demonstrated that the formula was still justified by "current needs." *Northwest Austin.* Congress learned of these conditions through a report, known as the Katz study, that looked at § 2 suits between 1982 and 2004. To Examine the Impact and Effectiveness of the Voting Rights Act: Hearing before the Subcommittee on the Constitution of the House Committee on the Judiciary, 109th Cong., 1st Sess., pp. 964–1124 (2005) (hereinafter Impact and Effectiveness). Because the private right of action authorized by § 2 of the VRA applies nationwide, a comparison of § 2 lawsuits in covered and noncovered jurisdictions provides an appropriate yardstick for measuring differences between covered and noncovered jurisdictions. If differences in the risk of voting discrimination between covered and noncovered jurisdictions had disappeared, one would expect that the rate of successful § 2 lawsuits would be roughly the same in both areas. The study's findings, however, indicated that racial discrimination in voting remains "concentrated in the jurisdictions singled out for preclearance." *Northwest Austin.*

Although covered jurisdictions account for less than 25 percent of the country's population, the Katz study revealed that they accounted for 56 percent of successful § 2 litigation since 1982. Impact and Effectiveness 974. Controlling for population, there were nearly *four* times as many successful § 2 cases in covered jurisdictions as there were in noncovered jurisdictions. The Katz study further found that § 2 lawsuits are more likely to succeed when they are filed in covered jurisdictions than in noncovered jurisdictions. Impact and Effectiveness 974. From these findings—ignored by the Court—Congress reasonably concluded that the coverage formula continues to identify the jurisdictions of greatest concern.

[Justice Ginsburg also invoked evidence before Congress that voting in the covered jurisdictions was more racially polarized than elsewhere in the country. H.R. Rep. No. 109–478, at 34–35. And she observed that the § 4 coverage regime was far from static, contrary to the Court's suggestions. Section 4(a), expanded in 1982, allows jurisdictions to bail out of § 4(b)'s coverage if they can demonstrate a history of voting regularity. Indeed, more than 200 jurisdictions have bailed out of the VRA since the 1982 Reauthorization.

[Justice Ginsburg took the Court to task for its treatment of the Court's own precedents for analyzing constitutional issues. Shelby County's challenge was a facial one: under the Court's precedents, such a challenge can succeed *only* if the challenger can show there is "no set of circumstances" to which the statute can constitutionally be applied. *United States* v. *Salerno*, 481 U.S. 739, 745 (1987). Why did the Court not engage the *Salerno* analysis? Apparently because Alabama is the classic case where the "old" formula applies in full force.]

Although circumstances in Alabama have changed, serious concerns remain. Between 1982 and 2005, Alabama had one of the highest rates of successful § 2 suits, second only to its VRA-covered neighbor Mississippi. In other words, even while subject to the restraining effect of § 5, Alabama was found to have "deni[ed] or abridge[d]" voting rights "on account of race or color" more frequently than nearly all other States in the Union. * * * Alabama's sorry history of § 2 violations alone provides sufficient justification for Congress' determination in 2006 that the State should remain subject to § 5's preclearance requirement.

A few examples suffice to demonstrate that, at least in Alabama, the "current burdens" imposed by § 5's preclearance requirement are "justified by current needs." *Northwest Austin.* In the interim between the VRA's 1982 and 2006 reauthorizations, this Court twice confronted purposeful racial discrimination in Alabama. In *Pleasant Grove* v. *United States*, 479

U.S. 462 (1987), the Court held that Pleasant Grove—a city in Jefferson County, Shelby County's neighbor—engaged in purposeful discrimination by annexing all-white areas while rejecting the annexation request of an adjacent black neighborhood. The city had "shown unambiguous opposition to racial integration, both before and after the passage of the federal civil rights laws," and its strategic annexations appeared to be an attempt "to provide for the growth of a monolithic white voting block" for "the impermissible purpose of minimizing future black voting strength." [Justice Ginsburg cited a second Supreme Court case and other court cases where Alabama was successfully charged with blatant violations of the Fifteenth Amendment and the VRA.]

A recent FBI investigation provides a further window into the persistence of racial discrimination in state politics. See *United States* v. *McGregor*, 824 F.Supp.2d 1339, 1344–1348 (MD Ala. 2011). Recording devices worn by state legislators cooperating with the FBI's investigation captured conversations between members of the state legislature and their political allies. The recorded conversations are shocking. Members of the state Senate derisively refer to African-Americans as "Aborigines" and talk openly of their aim to quash a particular gambling-related referendum because the referendum, if placed on the ballot, might increase African-American voter turnout. *Id.*, at 1345–1346 (internal quotation marks omitted). See also *id.*, at 1345 (legislators and their allies expressed concern that if the referendum were placed on the ballot, " '[e]very black, every illiterate' would be 'bused [to the polls] on HUD financed buses' "). These conversations occurred not in the 1870's, or even in the 1960's, they took place in 2010. * * *

The sad irony of today's decision lies in its utter failure to grasp why the VRA has proven effective. The Court appears to believe that the VRA's success in eliminating the specific devices extant in 1965 means that preclearance is no longer needed. With that belief, and the argument derived from it, history repeats itself. The same assumption—that the problem could be solved when particular methods of voting discrimination are identified and eliminated—was indulged and proved wrong repeatedly prior to the VRA's enactment. Unlike prior statutes, which singled out particular tests or devices, the VRA is grounded in Congress' recognition of the "variety and persistence" of measures designed to impair minority voting rights. *Katzenbach.* In truth, the evolution of voting discrimination into more subtle second-generation barriers is powerful evidence that a remedy as effective as preclearance remains vital to protect minority voting rights and prevent backsliding. * * *

NOTES ON SHELBY COUNTY

1. *The Doctrinal Debate.* Does the Chief Justice have satisfactory answers to the doctrinal issues raised by Justice Ginsburg's dissenting

opinion? To her examination of the record? The Chief Justice's primary strategy is to escape from the overwhelming congressional record of § 5 violations by Alabama and other covered jurisdictions, by leaving § 5 intact as a formal matter, and only striking down § 4(b)'s coverage formula. Is that a successful strategy, in your view?

Consider the Court's failure to engage Justice Ginsburg's charge that the majority was violating the doctrine established by *United States* v. *Salerno*, 481 U.S. 739, 745 (1987). That is, Shelby County's challenge to the VRA was a facial challenge; under *Salerno,* the challenger was required to show that there was "no set of circumstances" to which the VRA could constitutionally be applied. This seems hard to accomplish, as Justice Ginsburg demonstrated. How should the Chief Justice have responded? Does his response hinge upon his clever choice to focus his constitutional fire on § 4(b), and not § 5?

2. *The Equality of the States as a Strong Background Norm.* The Chief Justice's opinion in *Shelby County* is now a citation for a constitutional norm that all states must, presumptively, be treated the same. What is the source of this norm? It does not appear anywhere in the Constitution, or even in *The Federalist.* The Chief Justice cites *Coyle* v. *Smith* but immediately concedes that *Coyle* created the "equal footing doctrine," relating to the admission of new states under U.S. Const., art. IV, § 3, cl. 1; see Sonia Sotomayor de Noonen, Note, *Statehood and the Equal Footing Doctrine: The Case for Puerto Rican Seabed Rights*, 88 Yale L.J. 825 (1979) (demonstrating that the equal footing doctrine does not prevent different treatment for new states, grounded upon demonstrated need).

Justices Scalia and Thomas are strong adherents to the disciplining mechanism of "original meaning," but how can they join an opinion that relies centrally on an idea that has no textual basis in the Constitution? Moreover, they object to nontextual constitutional precepts on this ground as well: without a basis in the constitutional text, these precepts are ungrounded and prey to ad hoc judicial efforts to make up the rules as new cases arise.

How far does the Court's state equal treatment precept extend? For example, if Congress decided that all nuclear waste materials would be stored in Nevada, over the objections of its citizens, would *Shelby County* stand in the way? Would the Court require Congress to spread the waste proportionately among all 50 states? Does it make a difference in your analysis that Article I, § 9, cl. 4 of the Constitution imposes a proportionality requirement upon "direct" taxation by the federal government? Why is there need for a Direct Taxation Clause in the Constitution of 1789 if it already embodied a background norm of state equal treatment? The Sixteenth Amendment negated the Direct Taxation Clause: How does this affect the willingness of a strict textualist to create a norm of state equal treatment?

3. *The End of the Second Reconstruction?* Note the parallel to the Court's evolving *Brown II* jurisprudence, set forth in Chapter 2, § 2C2 of the Casebook. Justices Scalia and Thomas have insisted in the *Brown II* cases that there is a laches limitation to constitutional remedies: once extraordinary

remedies have been implemented for a period of time, and jurisdictions have formally acquiesced in them, courts must relinquish jurisdiction, even if (de facto) racial segregation continues. See also *Parents Involved in Community Schools v. Seattle School District No. 1* (Casebook, pp. 333–53), where the Court rebuked local efforts to create integrated schools through race-sensitive criteria.

In *Shelby County*, the Court majority reveals a similar impatience with longstanding remediation by Congress (rather than the Court) and terminates the process upon a finding that covered jurisdictions have formally acquiesced in the remedies. As in the school segregation cases, the liberal Justices dissent, on the ground that there is evidence of continuing exclusions based upon race. In the school context, the winding down of judicial monitoring has coincided with rising levels of segregation—precisely the phenomenon Justice Ginsburg warns will happen in the voting context.

Press accounts within days of the Court's decision announced that several southern states planned to implement new voter identification and other restrictive laws; some states will redistrict in the wake of the Court's ruling. Before *Shelby County,* all such actions would have required preclearance, and therefore a review and often negotiation process with the Department of Justice. After *Shelby County,* such laws might still be challenged under § 2, which the Court left in place but has interpreted narrowly.

Is this process a judicial renunciation of the Reconstruction Amendments? Or, less dramatically, a retreat from the deployment of significant judicial resources to solve a problem that seems intractable? Or a confession of pessimism that the federal government can assure progress in race relations through the dialectic approach pioneered in the *Brown II* cases and then expanded to focus on the Department of Justice in the VRA?

SECTION 4. BEYOND THE COMMERCE AND CIVIL RIGHTS ENFORCEMENT POWERS

C. THE TREATY POWER

Page 1031. Delete Problem 7–8 and insert the following materials at the end of Section 4:

Bond v. United States

134 S.Ct. 2077 (2014)

In 1997, the Senate ratified the Convention on the Prohibition of the Development, Production, Stockpiling, and Use of Chemical Weapons and on Their Destruction. S. Treaty Doc. No. 103–21, 1974 U. N. T. S. 317. To fulfill the United States' obligations under the Convention, Congress enacted the Chemical Weapons Convention Implementation Act of 1998. 112 Stat. 2681– 856. The Act forbids any person knowingly "to develop, produce, otherwise acquire, transfer directly or indirectly, receive, stockpile, retain, own, possess, or use, or threaten to use, any chemical weapon." 18 U.S.C. § 229(a)(1). It defines "chemical weapon" in relevant part as "[a] toxic chemical and its precursors, except where intended for a purpose not prohibited under this chapter as long as the type and quantity is consistent with such a purpose." § 229F(1)(A).

When Carol Anne Bond, a microbiologist, learned that her best friend was pregnant with a child whose father was her own husband, Bond spread an arsenic-based chemical on the other woman's car door, the front door of her house, and her mailbox. Bond's hope was to harass the cheating friend and make her sick, but the only injury sustained by the other woman was a slight burn on one finger. Because the chemical was "toxic," however, federal prosecutors charged Bond with two counts of violating the 1998 Implementation Act. Bond responded that Congress had no authority to adopt this statute. On appeal, the Government relied on Congress's Treaty Power, as understood in *Missouri v. Holland*. Bond urged the Court to overrule *Holland*.

Writing for the Court, **CHIEF JUSTICE ROBERTS** declined to rule on the constitutional issue, because a statutory issue resolved the case: Bond did not fall within the ambit of the statute. To be sure, she had used a chemical considered "toxic" under the Convention and as defined by the Implementation Act, but a literal application of the statute "would 'dramatically intrude[ ] upon traditional state criminal jurisdiction,' and we avoid reading statutes to have such reach in the absence of a clear indication that they do. *United States* v. *Bass*, 404 U.S. 336, 350 (1971)."

The Court held that that "it is appropriate to refer to basic principles of federalism embodied in the Constitution to resolve ambiguity in a federal statute. In this case, the ambiguity derives from the improbably broad reach of the key statutory definition given the term—'chemical weapon'—being defined; the deeply serious consequences of adopting such a boundless reading; and the lack of any apparent need to do so in light of the context from which the statute arose—a treaty about chemical warfare and terrorism. We conclude that, in this curious case, we can insist on a clear indication that Congress meant to reach purely local crimes, before interpreting the statute's expansive language in a way that intrudes on the police power of the States. See *Bass*."

Joined by Justices Thomas and Alito, **JUSTICE SCALIA** rejected the Court's interpretation of the statute, for it clearly covered Bond's vengeful activities. But Justice Scalia (joined by Justice Thomas) concurred in the Court's judgment on the ground that the Treaty Clause vests no authority in Congress to adopt statutes that do not fall within one of its enumerated powers (such as the Commerce Clause power, which had been waived as a basis for the statute in this appeal). Justices Scalia and Thomas would have overruled *Missouri v. Holland*.

Justice Scalia rejected the Government's *Holland*-based argument that the 1998 Implementation Act was "necessary and proper" to carry out Congress's and the President's exercise of the Treaty Power set forth in Article II. Under the Necessary and Proper Clause, Congress has the authority to facilitate treaty-making, such as funding presidential treaty negotiators. "But a power to help the President *make* treaties is not a power to *implement* treaties already made. See generally Rosenkranz, Executing the Treaty Power, 118 Harv. L. Rev. 1867 (2005) [Casebook, p. 1029]. Once a treaty has been made, Congress's power to do what is 'necessary and proper' to assist the making of treaties drops out of the picture. To legislate compliance with the United States' treaty obligations, Congress must rely upon its independent (though quite robust) Article I, § 8, powers."

Justice Scalia warned that strict compliance with the Constitution's structure is especially important in an era when treaties have become multilateral regulatory regimes, requiring signatories to regulate private businesses and persons as well as public activities. The constitutional limitations protecting private persons against federal governmental regulation, such as the limits enforced in *Lopez* and *Morrison*, would be easily negated under the Government's reading of *Missouri v. Holland.*

Thus, Justice Scalia worried about "the possibilities of what the Federal Government may accomplish, with the right treaty in hand, are endless and hardly farfetched. It could begin, as some scholars have suggested, with abrogation of this Court's constitutional rulings. For example, the holding that a statute prohibiting the carrying of firearms near schools went beyond Congress's enumerated powers, *Lopez*, could be reversed by negotiating a treaty with Latvia providing that neither sovereign would permit the carrying of guns near schools. Similarly, Congress could reenact the invalidated part of the Violence Against Women Act of 1994 that provided a civil remedy for victims of gender motivated violence, just so long as there were a treaty on point—and some authors think there already is, see MacKinnon, The Supreme Court, 1999 Term, Comment,114 Harv. L. Rev. 135, 167 (2000)."

In a separate concurring opinion, JUSTICE THOMAS (joined by Justices Scalia and Alito) argued for a narrow understanding of the Treaty Power itself. In other words, the President and the Senate have no authority to enter into a treaty that does not have a "nexus to foreign relations." Such a limitation on the Federal Government's treaty power is needed not only to preserve "the basic constitutional distinction between domestic and foreign powers, see *Curtiss-Wright Export Corp.* [Casebook, pp. 1190–91]," but also to protect the personal liberties that derive from the Constitution's diffusion of sovereign power, argued Justice Thomas. "And a treaty-based police power would pose an even greater threat when exercised through a self-executing treaty because it would circumvent the role of the House of Representatives in the legislative process."

Justice Thomas surveyed the leading pre-1789 treatises by Grotius, Pufendorf, and Vattel, as well as contemporary dictionaries and practice. When they adopted the Constitution in 1789, We the People would have understood the power to make "treaties" to have been a power to enter into agreements relating to "international intercourse" (i.e., war and peace, alliances with other countries, foreign trade) and *not* a power to regulate domestic activities. So the

United States could have entered into a treaty binding signatory nations to cease using chemical weapons, but no one in 1789 would have thought a treaty could make chemistry-based harassment by private persons a crime (the Bond case).

Justice Thomas argued that this original meaning was consistent with the actual ratifying debates as well. "In essays during the ratification campaign in New York, James Madison took the view that the Treaty Power was inherently limited. The Federal Government's powers, Madison wrote, 'will be exercised principally on external objects, as war, peace, negotiation, and foreign commerce'—the traditional subjects of treaty-making. The Federalist No. 45. If the 'external' Treaty Power contained a capacious domestic regulatory authority, that would plainly conflict with Madison's firm understanding that '[t]he powers delegated by the proposed Constitution to the Federal Government, are few and defined.' *Ibid*. Madison evidently saw no conflict, however, because the Treaty Power included authority to 'regulate the intercourse with foreign nations' rather than all domestic affairs. [The Federalist] No. 42." Madison elaborated on this position during the Virginia ratifying convention, which contained the most detailed discussion of the Treaty Power.

In an extensive discussion, Justice Thomas invoked Hamilton and other Framers, as well as post-ratification practice (such as the congressional debates over the Jay Treaty in 1796) and judicial precedent. Indeed, *Missouri v. Holland* is consistent with this understanding of the Treaty Power, for the treaty in that case covered only *migratory birds,* namely, those traversing national borders.

In a separate concurring opinion, **JUSTICE ALITO** agreed with Justice Scalia that the 1998 Implementation Act reached Bond's conduct but concurred in the Court's judgment because he found the statute unconstitutional. He did not have to reach the issue of overruling *Missouri v. Holland,* because he (like Justice Thomas) viewed the Treaty Power as limited to matters of "international intercourse."

Query: Unlike the commentators discussed in Casebook, pp. 1028–31, Justice Alito would narrow Congress's authority without overruling *Missouri v. Holland*. How about that as a constitutional strategy? Does Justice Thomas's original meaning case for such a position strike you as persuasive? Does Justice Thomas's precept for treaty invalidity represent an easily justiciable standard?

For example, can the United States enter into a treaty prohibiting torture by government officials? How is that a regulation of "international intercourse"? If an anti-torture treaty falls outside the Treaty Power, then hundreds of treaties are invalid: To what extent does the nation's practice in the last century augur against such a ruling? If an anti-torture treaty falls within the Treaty Power, then why shouldn't a treaty aimed at violence against women?

United States v. Windsor

570 U.S. 744 (2013)

Edith Windsor was legally married to her life partner, Thea Spyer, at the time her partner died. Nonetheless, pursuant to § 3 of the Defense of Marriage Act, Windsor did not have the benefit of the spousal exclusion for federal estate tax purposes and had to pay $363,000 in estate taxes that a different-sex married couple would have owed. Windsor challenged DOMA § 3 as an unconstitutional discrimination against her. The Supreme Court sustained Windsor's challenge, and we excerpt the Court's debate in Chapters 4 (the equal protection issue) and 9 (the constitutional standing issues) of this Supplement.

In Part III of his opinion for the Court, **JUSTICE KENNEDY** prefaced his discussion of the merits of the challenge to DOMA with a discussion of federalism. "By history and tradition the definition and regulation of marriage, as will be discussed in more detail, has been treated as being within the authority and realm of the separate States. Yet it is further established that Congress, in enacting discrete statutes, can make determinations that bear on marital rights and privileges."

Thus, Congress has not always felt confined to "marriages" as defined by state law. "In addressing the interaction of state domestic relations and federal immigration law Congress determined that marriages 'entered into for the purpose of procuring an alien's admission [to the United States] as an immigrant' will not qualify the noncitizen for that status, even if the noncitizen's marriage is valid and proper for state-law purposes. 8 U.S.C. § 1186a(b)(1). And in establishing income-based criteria for Social Security benefits, Congress decided that although state law would determine in general who qualifies as an applicant's spouse, common-law marriages also should be recognized, regardless of any particular State's view on these relationships. 42 U.S.C. § 1382c(d)(2)."

Justice Kennedy observed, however, that "DOMA has a far greater reach; for it enacts a directive applicable to over 1,000 federal statutes and the whole realm of federal regulations. And its operation is directed to a class of persons that the laws of New York, and of 11 other States, have sought to protect." This is significant, because "regulation of domestic relations" is "an area that has long been regarded as a virtually exclusive province of the States." *Sosna* v. *Iowa*, 419 U.S. 393, 404 (1976).

"The recognition of civil marriages is central to state domestic relations law applicable to its residents and citizens. See *Williams* v. *North Carolina*, 317 U.S. 287, 298 (1942) ('Each state as a sovereign has a rightful and legitimate concern in the marital status of persons domiciled within its borders'). The definition of marriage is the foundation of the State's broader authority to regulate the subject of domestic relations with respect to the '[p]rotection of offspring, property interests, and the enforcement of marital responsibilities.' *Ibid*. '[T]he states, at the time of the adoption of the Constitution, possessed full power over the subject of marriage and divorce . . .

[and] the Constitution delegated no authority to the Government of the United States on the subject of marriage and divorce.' *Haddock* v. *Haddock*, 201 U.S. 562, 575 (1906)."

For this reason, the large majority of federal statutes defer to state policy decisions with respect to domestic relations. E.g., *De Sylva* v. *Ballentine*, 351 U.S. 570 (1956) (Copyright Act). See also See *Ankenbrandt* v. *Richards*, 504 U.S. 689, 703 (1992) (federal courts generally abstain from adjudicating issues of marital or parental status or rights). From the very beginning of the Nation, "the common understanding was that the domestic relations of husband and wife and parent and child were matters reserved to the States." *Ohio ex rel. Popovici* v. *Agler*, 280 U.S. 379, 383–384 (1930)." Accordingly, each state has constructed the eligibility and rules for marriage in distinctive ways.

"Against this background DOMA rejects the long established precept that the incidents, benefits, and obligations of marriage are uniform for all married couples within each State, though they may vary, subject to constitutional guarantees, from one State to the next. Despite these considerations, it is unnecessary to decide whether this federal intrusion on state power is a violation of the Constitution because it disrupts the federal balance. The State's power in defining the marital relation is of central relevance in this case quite apart from principles of federalism. Here the State's decision to give this class of persons the right to marry conferred upon them a dignity and status of immense import. When the State used its historic and essential authority to define the marital relation in this way, its role and its power in making the decision enhanced the recognition, dignity, and protection of the class in their own community. DOMA, because of its reach and extent, departs from this history and tradition of reliance on state law to define marriage.

"[D]iscriminations of an unusual character especially suggest careful consideration to determine whether they are obnoxious to the constitutional provision." *Romer* v. *Evans*, 517 U.S. 620, 633 (1996) (quoting *Louisville Gas & Elec. Co.* v. *Coleman*, 277 U.S. 32, 37–38 (1928)). * * *

"The States' interest in defining and regulating the marital relation, subject to constitutional guarantees, stems from the understanding that marriage is more than a routine classification for purposes of certain statutory benefits. * * * By its recognition of the validity of same-sex marriages performed in other jurisdictions and then by authorizing same-sex unions and same-sex marriages, New York sought to give further protection and dignity to that bond. For same-sex couples who wished to be married, the State acted to give their lawful conduct a lawful status. This status is a far-reaching legal acknowledgment of the intimate relationship between two people, a relationship deemed by the State worthy of dignity in the community equal with all other marriages. It reflects both the community's considered perspective on the historical roots of the institution of marriage and its evolving understanding of the meaning of equality." In Part IV of his opinion for the Court, excerpted in Chapter 4 of this Supplement, Justice Kennedy ruled that DOMA § 3 violated the equal protection guarantee of the Fifth Amendment.

Four Justices dissented from Justice Kennedy's disposition; their arguments are excerpted an analyzed in Chapters 4 and 9 of this Supplement. But each of the dissenting opinions also addressed the Court's federalism discussion. **CHIEF JUSTICE ROBERTS'S** dissenting opinion said this: "The Court does not have before it, and the logic of its opinion does not decide, the distinct question whether the States, in the exercise of their 'historic and essential authority to define the marital relation,' may continue to utilize the traditional definition of marriage." Indeed, the Chief Justice maintained, the constitutionality of state (rather than national) discriminations in the definition of marriage ought to find support in the Court's analysis. "Thus, while '[t]he State's power in defining the marital relation is of central relevance' to the majority's decision to strike down DOMA here, that power will come into play on the other side of the board in future cases about the constitutionality of state marriage definitions. So too will the concerns for state diversity and sovereignty that weigh against DOMA's constitutionality in this case." Similar sentiments were expressed in the dissenting opinion of **JUSTICE ALITO**, joined by Justice Thomas.

In his dissenting opinion, **JUSTICE SCALIA** (also joined by Justice Thomas), opined that the Court's federalism discussion had no logical relevance to its constitutional holding. So why did the Court devote almost seven pages of its opinion to federalism? "My guess is that the majority, while reluctant to suggest that defining the meaning of 'marriage' in federal statutes is unsupported by any of the Federal Government's enumerated powers, nonetheless needs some rhetorical basis to support its pretense that today's prohibition of laws excluding same-sex marriage is confined to the Federal Government (leaving the second, state-law shoe to be dropped later, maybe next Term). But I am only guessing."

NOTES ON THE DOMA CASE AND FEDERALISM

1. *What Role Does the Federalism Discussion Play in the Court's Disposition in* Windsor? It appears that no Justice believed that DOMA § 3 was beyond the authority of Congress to legislate. If DOMA § 3 had defined marriage in federal statutes and regulations, across the board, as always *including* same-sex couples, would that inclusion have been unconstitutional, or constitutionally problematic in any way? At oral argument, the Solicitor General readily conceded that this would have been perfectly constitutional.

So what role, precisely, does the federalism discussion play in the Court's disposition? Put together Part III of *Windsor,* excerpted here, and Part IV, excerpted in Chapter 4 of this Supplement. Does the federalism discussion set up the equal protection discussion in any way? Consider *Village of Arlington Heights v. Metropolitan Housing Development Corp.,* 429 U.S. 252 (1977) (excerpted in Casebook, pp. 238–40), where the Court articulated a variety of considerations that might be the basis for a finding of "discriminatory intent" under *Washington v. Davis.*

2. *Federalism Values and the Next Round of Equal Protection Challenges to State Marriage Exclusions.* A key question after *Windsor* but before *Obergefell v. Hodges,* 135 S.Ct. 2584 (2015) (Chapter 5 of this Supplement) was decided was whether Justice Kennedy's federalism analysis would be relevant to federal challenges to mini-DOMAs like those at issue in *Obergefell* (namely, state exclusions of same-sex couples from their marriage laws, most of which were encoded in state constitutions). The key question in that period was whether *Windsor*'s emphasis on federalism would make federal courts more reluctant to strike down mini-DOMAs and declare a right of marriage equality in all 50 states. The *Windsor* court expressed no opinion on this matter, but the Chief Justice and Justices Thomas and Alito argued that federal courts should attend to the federalism reasoning, and give states a wider berth to exclude lesbian and gay couples from marriage than the Court gives the federal government.

Evaluate this last point in light of the constitutional values served by federalism (Casebook, pp. 897–900):

(1) **Liberty.** Does the "double security" promised by the Framers for people's "liberty" find protection in state regulatory authority to define civil marriage restrictively? Whose "liberty" matters: the liberty of lesbian and gay couples to enter civil marriage, or the liberty of parents and churches that do not want state validation of such relationships? If both, how does the liberty value of federalism cut in this debate?

(2) **Republicanism.** Not only are more citizens politically engaged at the state and local level, but the marriage equality issue has engaged the voters directly and deeply in most states, through ballot initiatives and referenda. California's Proposition 8 is an example. In 2012, marriage equality prevailed in all four states with ballot initiatives or referenda. DOMA resolved the marriage issue in a sweeping way at the national level. The *Windsor* dissenters argued that federal courts should be more reluctant to take this issue away from the political process at the state level.

(3) **Diversity.** Perhaps most important, leaving the marriage equality debate with the states, rather than imposing a national solution, would allow a diversity of regimes that would satisfy most Americans *and* provide useful information for undecided citizens to form or reform their views. As of July 25, 2014, nineteen states (and the District of Columbia) offered marriage licenses to same-sex couples, and another three offered civil unions or another form of recognition. Most LGBT citizens live in those states—while most citizens opposed to gay marriage on religious or other grounds live in nonrecognition states. What is wrong, the Chief Justice implores,

with letting the democratic process work through this issue, state by state?

Once *Obergefell* was decided only two years later, it became clear that the principles of federalism invoked in *Windsor* did not, ultimately, pose the bar to full marriage equality that the *Windsor* dissenters contemplated. Were these federalism values undervalued in *Obergefell*'s move to national marriage equality?

SECTION 6. NATIONALIST LIMITATIONS UPON STATE REGULATORY AUTHORITY

B. DORMANT COMMERCE CLAUSE DOCTRINE

1. *Discrimination Against Interstate Commerce*

Page 1121.   Add the following materials right after the *NOTE ON INTERSTATE TAXATION OF INTERSTATE COMMERCE*:

Comptroller of the Treasury of Maryland v. Wynne
135 S.Ct. 1787 (2015)

Maryland's personal income tax on state residents consists of a "state" income tax and a "county" income tax. Residents who pay income tax to another jurisdiction for income earned in that other jurisdiction are allowed a credit against the "state" tax but not the "county" tax. Nonresidents who earn income from sources within Maryland must pay the "state" income tax, and nonresidents not subject to the county tax must pay a "special nonresident tax" in lieu of the "county" tax. Brian and Karen Wynne were a Maryland married couple with income from many other jurisdictions; they challenged the state's refusal to give them credit against the county tax for similar taxes paid to other jurisdictions. **JUSTICE ALITO,** writing for a narrowly divided Court, ruled that this tax scheme violated the Dormant Commerce Clause, under the *Complete Auto Transit* test, refined for tax challenges by what the Court has called the "internal consistency" test. This test, which helps courts identify tax schemes that discriminate against interstate commerce, "looks to the structure of the tax at issue to see whether its identical application by every State in the Union would place interstate commerce at a disadvantage." *Oklahoma Tax Comm'n v. Jefferson Lines, Inc.,* 514 U.S. 179, 185 (1986)." By hypothetically assuming that every State has the same tax structure, the internal consistency test allows courts to isolate the effect of a defendant State's tax scheme. This is a virtue of the test because it allows courts to distinguish between (1) tax schemes that inherently discriminate against interstate commerce without regard to the tax policies of other States, and (2) tax schemes that create disparate incentives to engage in interstate commerce (and sometimes result in double taxation) only as a result of the interaction of two different but nondiscriminatory and internally consistent schemes. The first category of taxes is typically unconstitutional; the second is not. Tax schemes that fail the internal consistency test will fall into the first category, not the second: '[A]ny cross-border tax disadvantage that remains after application of the [test] cannot be due to tax disparities' but is instead attributable to the taxing State's discriminatory policies alone." See *J. D. Adams Mfg. Co.* v. *Storen*, 304 U.S. 307 (1938) (striking down Indiana statute taxing an in-state company's out-of-state gross receipts without providing a credit for taxes paid in other jurisdiction).

"Maryland's income tax scheme fails the internal consistency test. A simple example illustrates the point. Assume that every State imposed the following taxes, which are similar to Maryland's 'county' and 'special nonresident' taxes: (1) a 1.25% tax on income that residents earn in State, (2) a 1.25% tax on income that residents earn in other jurisdictions, and (3) a 1.25% tax on income that nonresidents earn in State. Assume further that two taxpayers, April and Bob, both live in State A, but that April earns her income in State A whereas Bob earns his income in State B. In this circumstance, Bob will pay more income tax than April solely because he earns income interstate. Specifically, April will have to pay a 1.25% tax only once, to State A. But Bob will have to pay a 1.25% tax twice: once to State A, where he resides, and once to State B, where he earns the income.

"Critically—and this dispels a central argument made by petitioner and the principal dissent—the Maryland scheme's discriminatory treatment of interstate commerce is not simply the result of its interaction with the taxing schemes of other States. Instead, the internal consistency test reveals what the undisputed economic analysis shows: Maryland's tax scheme is inherently discriminatory and operates as a tariff. This identity between Maryland's tax and a tariff is fatal because tariffs are '[t]he paradigmatic example of a law discriminating against interstate commerce.' *West Lynn* [Casebook, p. 1137]. Justice Alito also rejected the argument, posed by the Solicitor General as well as the dissenting Justices, that constitutional scrutiny may be abated because the "discriminatory" tax fell upon state individual residents (insiders) like the Wynnes, rather than out-of-state corporations (outsiders). "The argument is that this Court need not be concerned about state laws that burden the interstate activities of individuals because those individuals can lobby and vote against legislators who support such measures. But if a State's tax unconstitutionally discriminates against interstate commerce, it is invalid regardless of whether the plaintiff is a resident voter or nonresident of the State. This Court has thus entertained and even sustained dormant Commerce Clause challenges by individual residents of the State that imposed the alleged burden on interstate commerce, *Department of Revenue of Ky.* v. *Davis*, 553 U.S. 328, 336 (2008) [Casebook, p. 1119]; *Granholm* v. *Heald*, 544 U.S. 460, 469 (2005) [Casebook, p. 1133], and we have also sustained such a challenge to a tax whose burden was borne by in-state consumers, *Bacchus Imports, Ltd.* v. *Dias*, 468 U.S. 263, 272 (1984)."

JUSTICE SCALIA (joined by Justice Thomas) dissented, on the ground that the "negative Commerce Clause" is a "judicial fraud." It is not grounded in the text or original meaning of the Constitution, and judges should not expand the

Dormant Commerce Clause case law any further. Also dissenting, **JUSTICE THOMAS** (joined by Justice Scalia) found the negative understanding of the Commerce Clause inconsistent with the Constitution's regulation of state taxation through the Import Export Clause.

JUSTICE GINSBURG (joined by Justices Scalia and Kagan) dissented from the majority's application of the Court's Dormant Commerce Clause precedents. "Today's decision veers from a principle of interstate and international taxation repeatedly acknowledged by this Court: A nation or State 'may tax *all* the income of its residents, even income earned outside the taxing jurisdiction.' *Oklahoma Tax Comm'n* v. *Chickasaw Nation*, 515 U.S. 450, 462–463 (1995). In accord with this principle, the Court has regularly rejected claims that taxes on a resident's out-of-state income violate the Due Process Clause for lack of a sufficient 'connection' to the taxing State. *Quill Corp.* v. *North Dakota*, 504 U.S. 298, 306 (1992). But under dormant Commerce Clause jurisprudence, the Court decides, a State is not really empowered to tax a resident's income from whatever source derived. In taxing personal income, the Court holds, source-based authority, *i.e.,* authority to tax commerce conducted within a State's territory, boxes in the taxing authority of a taxpayer's domicile.

> "As I see it, nothing in the Constitution or in prior decisions of this Court dictates that one of two States, the domiciliary State or the source State, must recede simply because both have lawful tax regimes reaching the same income. True, Maryland elected to deny a credit for income taxes paid to other States in computing a resident's county tax liability. It is equally true, however, that the other States that taxed the Wynnes' income elected not to offer them a credit for their Maryland county income taxes. In this situation, the Constitution does not prefer one lawful basis for state taxation of a person's income over the other. Nor does it require one State, in this case Maryland, to limit its residence-based taxation, should the State also choose to exercise, to the full extent, its source-based authority. States often offer their residents credits for income taxes paid to other States, as Maryland does for state income tax purposes. States do so, however, as a matter of tax 'policy,' not because the Constitution compels that course."

As a general matter, "States have long favored their residents over nonresidents in the provision of local services. See *Reeves, Inc.* v. *Stake*, 447 U.S. 429, 442 (1980) (such favoritism does not violate the Commerce Clause). Excluding nonresidents from these services, this Court has observed, is rational for it is residents 'who fund the state treasury and whom the State was created to serve.' A taxpayer's home State, then, can hardly be faulted for making support of local government activities an obligation of every resident, regardless of any obligations residents may have to *other* States. Residents, moreover, possess political means, not shared by outsiders, to ensure that the power to tax their income is not abused. 'It is not,' this Court has observed, 'a purpose of the Commerce Clause to protect state residents from their own state taxes.' *Goldberg* v. *Sweet*, 488 U.S. 252, 266 (1989). The reason is evident. Residents are 'insider[s] who presumably [are] able to complain about and change the tax through the [State's] political process.' *Ibid.* Nonresidents, by contrast, are not similarly positioned to 'effec[t] legislative change.' *Ibid.* As Chief Justice Marshall, developer of the Court's Commerce Clause jurisprudence, reasoned: 'In imposing a tax the legislature acts upon its constituents. This is in general a sufficient security against erroneous and oppressive taxation.' *McCulloch* v. *Maryland.* The 'people of a State' can thus 'res[t] confidently on the interest of the legislator, and on the influence of the constituents over their representative, to guard them against . . . abuse" of the "right of taxing themselves and their property.' "

Additionally, Justice Ginsburg pointed to the longstanding state adherence to the rule announced in this case, namely, granting tax credits to residents who pay taxes elsewhere. "As Justice Holmes stated over a century ago, in regard to a 'mode of taxation . . . of long standing, . . . the fact that the system has been in force for a very long time is of itself a strong reason . . . for leaving any improvement that may be desired to the legislature.' *Paddell* v. *City of New York*, 211 U.S. 446, 448 (1908). Only recently, this Court followed that sound advice in resisting a dormant Commerce Clause challenge to a taxing practice with a pedigree as enduring as the practice in this case. See *Department of Revenue of Ky.* v. *Davis*, 553 U.S. 328, 356–357 (2008) [Casebook, p. 1119]. Surely that advice merits application here, where the challenged tax draws support from both historical practice and numerous decisions of this Court.

"The majority rejects Justice Holmes' counsel, observing that most States, over time, have chosen not to exercise plenary authority to tax residents' worldwide income. The Court, however, learns the wrong lesson from the 'independent *policy* decision[s]' States have made. This history demonstrates not that States 'doub[t]' their 'constitutiona[l]' authority to tax residents' income, wherever earned, as the majority speculates, but that the very political processes the Court disregards as 'fanciful' have in fact worked to produce policies the Court ranks as responsible—all the more reason to resist this Court's heavy-handed supervision."

Queries: What distinguishes *Wynne* from *United Haulers* [Casebook, p. 1116]. Justice Alito, a vigorous enforcer of the Dormant Commerce Clause precedents, wrote for the Court in *Wynne* but dissented in *United Haulers* and in *Davis* [Casebook, p. 1119]. Why would the Chief Justice, for example, vote differently in *Wynne* and *United Haulers*? Justice Ginsburg's dissenting opinion makes out a good case for the proposition (strongly echoed by Justice Scalia's dissent) that the Court's Dormant Commerce Clause jurisprudence has "jumped the shark" and has ventured into aggressive judicial management of state tax policy. But notice a pullback in the next big case.

SOUTH DAKOTA V. WAYFAIR, INC.
___ U.S. ___, 138 S.Ct. 2080, ___ L.Ed.2d ___ (2018)

JUSTICE KENNEDY delivered the opinion of the Court.

When a consumer purchases goods or services, the consumer's State often imposes a sales tax. This case requires the Court to determine when an out-of-state seller can be required to collect and remit that tax. All concede that taxing the sales in question here is lawful. The question is whether the out-of-state seller can be held responsible for its payment, and this turns on a proper interpretation of the Commerce Clause, U.S. Const., Art. I, § 8, cl. 3.

In two earlier cases the Court held that an out-of-state seller's liability to collect and remit the tax to the consumer's State depended on whether the seller had a physical presence in that State, but that mere shipment of goods into the consumer's State, following an order from a catalog, did not satisfy the physical presence requirement. *National Bellas Hess, Inc. v. Department of Revenue of Ill.,* 386 U.S. 753 (1967), [reaffirmed and followed in] *Quill Corp. v. North Dakota,* 504 U.S. 298 (1992). [South Dakota asks the Court to overrule those precedents.]

[Justice Kennedy reviewed the doctrinal history of the Court's general jurisprudence of the Dormant Commerce Clause.] The Court explained the now-accepted framework for state taxation in *Complete Auto Transit, Inc. v. Brady,* 430 U.S. 274 (1977). The Court held that a State "may tax exclusively interstate commerce so long as the tax does not create any effect forbidden by the Commerce Clause." *Id.,* at 285, 97 S.Ct. 1076. After all, "interstate commerce may be required to pay its fair share of state taxes." *D.H. Holmes Co. v. McNamara,* 486 U.S. 24, 31, 108 S.Ct. 1619, 100 L.Ed.2d 21 (1988). The Court will sustain a tax so long as it (1) applies to an activity with a substantial nexus with the taxing State, (2) is fairly apportioned, (3) does not discriminate against interstate commerce, and (4) is fairly related to the services the State provides. See *Complete Auto.* * * *

Each year, the physical presence rule becomes further removed from economic reality and results in significant revenue losses to the States. These critiques underscore that the physical presence rule, both as first formulated and as applied today, is an incorrect interpretation of the Commerce Clause.

Quill is flawed on its own terms. First, the physical presence rule is not a necessary interpretation of the requirement that a state tax must be "applied to an activity with a substantial nexus with the taxing State." *Complete Auto.* Second, *Quill* creates rather than resolves market distortions. And third, *Quill* imposes the sort of arbitrary, formalistic distinction that the Court's modern Commerce Clause precedents disavow. * * *

The *Quill* majority expressed concern that without the physical presence rule "a state tax might unduly burden interstate commerce" by subjecting retailers to tax-collection obligations in thousands of different taxing jurisdictions. But the administrative costs of compliance, especially in the modern economy with its Internet technology, are largely unrelated to whether a company happens to have a physical presence in a State. For example, a business with one salesperson in each State must collect sales taxes in every jurisdiction in which goods are delivered; but a business with 500 salespersons in one central location and a website accessible in every State need not collect sales taxes on otherwise identical nationwide sales. In other words, under *Quill,* a small company with diverse physical presence might be equally or more burdened by compliance costs than a large remote seller. The physical presence rule is a poor proxy for the compliance costs faced by companies that do business in multiple States. Other aspects of the Court's doctrine can better and more accurately address any potential burdens on interstate commerce, whether or not *Quill's* physical presence rule is satisfied.

The Court has consistently explained that the Commerce Clause was designed to prevent States from engaging in economic discrimination so they would not divide into isolated, separable units. See *Philadelphia v. New Jersey,* 437 U.S. 617, 623 (1978). But it is "not the purpose of the [C]ommerce [C]lause to relieve those engaged in interstate commerce from their just share of state tax burden." *Complete Auto.* And it is certainly not the purpose of the Commerce Clause to permit the Judiciary to create market distortions. "If the Commerce Clause was intended to put businesses on an even playing field, the [physical presence] rule is hardly a way to achieve that goal." *Quill* ([dissenting] opinion of White, J.).

Quill puts both local businesses and many interstate businesses with physical presence at a competitive disadvantage relative to remote sellers. Remote sellers can avoid the regulatory burdens of tax collection and can offer *de facto* lower prices caused by the widespread failure of consumers to pay the tax on their own. This "guarantees a competitive benefit to certain firms simply because of the organizational form they choose" while the rest of the Court's jurisprudence "is all about preventing discrimination between firms." *Direct Marketing* (Gorsuch, J., concurring). In effect, *Quill* has come to serve as a judicially created tax shelter for businesses that decide to limit their physical presence and still sell their goods and services to a State's consumers—something that has become easier and more prevalent as technology has advanced.

Worse still, the rule produces an incentive to avoid physical presence in multiple States. Distortions caused by the desire of businesses to avoid tax collection mean that the market may currently lack storefronts, distribution points, and employment centers that otherwise would be efficient or desirable. The Commerce Clause must not prefer interstate commerce only to the point where a merchant physically crosses state borders. Rejecting the physical presence rule is necessary to ensure that artificial competitive advantages are not created by this Court's precedents. This Court should not prevent States from collecting lawful taxes through a physical presence rule that can be satisfied only if there is an employee or a building in the State.

The *Quill* Court itself acknowledged that the physical presence rule is "artificial at its edges." That was an understatement when *Quill* was decided; and when the day-to-day functions of marketing and distribution in the modern economy are considered, it is all the more evident that the physical presence rule is artificial in its entirety.

Modern e-commerce does not align analytically with a test that relies on the sort of physical presence defined in *Quill*. In a footnote, *Quill* rejected the argument that "title to 'a few floppy diskettes' present in a State" was sufficient to constitute a "substantial nexus." But it is not clear why a single employee or a single warehouse should create a substantial nexus while "physical" aspects of pervasive modern technology should not. For example, a company with a website accessible in South Dakota may be said to have a physical presence in the State via the customers' computers. A website may leave cookies saved to the customers' hard drives, or customers may download the company's app onto their phones. Or a company may lease data storage that is permanently, or even occasionally, located in South Dakota. What may have seemed like a "clear," "bright-line tes[t]" when *Quill* was written now threatens to compound the arbitrary consequences that should have been apparent from the outset.

The "dramatic technological and social changes" of our "increasingly interconnected economy" mean that buyers are "closer to most major retailers" than ever before—"regardless of how close or far the nearest storefront." *Direct Marketing Assn. v. Brohl,* 135 S.Ct. 1124, 1135 (2015) (Kennedy, J., concurring). Between targeted advertising and instant access to most consumers via any internet-enabled device, "a business may be present in a State in a meaningful way without" that presence "being physical in the traditional sense of the term." *Id.,* at 1135. A virtual showroom can show far more inventory, in far more detail, and with greater opportunities for consumer and seller interaction than might be possible for local stores. Yet the continuous and pervasive virtual presence of retailers today is, under *Quill,* simply irrelevant. This Court should not maintain a rule that ignores these substantial virtual connections to the State.

The physical presence rule as defined and enforced in *Bellas Hess* and *Quill* is not just a technical legal problem—it is an extraordinary imposition by the Judiciary on States' authority to collect taxes and perform critical public functions. Forty-one States, two Territories, and the

District of Columbia now ask this Court to reject the test formulated in *Quill*. *Quill*'s physical presence rule intrudes on States' reasonable choices in enacting their tax systems. And that it allows remote sellers to escape an obligation to remit a lawful state tax is unfair and unjust. It is unfair and unjust to those competitors, both local and out of State, who must remit the tax; to the consumers who pay the tax; and to the States that seek fair enforcement of the sales tax, a tax many States for many years have considered an indispensable source for raising revenue.

[Justice Kennedy gave a deep bow to *stare decisis*, but the rule of law and reliance interests in following precedent are weaker in this case, and countervailing constitutional interests much stronger.] If it becomes apparent that the Court's Commerce Clause decisions prohibit the States from exercising their lawful sovereign powers in our federal system, the Court should be vigilant in correcting the error. While it can be conceded that Congress has the authority to change the physical presence rule, Congress cannot change the constitutional default rule. It is inconsistent with the Court's proper role to ask Congress to address a false constitutional premise of this Court's own creation. Courts have acted as the front line of review in this limited sphere; and hence it is important that their principles be accurate and logical, whether or not Congress can or will act in response. It is currently the Court, and not Congress, that is limiting the lawful prerogatives of the States.

Further, the real world implementation of Commerce Clause doctrines now makes it manifest that the physical presence rule as defined by *Quill* must give way to the "far-reaching systemic and structural changes in the economy" and "many other societal dimensions" caused by the Cyber Age. *Direct Marketing* (Kennedy, J., concurring). Though *Quill* was wrong on its own terms when it was decided in 1992, since then the Internet revolution has made its earlier error all the more egregious and harmful. * * *

[We omit the concurring opinion of **JUSTICE THOMAS.**]

CHIEF JUSTICE ROBERTS, joined by **JUSTICES BREYER, SOTOMAYOR,** and **KAGAN**, dissenting. * * *

I agree that *Bellas Hess* was wrongly decided, for many of the reasons given by the Court. The Court argues in favor of overturning that decision because the "Internet's prevalence and power have changed the dynamics of the national economy." But that is the very reason I oppose discarding the physical-presence rule. E-commerce has grown into a significant and vibrant part of our national economy against the backdrop of established rules, including the physical-presence rule. Any alteration to those rules with the potential to disrupt the development of such a critical segment of the economy should be undertaken by Congress. The Court should not act on this important question of current economic policy, solely to expiate a mistake it made over 50 years ago.

[The Chief Justice pointed out that *stare decisis* has much stronger bite in areas where Congress has the authority to regulate. Unlike most other constitutional issues, Congress has full authority to set baselines and override the Court's Dormant Commerce Clause decisions like *Bellas* and *Quill*.] Congress has in fact been considering whether to alter the rule established in *Bellas Hess* for some time. See Addendum to Brief for Four United States Senators as *Amici Curiae* 1–4 (compiling efforts by Congress between 2001 and 2017 to pass legislation respecting interstate sales tax collection); Brief for Rep. Bob Goodlatte et al. as *Amici Curiae* 20–23 (Goodlatte Brief) (same). Three bills addressing the issue are currently pending. Nothing in today's decision precludes Congress from continuing to seek a legislative solution. But by suddenly changing the ground rules, the Court may have waylaid Congress's consideration of the issue. Armed with today's decision, state officials can be expected to redirect their attention from working with Congress on a national solution, to securing new tax revenue from remote retailers. See, *e.g.,* Brief for Sen. Ted Cruz et al. as *Amici Curiae* 10–11 ("Overturning *Quill* would undo much of Congress' work to find a workable national compromise under the Commerce Clause.").

The Court proceeds with an inexplicable sense of urgency. It asserts that the passage of time is only increasing the need to take the extraordinary step of overruling *Bellas Hess* and *Quill*: "Each year, the physical presence rule becomes further removed from economic reality and results in significant revenue losses to the States." The factual predicates for that assertion include a Government Accountability Office (GAO) estimate that, under the physical-presence rule, States lose billions of dollars annually in sales tax revenue. But evidence in the same GAO report indicates that the pendulum is swinging in the opposite direction, and has been for some time. States and local governments are already able to collect approximately 80 percent of the tax revenue that would be available if there were no physical-presence rule. Among the top 100 Internet retailers that rate is between 87 and 96 percent. Some companies, including the online behemoth Amazon, now voluntarily collect and remit sales tax in every State that assesses one—even those in which they have no physical presence. To the extent the physical-presence rule is harming States, the harm is apparently receding with time.

The Court rests its decision to overrule *Bellas Hess* on the "present realities of the interstate marketplace." As the Court puts it, allowing remote sellers to escape remitting a lawful tax is "unfair and unjust." "[U]nfair and unjust to . . . competitors . . . who must remit the tax; to the consumers who pay the tax; and to the States that seek fair enforcement of the sales tax." But "the present realities of the interstate marketplace" include the possibility that the marketplace itself could be affected by abandoning the physical-presence rule. The Court's focus on unfairness and injustice does not appear to embrace consideration of that current public policy concern.

The Court, for example, breezily disregards the costs that its decision will impose on retailers. Correctly calculating and remitting sales taxes on all e-commerce sales will likely prove baffling for many retailers. Over 10,000 jurisdictions levy sales taxes, each with "different tax rates, different rules governing tax-exempt goods and services, different product category definitions, and different standards for determining whether an out-of-state seller has a substantial presence" in the jurisdiction. A few examples: New Jersey knitters pay sales tax on yarn purchased for art projects, but not on yarn earmarked for sweaters. Texas taxes sales of plain deodorant at 6.25 percent but imposes no tax on deodorant with antiperspirant. Illinois categorizes Twix and Snickers bars—chocolate-and-caramel confections usually displayed side-by-side in the candy aisle—as food and candy, respectively (Twix have flour; Snickers don't), and taxes them differently. [Citing *amicus* briefs for all these examples.]

The burden will fall disproportionately on small businesses. One vitalizing effect of the Internet has been connecting small, even "micro" businesses to potential buyers across the Nation. People starting a business selling their embroidered pillowcases or carved decoys can offer their wares throughout the country—but probably not if they have to figure out the tax due on every sale. And the software said to facilitate compliance is still in its infancy, and its capabilities and expense are subject to debate. The Court's decision today will surely have the effect of dampening opportunities for commerce in a broad range of new markets.

A good reason to leave these matters to Congress is that legislators may more directly consider the competing interests at stake. Unlike this Court, Congress has the flexibility to address these questions in a wide variety of ways. * * *

Here, after investigation, Congress could reasonably decide that current trends might sufficiently expand tax revenues, obviating the need for an abrupt policy shift with potentially adverse consequences for e-commerce. Or Congress might decide that the benefits of allowing States to secure additional tax revenue outweigh any foreseeable harm to e-commerce. Or Congress might elect to accommodate these competing interests, by, for example, allowing States to tax Internet sales by remote retailers only if revenue from such sales exceeds some set amount per year. See Goodlatte Brief 12–14 (providing varied examples of how Congress could address sales tax collection). In any event, Congress can focus directly on current policy concerns rather than past legal mistakes. Congress can also provide a nuanced answer to the troubling question whether any change will have retroactive effect. * * *

Query: Harbingers for the Future? There are three remarkable things about this case that speak to the future: (1) The Internet has changed the relationship among states, businesses, and consumers—and the Dormant Commerce Clause stands as a possible impediment to evolving state regulation and taxation. (2) Will *stare decisis* protect existing Dormant Commerce Clause precedents from being overruled? Our federalism chapter is filled with Supreme Court decisions overruling federalism precedents, and this is the most recent one, notwithstanding the Chief Justice's penetrating critique. (3) Expect to see more business-based challenges to state regulation—unless the Court retires the Dormant Commerce Clause. On the current Court, Justice Thomas is a longstanding critic of the entire line of cases, and newly appointed Justice Gorsuch made similar criticisms when he was serving on the Tenth Circuit. Notice that both are in the majority here.

C. SHOULD THE DORMANT COMMERCE CLAUSE BE LAID TO REST? ALTERNATE LIMITATIONS ON THE STATES

Page 1141. Add the following paragraphs right before the heading for The Import-Export Clause:

Justices Thomas and Scalia continued their attack on the "negative Commerce Clause" in *Comptroller of the Treasury of Maryland v. Wynne*, 135 S.Ct. 1787 (2015), the interstate taxation case excerpted earlier in this chapter of the Supplement. In separate dissenting opinions (each joined by the other), Thomas and Scalia maintained that the Court's jurisprudence is inconsistent with the original meaning of the Constitution. As they had argued previously, the Commerce Clause contains no "negative" language vetoing state regulation, and other provisions of the Constitution do regulate discriminatory state economic regulations and taxation. In *Wynne,* these Justices made out a more detailed case for the further propositions that in the founding era many states had taxes and regulations that did discriminate against interstate commercial activities and investments. Not only did the ratification debates say nothing about these laws, but they persevered after the Constitution of 1789 went into effect. For decades, no one suggested that such laws violated the Constitution. It was not until 1873 that the Supreme Court ruled that some laws of this nature did violate the Constitution. In his dissenting opinion, Justice Thomas said that he would not vote to invalidate a law for violating the Court's made-up "negative" Commerce Clause. In his dissenting opinion, Justice Scalia labeled the "negative" Commerce Clause a "judicial fraud," yet conceded that, for reasons of *stare decisis,* he would agree to invalidation of a state law openly discriminating against interstate commerce *or* falling within the four corners of one of the Court's Dormant Commerce Clause precedents.

As pointed out in the Casebook, p. 1121, there is at least one zealous enforcer of the Dormant Commerce Clause on the Court, namely, Justice Alito. And there are zealous opponents, namely, Justices Scalia and Thomas. (In 2016, Justice Scalia died. His successor, Justice Gorsuch is an even stronger critic of the Dormant Commerce Clause.) Among the middle group on the Court, however, it appears that Justices Ginsburg and Kagan may be reluctant enforcers at best.

Note that Justice Alito's opinion for the Court abandoned one justification for the Dormant Commerce Clause, namely, the process (representation-reinforcement) argument that the doctrine protects "outsiders" against predation by rent-seeking state "insiders." The Court emphasized two other justifications for the doctrine—namely, *stare decisis* and the Constitution's anti-balkinization (anti-tariff) purpose. Does this limited defense of Dormant Commerce Clause doctrine render it more vulnerable to its critics inside and outside the Court? Notice that *South Dakota v. Wayfair* overruled precedent to further constrict the reach of the Dormant Commerce Clause.

Is the Dormant Commerce Clause in more danger than ever before? If you were on the Court, would you be inclined to abrogate this line of cases? Or interpret the case law conservatively? If so, are the other constitutional protections against state intrusions onto interstate commerce (the balkanization concern) sufficient protections? Consider the possibilities in the materials that follow.

CHAPTER 8

SEPARATION OF POWERS

■ ■ ■

SECTION 1. ISSUES OF EXECUTIVE AGGRANDIZEMENT (IMPERIAL PRESIDENCY)

A. THE POST-NEW DEAL FRAMEWORK

Page 1189. Insert the following Case and Notes at the end of Section 1(A), right after Problem 8–1:

NATIONAL LABOR RELATIONS BOARD v. NOEL CANNING

572 U.S. ___, 134 S.Ct. 2550, 189 L.Ed.2d 538 (2014)

JUSTICE BREYER delivered the opinion of the Court.

Ordinarily the President must obtain "the Advice and Consent of the Senate" before appointing an "Office[r] of the United States." U.S. Const., Art. II, § 2, cl. 2. But the Recess Appointments Clause creates an exception. It gives the President alone the power "to fill up all Vacancies that may happen during the Recess of the Senate, by granting Commissions which shall expire at the End of their next Session." Art. II, § 2, cl. 3. We here consider three questions about the application of this Clause.

The first concerns the scope of the words "recess of the Senate." Does that phrase refer only to an inter-session recess (*i.e.,* a break between formal sessions of Congress), or does it also include an intra-session recess, such as a summer recess in the midst of a session? We conclude that the Clause applies to both kinds of recess.

The second question concerns the scope of the words "vacancies that may happen." Does that phrase refer only to vacancies that first come into existence during a recess, or does it also include vacancies that arise prior to a recess but continue to exist during the recess? We conclude that the Clause applies to both kinds of vacancy.

The third question concerns calculation of the length of a "recess." The President made the appointments here at issue on January 4, 2012. At that time the Senate was in recess pursuant to a December 17, 2011, resolution providing for a series of brief recesses punctuated by *pro forma* session[s]," with "no business ... transacted," every Tuesday and Friday through January 20, 2012. S. J., 112th Cong., 1st Sess., 923 (2011) (hereinafter 2011

193

S. J.). In calculating the length of a recess are we to ignore the *pro forma* sessions, thereby treating the series of brief recesses as a single, month-long recess? We conclude that we cannot ignore these *pro forma* sessions.

Our answer to the third question means that, when the appointments before us took place, the Senate was in the midst of a 3-day recess. Three days is too short a time to bring a recess within the scope of the Clause. Thus we conclude that the President lacked the power to make the recess appointments here at issue.

[II] Before turning to the specific questions presented, we shall mention two background considerations that we find relevant to all three. First, *the Recess Appointments Clause sets forth a subsidiary, not a primary, method for appointing officers of the United States.* The immediately preceding Clause—Article II, Section 2, Clause 2—provides the primary method of appointment. It says that the President "shall nominate, *and by and with the Advice and Consent of the Senate,* shall appoint Ambassadors, other public Ministers and Consuls, Judges of the supreme Court, and all other Officers of the United States" (emphasis added).

The Federalist Papers make clear that the Founders intended this method of appointment, requiring Senate approval, to be the norm (at least for principal officers). Alexander Hamilton wrote that the Constitution vests the power of *nomination* in the President alone because "one man of discernment is better fitted to analise and estimate the peculiar qualities adapted to particular offices, than a body of men of equal, or perhaps even of superior discernment." The Federalist No. 76, p. 510 (J. Cooke ed. 1961).

At the same time, the need to secure Senate approval provides "an excellent check upon a spirit of favoritism in the President, and would tend greatly to preventing the appointment of unfit characters from State prejudice, from family connection, from personal attachment, or from a view to popularity." *Id.,* at 513.

Thus the Recess Appointments Clause reflects the tension between, on the one hand, the President's continuous need for "the assistance of subordinates," *Myers* v. *United States,* 272 U.S. 52, 117 (1926), and, on the other, the Senate's practice, particularly during the Republic's early years, of meeting for a single brief session each year, see Art. I, § 4, cl. 2; Amdt. 20, § 2 (requiring the Senate to "assemble" only "once in every year"). We seek to interpret the Clause as granting the President the power to make appointments during a recess but not offering the President the authority routinely to avoid the need for Senate confirmation.

Second, *in interpreting the Clause, we put significant weight upon historical practice.* For one thing, the interpretive questions before us concern the allocation of power between two elected branches of Government. Long ago Chief Justice Marshall wrote that "a doubtful question, one on which human reason may pause, and the human judgment be suspended, in the decision of which the great principles of liberty are not concerned, but the respective powers of those who are equally the representatives of the people, are to be adjusted; if not put at rest by the practice of the government, ought to receive a considerable impression from that practice." *McCulloch* v. *Maryland*, 4 Wheat. 316, 401 (1819).

And we later confirmed that "[l]ong settled and established practice is a consideration of great weight in a proper interpretation of constitutional provisions" regulating the relationship between Congress and the President. *The Pocket Veto Case*, 279 U.S. 655, 689 (1929); see also *id.*, at 690 ("[A] practice of at least twenty years duration 'on the part of the executive department, acquiesced in by the legislative department, . . . is entitled to great regard in determining the true construction of a constitutional provision the phraseology of which is in any respect of doubtful meaning'" (quoting *State* v. *South Norwalk*, 77 Conn. 257, 264, 58 A. 759, 761 (1904))). * * *

There is a great deal of history to consider here. Presidents have made recess appointments since the beginning of the Republic. Their frequency suggests that the Senate and President have recognized that recess appointments can be both necessary and appropriate in certain circumstances. We have not previously interpreted the Clause, and, when doing so for the first time in more than 200 years, we must hesitate to upset the compromises and working arrangements that the elected branches of Government themselves have reached.

[III] The first question concerns the scope of the phrase *"the recess* of the Senate." Art. II, § 2, cl. 3 (emphasis added). The Constitution provides for congressional elections every two years. And the 2-year life of each elected Congress typically consists of two formal 1-year sessions, each separated from the next by an "inter-session recess." The Senate or the House of Representatives announces an inter-session recess by approving a resolution stating that it will "adjourn *sine die,*" *i.e.,* without specifying a date to return (in which case Congress will reconvene when the next formal session is scheduled to begin). The Senate and the House also take breaks in the midst of a session.

The Senate or the House announces any such "intra-session recess" by adopting a resolution stating that it will "adjourn" to a fixed date, a few days or weeks or even months later. All agree that the phrase "the recess of the Senate" covers inter-session recesses. The question is whether it includes intra-session recesses as well. In our view, the phrase "the recess" includes an intra-session recess of substantial length. Its words taken literally can refer to both types of recess. Founding-era dictionaries define the word "recess," much as we do today, simply as "a period of cessation from usual work." 13 The Oxford English Dictionary 322–323 (2d ed. 1989) (hereinafter OED) (citing 18th-and 19th-century sources for that definition of "recess"). The Founders themselves used the word to refer to intra-session, as well as to intersession, breaks. See, *e.g.,* 3 Records of the Federal Convention of 1787, p. 76 (M. Farrand rev. 1966) (hereinafter Farrand) (letter from George Washington to John Jay using "the recess" to refer to an intra-session break of the Constitutional Convention).

We recognize that the word "the" in "*the* recess" might suggest that the phrase refers to the single break separating formal sessions of Congress. * * * But the word can also refer "to a term used generically or universally." 17 OED 879. The Constitution, for example, directs the Senate to choose a President *pro tempore* "in *the* Absence of the Vice-President." Art. I, § 3, cl. 5 (emphasis added). And the Federalist Papers refer to the chief magistrate of an ancient Achaean league who "administered the government in *the* recess of the Senate." The Federalist No. 18, at 113 (J. Madison) (emphasis added). Reading "the" generically in this way, there is no linguistic problem applying the Clause's phrase to both kinds of recess. And, in fact, the phrase "the recess" was used to refer to intra-session recesses at the time of the founding. See, *e.g.,* 3 Farrand 76 (letter from Washington to Jay); New Jersey Legislative-Council Journal, 5th Sess., 1st Sitting 70, 2d Sitting 9 (1781) (twice referring to a 4-month, intra-session break as "the Recess").

The constitutional text is thus ambiguous. And we believe the Clause's purpose demands the broader interpretation. The Clause gives the President authority to make appointments during "the recess of the Senate" so that the President can ensure the continued functioning of the Federal Government when the Senate is away. The Senate is equally away during both an inter-session and an intra-session recess, and its capacity to participate in the appointments process has nothing to do with the words it uses to signal its departure.

History also offers strong support for the broad interpretation. We concede that pre-Civil War history is not helpful. But it shows only that Congress generally took long breaks between sessions, while taking no significant intra-session breaks at all (five times it took a break of a week or so at Christmas). * * * In 1867 and 1868, Congress for the first time took substantial, nonholiday intra-session breaks, and President Andrew Johnson made dozens of recess appointments. The Federal Court of Claims upheld one of those specific appointments, writing "[w]e have *no doubt* that a vacancy occurring while the Senate was thus temporarily adjourned" during the "first session of the Fortieth Congress" was "legally filled by appointment of the President alone." *Gould* v. *United States*, 19 Ct. Cl. 593, 595–596 (1884) (emphasis added). Attorney General Evarts also issued three opinions concerning the constitutionality of President Johnson's appointments, and it apparently did not occur to him that the distinction between intra-session and inter-session recesses was significant. See 12 Op. Atty. Gen. 449 (1868); 12 Op. Atty. Gen. 455 (1868); 12 Op. Atty. Gen. 469 (1868). Similarly, though the 40th Congress impeached President Johnson on charges relating to his appointment power, he was not accused of violating the Constitution by making intra-session recess appointments. Hartnett, Recess Appointments of Article III Judges: Three Constitutional Questions, 26 Cardozo L. Rev. 377, 409 (2005).

In all, between the founding and the Great Depression, Congress took substantial intra-session breaks (other than holiday breaks) in four years: 1867, 1868, 1921, and 1929. And in each of those years the President made intra-session recess appointments. [Justice Breyer included an Appendix to his opinion for the Court, with documentation of recess appointments.]

Since 1929, and particularly since the end of World War II, Congress has shortened its inter-session breaks as it has taken longer and more frequent intra-session breaks; Presidents have correspondingly made more intra-session recess appointments. Indeed, if we include military appointments, Presidents have made thousands of intra-session recess appointments. President Franklin Roosevelt, for example, commissioned Dwight Eisenhower as a permanent Major General during an intra-session recess; President Truman made Dean Acheson Under Secretary of State; and President George H. W. Bush reappointed Alan Greenspan as Chairman of the Federal Reserve Board.

Not surprisingly, the publicly available opinions of Presidential legal advisers that we have found are nearly unanimous in determining that the Clause authorizes these appointments. In 1921, for example, Attorney General Daugherty advised President Harding that he could make intra-session recess appointments. He reasoned:

> "If the President's power of appointment is to be defeated because the Senate takes an adjournment to a specified date, the painful and inevitable result will be measurably to prevent the exercise of governmental functions. I can not bring myself to believe that the framers of the Constitution ever intended such a catastrophe to happen." 33 Op. Atty. Gen. 20, 23.

We have found memoranda offering similar advice to President Eisenhower and to every President from Carter to the present. * * *

Similarly, in 1940 the Senate helped to enact a law regulating the payment of recess appointees, and the Comptroller General of the United States has interpreted that law functionally. An earlier 1863 statute had denied pay to individuals appointed to fill up vacancies first arising prior to the beginning of a recess. The Senate Judiciary Committee then believed that those vacancies fell outside the scope of the Clause. In 1940, however, the Senate amended the law to permit many of those recess appointees to be paid. Act of July 11, 1940, 54 Stat. 751. Interpreting the amendments in

1948, the Comptroller General—who, unlike the Attorney General, is an "officer of the Legislative Branch," *Bowsher*—wrote:

> "I think it is clear that [the Pay Act amendments'] primary purpose was to relieve 'recess appointees' of the burden of serving without compensation during periods when the Senate is not actually sitting and is not available to give its advice and consent in respect to the appointment, irrespective of whether the recess of the Senate is attributable to a final adjournment *sine die* or to an adjournment to a specified date." 28 Comp. Gen. 30, 37.

[Justice Breyer concluded that historical practice supported presidential appointments during intra-session recesses but further ruled that the President could not act when the Senate is in recess for fewer than 3 days, as the Constitution (Article I, § 5, cl. 4) bars the Senate from adjourning for more than 3 days without the consent of the House. Additionally, the Court ruled,] in light of historical practice, that a recess of more than 3 days but less than 10 days is presumptively too short to fall within the Clause. We add the word "presumptively" to leave open the possibility that some very unusual circumstance—a national catastrophe, for instance, that renders the Senate unavailable but calls for an urgent response—could demand the exercise of the recess-appointment power during a shorter break.

[IV] [The second issue was whether the "Vacancies that may *happen*" must be vacancies that arise during the recess, and not vacancies that persist during the recess. Justice Breyer favored the latter, broader interpretation.] We believe that the Clause's language, read literally, permits, though it does not naturally favor, our broader interpretation. We concede that the most natural meaning of "happens" as applied to a "vacancy" (at least to a modern ear) is that the vacancy "happens" when it initially occurs. But that is not the only possible way to use the word.

Thomas Jefferson wrote that the Clause is "certainly susceptible of [two] constructions." Letter to Wilson Cary Nicholas (Jan. 26, 1802), in 36 Papers of Thomas Jefferson 433 (B. Oberg ed., 2009). It "may mean 'vacancies that may happen to be' or 'may happen to fall'" during a recess. *Ibid.* Jefferson used the phrase in the first sense when he wrote to a job seeker that a particular position was unavailable, but that he (Jefferson) was "happy that *another vacancy happens* wherein I can . . . avail the public of your integrity & talents," for "the office of Treasurer of the US. *is vacant* by the resignation of Mr. Meredith." Letter to Thomas Tudor Tucker (Oct. 31, 1801), in 35 *id.*, at 530 (B. Oberg ed. 2008) (emphasis added).

Similarly, when Attorney General William Wirt advised President Monroe to follow the broader interpretation, he wrote that the "expression seems not perfectly clear. It may mean 'happen to take place:' that is, '*to originate*,'" or it "may mean, also, without violence to the sense, 'happen to exist.'" 1 Op. Atty. Gen. 631, 631–632 (1823). The broader interpretation, he added, is "most accordant with" the Constitution's "reason and spirit." *Id.,* at 632. * * *

The Clause's purpose strongly supports the broader interpretation. That purpose is to permit the President to obtain the assistance of subordinate officers when the Senate, due to its recess, cannot confirm them. Attorney General Wirt clearly described how the narrower interpretation would undermine this purpose:

> "Put the case of a vacancy occurring in an office, held in a distant part of the country, on the last day of the Senate's session. Before the vacancy is made known to the President, the Senate rises. The office may be an important one; the vacancy may paralyze a whole line of action in some essential branch of our internal police; the public interests may imperiously demand that it shall be immediately filled. But the vacancy happened to occur during the session of the Senate; and if the President's power is to be limited to such vacancies only as happen to occur during the recess of the Senate, the vacancy in the case put must continue, however ruinous the consequences may be to the public." 1 Op. Atty. Gen., at 632.

[What does history have to teach us? Justice Breyer found little relevant practice from the Washington, Adams, and Jefferson Administrations.] But the evidence suggests that James Madison—as familiar as anyone with the workings of the Constitutional Convention—appointed Theodore Gaillard to replace a district judge who had left office before a recess began. It also appears that in 1815 Madison signed a bill that created two new offices prior to a recess which he then filled later during the recess. See Act of Mar. 3, ch. 95, 3 Stat. 235; S. J. 13th Cong., 3d Sess., 689–690 (1815); 3 S. Exec. J. 19 (1828) (for Monday, Jan. 8, 1816). He also made recess appointments to "territorial" United States attorney and marshal positions, both of which had been created when the Senate was in session more than two years before. Act of Feb. 27, 1813, ch. 35, 2 Stat. 806; 3 S. Exec. J. 19.

[Upon the advice of Attorney General Wirt, the Monroe Administration followed the same understanding, as did every other Attorney General to opine on this issue.] Indeed, as early as 1862, Attorney General Bates advised President Lincoln that his power to fill pre-recess vacancies was "settled . . . as far . . . as a constitutional question can be settled," 10 Op. Atty. Gen., at 356, and a century later Acting Attorney General Walsh gave President Eisenhower the same advice "without any doubt," 41 Op. Atty. Gen., at 466. * * *

* * * No one disputes that every President since James Buchanan has made recess appointments to preexisting vacancies. * * *

[Did the Senate object? Not early on.] Then in 1863 the Senate Judiciary Committee disagreed with the broad interpretation. It issued a report concluding that a vacancy "must have its inceptive point after one session has closed and before another session has begun." S. Rep. No. 80, 37th Cong., 3d Sess., p. 3. And the Senate then passed the Pay Act, which provided that "no money shall be paid . . . as a salary, to any person appointed during the recess of the Senate, to fill a vacancy . . . which . . . existed while the Senate was in session." Act of Feb. 9, 1863, § 2, 12 Stat. 646. [Justice Breyer minimized the extent to which the 1863 Pay Act was a constitutional pushback from the Senate.]

In any event, the Senate subsequently abandoned its hostility. In the debate preceding the 1905 Senate Report regarding President Roosevelt's "constructive" recess appointments, Senator Tillman—who chaired the Committee that authored the 1905 Report—brought up the 1863 Report, and another Senator responded: "Whatever that report may have said in 1863, I do not think that has been the view the Senate has taken" of the issue. 38 Cong. Rec. 1606 (1904). Senator Tillman then agreed that "the Senate has acquiesced" in the President's "power to fill" pre-recess vacancies. *Ibid.* And Senator Tillman's 1905 Report described the Clause's purpose in terms closely echoing Attorney General Wirt. 1905 Senate Report, at 2 ("Its sole purpose was to render it *certain* that at all times there should be, whether the Senate was in session or not, an officer for every office" (emphasis added)).

[The President continued to make recess appointments for vacancies that arose before the recesses.] Then in 1940 Congress amended the Pay Act to authorize salary payments (with some exceptions) where (1) the "vacancy arose within thirty days prior to the termination of the session," (2) "at the termination of the session" a nomination was "pending," or (3) a nominee was "rejected by the Senate within thirty days prior to the termination of the session." Act of July 11, 54 Stat. 751 (codified, as amended, at 5 U.S.C. § 5503). All three circumstances concern a vacancy that did not initially occur during a recess but happened to exist during that recess. By paying salaries to this kind of recess appointee, the 1940 Senate (and later Senates) in effect supported the President's interpretation of the Clause.

[V] The third question concerns the calculation of the length of the Senate's "recess." On December 17, 2011, the Senate by unanimous consent adopted a resolution to convene "*pro forma* session[s]" only, with "no business . . . transacted," on every Tuesday and Friday from December 20, 2011, through January 20, 2012. At the end of each *pro forma* session, the Senate would "adjourn until" the following *pro forma* session. *Ibid.* During that period, the Senate convened and adjourned as agreed. It held *pro forma* sessions on December 20, 23, 27, and 30, and on January 3, 6, 10, 13, 17, and 20; and at the end of each *pro forma* session, it adjourned until the time and date of the next. The President made the recess appointments before us on January 4, 2012, in between the January 3 and the January 6 *pro forma* sessions. We must determine the significance of these sessions— that is, whether, for purposes of the Clause, we should treat them as periods when the Senate was in session or as periods when it was in recess. If the former, the period between January 3 and January 6 was a 3-day recess, which is too short to trigger the President's recess-appointment power. If the latter, however, then the 3-day period was part of a much longer recess during which the President did have the power to make recess appointments.

[The Court unanimously rejected the Solicitor General's argument that the *pro forma* sessions did not count as sessions, and hence did not break up the periods of recess.] We hold that, for purposes of the Recess Appointments Clause, the Senate is in session when it says it is, provided that, under its own rules, it retains the capacity to transact Senate business. The Senate met that standard here.

The standard we apply is consistent with the Constitution's broad delegation of authority to the Senate to determine how and when to conduct its business. The Constitution explicitly empowers the Senate to "determine the Rules of its Proceedings." Art. I, § 5, cl. 2. And we have held that "all matters of method are open to the determination" of the Senate, as long as there is "a reasonable relation between the mode or method of proceeding established by the rule and the result which is sought to be attained" and the rule does not "ignore constitutional restraints or violate fundamental rights." *United States* v. *Ballin*, 144 U.S. 1, 5 (1892).

In addition, the Constitution provides the Senate with extensive control over its schedule. There are only limited exceptions. See Amdt. 20, § 2 (Congress must meet once a year on January 3, unless it specifies another day by law); Art. II, § 3 (Senate must meet if the President calls it into special session); Art. I, § 5, cl. 4 (neither House may adjourn for more than three days without consent of the other). The Constitution thus gives the Senate wide latitude to determine whether and when to have a session, as well as how to conduct the session. This suggests that the Senate's determination about what constitutes a session should merit great respect. [Accordingly, Justice Breyer ruled that the Senate was in session during the *pro forma* sessions and, hence, that the short breaks between *pro forma* sessions could not trigger the Recess Appointments Clause.]

[VI] The Recess Appointments Clause responds to a structural difference between the Executive and Legislative Branches: The Executive Branch is perpetually in operation, while the Legislature only acts in intervals separated by recesses. The purpose of the Clause is to allow the Executive to continue operating while the Senate is unavailable. We believe that the Clause's text, standing alone, is ambiguous. It does not resolve whether the President may make appointments during intra-session recesses, or whether he may fill pre-recess vacancies. But the broader reading better serves the Clause's structural function. Moreover, that broader reading is reinforced by centuries of history, which we are hesitant to disturb. We thus hold that the Constitution empowers the President to fill any existing vacancy during any recess—intra-session or inter-session—of sufficient length.

[Joined by **CHIEF JUSTICE ROBERTS** and **JUSTICES THOMAS** and **ALITO, JUSTICE SCALIA** rejected the Court's analysis and maintained that the Recess Appointments Clause allowed presidential appointments *only* for vacancies that *arise* during *inter-session* recesses. Because these Justices agreed that the Obama appointments in this case violated the Constitution, they concurred in the Court's judgment. We discuss many of Justice Scalia's arguments in the Notes that follow.]

NOTES ON THE RECESS APPOINTMENTS CASE: THE MANY FACES OF HISTORY IN CONSTITUTIONAL INTERPRETATION

Noel Canning reflects the increasingly important role of history in the Supreme Court's interpretation of the Constitution's structure and particular provisions.

1.   *Original Meaning of Constitutional Text.* Like the Justices in the Second Amendment Cases, *Heller* (2008) and *McDonald* (2010) (Casebook, pp. 199–210), as well as the Brady Act Case, *Printz* (1997) (Casebook, pp. 1055–65), all nine Justices in the Recess Appointments Case trained their attention on the original meaning of the relevant text. The continued, even accelerating, rise of original meaning is significant. But it is not clear that methodology makes a difference. Original meaning theorists maintain that this interpretive approach is the only one that constrains result-oriented judges to rule neutrally and predictably. Is that correct?

Or does the debate among the Justices in *Noel Canning* support the critics, who say that original meaning inquiries are like looking out over the crowd and picking out your friends? For example, does Justice Breyer present a good case for the propositions that the "original meaning" of "recess" can include intra-session recesses and that a vacancy "happens" not only when it arises but also when it persists over time? Or is original meaning just window dressing?

As to the first issue, one historian has opined that "in government practice the phrase 'the Recess' *always* referred to the gap between sessions." Robert Natelson, *The Origins and Meaning of "Vacancies that May Happen During the Recess" in the Constitution's Recess Appointments Clause*, 37 Harv. J. L. & Pub. Pol'y 199, 213 (2014). Indeed, the Constitution uses the verb "adjourn" rather than "recess" to refer to the commencement of breaks *during* a formal legislative session. U.S. Const. art. I, § 5, cl. 1 and 4. In *Federalist* No. 67, Publius explained to the ratifying audience that appointments would require Senate consent "during the *session* of the Senate" but would be made by the

President alone *"in their recess,"* apparently using the term as a break between sessions.

As to the second issue, even Justice Breyer conceded that the narrow reading of "happens" is the "most natural" one. Justice Scalia maintained that it is the only "plausible" one, a view he felt was confirmed by early practice. "In 1792, Attorney General Edmund Randolph, who had been a leading member of the Constitutional Convention, provided the Executive Branch's first formal interpretation of the Clause. He advised President Washington that the Constitution did not authorize a recess appointment to fill the office of Chief Coiner of the United States Mint, which had been created by Congress on April 2, 1792, during the Senate's session. Randolph wrote: '[I]s it a vacancy which has *happened* during the recess of the Senate? It is now the same and no other vacancy, than that, which existed on the 2nd. of April 1792. It commenced therefore on that day or may be said to have *happened* on that day.' Opinion on Recess Appointments (July 7, 1792), in 24 Papers of Thomas Jefferson 165–166 (J. Catanzariti ed. 1990). Randolph added that his interpretation was the most congruent with the Constitution's structure, which made the recess-appointment power "an exception to the general participation of the Senate.' *Ibid.*" President Adams's Attorney General, Charles Lee, came to the same conclusion. Even Attorney General Wirt in 1823 admitted that the letter of the Constitution did not support his broad reading.

The asserted virtue of the original meaning methodology is that it yields more predictable interpretations and constrains judges better than any other method. Was the Court's interpretation of the Recess Appointments Clause (to include intra-session recesses of more than ten days, and sometimes for 3–10 days, to fill preexisting vacancies) *predictable*? Did the methodology *constrain* any Justice? It's hard to see how: the Court's four most conservative GOP-appointed Justices (all of whom served in the executive branch before becoming judges) voted with the Republican Senators challenging the President's action and giving the pro-labor NLRB a hard time, while the Court's four liberal Democrat-appointed Justices (only one of whom served in the executive branch) voted with the Democratic Solicitor General on most issues and gave hundreds of recess appointees a break. For all the argumentation in the opinions, it is hard to imagine that original meaning explains the Court's judgment—and it is far from clear that any Justice really voted with nothing else in mind.

2. *Historical Purposes of Constitutional Text.* Another way that history figures into the Justices' debate in *Noel Canning* is figuring out the purpose of the Recess Appointments Clause. Indeed, because he finds the text ambiguous, Justice Breyer's opinion for the Court relies mainly on the historical purpose of the Clause. But is he any more persuasive on that front than in his treatment of original meaning?

Justice Breyer said the purpose of the Clause is to keep the government running efficiently when the Senate is not prepared to do business (and confirm appointees)—but his main evidence for that proposition is the Opinion of Attorney General Wirt other executive branch officers far removed from the founding era. Justice Scalia responded: "The majority disregards another self-evident purpose of the Clause: to preserve the Senate's role in the appointment process—which the founding generation regarded as a critical protection against 'despotism'—by clearly delineating the times when the President can appoint officers without the Senate's consent. Today's decision seriously undercuts *that* purpose."

Indeed, viewed structurally, the Constitution protects the liberty of citizens and corporations by making it harder for potentially tyrannical officials to act without the cooperation of officials in other branches. See *Federalist* No. 51 (Madison) (the Constitution's system of checks and balances provides a "double security" for citizens). Thus, the obvious purpose of the Appointments Clauses is to check the President's ability to make appointments without considering the views of the Senate; that purpose is liberty-protecting and democracy-enhancing, as it assures the country that persons acceptable to both the nationally elected President and the state-representing Senate will serve in high office. In this scheme of things, the Recess Appointments Clause is an *exception*, to accommodate practical problems when the Senate is unavailable to participate. Exceptions are supposed to be narrowly construed, not broadly, as Justice Breyer urged. And the Court's broad interpretation of the Recess Appointments Clause opens the way for the already imperial President to secure even more power vis-à-vis Congress.

Justice Scalia made another point about purposive interpretation: "The rise of intra-session adjournments has occurred in tandem with the development of modern forms of communication and transportation that mean the Senate 'is always available' to consider nominations, even when its Members are temporarily dispersed for an intra-session break. Tr. of Oral Arg. 21 (Ginsburg, J.). The Recess Appointments Clause therefore is, or rather, should be, an anachronism—'essentially an historic relic, something whose original purpose has disappeared.' *Id.*, at 19 (Kagan, J.). The need it was designed to fill no longer exists, and its only remaining use is the ignoble one of enabling the President to circumvent the Senate's role in the appointment process." Justice Breyer responded that Justice Scalia was trying to read the Recess Appointments Clause out of the Constitution—which is not correct: Justice Scalia was merely responding to the purpose argument with the observation that the *original* purpose is no longer so pressing and, hence, provides even less reason to read the Clause broadly.

Consider Justice Scalia's analysis in light of what has transpired in Washington, D.C. in the last several years—Congress has shut down. Due to hyperpartisan bickering between the parties and to the fractured GOP caucus in the House (which the Republicans have controlled since 2011), not only does Congress not enact substantive legislation anymore, but even routine legislative activities such as budgets, debt ceiling adjustments, and confirmations have slowed or stalled. Like the Bush-Cheney Administration, the Obama Administration has responded to an exacerbated congressional gridlock with aggressive executive action—including more recess appointments to positions that were once routine matters. Can you blame the Court majority for giving the President some slack, given his efforts to press onward with governance and given the contrast with an obstructionist and deeply unpopular Congress?

3. *Practice as Constitutional Adverse Possession.* As in the Steel Seizure Case (Casebook, pp. 1175–88), the Justices in the Recess Appointments Case took a variety of positions regarding the relevance of executive practice when judges set the meaning of constitutional provisions. Justice Breyer posited that constitutional ambiguities may be resolved by consulting a longstanding presidential practice which Congress has not decisively resisted. Like Chief Justice Vinson in the Steel Seizure Case (Casebook, pp. 1184–85), Justice Breyer applied the practice-as-adverse-possession standard pretty liberally. Following Justice Frankfurter's formulation of the constitutional adverse possession idea (Casebook, pp. 1179–80), Justice Scalia opined that "where a governmental practice has been open, widespread, and unchallenged since the early days of the Republic, the practice should guide our interpretation of an ambiguous constitutional provision."

Even if the constitutional text were in any way ambiguous and even if the Breyer/Vinson standard were the proper one, Justice Scalia argued that the majority did not make its case. "Intra-session recess appointments were virtually unheard of for the first 130 years of the Republic, were deemed unconstitutional by the first Attorney General to address them [Attorney General Philander Knox in 1901], were not openly defended by the Executive until 1921 [Attorney General Harry Daugherty], were not made in significant numbers until after World War II, and have been repeatedly criticized as unconstitutional by Senators of both parties."

On the availability of recess appointments arising beforehand, Justice Scalia had an even stronger historical response. Few Presidents made such appointments in the first century of the republic—and when they did there was sometimes pushback. After President Lincoln appointed David Davis to the Supreme Court through a recess appointment to a preexisting vacancy, a number of Senators strenuously objected. And in 1863 Congress enacted the Pay Act, which provided that "no money shall be paid . . . out of the Treasury, as salary, to any person appointed during the recess of the Senate, to fill a vacancy . . . which . . . existed while the Senate was in session." Act of Feb. 9, 1863, § 2, 12 Stat. 646. Between 1863 and 1940, there were few recess appointments to fill preexisting vacancies.

As Justice Breyer observed, Congress amended the Pay Act in 1940. Under the current version of the Act, "[p]ayment for services may not be made from the Treasury of the United States to an individual appointed during a recess of the Senate to fill a vacancy" that "existed while the Senate was in session" *unless* either the vacancy arose, or a different individual's nomination to fill the vacancy was rejected, "within 30 days before the end of the session"; or a nomination was pending before the Senate at the end of the session, and the individual nominated was not himself a recess appointee. § 5503(a)(1)–(3).

And if the President fills a pre-recess vacancy under one of the circumstances specified in the Act, the law requires that he submit a nomination for that office to the Senate "not later than 40 days after the beginning of the next session." § 5503(b).

Since the 1940 Amendment to the Pay Act, Presidents have made several dozen recess appointments to fill preexisting vacancies. Even as amended, the Pay Act seems disapproving of the practice generally, and certainly regulates it stringently. (If the President has the constitutional authority described by the Court, isn't the Pay Act unconstitutional, because it burdens officials validly appointed by the President?) Senators, including the GOP Senators who participated in *Noel Canning,* have continued to object to the practice. Concluded Justice Scalia: "I can conceive of no sane constitutional theory under which this evidence of 'historical practice'—which is actually evidence of a long-simmering inter-branch conflict—would require us to defer to the views of the Executive Branch." Can you disagree with this assertion?

Return to first principles, and the Steel Seizure Case. Why should executive practice be relevant to the meaning of the Constitution? Understood thus, executive practice can easily bootstrap an institutionally biased viewpoint into the law of the land: Is that not disturbing—especially in light of the first-mover advantage the President already has and the imperial power the office has accumulated. The contrast between the President and the Senate is quite stark: the Presidency can mobilize quickly because one man or woman makes ultimate decisions, whereby the Senate cannot act on most matters (including adjournment!) without the cooperation of the House and is internally hamstrung by the filibuster and other vetogates that block legislative initiatives.

In light of these concerns, has the *Noel Canning* majority stacked the deck in its adverse possession analysis? If it has done so, perhaps that is defensible because the adverse possession idea is defensible. After all, property law, the home to rule-of-law values and bright line directives, originated the adverse possession idea, where it has served a useful role of protecting reliance interests and providing incentives for property owners to assert their rights. The big problem for adverse possession in constitutional law, however, is that it is usually easier for the President to assert executive authority than it is for a diffused and often disorganized Congress to assert its prerogatives. The easiest way for Congress to resist a presidential initiative is to refuse to fund it or to limit the initiative through a rider to an appropriations measure or even a framework statute such as the Pay Act.

What is the right answer to the Case of the Recess Appointments? Does John Hart Ely's representation-reinforcement theory have any insights here (Casebook, pp. 161–71)? How about Alexander Bickel's theory of the passive virtues: Is passivity virtuous in this kind of case?

B. FOREIGN RELATIONS AND WAR

Page 1216. Insert new subsections B.4 and B.5 at the end of subsection B.3:

4. *Presidential Authority in Conducting Diplomacy*

Zivotofsky v. Kerry

___ U.S. ___, 135 S.Ct. 2076 (2015)

Since 1948, the United States, acting through the President, has recognized the state of Israel but has taken no position on the delicate issue of which state has sovereignty over Jerusalem. Consistent with this policy, the State Department will not identify Israel as the nation of citizenship for anyone born in Jerusalem; the passport will simply say "Jerusalem." This is considered objectionable by many supporters of Israel.

In 2002, Congress passed the Foreign Relations Authorization Act, Fiscal Year 2003, 116 Stat. 1350. Section 214 of the Act is titled "United States Policy with Respect to Jerusalem as the Capital of Israel." Section 214(d) allows citizens born in Jerusalem to list their place of birth as "Israel." "For purposes of the registration of birth, certification of nationality, or issuance of a passport of a United States citizen born in the city of Jerusalem, the Secretary shall, upon the request of the citizen or the citizen's legal guardian, record the place of birth as Israel." Did this statutory override of State Department and Presidential policy violate Article II?

Writing for the Court, **Justice Kennedy** applied the Steel Seizure framework and found that the President's assertion of authority fell under Category 3—"measures incompatible with the expressed or implied will of Congress," which can only be allowed when the President's own constitutional authority disables Congress from acting. Unlike the Steel Seizure Case, where President Truman did not satisfy the stringent requirements of Category 3, the Court here upheld the President and ruled that the 2002 statute was invalid because Article II vested the President with exclusive authority to "recognize" foreign states.

The Constitution does not use the term "recognition," but Secretary Kerry relied on the Reception Clause, which directs that the President "shall receive Ambassadors and other public Ministers." Art. II, § 3. The Reception Clause received little attention at the Constitutional Convention, see Reinstein, Recognition: A Case Study on the Original Understanding of Executive Power, 45 U. Rich. L. Rev. 801, 860–862 (2011), and during the ratification debates, Alexander Hamilton claimed that the power to receive ambassadors was "more a matter of dignity than of authority," a ministerial duty largely "without consequence." The Federalist No. 69, p. 420 (C. Rossiter ed. 1961).

"At the time of the founding, however, prominent international scholars suggested that receiving an ambassador was tantamount to recognizing the sovereignty of the sending state. See E. de Vattel, The Law of Nations § 78, p.

461 (1758) (J. Chitty ed. 1853) ('[E]very state, truly possessed of sovereignty, has a right to send ambassadors' and 'to contest their right in this instance' is equivalent to 'contesting their sovereign dignity'); [other sources omitted]. It is a logical and proper inference, then, that a Clause directing the President alone to receive ambassadors would be understood to acknowledge his power to recognize other nations."

"This in fact occurred early in the Nation's history when President Washington recognized the French Revolutionary Government by receiving its ambassador. After this incident the import of the Reception Clause became clear—causing Hamilton to change his earlier view. He wrote that the Reception Clause 'includes th[e power] of judging, in the case of a revolution of government in a foreign country, whether the new rulers are competent organs of the national will, and ought to be recognised, or not.' See A. Hamilton, Pacificus No. 1, in The Letters of Pacificus and Helvidius 5, 13–14 (1845) (reprint 1976) (President 'acknowledged the republic of France, by the reception of its minister'). [S]ee also 3 J. Story, Commentaries on the Constitution of the United States § 1560, p. 416 (1833) ('If the executive receives an ambassador, or other minister, as the representative of a new nation . . . it is an acknowledgment of the sovereign authority *de facto* of such new nation, or party'). As a result, the Reception Clause provides support, although not the sole authority, for the President's power to recognize other nations."

Justice Kennedy found the foregoing inference supported by the President's other Article II powers. The President, "by and with the Advice and Consent of the Senate," is to "make Treaties, provided two thirds of the Senators present concur." Art. II, § 2, cl. 2. Also, "he shall nominate, and by and with the Advice and Consent of the Senate, shall appoint Ambassadors" as well as "other public Ministers and Consuls." *Ibid.*

"As a matter of constitutional structure, these additional powers give the President control over recognition decisions. At international law, recognition may be effected by different means, but each means is dependent upon Presidential power. In addition to receiving an ambassador, recognition may occur on 'the conclusion of a bilateral treaty,' or the 'formal initiation of diplomatic relations,' including the dispatch of an ambassador. The President has the sole power to negotiate treaties, and the Senate may not conclude or ratify a treaty without Presidential action. The President, too, nominates the Nation's ambassadors and dispatches other diplomatic agents. Congress may not send an ambassador without his involvement. Beyond that, the President himself has the power to open diplomatic channels simply by engaging in direct diplomacy with foreign heads of state and their ministers. The Constitution thus assigns the President means to effect recognition on his own initiative. Congress, by contrast, has no constitutional power that would enable it to initiate diplomatic relations with a foreign nation. Because these specific Clauses confer the recognition power on the President, the Court need not consider whether or to what extent the Vesting Clause, which provides that the 'executive Power' shall be vested in the President, provides further support for the President's action here. Art. II, § 1, cl. 1.

"The text and structure of the Constitution grant the President the power to recognize foreign nations and governments. The question then becomes whether that power is exclusive. The various ways in which the President may unilaterally effect recognition—and the lack of any similar power vested in Congress—suggest that it is. So, too, do functional considerations. Put simply, the Nation must have a single policy regarding which governments are legitimate in the eyes of the United States and which are not. Foreign countries need to know, before entering into diplomatic relations or commerce with the United States, whether their ambassadors will be received; whether their officials will be immune from suit in federal court; and whether they may initiate lawsuits here to vindicate their rights. These assurances cannot be equivocal."

Justice Kennedy also found it significant that "the President since the founding has exercised this unilateral power to recognize new states—and the Court has endorsed the practice. See *Banco Nacional de Cuba v. Sabbatino*, 376 U.S. 398, 410, 84 S.Ct. 923, 11 L.Ed.2d 804 (1964); [*United States v. Pink*, 315 U.S. 203, 229, 62 S.Ct. 552, 86 L.Ed. 796 (1942)]; *Williams v. Suffolk Ins. Co.*, 13 Pet. 415, 420, 10 L.Ed. 226 (1839). Texts and treatises on international law treat the President's word as the final word on recognition. See, *e.g.*, Restatement (Third) of Foreign Relations Law § 204, at 89 ('Under the Constitution of the United States the President has exclusive authority to recognize or not to recognize a foreign state or government'). In light of this authority all six judges who considered this case in the Court of Appeals agreed that the President holds the exclusive recognition power." Justice Kennedy found *Sabbatino* especially relevant, for the Court held that "[p]olitical recognition is exclusively a function of the Executive."

Secretary Kerry urged the Court to define the executive power broadly, namely, "exclusive authority to conduct diplomatic relations," along with "the bulk of foreign-affairs powers." Brief for Respondent 18, 16. The Court refused to go that far. "In a world that is ever more compressed and interdependent, it is essential the congressional role in foreign affairs be understood and respected. For it is Congress that makes laws, and in countless ways its laws will and should shape the Nation's course. The Executive is not free from the ordinary controls and checks of Congress merely because foreign affairs are at issue."

Finally, Justice Kennedy considered the extensive historical record to discern whether there had been congressional acquiescence in the exclusive power claimed by the President and the Secretary of State. As Judge Tatel had remarked in the proceedings below, what is most remarkable is that, since the Washington Administration, the President had openly claimed the exclusive authority to recognize foreign states (or not) and had not been met with a congressional statute to the contrary—until the 2002 law at issue in this case.

Justice Breyer joined the opinion for the Court but noted his view, rejected by the Court in *Zivotofsky v. Clinton*, 132 S.Ct. 1421 (2012), that the controversy was a nonjusticiable political question. See Chapter 9 of the Casebook, as well as *Sabbatino*, where the Court ruled that the President's recognition of Cuba was not reviewable.

Justice Thomas concurred in part of the Court's judgment and rejected the Court's constitutional analysis. He argued that the Article II Vesting Clause ("executive power," without qualification) gives the President plenary authority to act in matters of foreign affairs or military deployment. Because Congress's Article I Vesting Clause only gives Congress "[a]ll legislative Powers herein granted," Congress can trump the President only where the Constitution has explicitly authorized congressional action, such as confirming ambassadors and providing funds for foreign affairs and military operations. See Saikrishna Prakash & Michael Ramsey, *The Executive Power Over Foreign Affairs*, 111 Yale L.J. 231, 298–346 (2001). Under his framework, Justice Thomas would have invalidated § 214(d) as applied to passports (fully within the "executive Power" as understood in 1789) but would have applied it to matters of naturalization, fully within Congress's enumerated powers. U.S. Const. art. I, § 8, cl. 4.

In a dissenting opinion, **Chief Justice Roberts** (joined by Justice Alito) noted that this was the first time the Supreme Court has allowed the President to defy an explicit congressional statute regulating foreign affairs. The Court's holding was not properly attentive to the "caution" urged by Justice Jackson in Steel Seizure Category 3 cases.

Justice Scalia (joined by the Chief Justice and Justice Alito) also dissented. In a significant break from Justice Thomas's broad reading of the Article II Vesting Clause, Justice Scalia worked within the analytical structure of a balanced government, where both Congress and the President share foreign affairs authority.

"Congress's power to 'establish an uniform Rule of Naturalization,' Art. I, § 8, cl. 4, enables it to grant American citizenship to someone born abroad. The naturalization power also enables Congress to furnish the people it makes citizens with papers verifying their citizenship—say a consular report of birth abroad (which certifies citizenship of an American born outside the United States) or a passport (which certifies citizenship for purposes of international travel). As the Necessary and Proper Clause confirms, every congressional power 'carries with it all those incidental powers which are necessary to its complete and effectual execution.' *Cohens v. Virginia*, 6 Wheat. 264, 429, 5 L.Ed. 257 (1821). Even on a miserly understanding of Congress's incidental authority, Congress may make grants of citizenship 'effectual' by providing for the issuance of certificates authenticating them.

"One would think that if Congress may grant Zivotofsky a passport and a birth report, it may also require these papers to record his birthplace as 'Israel.' The birthplace specification promotes the document's citizenship-authenticating function by identifying the bearer, distinguishing people with similar names but different birthplaces from each other, helping authorities uncover identity fraud, and facilitating retrieval of the Government's citizenship records."

Having found that Congress possessed constitutional authority to enact § 214(d), Justice Scalia posed the question whether Article II trumps that authority. Without resolving the thorny question of whether Article II trumps Article I, Justice Scalia found no conflict between the legislative and executive powers at issue, because "§ 214(d) has nothing to do with recognition," the core executive power the majority jealously protected. "Section 214(d) does not require the Secretary to make a formal declaration about Israel's sovereignty over Jerusalem. And nobody suggests that international custom infers acceptance of sovereignty from the birthplace designation on a passport or birth report, as it does from bilateral treaties or exchanges of ambassadors. Recognition would preclude the United States (as a matter of international law) from later contesting Israeli sovereignty over Jerusalem. But making a notation in a passport or birth report does not encumber the Republic with any international obligations. It leaves the Nation free (so far as international law is concerned) to change its mind in the future. That would be true even if the statute required *all* passports to list 'Israel.' But in fact it requires only those passports to list 'Israel' for which the citizen (or his guardian) *requests* 'Israel'; all the rest, under the Secretary's policy, list 'Jerusalem.' It is utterly impossible for this deference to private requests to constitute an act that unequivocally manifests an intention to grant recognition.

"Section 214(d) performs a more prosaic function than extending recognition. Just as foreign countries care about what our Government has to say about their borders, so too American citizens often care about what our Government has to say about their identities."

What of the Court's concern that the nation speak in one voice on matters of foreign relations? Nonsense, replied Justice Scalia. There is nothing in the Constitution that says Congress and the President must operate along exactly the same assumptions about foreign relations matters. Consider the President's power "to make Treaties," Art. II, § 2, cl. 2. "There is no question that Congress may, if it wishes, pass laws that openly flout treaties made by the President. Would anyone have dreamt that the President may refuse to carry out such laws—or, to bring the point closer to home, refuse to execute federal courts' judgments under such laws—so that the Executive may 'speak with one voice' about the country's international obligations? To ask is to answer. Today's holding puts the implied power to recognize territorial claims (which the Court infers from the power to recognize states, which it infers from the responsibility to receive ambassadors) on a higher footing than the express power to make treaties."

Justice Scalia concluded: "In the end, the Court's decision does not rest on text or history or precedent. It instead comes down to 'functional considerations'—principally the Court's perception that the Nation 'must speak with one voice' about the status of Jerusalem. The vices of this mode of analysis go beyond mere lack of footing in the Constitution. Functionalism of the sort the Court practices today will *systematically* favor the unitary President over the plural Congress in disputes involving foreign affairs. It is possible that this approach will make for more effective foreign policy, perhaps as effective as that of a monarchy. It is certain that, in the long run, it will erode the structure of separated powers that the People established for the protection of their liberty."

NOTE ON THE PRESIDENT'S EXPANDING AUTHORITY IN FOREIGN AFFAIRS

As reflected in Justice Kennedy's opinion, as well as those of the dissenters, the Prakash and Ramsey Foreign Affairs Vesting Thesis (Casebook, pp. 1191–94) has little constituency among the Justices (except for Justice Thomas). But if you read the Reception Clause as broadly as Justice Kennedy does, and then afford the same broad reading to the Commander-in-Chief Clause, you have accepted a significant amount of little-restricted power to the President. Is this process of expanding presidential power inevitable, given the circumstances of the modern world? Can the Constitution accommodate it? Ought the Constitution set some limits? How can they be enforced?

Recall Edward Swaine's argument that decisive, initiative-seizing Presidents have deployed the Steel Seizure (Jackson) framework much more successfully than plodding Congress has been. Edward T. Swaine, *The Political Economy of* Youngstown, 83 S. Cal. L. Rev. 263 (2010) (Casebook, pp. 1187–88). Functionalism is the President's best friend in constitutional theory—a point that the Chief Justice and Justice Scalia join in making. But cf. *Chadha*, where the President's highly formalist point of view prevailed with the Justices, at the expense of Congress's enactment of legislative veto provisions.

Consider the cogency of Justice Scalia's critique of functionalism in light of the arguments made by the Obama Administration in the Libyan Bombing Problem. See Problem 8–2(c) (Casebook, pp. 1209–11). Does the majority opinion provide ammunition for the Obama Administration's narrowing interpretation of the War Powers Resolution? If a justiciable controversy had brought the Libyan Bombing Campaign to the Supreme Court after *Zivotofsky*, how would the Justices have ruled?

5. *Presidential Authority over Immigration and Naturalization*

Texas v. United States
109 F.3d 134 (5 Cir. Nov. 2015), aff'd by an equally divided Court, 136 S.Ct. 2271 (2016)

In June 2012, the Department of Homeland Security ("DHS") implemented the Deferred Action for Childhood Arrivals program ("DACA"). DHS described the program as an exercise of "prosecutorial discretion": The Department would defer action against undocumented immigrants who had come to this country before the age of sixteen and met other criteria; for such persons, the government would also accept applications for work authorization. But the memo disclaimed any new "substantive right, immigration status or pathway to citizenship" for the 1.2 million persons qualifying for DACA.

In November 2014, DHS expanded DACA by making millions more persons eligible for the program and extending the period for employment authorization. DHS also created a new process called Deferred Action for Parents of Americans and Lawful Permanent Residents program ("DAPA"), which applied to individuals who then had a son or daughter who was a U.S. citizen or lawful permanent resident and meet five additional criteria. Although "[d]eferred action does not confer any form of legal status in this country, much less citizenship [,] it [does] mean[ ] that, for a specified period of time, an individual is permitted to be *lawfully present* in the United States," according to the DAPA Memo. Of the approximately 11.3 million undocumented immigrants then in the United States, 4.3 million would be eligible for lawful presence pursuant to DAPA, according to the District Court.

"Lawful presence" is not an enforceable right to remain in the United States and can be revoked at any time, but that classification nevertheless has significant legal consequences. Unlawfully present aliens are generally not eligible to receive federal public benefits or state and local public benefits unless the state otherwise provides, but DAPA-qualified persons granted lawful presence are no longer barred from receiving social security and Medicare benefits, pursuant to the authorizing statutes for the various programs. The Government conceded that, under federal statutory law, an undocumented immigrant "lawfully present" and with a work authorization may obtain a social security number, would accrue social security credit for employment, and would be eligible for earned income tax credits. Some state benefits turn on the distinction. Texas, for example, will not issue driver's licenses to immigrants who are not "lawfully present" but will do so for DAPA-qualified immigrants. Complaining about the extra costs for its driver's license and other state programs, Texas and twenty-five other states brought suit against the federal government and secured a nationwide injunction barring DHS from implementing the DAPA program. (The lawsuit did not challenge DACA.)

The Fifth Circuit, in an opinion by **Judge Jerry Smith**, affirmed the lower court's nationwide injunction. Judge Smith's opinion concluded that (1) Texas and the other states had Article III standing to challenge DAPA, because the program imposed administrative costs on them, such as Texas's burdened driver's license system; (2) DAPA changed the substantive rights of both immigrants and the states and was therefore an invalid legislative rule because it did not follow the notice-and-comment process required by the Administrative Procedure Act (APA), 5 U.S.C. § 553, for most legislative rules; and (3) DAPA's rule is inconsistent with the nation's immigration statutes and violates the President's "take Care" duties. U.S. Const., art. II, § 3.

On the second holding, the Government maintained that DAPA was merely a policy statement guiding administrators' exercise of "prosecutorial discretion," which is unreviewable under the APA, 5 U.S.C. § 702(a). Judge Smith rejected this claim in Part VI of his opinion. To determine whether DAPA is a general policy guidance, and not a binding rule, the court asked whether DAPA "impose[s] any rights and obligations" (substantive rule) or "genuinely leaves the agency and its decision-makers free to exercise discretion" (policy guidance). "[A]n agency pronouncement will be considered binding as a practical matter if it either appears on its face to be binding, or is applied by the agency in a way that indicates it is binding." Relying repeatedly on statements by President Obama, to the effect that DAPA was a broad measure opening up the process of citizenship to millions of undocumented immigrants, the lower court found that the preexisting DACA program was written to bind the hands of administrators and in fact was implemented that way. Like the DAPA Memo, the DACA Memo instructed agencies to review applications on a case-by-case basis and exercise discretion, but the district court found that those statements were "merely pretext," because only about 5% of the 723,000 applications accepted for evaluation had been denied, and because testimony by an administrator established that DHS pressured decisionmakers to rubber-stamp applications by DACA-eligible immigrants. Because DAPA was modeled upon and tied to the earlier program, the lower court ruled, and the Fifth Circuit affirmed, that DAPA was something more than a policy guidance.

"A binding rule is not required to undergo notice and comment if it is one 'of agency organization, procedure, or practice.' § 553(b)(A). '[T]he substantial impact test is the primary means by which [we] look beyond the label 'procedural' to determine whether a rule is of the type Congress thought appropriate for public participation.' 'An agency rule that modifies substantive rights and interests can only be nominally procedural, and the exemption for such rules of agency procedure cannot apply.' DAPA undoubtedly meets that test—conferring lawful presence on 500,000 illegal aliens residing in Texas forces the state to choose between spending millions of dollars to subsidize driver's licenses and amending its statutes."

In Part VII of his opinion, Judge Smith went beyond the lower court (which rested its judgment on the APA) and ruled that DAPA is also inconsistent with Congress's immigration statutory scheme and therefore violates the Take Care Clause. "The limited ways in which illegal aliens can lawfully reside in the United States reflect Congress's concern that 'aliens have been applying for and receiving public benefits from Federal, State, and local governments at increasing rates,' 8 U.S.C. § 1601(3), and that '[i]t is a compelling government interest to enact new rules for eligibility and sponsorship agreements in order to assure that aliens be self-reliant in accordance with national immigration policy,' § 1601(5).

"In specific and detailed provisions, the INA expressly and carefully provides legal designations allowing defined classes of aliens to be lawfully present and confers eligibility for 'discretionary relief allowing [aliens in deportation proceedings] to remain in the country.' Congress has also identified narrow classes of aliens eligible for deferred action, including certain petitioners for immigration status under the Violence Against Women Act of 1994, immediate family members of lawful permanent residents ('LPRs') killed by terrorism, and immediate family members of LPRs killed in combat and granted posthumous citizenship. Entirely absent from those specific classes is the group of 4.3 million illegal aliens who would be eligible for lawful presence under DAPA were it not enjoined.

"Congress has enacted an intricate process for illegal aliens to derive a lawful immigration classification from their children's immigration status: In general, an applicant must (i) have a U.S. citizen child who is at least twenty-one years old, (ii) leave the United States, (iii) wait ten years, and then (iv) obtain one of the limited number of family-preference visas from a United States consulate. Although DAPA does not confer the full panoply of benefits that a visa gives, DAPA would allow illegal aliens to receive the benefits of lawful presence solely on account of their children's immigration status without complying with any of the requirements, enumerated above, that Congress has deliberately imposed. DAPA requires only that prospective beneficiaries 'have . . . a son or daughter who is a U.S. citizen or lawful permanent resident'—without regard to the age of the child—and there is no need to leave the United States or wait ten years or obtain a visa. Further, the INA does not contain a family-sponsorship process for parents of an LPR child, but DAPA allows a parent to derive lawful presence from his child's LPR status.

"The INA authorizes cancellation of removal and adjustment of status if, *inter alia,* 'the alien has been physically present in the United States for a continuous period of *not less than 10 years* immediately preceding the date of such application' and if 'removal would result in *exceptional and extremely unusual hardship* to the alien's spouse, parent, or child, who is a citizen of the United States or an alien lawfully admitted for permanent residence.' 8 U.S.C. § 1229b(b)(1)(A) (emphasis added). Although LPR status is more substantial than is lawful presence, § 1229b(b)(1) is the most specific delegation of authority to the Secretary to change the immigration classification of removable aliens that meet only the DAPA criteria and do not fit within the specific categories set forth in § 1229b(b)(2)–(6).

"Instead of a ten-year physical-presence period, DAPA grants lawful presence to persons who 'have continuously resided in the United States since before January 1, 2010,' and there is no requirement that removal would result in exceptional and extremely unusual hardship. Although the Secretary has discretion to make immigration decisions based on humanitarian grounds, that discretion is conferred only for particular family relationships and specific forms of relief—none of which includes granting lawful presence, on the basis of a child's immigration status, to the class of aliens that would be eligible for DAPA.

"The INA also specifies classes of aliens eligible and ineligible for work authorization, including those 'eligible for work authorization and deferred action'—with no mention of the class of persons whom DAPA would make eligible for work authorization. Congress " 'forcefully' made combating the employment of illegal aliens central to '[t]he policy of immigration law,' " in part by 'establishing an extensive "employment verification system," designed to deny employment to aliens who . . . are not *lawfully present* in the United States.'

"The INA's careful employment-authorization scheme 'protect[s] against the displacement of workers in the United States,' and a 'primary purpose in restricting immigration is to preserve jobs for American workers.' DAPA would dramatically increase the number of aliens eligible for work authorization, thereby undermining Congress's stated goal of closely guarding access to work authorization and preserving jobs for those lawfully in the country." Moreover, DAPA would reflect a major shifts in the nation's social and economic policies that Congress presumably does not vest in agency discretion. E.g., *King v. Burwell*, 135 S.Ct. 2480 (2015).

"Presumably because DAPA is not authorized by statute, the United States posits that its authority is grounded in historical practice, but that 'does not, by itself, create power,' and in any event, previous deferred-action programs are not analogous to DAPA. '[M]ost . . . discretionary deferrals have been done on a country-specific basis, usually in response to war, civil unrest, or natural disasters,' but DAPA is not such a program. Likewise, many of the previous programs were bridges from one legal status to another, whereas DAPA awards lawful presence to persons who have never had a legal status and may never receive one.

"Although the 'Family Fairness' program did grant voluntary departure to family members of legalized aliens while they 'wait[ed] for a visa preference number to become available for family members,' that program was interstitial to a statutory legalization scheme. DAPA is far from interstitial: Congress has repeatedly declined to enact the Development, Relief, and Education for Alien Minors Act ("DREAM Act"), features of which closely resemble DACA and DAPA.

"Historical practice that is so far afield from the challenged program sheds no light on the Secretary's authority to implement DAPA. Indeed, as the district court recognized, the President explicitly stated that 'it was the failure of Congress to enact such a program that prompted him . . . to "change the law." ' At oral argument, and despite being given several opportunities, the attorney for the United States was unable to reconcile that remark with the position that the government now takes." Judge Smith flatly rejected the Government's view that "congressional silence" can confer great and unprecedented power to DHS to alter the nation's immigration policies.

Judge King dissented from the judgment affirming the lower court. "Although there are approximately 11.3 million removable aliens in this country today, for the last several years Congress has provided the Department of Homeland Security (DHS) with only enough resources to remove approximately 400,000 of those aliens per year. Recognizing DHS's congressionally granted prosecutorial discretion to set removal enforcement priorities, Congress has exhorted DHS to use those resources to 'mak[e] our country safer.' In response, DHS has focused on removing 'those who represent threats to national security, public safety, and border security.' The DAPA Memorandum at issue here focuses on a subset of removable aliens who are unlikely to be removed unless and until more resources are made available by Congress: those who are the parents of United States citizens or legal permanent residents, who have resided in the United States for at least the last five years, who lack a criminal record, and who are not otherwise removal priorities as determined by DHS. The DAPA Memorandum has three primary objectives for these aliens: (1) to permit them to be lawfully employed and thereby enhance their ability to be self-sufficient, a goal of United States immigration law since this country's earliest immigration statutes; (2) to encourage them to come out of the shadows and to identify themselves and where they live, DHS's prime law enforcement objective; and (3) to maintain flexibility so that if Congress is able to make more resources for removal available, DHS will be able to respond."

Moreover, Congress has delegated to the Secretary of Homeland Security the authority to "[e]stablish[ ] national immigration enforcement policies and priorities," 6 U.S.C. § 202(5), and to "establish such regulations; [to] issue such instructions; and [to] perform such other acts as he deems necessary for carrying out" his responsibilities, 8 U.S.C. § 1103(a)(3). Congress has given the Secretary some direction, in appropriations bills, as to how removal resources should be spent—by specifically devoting funding toward "identify[ing] aliens convicted of a crime who may be deportable, and * * * remov[ing] them from the United States once they are judged deportable," and by making clear that the Secretary "shall prioritize the identification and removal of aliens convicted of a crime by the severity of that crime." Department of Homeland Security Appropriations Act, Pub.L. No. 114–4, 129 Stat. 39, 43 (2015).

Judge King argued that the DAPA Memorandum was consistent with the foregoing institutional structure. The Memorandum established new deferred action guidance, "direct[ing] USCIS to establish a process, similar to DACA, for exercising prosecutorial discretion through the use of deferred action, on a case-by-case basis, to those individuals" who could meet six criteria:

- they have, on the date of this memorandum, a son or daughter who is a U.S. citizen or lawful permanent resident;
- they have continuously resided in the United States since before January 1, 2010;
- they are physically present in the United States on the date of this memorandum, *and* at the time of making a request for consideration of deferred action with USCIS;
- they have no lawful status on the date of this memorandum;

- they are not an enforcement priority as reflected in the [Enforcement Priorities Memorandum]; and

- they present no other factors that, in the exercise of discretion, makes the grant of deferred action inappropriate.

The DAPA Memorandum described deferred action as a "form of prosecutorial discretion by which the Secretary deprioritizes an individual's case for humanitarian reasons, administrative convenience, or in the interest of the Department's overall enforcement mission." The Memorandum made clear that deferred action must be "granted on a case-by-case basis"; "may be terminated at any time at the agency's discretion"; and "does not confer any form of legal status in this country, much less citizenship." Based upon this reading of the DAPA Memorandum, Judge King concluded that it was a policy document guiding prosecutorial discretion, and not a substantive rule requiring notice and comment under the APA.

As to the Take Care Clause claim, Judge King would have required more deliberation, as the parties did not brief it in detail. On the merits, the Government had the better arguments, however. "Congress has never prohibited or limited *ad hoc* deferred action, which is no different than DAPA other than scale. In fact, each time Congress spoke to this general issue, it did so incidentally and as part of larger statutes not concerned with deferred action. *See, e.g.,* USA PATRIOT ACT of 2001, Pub L. No. 107–56, § 423(b), 115 Stat. 272, 361 (discussing deferred action for family members of LPRs killed by terrorism within a far larger statute aimed primarily at combatting terrorism). And the language regarding deferred action was worded in permissive terms, not prohibitive terms. *See, e.g.,* 8 U.S.C. § 1154(a)(1)(D)(i)(II) (stating that a qualifying individual 'is eligible for deferred action and work authorization'). More importantly, in enacting these provisos, Congress was legislating against a backdrop of longstanding practice of federal immigration officials exercising *ad hoc* deferred action. By the time Congress specified categories of aliens eligible for deferred action, immigration officials were already "engaging in a regular practice . . . of exercising [deferred action] for humanitarian reasons or simply for its own convenience." [*Reno v. American-Arab Anti-Discrimination Comm.*, 525 U.S. 471, 484 (1999).]

"Yet Congress did nothing to upset this practice. The provisions cited by the majority, if anything, highlight Congress's continued acceptance of flexible and discretionary deferred action." Judge King concluded: "It is hard to see how DAPA is unreasonable on the record before us. DAPA does not negate or conflict with any provision of the INA. DHS has repeatedly asserted its right to engage in deferred action. *Cf. FDA v. Brown & Williamson Tobacco Corp.,* 529 U.S. 120, 146, 120 S.Ct. 1291, 146 L.Ed.2d 121 (2000) (concluding an agency was not entitled to deference where it previously disavowed its enforcement authority). And DAPA appears to further DHS's mission of '[e]stablishing national immigration enforcement policies and priorities.' 6 U.S.C. § 202(5).

"Indeed, if DAPA were unreasonable under the INA, then it follows that *ad hoc* grants of deferred action are unreasonable as well—something the majority declines to reach. But, as previously mentioned, there is no difference between the two other than scale, and *ad hoc* deferred action has been repeatedly acknowledged by Congress and the courts as a key feature of immigration enforcement. *See Reno,* 525 U.S. at 483–84.

NOTE ON THE *DAPA* CASE AND PRESIDENTIAL AUTHORITY OVER IMMIGRATION AND NATURALIZATION

As the caption indicates, the eight-Justice Supreme Court deadlocked on appeal: four Justices would have affirmed Judge Smith and four would have reversed. If you were the decisive ninth Justice, how would you vote? (Remember, as the Justice who breaks a 4–4 tie, you may devise your own solution to this constitutional riddle, to some extent.) Before you cast your vote, you might want to consider an excellent scholarly introduction to these issues in Adam B. Cox & Cristina M. Rodriguez, *The President and Immigration Law Redux,* 125 Yale L. J. 104 (2015), as well as the following notes.

1.　*The Applicability of the Jackson Framework to Agency Actions?* As the Texas Immigration Case illustrates, a great deal of presidential power is exercised by executive agencies operating under White House directives. See Elena Kagan, *Presidential Administration,* 114 Harv. L. Rev. 2245 (2001). Sometimes, as with DAPA, the presidential influence is open and claimed. Under those circumstances, should the Jackson framework carry much weight? Both opinions in the DAPA Case frame the issues as ordinary administrative law issues, and not in separation of powers terms—but each opinion notes the congressional acquiescence arguments at the end, which are relevant if the case were in Jackson's Category 2 (as the dissent says) and not Category 3 (the majority's view).

The administrative law debate—whether DAPA is simply an exercise of the executive branch's prosecutorial discretion (the Government's view) or is an exercise in lawmaking (Texas's view, accepted by the court)—is deeply intertwined with separation of powers. The President and her/his executive officials have almost unreviewable discretion as to prosecution but must go through Article I, Section 7 for lawmaking (the Steel Seizure majority opinion) and must go through notice and comment for legislative rulemaking (the APA). Where does DAPA properly fit within this constitutional-legal framework?

2.　*Does the Executive Branch Deserve an Article II Bounce in Immigration Cases?* In military, diplomatic, and foreign affairs cases, the President's inherent Article II powers seem to give her/him a bounce in the Jackson framework: Not only does the President "win" those challenges, in the face of congressional nonacquiescence, but sometimes the President's authority has actually trumped that of Congress. See, for example, the surprising triumph of the President's position in *Zivotofsky ex rel. Zivotofsky v. Kerry,* 135 S.Ct. 2076 (2015), immediately preceding in this Supplement.

What is the best normative constitutional basis for the President's bounce in cases like *Zivotofsky*? Is it applicable to the President's role in immigration and naturalization? Please reread the text and ponder the structure of the Constitution as you think about this issue. And consider your answer in light of the original meaning and historical materials introduced earlier in the Casebook and in this Supplement.

3.   *How Does Gridlock Affect the Proper Analysis?* President Obama explicitly invoked congressional gridlock over the proposed DREAM Act as a reason for acting. This was politically astute but came back to haunt the Administration in the Fifth Circuit. Should the existence of an intractable problem that Congress is incapable of addressing influence your analysis? Does the problem have to be urgent?

PROBLEM 8–2A:
PRESIDENTIAL AUTHORITY TO RESTRICT IMMIGRATION

During the 2016 presidential campaign, GOP nominee Donald Trump promised that, if elected, he would ban immigration of Muslims into the United States, on the ground that Islam, by his lights, is an extremist and violent religion and that Muslims pose an unusually high threat of terrorist activities. To the surprise of the pundits (and the Democrats and not a few Republicans), Trump won the election.

One week after his inauguration as President and without interagency review, President Donald J. Trump issued Executive Order 13769 ("EO1"). Exec. Order No. 13769, 82 Fed. Reg. 8977 (Jan. 27, 2017). Entitled "Protecting the Nation From Foreign Terrorist Entry Into the United States," EO1's stated purpose was to "protect the American people from terrorist attacks by foreign nationals admitted to the United States." "Numerous foreign-born individuals have been convicted or implicated in terrorism-related crimes since September 11, 2001, including foreign nationals who entered the United States after receiving visitor, student, or employment visas, or who entered through the United States refugee resettlement program."

In response, EO1 mandated two main courses of action to assure that the United States remain "vigilant during the visa-issuance process to ensure that those approved for admission do not intend to harm Americans and that they have no ties to terrorism." In Section 3, the President invoked his authority under 8 U.S.C. § 1182(f) to suspend for 90 days immigrant and nonimmigrant entry into the United States of nationals from seven majority-Muslim countries: Iraq, Iran, Libya, Sudan, Somalia, Syria, and Yemen. In Section 5, the President made important changes to refugee screening that will not be a focus on this Problem (but are important policy changes raising their own legal and constitutional issues).

EO1 took immediate effect—but had the immediate effect of causing mass confusion at airports and other points of entry. Various states, private organizations, and individuals filed a series of lawsuits to enjoin the implementation of EO1. Courts in the Ninth Circuit and elsewhere issued injunctions to that effect, and after the Ninth Circuit declined to overturn such an injunction, the President retired EO1 and issued EO2, also entitled "Protecting the Nation From Foreign Terrorist Entry Into the United States." Exec. Order No. 13780, 82 Fed. Reg. 13209 (Mar. 6, 2017). The revised Executive Order was to take effect on March 16, 2017, at which point EO1 would be revoked. EO2 expressly stated that EO1 "did not provide a basis for discriminating for or against members of any particular religion" and was "not motivated by animus toward any religion."

Section 2 of EO2—"Temporary Suspension of Entry for Nationals of Countries of Particular Concern During Review Period"—reinstated the 90-day ban on travel for nationals of six of the seven majority-Muslim countries identified in EO1: Iran, Libya, Somalia, Sudan, Syria, and Yemen. Section 2 also directed the Secretary of Homeland Security, the Secretary of State, and the Director of National Intelligence to "conduct a worldwide review to identify whether, and if so what, additional information will be needed from each foreign country to adjudicate an application by a national of that country for a visa, admission, or other benefit under the INA (adjudications) in order to determine that the individual is not a security or public-safety threat." Section 2(c) stated in full:

> To temporarily reduce investigative burdens on relevant agencies during the review period described in subsection (a) of this section, to ensure the proper review and maximum utilization of available resources for the screening and vetting of foreign nationals, to ensure that adequate standards are established to prevent infiltration by foreign terrorists, and in light of the national security concerns referenced in section 1 of this order, I hereby proclaim, pursuant to sections 212(f) and 215(a) of the INA, 8 U.S.C. [§§] 1182(f) and 1185(a), that the unrestricted entry into the United States of nationals of Iran, Libya, Somalia, Sudan, Syria, and Yemen would be detrimental to the interests of the United States. I therefore direct that the entry into the United States of nationals of those six countries be suspended for 90 days from the effective date of this order, subject to the limitations, waivers, and exceptions set forth in sections 3 and 12 of this order.

Regarding the six identified countries, EO2 explained:

> Each of these countries is a state sponsor of terrorism, has been significantly compromised by terrorist organizations, or contains active conflict zones. Any of these circumstances diminishes the foreign government's willingness or ability to share or validate important information about individuals seeking to travel to the United States. Moreover, the significant presence in each of these countries of terrorist organizations, their members, and others exposed to those organizations increases the chance that conditions will be exploited to enable terrorist operatives or sympathizers to travel to the United States. Finally, once foreign nationals from these

countries are admitted to the United States, it is often difficult to remove them, because many of these countries typically delay issuing, or refuse to issue, travel documents.

Based on the conditions of these six countries, "the risk of erroneously permitting entry of a national of one of these countries who intends to commit terrorist acts or otherwise harm the national security of the United States is unacceptably high."

EO2 stated that it no longer included Iraq on the list of designated countries because of Iraq's "close cooperative relationship" with the United States and its recent efforts to enhance its travel documentation procedures. The Order also stated that its scope has been narrowed from EO1 in response to "judicial concerns" about the suspension of entry with respect to certain categories of aliens. EO2 applied only to individuals outside of the United States who did not have a valid visa as of the issuance of EO1 or EO2. EO2, unlike EO1, expressly exempted lawful permanent residents, dual citizens traveling under a passport issued by a country not on the banned list, asylum-seekers, and refugees already admitted to the United States. The Order also provided that consular officers or Customs and Border Protection officials could exercise discretion in authorizing case-by-case waivers to issue visas and grant entry during the suspension period, and offers examples of when waivers "could be appropriate."

EO2 supplied additional information relevant to national security concerns. The Order included excerpts from the State Department's 2015 Country Reports on Terrorism, to demonstrate "why . . . nationals [from the designated countries] continue to present heightened risk to the security of the United States." EO2 stated that foreign nationals and refugees have committed acts of terrorism:

> Recent history shows that some of those who have entered the United States through our immigration system have proved to be threats to our national security. Since 2001, hundreds of persons born abroad have been convicted of terrorism-related crimes in the United States. They have included not just persons who came here legally on visas but also individuals who first entered the country as refugees. For example, in January 2013, two Iraqi nationals admitted to the United States as refugees in 2009 were sentenced to 40 years and to life in prison, respectively, for multiple terrorism-related offenses. And in October 2014, a native of Somalia who had been brought to the United States as a child refugee and later became a naturalized United States citizen was sentenced to 30 years in prison for attempting to use a weapon of mass destruction as part of a plot to detonate a bomb at a crowded Christmas-tree-lighting ceremony in Portland, Oregon. The Attorney General has reported to me that more than 300 persons who entered the United States as refugees are currently the subjects of counterterrorism investigations by the Federal Bureau of Investigation.

EO2 does not discuss any instances of domestic terrorism involving nationals from Iran, Libya, Sudan, Syria, or Yemen.

A report from the Department of Homeland Security ("DHS") surfaced after EO1 issued. First, a draft report from DHS, prepared about one month after EO1 issued and two weeks prior to EO2's issuance, concluded that citizenship "is unlikely to be a reliable indicator of potential terrorist activity" and that citizens of countries affected by EO1 are "[r]arely [i]mplicated in U.S.-[b]ased [t]errorism." Specifically, the DHS report determined that since the spring of 2011, at least eighty-two individuals were inspired by a foreign terrorist group to carry out or attempt to carry out an attack in the United States. Slightly more than half were U.S. citizens born in the United States, and the remaining persons were from twenty-six different countries—with the most individuals originating from Pakistan, followed by Somalia, Bangladesh, Cuba, Ethiopia, Iraq, and Uzbekistan. Of the six countries included in EO2, only Somalia was identified as being among the "top" countries-of-origin for the terrorists analyzed in the report. During the time period covered in the report, three offenders were from Somalia; one was from Iran, Sudan, and Yemen each; and none was from Syria or Libya. The final version of the report, issued five days prior to EO2, concluded "that most foreign-born, [U.S.]-based violent extremists likely radicalized several years *after* their entry to the United States, [thus] limiting the ability of screening and vetting officials to prevent their entry because of national security concerns" (emphasis added).

Both executive orders were issued pursuant to authority vested in the President by § 212(f) of the Immigration and Nationalization Act of 1952:

> Whenever the President finds that the entry of any aliens or of any class of aliens into the United States would be detrimental to the interests of the United States, he may by proclamation, and for such period as he shall deem necessary, suspend the entry of all aliens or any class of aliens as immigrants or nonimmigrants, or impose on the entry of aliens any restrictions he may deem to be appropriate.

8 U.S.C. § 1182(f). Added by a later amendment to the 1952 Act, section 1182(a)(3) requires that immigration officials bar entry into this country to an alien for whom there is "reasonable ground to believe" that he or she "is likely to engage after entry in any [specifically defined] terrorist activity," 8 U.S.C. § 1182(a)(3)(B)(i)(II).

Contemporaneous to enacting the Civil Rights Act of 1964, Congress amended the INA in 1965 to eliminate the "national origins system as the basis for the selection of immigrants to the United States." H.R. Rep. No. 89–745, at 8 (1965). Section 1152(a)(1)(A) says this:

> [N]o person shall receive any preference or priority or be discriminated against in the issuance of an immigrant visa because of the person's race, sex, nationality, place of birth, or place of residence.

8 U.S.C. § 1152(a)(1)(A).

Like EO1, EO2 found a hostile reception among judges. See *Hawaii v. Trump*, 859 F.3d 741 (9th Cir. 2017), *cert. granted*, 137 S.Ct. 2080 (June 2017) (also narrowing the nationwide injunctions entered in the Ninth Circuit). In September 2017, the President issued Proclamation No. 9645—widely referred to as EO3. The Proclamation revoked EO2 and revamped the justifications and restrictions for entry into this country by nationals of specified countries. Specifically, EO3 placed entry restrictions on the nationals of eight foreign states whose systems for managing and sharing information about their nationals the President deemed inadequate.

Foreign states were selected for inclusion in EO3 based on a review undertaken pursuant to EO1 and EO2. As part of that review, the DHS, in consultation with the State Department and intelligence agencies, developed an information and risk assessment "baseline." DHS then collected and evaluated data for all foreign governments, identifying those having deficient information-sharing practices and presenting national security concerns, as well as other countries "at risk" of failing to meet the baseline. After a 50-day period during which the State Department made diplomatic efforts to encourage foreign governments to improve their practices, the Acting Secretary of Homeland Security concluded that eight countries—Chad, Iran, Iraq, Libya, North Korea, Syria, Venezuela, and Yemen—remained deficient. She recommended entry restrictions for certain nationals from all of those countries but Iraq, which had a close cooperative relationship with the U.S. She also recommended including Somalia, which met the information-sharing component of the baseline standards but had other special risk factors, such as a significant terrorist presence.

After consulting with Cabinet members, the President adopted the recommendations and issued the Proclamation. Invoking his authority under §§ 1182(f) and 1185(a), the President determined that certain restrictions were necessary to "prevent the entry of those foreign nationals about whom the United States Government lacks sufficient information" and "elicit improved identity-management and information-sharing protocols and practices from foreign governments." The Proclamation imposed a range of entry restrictions that vary based on the "distinct circumstances" in each of the eight countries. It exempted lawful permanent residents and provided case-by-case waivers under certain circumstances. It also directed DHS to assess on a continuing basis whether the restrictions should be modified or continued, and to report to the President every 180 days. At the completion of the first such review period, the President determined that Chad had sufficiently improved its practices, and he lifted restrictions on its nationals.

PROBLEM 8–2B:
PRESIDENTIAL AUTHORITY TO RESTRICT IMMIGRATION BY RELIGION-INSPIRED TRAVEL BANS?

In Problem 8–2A, we largely removed the issue of religion, so that the student could focus on the pure separation of powers issues presented by the

Travel Ban. What follows is the political history of the Travel Bans, with reference to the role that rhetoric hostile to Muslims played in the 2016 election and the first year and a half of the Trump Administration. (All quotations are taken from the Record on Appeal to the Supreme Court.)

During his presidential campaign in 2015–16, candidate Donald Trump pledged that, if elected, he would ban Muslims from entering the United States. On December 7, 2015, he issued a formal statement "calling for a total and complete shutdown of Muslims entering the United States." That statement, which remained on his campaign website until May 2017 (several months into his Presidency), read in full:

> "Donald J. Trump is calling for a total and complete shutdown of Muslims entering the United States until our country's representatives can figure out what is going on. According to Pew Research, among others, there is great hatred towards Americans by large segments of the Muslim population. Most recently, a poll from the Center for Security Policy released data showing '25% of those polled agreed that violence against Americans here in the United States is justified as a part of the global jihad' and 51% of those polled 'agreed that Muslims in America should have the choice of being governed according to Shariah.' Shariah authorizes such atrocities as murder against nonbelievers who won't convert, beheadings and more unthinkable acts that pose great harm to Americans, especially women.

> "Mr. Trum[p] stated, 'Without looking at the various polling data, it is obvious to anybody the hatred is beyond comprehension. Where this hatred comes from and why we will have to determine. Until we are able to determine and understand this problem and the dangerous threat it poses, our country cannot be the victims of the horrendous attacks by people that believe only in Jihad, and have no sense of reason or respect of human life. If I win the election for President, we are going to Make America Great Again.'—Donald J. Trump."

On December 8, 2015, candidate Trump justified his proposal during a television interview by noting that President Franklin D. Roosevelt "did the same thing" with respect to the internment of Japanese Americans during World War II. In January 2016, during a Republican primary debate, Trump was asked whether he wanted to "rethink [his] position" on "banning Muslims from entering the country." He answered, "No."

A month later, at a rally, Trump told an apocryphal story about United States General John J. Pershing killing a large group of Muslim insurgents in the Philippines with bullets dipped in pigs' blood in the early 1900's. In March 2016, he said: "Islam hates us. * * * [W]e can't allow people coming into this country who have this hatred of the United States * * * [a]nd of people that are not Muslim." That same month, Trump asserted that "[w]e're having problems with the Muslims, and we're having problems with Muslims coming into the country." He called for surveillance of mosques in the United States, blaming terrorist attacks on Muslims' lack of "assimilation" and their commitment to "sharia law." A day later, he opined that Muslims "do not respect us at all" and "don't respect a lot of the things that are happening throughout not only our country, but they don't respect other things."

As Trump's presidential campaign progressed, he adapted his rhetoric to meet criticisms. In June 2016, he characterized his proposal as a suspension of immigration from countries "where there's a proven history of terrorism." He also described the proposal as rooted in the need to stop "importing radical Islamic terrorism to the West through a failed immigration system." Asked in July 2016 whether he was "pull[ing] back from" his pledged Muslim ban, Trump responded, "I actually don't think it's a rollback. In fact, you could say it's an expansion." He confessed that he used different terminology because "[p]eople were so upset when [he] used the word Muslim."

A month before the 2016 election, Trump, the GOP presidential nominee, reiterated that his proposed "Muslim ban" had "morphed into a[n] extreme vetting from certain areas of the world." Then, on December 21, 2016, President-elect Trump was asked whether he would "rethink" his previous "plans to create a Muslim registry or ban Muslim immigration." He replied: "You know my plans. All along, I've proven to be right."

On January 27, 2017, one week after taking office, President Trump signed EO1, "Protecting the Nation From Foreign Terrorist Entry Into the United States." As he signed it, President Trump read the title, looked up, and said "We all know what that means." That same day, President Trump explained to the media that, under EO1, Christians would be given priority for entry as refugees into the United States. In particular, he bemoaned the fact that in the past, "[i]f you were a Muslim [refugee from Syria] you could come in, but if you were a Christian, it was almost impossible." Considering that past policy "very unfair," President Trump explained that EO1 was designed "to help" the Christians in Syria. The following day, one of President Trump's key advisers candidly drew the connection between EO1 and the "Muslim ban" that the President had pledged to implement if elected. According to that adviser, "[W]hen [Donald Trump] first announced it, he said, 'Muslim ban.' He called me up. He said, 'Put a commission together. Show me the right way to do it legally.' " After suffering a series of judicial rebukes, the White House revoked EO1 and, on March 6, 2017, issued EO2.

One of President Trump's senior advisers publicly explained that EO2 would "have the same basic policy outcome" as EO1, and that any changes would address "very technical issues that were brought up by the court." After EO2 was issued, the White House Press Secretary told reporters that, by issuing EO2, President Trump "continue[d] to deliver on * * * his most significant campaign promises." That statement was consistent with President Trump's own declaration that "I keep my campaign promises, and our citizens will be very happy when they see the result."

Before EO2 took effect, it was enjoined by several federal courts. During the EO2 litigation, President Trump repeatedly made statements alluding to a desire to keep Muslims out of the country. For instance, he said at a rally of his supporters that EO2 was just a "watered down version of the first one" and had been "tailor[ed]" at the behest of "the lawyers." He further added that he would prefer "to go back to the first [executive order] and go all the way" and reiterated his belief that it was "very hard" for Muslims to assimilate into Western culture. During a rally in April 2017, President Trump recited the lyrics to a song called "The Snake," a song about a woman who nurses a sick snake back to health but then is attacked by the snake, as a warning about Syrian refugees entering the country.

In June 2017, the President stated on Twitter that the Justice Department had submitted a "watered down, politically correct version" of the "original Travel Ban" "to S[upreme] C[ourt]." The President went on to tweet: "People, the lawyers and the courts can call it whatever they want, but I am calling it what we need and what it is, a TRAVEL BAN!" He added: "That's right, we need a TRAVEL BAN for certain DANGEROUS countries, not some politically correct term that won't help us protect our people!" Then, on August 17, 2017, President Trump issued yet another tweet about Islam, once more referencing the story about General Pershing's massacre of Muslims in the Philippines: "Study what General Pershing . . . did to terrorists when caught. There was no more Radical Islamic Terror for 35 years."

In September 2017, President Trump tweeted that "[t]he travel ban into the United States should be far larger, tougher and more specific—but stupidly, that would not be politically correct!" On September 24, the President issued the Proclamation dubbed EO3. On November 29, he "retweeted" three anti-Muslim videos, entitled "Muslim Destroys a Statue of Virgin Mary!", "Islamist mob pushes teenage boy off roof and beats him to death!", and "Muslim migrant beats up Dutch boy on crutches." Those videos were initially tweeted by a British political party whose mission was to oppose "all alien and destructive politic [al] or religious doctrines, including * * * Islam." When asked about these videos, the White House Deputy Press Secretary connected them to the Proclamation: "The President has been talking about these security issues for years now, from the campaign trail to the White House" and "has addressed these issues with the travel order that he issued earlier this year and the companion proclamation."

Review the materials on the Religion Clauses in Chapter 6 of the main book. Considering the final wording and structure of the September 2017 Proclamation, EO3, as well as the materials set forth above, does EO3 violate the First Amendment? Jot down your thoughts and read the Supreme Court's disposition below.

TRUMP V. HAWAII

__ U.S. __, 138 S.Ct. 2392, __ L.Ed.2d __ (2018)

CHIEF JUSTICE ROBERTS delivered the opinion of the Court. * * *

Plaintiffs—the State of Hawaii, three individuals with foreign relatives affected by the entry suspension, and the Muslim Association of Hawaii—argue that the Proclamation violates the Immigration and Nationality Act (INA) and the Establishment Clause. The District Court granted a nationwide preliminary injunction barring enforcement of the restrictions. The Ninth Circuit affirmed, concluding that the Proclamation contravened two provisions of the INA: § 1182(f), which authorizes the President to "suspend the entry of all aliens or any class of aliens" whenever he "finds" that their entry "would be detrimental to the interests of the United States," and § 1152(a)(1)(A), which provides that "no person shall . . . be discriminated against in the issuance of an immigrant visa because of the person's race, sex, nationality, place of birth, or place of residence." * * *

The text of § 1182(f) states:

> "Whenever the President finds that the entry of any aliens or of any class of aliens into the United States would be detrimental to the interests of the United States, he may by proclamation, and for such period as he shall deem necessary, suspend the entry of all aliens or any class of aliens as immigrants or nonimmigrants, or impose on the entry of aliens any restrictions he may deem to be appropriate."

By its terms, § 1182(f) exudes deference to the President in every clause. It entrusts to the President the decisions whether and when to suspend entry ("[w]henever [he] finds that the entry" of aliens "would be detrimental" to the national interest); whose entry to suspend ("all aliens or any class of aliens"); for how long ("for such period as he shall deem necessary"); and on what conditions ("any restrictions he may deem to be appropriate"). It is therefore unsurprising that we have previously observed that § 1182(f) vests the President with "ample power" to impose entry restrictions in addition to those elsewhere enumerated in the INA. [*Sale v. Haitian Centers Council, Inc.,* 509 U.S. 155 (1993).]

The Proclamation falls well within this comprehensive delegation. The sole prerequisite set forth in § 1182(f) is that the President "find[ ]" that the entry of the covered aliens "would be detrimental to the interests of the United States." The President has undoubtedly fulfilled that requirement here. He first ordered DHS and other agencies to conduct a comprehensive evaluation of every single country's compliance with the information and risk assessment baseline. The President then issued a Proclamation setting forth extensive findings describing how deficiencies in the practices of select foreign governments—several of which are state sponsors of terrorism—deprive the Government of "sufficient information to assess the risks [those countries' nationals] pose to the United States." Proclamation § 1(h)(i). Based on that review, the President found that it was in the national interest to restrict entry of aliens who could not be vetted with adequate information—both to protect national security and public safety, and to induce improvement by their home countries. The Proclamation therefore "craft[ed] . . . country-specific restrictions that would be most likely to encourage cooperation given each country's distinct circumstances," while securing the Nation "until such time as improvements occur." *Ibid.*

Plaintiffs believe that these findings are insufficient. They argue, as an initial matter, that the Proclamation fails to provide a persuasive rationale for why nationality alone renders the covered foreign nationals a security risk. And they further discount the President's stated concern about deficient vetting because the Proclamation allows many aliens from the designated countries to enter on nonimmigrant visas.

Such arguments are grounded on the premise that § 1182(f) not only requires the President to *make* a finding that entry "would be detrimental to the interests of the United States," but also to explain that finding with sufficient detail to enable judicial review. That premise is questionable. See *Webster v. Doe,* 486 U.S. 592, 600 (1988) (concluding that a statute authorizing the CIA Director to terminate an employee when the Director "shall deem such termination necessary or advisable in the interests of the United States" forecloses "any meaningful judicial standard of review"). But even assuming that some form of review is appropriate, plaintiffs' attacks on the sufficiency of the President's findings cannot be sustained. The 12-page Proclamation—which thoroughly describes the process, agency evaluations, and recommendations underlying the President's chosen restrictions—is more detailed than any prior order a President has issued under § 1182(f).

Moreover, plaintiffs' request for a searching inquiry into the persuasiveness of the President's justifications is inconsistent with the broad statutory text and the deference traditionally accorded the President in this sphere. "Whether the President's chosen method" of addressing perceived risks is justified from a policy perspective is "irrelevant to the scope of his [§ 1182(f)] authority." *Sale.* And when the President adopts "a preventive measure . . . in the context of international affairs and national security," he is "not required to conclusively link all of the pieces in the puzzle before [courts] grant weight to [his] empirical conclusions." *Holder v. Humanitarian Law Project,* 561 U.S. 1, 35 (2010). * * *

For more than a century, this Court has recognized that the admission and exclusion of foreign nationals is a "fundamental sovereign attribute exercised by the Government's political departments largely immune from judicial control." *Fiallo v. Bell,* 430 U.S. 787, 792 (1977). Because decisions in these matters may implicate "relations with foreign powers," or involve "classifications defined in the light of changing political and economic circumstances," such judgments "are frequently of a character more appropriate to either the Legislature or the Executive." *Mathews v. Diaz,* 426 U.S. 67, 81 (1976).

Nonetheless, although foreign nationals seeking admission have no constitutional right to entry, this Court has engaged in a circumscribed judicial inquiry when the denial of a visa allegedly burdens the constitutional rights of a U.S. citizen. In *Kleindienst v. Mandel,* [408 U.S. 753 (1972),] the Attorney General denied admission to a Belgian journalist and self-described "revolutionary Marxist," Ernest Mandel, who had been invited to speak at a conference at Stanford University. The professors who wished to hear Mandel speak challenged that decision under the First Amendment, and we acknowledged that their constitutional "right to receive information" was implicated. But we limited our review to whether the Executive gave a "facially legitimate and bona fide" reason for its action. Given the authority of the political branches over admission, we held that "when the Executive exercises this [delegated] power negatively on the basis of a facially legitimate and bona fide reason, the courts will neither look behind the exercise of that discretion, nor test it by balancing its justification" against the asserted constitutional interests of U.S. citizens.

The upshot of our cases in this context is clear: "Any rule of constitutional law that would inhibit the flexibility" of the President "to respond to changing world conditions should be adopted only with the greatest caution," and our inquiry into matters of entry and national security is highly constrained. *Mathews.* We need not define the precise contours of that inquiry in this case. A conventional application of *Mandel,* asking only whether the policy is facially legitimate and bona fide, would put an end to our review. But the Government has suggested that it may be appropriate here for the inquiry to extend beyond the facial neutrality of the order. See Tr. of Oral Arg. 16–17, 25–27 (describing *Mandel* as "the starting point" of the analysis). For our purposes today, we assume that we may look behind the face of the Proclamation to the extent of applying rational basis review. That standard of review considers whether the entry policy is plausibly related to the Government's stated objective to protect the country and improve vetting processes. See *Railroad Retirement Bd. v. Fritz,* 449 U.S. 166, 179 (1980). As a result, we may consider plaintiffs' extrinsic evidence, but will uphold the policy so long as it can reasonably be understood to result from a justification independent of unconstitutional grounds. * * *

The Proclamation is expressly premised on legitimate purposes: preventing entry of nationals who cannot be adequately vetted and inducing other nations to improve their practices. The text says nothing about religion. Plaintiffs and the dissent nonetheless emphasize that five of the seven nations currently included in the Proclamation have Muslim-majority populations. Yet that fact alone does not support an inference of religious hostility, given that the policy covers just 8% of the world's Muslim population and is limited to countries that were previously designated by Congress or prior administrations as posing national security risks. See 8 U.S.C. § 1187(a)(12)(A) (identifying Syria and state sponsors of terrorism such as Iran as "countr[ies] or area[s] of concern" for purposes of administering the Visa Waiver Program); Dept. of Homeland Security, DHS Announces Further Travel Restrictions for the Visa Waiver Program (Feb. 18, 2016) (designating Libya, Somalia, and Yemen as additional countries of concern). * * *

Finally, the dissent invokes *Korematsu v. United States,* 323 U.S. 214 (1944). Whatever rhetorical advantage the dissent may see in doing so, *Korematsu* has nothing to do with this case. The forcible relocation of U.S. citizens to concentration camps, solely and explicitly on the basis of race, is objectively unlawful and outside the scope of Presidential authority. But it is wholly inapt to liken that morally repugnant order to a facially neutral policy denying certain foreign nationals the privilege of admission. The entry suspension is an act that is well within executive authority and could have been taken by any other President—the only question is evaluating the actions of this particular President in promulgating an otherwise valid Proclamation.

The dissent's reference to *Korematsu,* however, affords this Court the opportunity to make express what is already obvious: *Korematsu* was gravely wrong the day it was decided, has been overruled in the court of history, and—to be clear—"has no place in law under the Constitution." [*Korematsu,*] 323 U.S. at 248 (Jackson, J., dissenting). * * *

JUSTICE KENNEDY concurring.

There may be some common ground between the opinions in this case, in that the Court does acknowledge that in some instances, governmental action may be subject to judicial review to determine whether or not it is "inexplicable by anything but animus," *Romer v. Evans,* 517 U.S. 620, 632 (1996), which in this case would be animosity to a religion. Whether judicial proceedings may properly continue in this case, in light of the substantial deference that is and must be accorded to the Executive in the conduct of foreign affairs, and in light of today's decision, is a matter to be addressed in the first instance on remand. And even if further proceedings are permitted, it would be necessary to determine that any discovery and other preliminary matters would not themselves intrude on the foreign affairs power of the Executive.

[We omit the concurring opinion of **JUSTICE THOMAS**, who also objected to the nationwide injunction issued by the district courts in these cases.]

[**JUSTICE BREYER**, joined by **JUSTICE KAGAN**, dissented. In their view, "the Proclamation's elaborate system of exemptions and waivers" were relevant. They would provide "case-by-case consideration of persons who may qualify for visas despite the Proclamation's general ban. Those persons include lawful permanent residents, asylum seekers, refugees, students, children, and numerous others." Briefs filed in the case suggest that that system was not being applied, and these Justices would have remanded the case for district court hearings on this issue. If the record could not be enriched in that way, these Justices agreed with Justice Sotomayor's constitutional objection.]

JUSTICE SOTOMAYOR, joined by **JUSTICE GINSBURG**, dissented.

The United States of America is a Nation built upon the promise of religious liberty. Our Founders honored that core promise by embedding the principle of religious neutrality in the First Amendment. The Court's decision today fails to safeguard that fundamental principle. It leaves undisturbed a policy first advertised openly and unequivocally as a "total and complete shutdown of Muslims entering the United States" because the policy now masquerades behind a facade of national-security concerns. But this repackaging does little to cleanse Presidential Proclamation No. 9645 of the appearance of discrimination that the President's words have created. Based on the evidence in the record, a reasonable observer would conclude that the Proclamation was motivated by anti-Muslim animus. That alone suffices to show that plaintiffs are likely to succeed on the merits of their Establishment Clause claim. The majority holds otherwise by ignoring the facts, misconstruing our legal precedent, and turning a blind eye to the pain and suffering the Proclamation inflicts upon countless families and individuals, many of whom are United States citizens. Because that troubling result runs contrary to the Constitution and our precedent, I dissent. * * *

The Establishment Clause forbids government policies "respecting an establishment of religion." U.S. Const., Amdt. 1. The "clearest command" of the Establishment Clause is that the Government cannot favor or disfavor one religion over another. *Larson v. Valente,* 456 U.S. 228, 244 (1982); *Church of Lukumi Babalu Aye, Inc. v. Hialeah,* 508 U.S. 520, 532 (1993). Consistent with that clear command, this Court has long acknowledged that governmental actions that favor one religion "inevitabl[y]" foster "the hatred, disrespect and even contempt of those who [hold] contrary beliefs." *Engel v. Vitale,* 370 U.S. 421, 431 (1962). That is so, this Court has held, because such acts send messages to members of minority faiths " 'that they are outsiders, not full members of the political community.' " *Santa Fe Independent School Dist. v. Doe,* 530 U.S. 290, 309 (2000). To guard against this serious harm, the Framers mandated a strict "principle of denominational neutrality." *Larson.*

"When the government acts with the ostensible and predominant purpose" of disfavoring a particular religion, "it violates that central Establishment Clause value of official religious neutrality, there being no neutrality when the government's ostensible object is to take sides." *McCreary County v. American Civil Liberties Union of Ky.,* 545 U.S. 844, 860 (2005). To determine whether plaintiffs have proved an Establishment Clause violation, the Court asks whether a reasonable observer would view the government action as enacted for the purpose of disfavoring a religion. See *id.*

In answering that question, this Court has generally considered the text of the government policy, its operation, and any available evidence regarding "the historical background of the decision under challenge, the specific series of events leading to the enactment or official policy in question, and the legislative or administrative history, including contemporaneous statements made by" the decisionmaker. *Lukumi; McCreary.*

[Justice Sotomayor recounted the history of the President's religion-based justification for a travel ban. Our quotations in Problem 8–2B are taken from her dissenting opinion; the majority did not dispute the accuracy or attribution of any of the quotations.]

Taking all the relevant evidence together, a reasonable observer would conclude that the Proclamation was driven primarily by anti-Muslim animus, rather than by the Government's asserted national-security justifications. Even before being sworn into office, then-candidate Trump stated that "Islam hates us," warned that "[w]e're having problems with the Muslims, and we're having problems with Muslims coming into the country," promised to enact a "total and complete shutdown of Muslims entering the United States," and instructed one of his advisers to find a "lega[l]" way to enact a Muslim ban. The President continued to make similar statements well after his inauguration * * *.

Moreover, despite several opportunities to do so, President Trump has never disavowed any of his prior statements about Islam. Instead, he has continued to make remarks that a reasonable observer would view as an unrelenting attack on the Muslim religion and its followers. Given President Trump's failure to correct the reasonable perception of his apparent hostility toward the Islamic faith, it is unsurprising that the President's lawyers have, at every step in the lower courts, failed in their attempts to launder the Proclamation of its discriminatory taint. * * *

In light of the Government's suggestion "that it may be appropriate here for the inquiry to extend beyond the facial neutrality of the order," the majority rightly declines to apply *Mandel's* "narrow standard of review" and "assume[s] that we may look behind the face of the Proclamation." In doing so, however, the Court, without explanation or precedential support, limits its review of the Proclamation to rational-basis scrutiny. That approach is perplexing, given that in other Establishment Clause cases, including those involving claims of religious animus or discrimination, this Court has applied a more stringent standard of review. As explained above, the Proclamation is plainly unconstitutional under that heightened standard.

But even under rational-basis review, the Proclamation must fall. That is so because the Proclamation is " 'divorced from any factual context from which we could discern a relationship to legitimate state interests,' and 'its sheer breadth [is] so discontinuous with the reasons offered for it' " that the policy is " 'inexplicable by anything but animus.' " *Ante* (quoting *Romer*); see also *Cleburne v. Cleburne Living Center, Inc.,* 473 U.S. 432, 448 (1985) (recognizing that classifications predicated on discriminatory animus can never be legitimate because the Government has no legitimate interest in exploiting "mere negative attitudes, or fear" toward a disfavored group). The President's statements, which the majority utterly fails to address in its legal analysis, strongly support the conclusion that the Proclamation was issued to express hostility toward Muslims and exclude them from the country. Given the overwhelming record evidence of anti-Muslim animus, it simply cannot be said that the Proclamation has a legitimate basis.

The majority insists that the Proclamation furthers two interrelated national-security interests: "preventing entry of nationals who cannot be adequately vetted and inducing other nations to improve their practices." But the Court offers insufficient support for its view "that the entry suspension has a legitimate grounding in [those] national security concerns, quite apart from any religious hostility." Indeed, even a cursory review of the Government's asserted national-security rationale reveals that the Proclamation is nothing more than a " 'religious gerrymander.' " *Lukumi.*

The majority first emphasizes that the Proclamation "says nothing about religion." Even so, the Proclamation, just like its predecessors, overwhelmingly targets Muslim-majority nations. Given the record here, including all the President's statements linking the Proclamation to his apparent hostility toward Muslims, it is of no moment that the Proclamation also includes minor restrictions on two non-Muslim majority countries, North Korea and Venezuela, or that the Government has removed a few Muslim-majority countries from the list of covered countries since EO-1 was issued. Consideration of the entire record supports the conclusion that the inclusion of North Korea and Venezuela, and the removal of other countries, simply reflect subtle efforts to start "talking territory instead of Muslim," precisely so the Executive Branch could evade criticism or legal consequences for the Proclamation's otherwise clear targeting of Muslims. The Proclamation's effect on North Korea and Venezuela, for example, is insubstantial, if not entirely symbolic. A prior sanctions order already restricts entry of North Korean nationals, see Exec. Order No. 13810, 82 Fed. Reg. 44705 (2017), and the Proclamation targets only a handful of Venezuelan government officials and their immediate family members, 82 Fed. Reg. 45166. As such, the President's inclusion of North Korea and Venezuela does little to mitigate the anti-Muslim animus that permeates the Proclamation.

[Justice Sotomayor also contended that Congress had already provided procedures that were a better-tailored mechanism for protecting national security concerns. Even after opportunity for briefing in the various court challenges, President Trump had not demonstrated how the broad travel ban added anything to national security. The failure to make such a showing was further evidence that EO3 was, like EO1 and EO2, nothing more than a mechanism to implement Trump's repeated promises of a Muslim travel ban.]

Today's holding is all the more troubling given the stark parallels between the reasoning of this case and that of Korematsu v. United States, 323 U.S. 214 (1944). In Korematsu, the Court gave "a pass [to] an odious, gravely injurious racial classification" authorized by an executive order. Adarand Constructors, Inc. v. Peña, 515 U.S. 200, 275 (1995) (Ginsburg, J., dissenting). As here, the Government invoked an ill-defined national-security threat to justify an exclusionary policy of sweeping proportion. As here, the exclusion order was rooted in dangerous stereotypes about, inter alia, a particular group's supposed inability to assimilate and desire to harm the United States. As here, the Government was unwilling to reveal its own intelligence agencies' views of the alleged security concerns to the very citizens it purported to protect. And as here, there was strong evidence that impermissible hostility and animus motivated the Government's policy.

Although a majority of the Court in *Korematsu* was willing to uphold the Government's actions based on a barren invocation of national security, dissenting Justices warned of that decision's harm to our constitutional fabric. Justice Murphy recognized that there is a need for great deference to the Executive Branch in the context of national security, but cautioned that "it is essential that there be definite limits to [the government's] discretion," as "[i]ndividuals must not be left impoverished of their constitutional rights on a plea of military necessity that has neither substance nor support." Justice Jackson lamented that the Court's decision upholding the Government's policy would prove to be "a far more subtle blow to liberty than the promulgation of the order itself," for although the executive order was not likely to be long lasting, the Court's willingness to tolerate it would endure. * * *

NOTES ON THE TRAVEL BAN CASE AND PRESIDENTIAL AUTHORITY OVER IMMIGRATION AND NATURALIZATION

1.   *Justiciability Issues.* In the travel ban cases, the courts had to determine whether there was an Article III case or controversy. The Trump Administration maintained that the plaintiffs' statutory claims (under the INA) were nonjusticiable. Based on the doctrine of consular nonreviewability, the Administration argued that because aliens have no "claim of right" to enter the United States, and because exclusion of aliens is "a fundamental act of sovereignty" by the political branches, review of an exclusion decision "is not within the province of any court, unless expressly authorized by law." *United States ex rel. Knauff v. Shaughnessy,* 338 U.S. 537, 542–43 (1950). The INA itself sets forth a comprehensive framework for review of orders of removal, but authorizes judicial review only for aliens physically present in the United State. Without dissent, the Chief Justice sidestepped that issue, which did not affect the Court's jurisdiction, and declined to resolve it.

As Chapter 9 will note, many Establishment Clause cases are dismissed because the plaintiffs cannot claim an individuated harm, which is fatal under the Court's Article III "standing" jurisprudence. For that reason, the plaintiffs were not the people directly subject to the travel ban, but were instead their American relatives. In *Trump v. Hawaii,* the Chief Justice's opinion held, without dissent, that American relatives of excluded foreign visitors had standing to sue.

2.   *Which Jackson Category?* As in *Steel Seizure* and the DAPA Case (above), a central debate in the Travel Ban Cases was whether the President's action was at its "lowest ebb," because contrary to specific direction from Congress, acting through statutes that were on point and disregarded by the President. As is commonly the case now, the *Steel Seizure* constitutional authority issue boils down to a series of statutory interpretation issues: If the President is acting pursuant to an explicit congressional delegation—as he did in *Curtiss-Wright*—the Supreme Court will uphold his action against separation of powers claims.

The lower courts found that the President went beyond his congressionally delegated authority in § 1182(f) and, further, contravened the anti-discrimination rule of § 1152(a)(1)(A). The Chief Justice's opinion rejected those findings and ruled, without explicit dissent, that EO3 complied with the former and was not at war with the latter. The Ninth Circuit applied normal principles of statutory interpretation to find a clash between EO3 and the immigration statutes—but the President argued that judges should defer to his interpretation of the laws (meaning broad interpretation of the delegations and avoidance of hard restrictions). Should the Court have been more deferential, before determining the direct conflict found here?

Plaintiffs also maintained that EO3 violated the Religion Clauses. Even though it disclaims discrimination based on religion and does not have an explicit religion-based allowance (as EO1 did), plaintiffs argued that the President's own statements confirmed the inference (from the named Muslim countries) that the order favors Christianity over Islam, thereby effecting an establishment of religion. (Because the plaintiffs were not immigrants who were themselves allegedly excluded, but were instead their American relatives, there were no free exercise claims.)

Ought a judge be able to use the dozens of anti-Muslim statements made by presidential candidate Trump to show religion-based animus? Statements by President Trump showing such animus or referring to his campaign statements and promises? See Katherine Shaw, *Beyond the Bully Pulpit: Presidential Speech in the Courts*, 96 Tex. L. Rev. 1 (2017), who argues that presidential speech should generally not be probative, except in cases where it evidences a clear intent to enter the legal (and not just political) arena, or involves foreign relations or national security, or is relevant to government purpose as a proper constitutional inquiry.

For Religion Clause claims, purpose is a central inquiry. Just weeks before the Court decided the Travel Ban Cases, it applied the Religion Clauses to invalidate a state commission order against a baker who invoked conscience reasons not to cater a gay wedding. Justice Kennedy's opinion for a 7–2 Court in *Masterpiece Cakeshop, Ltd. v. Colorado Civil Rights Commission,* 138 S.Ct. 1719 (June 2, 2018), which is excerpted in Chapter 6 of this Supplement, found a violation of state neutrality required by the Religion Clauses based upon statements by two of the seven commissioners, who endorsed the view that religious beliefs cannot legitimately be carried into the public sphere or commercial domain, disparaged the baker's faith as despicable and characterized it as merely rhetorical, and compared his invocation of his sincerely held religious beliefs to defenses of slavery and the Holocaust. No commissioners objected to the comments. The Court also relied on the commission's disparate treatment of cases where bakers objected on nonreligious grounds to making cakes with objectionable messages.

The evidence of anti-religious animus seems much stronger in the Travel Ban Cases: What might be a constitutional basis for reading the evidence so differently?

3.   *Should the President Get a Bounce from the National Security Context?* Dissenting from the Fourth Circuit's decision invalidating EO2, Judge Niemeyer argued that the Religion Clauses challenge had to be evaluated under the standards of *Kleindienst v. Mandel,* 408 U.S. 753 (1972). There, the Supreme Court upheld a decision by immigration officials to bar a Belgian Marxist from entering the country to participate in academic conferences. Although the Court recognized that First Amendment rights were implicated by the travel ban, the constitutional concern was tempered by the fact that "the power to exclude aliens is inherent in sovereignty, necessary for maintaining normal international relations and defending the country against

foreign encroachments and dangers—a power to be exercised exclusively by the political branches of government." The government's power "to exclude aliens altogether from the United States, or to prescribe the terms and conditions upon which they may come to this country, and to have its declared policy in that regard enforced exclusively through executive officers, without judicial intervention, is settled by our previous adjudications." Because "Congress has delegated conditional exercise of this power [of exclusion] to the Executive," the Court held that "when the Executive exercises this power negatively on the basis of a facially legitimate and bona fide reason, *the courts will neither look behind the exercise of that discretion, nor test it by balancing its justification against the First Amendment interests* of those who seek personal communication with the applicant." Accord, *Fiallo v. Bell*, 430 U.S. 787 (1977); *Kerry v. Din*, 135 S.Ct. 2128, 2139 (2015) (Kennedy, J., concurring in the judgment).

Even the Trump Administration did not push *Mandel* that far, nor did the Chief Justice's majority opinion, but both clearly read the Constitution and the Court's national security precedents to support a significant interpretive thumb on the scales in favor of the President's interpretation of both immigration statutes and the Constitution. That explains the difference between the Court majorities in the Travel Ban Cases and the Cakeshop Case, but is this a constitutionally defensible interpretive norm?

In support of such a norm are a number of constitutional precedents, as well as the sovereignty theory evoked in *Mandel*. Institutionally, the Supreme Court has been concerned that it does not have much to add to our government's politically volatile immigration policy. And some Justices believe that such policies are political questions for which serious judicial review would be inconsistent with Article III as well as Articles I and II.

On the other hand, scholars have praised the Court for more modest interventions, as when the Justices have trimmed back presidential or agency overreaching through narrow interpretations of the immigration laws. E.g., Philip Frickey, *Getting from Joe to Gene (McCarthy): The Avoidance Canon, Legal Process Theory, and Narrowing Statutory Interpretation in the Early Warren Court*, 93 Calif. L. Rev. 397 (2005). Why should the Roberts Court not have followed that approach in the Travel Ban Cases? Justice Breyer's dissenting opinion offered a similar legal process strategy for mild judicial pushback.

PROBLEM 8–2C:
PRESIDENTIAL AUTHORITY TO RESTRICT IMMIGRATION (REVISITED)

Recall that EO1 rested on the following statement from the White House: "Numerous foreign-born individuals have been convicted or implicated in terrorism-related crimes since September 11, 2001, including foreign nationals who entered the United States after receiving visitor, student, or employment visas, or who entered through the United States refugee resettlement program." In order to remain "vigilant during the visa-issuance process to ensure that those approved for admission do not intend to harm Americans and that they have no ties to terrorism," the President invoked his authority under 8 U.S.C. § 1182(f) to suspend for 90 days immigrant and nonimmigrant entry into the United States of nationals from seven majority-Muslim countries: Iraq, Iran, Libya, Sudan, Somalia, Syria, and Yemen. Given the context of this original travel ban *and* its terms *and* the President's statements, would EO1 have been sustained by the Supreme Court, given the reasoning of the Chief Justice's opinion for the Court? Does your analysis change if you also consider Justice Kennedy's concurring opinion?

Same question for EO2, described in some detail in Problem 8–2A. How do your answers to these questions change your understanding of the Chief Justice's and Justice Kennedy's opinions in *Trump v. Hawaii*?

SECTION 2. ISSUES OF LEGISLATIVE OVERREACHING

B. CONGRESSIONAL AND PRESIDENTIAL POWER TO CONTROL "EXECUTIVE" OFFICIALS

Page 1290. Insert the following materials right before Problem 8–5:

PROBLEM 8–4A:
IS THE STRUCTURE OF THE CONSUMER FINANCIAL PROTECTION BUREAU UNCONSTITUTIONAL?

The 2008 financial crisis destabilized the economy and left millions of Americans economically devastated. After hearings, Congress concluded that the financial services industry had pushed consumers into unsustainable forms of debt and that federal regulators had failed to prevent mounting risks to the economy, in part because those regulators were overly responsive to the industry they purported to police. Congress saw a need for an agency to help restore public confidence in markets: a regulator attentive to individuals and families. In the Dodd-Frank Wall Street Reform and Consumer Protection Act of 2010, P.L. 111-203, Congress established the Consumer Financial Protection Bureau (CFPB).

The CFPB is a financial regulator that applies a set of preexisting statutes to financial services marketed "primarily for personal, family, or household purposes." 12 U.S.C. § 5481(5)(A); *see also id.* §§ 5481(4), (6), (15). Congress has historically given a modicum of independence to financial regulators like the Federal Reserve, the FTC, and the Office of the Comptroller of the Currency. Rather than a multi-member commission, the CFPB's chief decision-maker is its Director, who is appointed by the President for a five-year term. The Director in 2017 would have seen his term expire in 2018; the next expiration date would be 2023, and so forth. The Director may be fired only for "inefficiency, neglect of duty, or malfeasance in office," 12 U.S.C. § 5491(c)(3)—the same language the Supreme Court approved for the independent commission in *Humphrey's*.

The Director has a considerable amount of authority. He or she sets the agency's general agenda; determines what proposed rules ought to be advanced for public comment; decides whether to issue a final rule, after notice and comment; manages the agency's budget; and accepts or rejects adjudicatory decisions rendered by administrative law judges (ALJs), who conduct the formal hearings and draft proposed orders and decisions.

You represent a company that has been sanctioned by the CFPB, based upon an agency adjudication presided over by an ALJ appointed by the Chief ALJ within the SEC (pursuant to an agreement between the SEC and the CFPB) and applying consumer-protective rules promulgated by the Director. Your main argument is that the order is inconsistent with the regulatory statute, but you are also considering an argument is that the decision-making structure of the agency violates the Constitution's separation of powers and/or Article II. Jot down the points you would make and the precedent(s) you would invoke. Think about the relevance of *Humphrey's Executor, Morrison v. Olson,* and *Free Enterprise,* among other precedents. Also consider the narrowest possible basis for invalidating the CFPB order (after the substantive statutory argument, of course).

Would such arguments succeed in federal court? Why or why not? See *PHH Corp. v. Consumer Financial Protection Bureau,* 881 F.3d 75 (D.C. Cir. en banc, Jan. 31, 2018). If you consult the D.C. Circuit's debate in *PHH,* you might pay special attention to Judge Kavanaugh's dissenting opinion; half a year later, he was nominated by President Trump to replace retiring Justice Anthony Kennedy.

If a court were to strike down the "for cause" removal protection for the Director, could that be severed from the remainder of the statute? After you have jotted down your thoughts, read the subsequent Supreme Court decision, and see if that decision changes your analysis in any way.

Lucia v. Securities and Exchange Commission
138 S.Ct. 2044 (2018).

One way the SEC administers the nation's securities laws is by instituting an administrative proceeding against an alleged wrongdoer. Typically, the Commission delegates the task of presiding over such a proceeding to one of the agency's five ALJs, all selected by the agency's staff and not appointed by the Commission. An ALJ assigned to hear an SEC enforcement action has the "authority to do all things necessary and appropriate" to ensure a "fair and orderly" adversarial proceeding. 17 C.F.R. §§ 201.111, 200.14(a). After a hearing ends, the ALJ issues an initial decision. The Commission can review that decision, but if it opts against review, it issues an order that the initial decision has become final. See § 201.360(d). The initial decision is then "deemed the action of the Commission." 15 U.S.C. § 78d–1(c).

Raymond Lucia was charged with violating certain securities laws. ALJ Cameron Elliot conducted the hearing and issued an initial decision concluding that Lucia had violated the law and imposing sanctions. On appeal to the SEC, Lucia objected that the ALJ was an "Officer of the United States" who had not been properly appointed. The SEC disagreed and ruled that an ALJ is just an "employee" of the agency, not an "Officer." The Supreme Court agreed with Lucia. Under Supreme Court precedent, to qualify as an Officer, rather than an employee, an individual must occupy a "continuing" position established by law and must "exercis[e] significant authority pursuant to the laws of the United States."

In *Freytag v. Commissioner,* 501 U.S. 868 (1991), the Supreme Court applied this framework to "special trial judges" (STJs) of the United States Tax Court. STJs could issue the final decision of the Tax Court in "comparatively narrow and minor matters." In major matters, they could preside over the hearing but could not issue a final decision. Instead, they were to "prepare proposed findings and an opinion" for a regular Tax Court judge to consider. The proceeding challenged in *Freytag* was a major one. The losing parties argued on appeal that the STJ who presided over their hearing was not constitutionally appointed.

Freytag held that STJs are Officers for purposes of the Appointments Clause. Such persons occupy a "continuing office established by law" and exercised "significant" authority" pursuant to the laws of the United States. The Tax Court argued that STJs were employees in all cases in which they could not enter a final decision. But the focus on finality "ignore[d] the significance of the duties and discretion that [STJs] possess." STJs "take testimony, conduct trials, rule on the admissibility of evidence, and have the power to enforce compliance with discovery orders. * * * [I]n the course of carrying out these important functions," STJs "exercise significant discretion."

Justice Kagan's opinion for the Court followed *Freytag* and ruled that the SEC's ALJs were "Officers" who had to be appointed by one of the bodies listed in the Appointments Clause. Like the Tax Court's STJs, the SEC's ALJs hold a continuing office established by law. SEC ALJs "receive[ ] a career appointment," 5 C.F.R. § 930.204(a), to a position created by statute, see 5 U.S.C. §§ 556–557, 5372, 3105. And they exercise the same "significant discretion" when carrying out the same "important functions" as STJs do. Both sets of officials have all the authority needed to ensure fair and orderly adversarial hearings—indeed, nearly all the tools of federal trial judges. The Commission's ALJs, like the Tax Court's STJs, "take testimony," "conduct trials," "rule on the admissibility of evidence," and "have the power to enforce compliance with discovery orders." So point for point from *Freytag*'s list, SEC ALJs have equivalent duties and powers as STJs in conducting adversarial inquiries.

Moreover, at the close of those proceedings, SEC ALJs issue decisions much like that in *Freytag*. STJs prepare proposed findings and an opinion adjudicating charges and assessing tax liabilities. Similarly, the Commission's

ALJs issue initial decisions containing factual findings, legal conclusions, and appropriate remedies. And what happens next reveals that the ALJ can play the more autonomous role. In a major Tax Court case, a regular Tax Court judge must always review an STJ's opinion, and that opinion comes to nothing unless the regular judge adopts it. By contrast, the SEC can decide against reviewing an ALJ's decision, and when it does so the ALJ's decision itself "becomes final" and is "deemed the action of the Commission."

Writing also for Justices Ginsburg and Sotomayor, **Justice Breyer** would have resolved the case on statutory rather than constitutional grounds. Dissenting, **Justice Sotomayor** (joined by Justice Ginsburg) would interpret the "significant authority" requirement to exclude agency personnel (such as the SEC ALJs) who did not have the authority to issue final, binding decisions.

Query: Revisit Problem 8–4A. Do you want to supplement your constitutional analysis for that problem?

CHAPTER 9

LIMITS ON THE JUDICIAL POWER

■ ■ ■

SECTION 2. "CASES" OR "CONTROVERSIES"

Page 1425.   Insert before Section 3:

CLAPPER V. AMNESTY INTERNATIONAL
568 U.S. 398, 133 S.Ct. 1138, 185 L.Ed.2d 264 (2013)

JUSTICE ALITO delivered the opinion of the Court.

Section 702 of the Foreign Intelligence Surveillance Act of 1978, 50 U.S.C. § 1881a, allows the Attorney General and the Director of National Intelligence to acquire foreign intelligence information by jointly authorizing the surveillance of individuals who are not "United States persons" and are reasonably believed to be located outside the United States. Before doing so, the Attorney General and the Director of National Intelligence normally must obtain the Foreign Intelligence Surveillance Court's approval. Respondents are United States persons whose work, they allege, requires them to engage in sensitive international communications with individuals who they believe are likely targets of surveillance under § 1881a. Respondents seek a declaration that § 1881a is unconstitutional, as well as an injunction against § 1881a-authorized surveillance. The question before us is whether respondents have Article III standing to seek this prospective relief.

Respondents assert that they can establish injury in fact because there is an objectively reasonable likelihood that their communications will be acquired under § 1881a at some point in the future. But respondents' theory of future injury is too speculative to satisfy the well-established requirement that threatened injury must be "certainly impending." And even if respondents could demonstrate that the threatened injury is certainly impending, they still would not be able to establish that this injury is fairly traceable to § 1881a. As an alternative argument, respondents contend that they are suffering present injury because the risk of § 1881a-authorized surveillance already has forced them to take costly and burdensome measures to protect the confidentiality of their international communications. But respondents cannot manufacture standing by choosing to make expenditures based on hypothetical future harm that is not certainly impending. We therefore hold that respondents lack Article III standing. * * *

In 1978, after years of debate, Congress enacted the Foreign Intelligence Surveillance Act (FISA) to authorize and regulate certain governmental electronic surveillance of communications for foreign intelligence purposes.

In constructing such a framework for foreign intelligence surveillance, Congress created two specialized courts. In FISA, Congress authorized judges of the Foreign Intelligence Surveillance Court (FISC) to approve electronic surveillance for foreign intelligence purposes if there is probable cause to believe that "the target of the electronic surveillance is a foreign power or an agent of a foreign power," and that each of the specific "facilities or places at which the electronic surveillance is directed is being used, or is about to be used, by a foreign power or an agent of a foreign power." Additionally, Congress vested the Foreign Intelligence Surveillance Court of Review with jurisdiction to review any denials by the FISC of applications for electronic surveillance. * * *

When Congress enacted the FISA Amendments Act of 2008 (FISA Amendments Act), it left much of FISA intact, but it "established a new and independent source of intelligence collection authority, beyond that granted in traditional FISA." As relevant here, § 702 of FISA, which was enacted as part of the FISA Amendments Act, supplements pre-existing FISA authority by creating a new framework under which the Government may seek the FISC's authorization of certain foreign intelligence surveillance targeting the communications of non-U.S. persons located abroad. Unlike traditional FISA surveillance, § 1881a does not require the Government to demonstrate probable cause that the target of the electronic surveillance is a foreign power or agent of a foreign power. And, unlike traditional FISA, § 1881a does not require the Government to specify the nature and location of each of the particular facilities or places at which the electronic surveillance will occur. * * *

The Foreign Intelligence Surveillance Court's role includes determining whether the Government's certification contains the required elements. Additionally, the Court assesses whether the targeting procedures are "reasonably designed" (1) to "ensure that an acquisition . . . is limited to targeting persons reasonably believed to be located outside the United States" and (2) to "prevent the intentional acquisition of any communication as to which the sender and all intended recipients are known . . . to be located in the United States." The Court analyzes whether the minimization procedures "meet the definition of minimization procedures under section 1801(h) . . . , as appropriate." The Court also assesses whether the targeting and minimization procedures are consistent with the statute and the Fourth Amendment.

Respondents are attorneys and human rights, labor, legal, and media organizations whose work allegedly requires them to engage in sensitive and sometimes privileged telephone and e-mail communications with colleagues, clients, sources, and other individuals located abroad. Respondents believe that some of the people with whom they exchange foreign intelligence information are likely targets of surveillance under § 1881a. Specifically, respondents claim that they communicate by telephone and e-mail with people the Government "believes or believed to be associated with terrorist organizations," "people located in geographic areas that are a special focus" of the Government's counterterrorism or diplomatic efforts, and activists who oppose governments that are supported by the United States Government.

Respondents claim that § 1881a compromises their ability to locate witnesses, cultivate sources, obtain information, and communicate confidential information to their clients. Respondents also assert that they "have ceased engaging" in certain telephone and e-mail conversations. According to respondents, the threat of surveillance will compel them to travel abroad in order to have in-person conversations. In addition, respondents declare that they have undertaken "costly and burdensome measures" to protect the confidentiality of sensitive communications. * * *

The law of Article III standing, which is built on separation-of-powers principles, serves to prevent the judicial process from being used to usurp the powers of the political branches. In keeping with the purpose of this doctrine, "[o]ur standing inquiry has been especially rigorous when reaching the merits of the dispute would force us to decide whether an action taken by one of the other two branches of the Federal Government was unconstitutional "Relaxation of standing requirements is directly related to the expansion of judicial power," and we have often found a lack of standing in cases in which the Judiciary has been requested to review actions of the political branches in the fields of intelligence gathering and foreign affairs.

To establish Article III standing, an injury must be "concrete, particularized, and actual or imminent; fairly traceable to the challenged action; and redressable by a favorable ruling." "Although imminence is concededly a somewhat elastic concept, it cannot be stretched beyond its purpose, which is to ensure that the alleged injury is not too speculative for Article III purposes—that the injury is certainly impending." Thus, we have repeatedly reiterated that "threatened injury must be certainly impending to constitute injury in fact," and that "[a]llegations of possible future injury" are not sufficient.

Respondents assert that they can establish injury in fact that is fairly traceable to § 1881a because there is an objectively reasonable likelihood that their communications with their foreign contacts will be intercepted under § 1881a at some point in the future. This argument fails. As an initial matter, the Second Circuit's "objectively reasonable likelihood" standard is inconsistent with our requirement that "threatened injury must be certainly impending to constitute injury in fact. Furthermore, respondents' argument rests on their highly speculative fear that: (1) the Government will decide to target the communications of non-U.S. persons with whom they communicate; (2) in doing so, the Government will choose to invoke its authority under § 1881a rather than utilizing another method of surveillance; (3) the Article III judges who serve on the Foreign Intelligence Surveillance Court will conclude that the Government's proposed surveillance procedures satisfy § 1881a's many safeguards and are consistent with the Fourth Amendment; (4) the Government will succeed in intercepting the communications of respondents' contacts; and (5) respondents will be parties to the particular communications that the Government intercepts. As discussed below, respondents' theory of standing, which relies on a highly attenuated chain of possibilities, does not satisfy the requirement that threatened injury must be certainly impending. * * *

Second, even if respondents could demonstrate that the targeting of their foreign contacts is imminent, respondents can only speculate as to whether the Government will seek to use § 1881a-authorized surveillance (rather than other methods) to do so. The Government has numerous other methods of conducting surveillance, none of which is challenged here. * * *

Third, even if respondents could show that the Government will seek the Foreign Intelligence Surveillance Court's authorization to acquire the communications of respondents' foreign contacts under § 1881a, respondents can only speculate as to whether that court will authorize such surveillance. In the past, we have been reluctant to endorse standing theories that require guesswork as to how independent decisionmakers will exercise their judgment. * * *

Fourth, even if the Government were to obtain the Foreign Intelligence Surveillance Court's approval to target respondents' foreign contacts under § 1881a, it is unclear whether the Government would succeed in acquiring the communications of respondents' foreign contacts. And fifth, even if the Government were to conduct surveillance of respondents' foreign contacts, respondents can only speculate as to whether their own communications with their foreign contacts would be incidentally acquired.

Respondents' alternative argument—namely, that they can establish standing based on the measures that they have undertaken to avoid § 1881a-authorized surveillance—fares no better. Respondents assert that they are suffering ongoing injuries that are fairly traceable to § 1881a because the risk of surveillance under § 1881a requires them to take costly and burdensome measures to protect the confidentiality of their communications. Respondents claim, for instance, that the threat of surveillance sometimes compels them to avoid certain e-mail and phone conversations, to "tal[k] in generalities rather than specifics," or to travel so that they can have in-person conversations. * * *

The Second Circuit's analysis improperly allowed respondents to establish standing by asserting that they suffer present costs and burdens that are based on a fear of surveillance, so long as that fear is not "fanciful, paranoid, or otherwise unreasonable." This improperly waters down the fundamental requirements of Article III. Respondents' contention that they have standing because they incurred certain costs as a reasonable reaction to a risk of harm is unavailing—because the harm respondents seek to avoid is not certainly impending. In other words, respondents cannot manufacture standing merely by inflicting harm on themselves based on their fears of hypothetical future harm that is not certainly impending. Any ongoing injuries that respondents are suffering are not fairly traceable to § 1881a.

If the law were otherwise, an enterprising plaintiff would be able to secure a lower standard for Article III standing simply by making an expenditure based on a nonparanoid fear. As Judge Raggi accurately noted, under the Second Circuit panel's reasoning, respondents could, "for the price of a plane ticket, . . . transform their standing burden from one requiring a showing of actual or imminent . . . interception to one requiring a showing that their subjective fear of such interception is not fanciful, irrational, or clearly unreasonable." Thus, allowing respondents to bring this action based on costs they incurred in response to a speculative threat would be tantamount to accepting a repackaged version of respondents' first failed theory of standing. * * *

Respondents incorrectly maintain that "[t]he kinds of injuries incurred here—injuries incurred because of [respondents'] reasonable efforts to avoid greater injuries that are otherwise likely to flow from the conduct they challenge—are the same kinds of injuries that this Court held to support standing in cases such as" *Laidlaw* * * * As an initial matter, none of these cases holds or even suggests that plaintiffs can establish standing simply by claiming that they experienced a "chilling effect" that resulted from a governmental policy that does not regulate, constrain, or compel any action on their part. Moreover, each of these cases was very different from the present case.

In *Laidlaw*, plaintiffs' standing was based on "the proposition that a company's continuous and pervasive illegal discharges of pollutants into a river would cause nearby residents to curtail their recreational use of that waterway and would subject them to other economic and aesthetic harms." Because the unlawful discharges of pollutants were "concededly ongoing," the only issue was whether "nearby residents"—who were members of the organizational plaintiffs—acted reasonably in refraining from using the polluted area. *Laidlaw* is therefore quite unlike the present case, in which it is not "concede[d]" that respondents would be subject to unlawful surveillance but for their decision to take preventive measures. *Laidlaw* would resemble this case only if (1) it were undisputed that the Government was using § 1881a-authorized surveillance to acquire respondents' communications and (2) the sole dispute concerned the reasonableness of respondents' preventive measures.

JUSTICE BREYER, with whom **JUSTICE GINSBURG**, **JUSTICE SOTOMAYOR**, and **JUSTICE KAGAN** join, dissenting.

[U]sing the authority of § 1881a, the Government can obtain court approval for its surveillance of electronic communications between places within the United States and targets in foreign territories by showing the court (1) that "a significant purpose of the acquisition is to obtain foreign intelligence information," and (2) that it will use general targeting and privacy-intrusion minimization procedures of a kind that the court had previously approved

Several considerations, based upon the record along with commonsense inferences, convince me that there is a very high likelihood that Government, acting under the authority of § 1881a, will intercept at least some of the communications just described. First, the plaintiffs have engaged, and continue to engage, in electronic communications of a kind that the 2008 amendment, but not the prior Act, authorizes the Government to intercept. These communications include discussions with family members of those detained at Guantanamo, friends and acquaintances of those persons, and investigators, experts and others with knowledge of circumstances related to terrorist activities. These persons are foreigners located outside the United States. They are not "foreign power[s]" or "agent[s] of . . . foreign power [s]." And the plaintiffs state that they exchange with these persons "foreign intelligence information," defined to include information that "relates to" "international terrorism" and "the national defense or the security of the United States."

Second, the plaintiffs have a strong motive to engage in, and the Government has a strong motive to listen to, conversations of the kind described. A lawyer representing a client normally seeks to learn the circumstances surrounding the crime (or the civil wrong) of which the client is accused. A fair reading of the affidavit of Scott McKay, for example, taken together with elementary considerations of a lawyer's obligation to his client, indicates that McKay will engage in conversations that concern what suspected foreign terrorists, such as his client, have done; in conversations that concern his clients' families, colleagues, and contacts; in conversations that concern what those persons (or those connected to them) have said and done, at least in relation to terrorist activities; in conversations that concern the political, social, and commercial environments in which the suspected terrorists have lived and worked; and so forth. Journalists and human rights workers have strong similar motives to conduct conversations of this kind. * * *

The majority more plausibly says that the plaintiffs have failed to show that the threatened harm is "certainly impending." But, as the majority appears to concede, certainty is not, and never has been, the touchstone of standing. The future is inherently uncertain. Yet federal courts frequently entertain actions for injunctions and for declaratory relief aimed at preventing future activities that are reasonably likely or highly likely, but not absolutely certain, to take place. And that degree of certainty is all that is needed to support standing here. * * *

The majority cannot find support in cases that use the words "certainly impending" to deny standing. While I do not claim to have read every standing case, I have examined quite a few, and not yet found any such case. * * *

In sum, as the Court concedes, the word "certainly" in the phrase "certainly impending" does not refer to absolute certainty. As our case law demonstrates, what the Constitution requires is something more akin to "reasonable probability" or "high probability." The use of some such standard is all that is necessary here to ensure the actual concrete injury that the Constitution demands.

NOTES

1.   *The Plaintiffs' Dilemma.* The Court faulted the plaintiffs for being unable to show that their calls have been intercepted under authority of § 1881a. But the possible existence of any surveillance of their calls, let alone the legal basis invoked by the agency in particular cases, was top secret, so there's no way the plaintiffs can offer direct evidence. Yet the Court wouldn't let them establish their standing indirectly, so they seem to have no way of protesting what could well be a violation of their constitutional rights.

2.   *What About* Laidlaw? *Is* it fair to say that the majority distinguishes *Laidlaw* on the ground that in *Laidlaw*, there was no doubt that the defendant's conduct was taking place, and the only issue was the impact on the plaintiffs, whereas here it was unclear whether the conduct was even taking place? Doesn't that really go to the fairly traceable requirement rather than injury in fact?

3.   *What Is "Imminent"?* Imminent seems to carry an implication of certainty and immediacy. Susan B. Anthony List v. Driehaus, 134 S.Ct. 2334 (2014), makes it clear that neither temporal proximity nor certainty is required in order to obtain standing. Ohio has a law prohibiting false statements in connection with elections. The lead plaintiff was accused by a candidate of making such statements, and the candidate filed a complaint with the Ohio

Elections Commission. When the candidate lost, however, the complaint was dropped. The Court nevertheless held that the plaintiff had standing to challenge the law because it said it intended to make similar statements about other candidates in the future elections, and if doing so could then face the burden of defending administrative proceedings as well as possible criminal charges. It was enough that the plaintiff established "an intention to engage in a course of conduct arguably affected with a constitutional interest, but proscribed by statute, and there exists a credible threat of prosecution thereunder."

HOLLINGSWORTH V. PERRY
570 U.S. 693, 133 S.Ct. 2652, 186 L.Ed.2d 768 (2013)

[An initiative measure (Proposition 8) in California limited marriage to members of the opposite sexes. After a lengthy trial, the federal district court ruled the initiative measure unconstitutional. State officials decided not to appeal. The individuals who had led the effort to place Proposition 8 on the ballot filed an appeal. The federal appellate court certified the following question to the California Supreme Court:

> "Whether under Article II, Section 8 of the California Constitution, or otherwise under California law, the official proponents of an initiative measure possess either a particularized interest in the initiative's validity or the authority to assert the State's interest in the initiative's validity, which would enable them to defend the constitutionality of the initiative upon its adoption or appeal a judgment invalidating the initiative, when the public officials charged with that duty refuse to do so."

The California Supreme Court responded that:

> "In a postelection challenge to a voter-approved initiative measure, the official proponents of the initiative are authorized under California law to appear and assert the state's interest in the initiative's validity and to appeal a judgment invalidating the measure when the public officials who ordinarily defend the measure or appeal such a judgment decline to do so."

Perry v. Brown, 52 Cal. 4th 1116, 1127, 265 P. 3d 1002, 1007 (2011). On certiorari, the Court considered whether a case or controversy continued to exist after the state officials dropped out of the case.]

CHIEF JUSTICE ROBERTS delivered the opinion of the Court.

Petitioners argue that the California Constitution and its election laws give them a " 'unique,' 'special,' and 'distinct' role in the initiative process— one 'involving both authority and responsibilities that differ from other supporters of the measure.' " True enough—but only when it comes to the process of enacting the law. Upon submitting the proposed initiative to the attorney general, petitioners became the official "proponents" of Proposition 8. As such, they were responsible for collecting the signatures required to qualify the measure for the ballot. After those signatures were collected, the proponents alone had the right to file the measure with election officials to put it on the ballot. Petitioners also possessed control over the arguments in favor of the initiative that would appear in California's ballot pamphlets.

But once Proposition 8 was approved by the voters, the measure became "a duly enacted constitutional amendment or statute." Petitioners have no role—special or otherwise—in the enforcement of Proposition 8. They therefore have no "personal stake" in defending its enforcement that is distinguishable from the general interest of every citizen of California. * * *

Without a judicially cognizable interest of their own, petitioners attempt to invoke that of someone else. They assert that even if *they* have no cognizable interest in appealing the District Court's judgment, the State of California does, and they may assert that interest on the State's behalf. * * *

Petitioners contend that this case is different, because the California Supreme Court has determined that they are "authorized under California law to appear and assert the state's interest" in the validity of Proposition 8. The court below agreed: "All a federal court need determine is that the state has suffered a harm sufficient to confer standing and that the party seeking to invoke the jurisdiction of the court is authorized by the state to represent its interest in remedying that harm." * * *

Both petitioners and respondents seek support from dicta in *Arizonans for Official English* v. *Arizona*, 520 U.S. 43. The plaintiff in *Arizonans for Official English* filed a constitutional challenge to an Arizona ballot initiative declaring English " 'the official language of the State of Arizona.' " After the District Court declared the initiative unconstitutional, Arizona's Governor announced that she would not pursue an appeal. Instead, the principal sponsor of the ballot initiative—the Arizonans for Official English Committee—sought to defend the measure in the Ninth Circuit. Analogizing the sponsors to the Arizona Legislature, the Ninth Circuit held that the Committee was "qualified to defend [the initiative] on appeal," and affirmed the District Court.

Before finding the case mooted by other events, this Court expressed "grave doubts" about the Ninth Circuit's standing analysis. We reiterated that "[s]tanding to defend on appeal in the place of an original defendant ... demands that the litigant possess 'a direct stake in the outcome.' " We recognized that a legislator authorized by state law to represent the State's interest may satisfy standing requirements * * *, but noted that the Arizona committee and its members were "not elected representatives, and we [we}re aware of no Arizona law appointing initiative sponsors as agents of the people of Arizona to defend, in lieu of public officials, the constitutionality of initiatives made law of the State."

Petitioners argue that, by virtue of the California Supreme Court's decision, they *are* authorized to act " 'as agents of the people' of California." But that Court never described petitioners as "agents of the people," or of anyone else. * * * All that the California Supreme Court decision stands for is that, so far as California is concerned, petitioners may argue in defense of Proposition 8. This "does not mean that the proponents become de facto public officials"; the authority they enjoy is "simply the authority to participate as parties in a court action and to assert legal arguments in defense of the state's interest in the validity of the initiative measure." That interest is by definition a generalized one, and it is precisely because proponents assert such an interest that they lack standing under our precedents. * * *

More to the point, the most basic features of an agency relationship are missing here. Agency requires more than mere authorization to assert a particular interest. "An essential element of agency is the principal's right to control the agent's actions." Yet petitioners answer to no one; they decide for themselves, with no review, what arguments to make and how to make them. Unlike California's attorney general, they are not elected at regular intervals—or elected at all. See Cal. Const., Art. V, § 11. No provision provides for their removal. As one *amicus* explains, "the proponents apparently have an unelected appointment for an unspecified period of time as defenders of the initiative, however and to whatever extent they choose to defend it."

"If the relationship between two persons is one of agency . . . , the agent owes a fiduciary obligation to the principal." 1 Restatement § 1.01, Comment *e*. But petitioners owe nothing of the sort to the people of California. Unlike California's elected officials, they have taken no oath of office. As the California Supreme Court explained, petitioners are bound simply by "the same ethical constraints that apply to all other parties in a legal proceeding." They are free to pursue a purely ideological commitment to the law's constitutionality without the need to take cognizance of resource constraints, changes in public opinion, or potential ramifications for other state priorities.

Finally, the California Supreme Court stated that "[t]he question of who should bear responsibility for any attorney fee award . . . is *entirely distinct* from the question" before it. But it is hornbook law that "a principal has a duty to indemnify the agent against expenses and other losses incurred by the agent in defending against actions brought by third parties if the agent acted with actual authority in taking the action challenged by the third party's suit." 2 Restatement § 8.14, Comment *d*. If the issue of fees is entirely distinct from the authority question, then authority cannot be based on agency. * * *

We have never before upheld the standing of a private party to defend the constitutionality of a state statute when state officials have chosen not to. We decline to do so for the first time here.

Because petitioners have not satisfied their burden to demonstrate standing to appeal the judgment of the District Court, the Ninth Circuit was without jurisdiction to consider the appeal. The judgment of the Ninth Circuit is vacated, and the case is remanded with instructions to dismiss the appeal for lack of jurisdiction.

JUSTICE KENNEDY, with whom JUSTICE THOMAS, JUSTICE ALITO, and JUSTICE SOTOMAYOR join, dissenting.

The Court's opinion is correct to state, and the Supreme Court of California was careful to acknowledge, that a proponent's standing to defend an initiative in federal court is a question of federal law. Proper resolution of the justiciability question requires, in this case, a threshold determination of state law. The state-law question is how California defines and elaborates the status and authority of an initiative's proponents who seek to intervene in court to defend the initiative after its adoption by the electorate. Those state-law issues have been addressed in a meticulous and unanimous opinion by the Supreme Court of California.

Under California law, a proponent has the authority to appear in court and assert the State's interest in defending an enacted initiative when the public officials charged with that duty refuse to do so. The State deems such an appearance essential to the integrity of its initiative process. Yet the Court today concludes that this state-defined status and this state-conferred right fall short of meeting federal requirements because the proponents cannot point to a formal delegation of authority that tracks the requirements of the Restatement of Agency. But the State Supreme Court's definition of proponents' powers is binding on this Court. And that definition is fully sufficient to establish the standing and adversity that are requisites for justiciability under Article III of the United States Constitution.

In my view Article III does not require California, when deciding who may appear in court to defend an initiative on its behalf, to comply with the Restatement of Agency or with this Court's view of how a State should make its laws or structure its government. The Court's reasoning does not take into account the fundamental principles or the practical dynamics of the initiative system in California, which uses this mechanism to control and to bypass public officials—the same officials who would not defend the initiative, an injury the Court now leaves unremedied. The Court's decision also has implications for the 26 other States that use an initiative or popular referendum system and which, like California, may choose to have initiative proponents stand in for the State when public officials decline to defend an initiative in litigation. In my submission, the Article III requirement for a justiciable case or controversy does not prevent proponents from having their day in court. * * *

The Court concludes that proponents lack sufficient ties to the state government. It notes that they "are not elected," "answer to no one," and lack " 'a fiduciary obligation' " to the State. *Ante,* at 15 (quoting 1 Restatement (Third) of Agency § 1.01, Comments *e, f* (2005)). But what the Court deems deficiencies in the proponents' connection to the State government, the State Supreme Court saw as essential qualifications to defend the initiative system. The very object of the initiative system is to establish a lawmaking process that does not depend upon state officials. In California, the popular initiative is necessary to implement "the theory that all power of government ultimately resides in the people." The right to adopt initiatives has been described by the California courts as "one of the most precious rights of [the State's] democratic process." That historic role for the initiative system "grew out of dissatisfaction with the then governing public officials and a widespread belief that the people had lost control of the political process." *Ibid.* The initiative's "primary purpose," then, "was to afford the people the ability to propose and to adopt constitutional amendments or statutory provisions that their elected public officials had refused or declined to adopt."

The California Supreme Court has determined that this purpose is undermined if the very officials the initiative process seeks to circumvent are the only parties who can defend an enacted initiative when it is challenged in a legal proceeding. Giving the Governor and attorney general this *de facto* veto will erode one of the cornerstones of the State's governmental structure. And in light of the frequency with which initiatives' opponents resort to litigation, the impact of that veto could be substantial. As a consequence, California finds it necessary to vest the responsibility and right to defend a voter-approved initiative in the initiative's proponents when the State Executive declines to do so.

Yet today the Court demands that the State follow the Restatement of Agency. There are reasons, however, why California might conclude that a conventional agency relationship is inconsistent with the history, design, and purpose of the initiative process. The State may not wish to associate itself with proponents or their views outside of the "extremely narrow and limited" context of this litigation, or to bear the cost of proponents' legal fees. The State may also wish to avoid the odd conflict of having a formal agent of the State (the initiative's proponent) arguing in favor of a law's validity while state officials (*e.g.,* the attorney general) contend in the same proceeding that it should be found invalid. * * *

Arizonans for Official English v. *Arizona*, 520 U.S. 43 (1997), is consistent with the premises of this dissent, not with the rationale of the Court's opinion. There, the Court noted its serious doubts as to the aspiring defenders' standing because there was "no Arizona law appointing initiative sponsors as agents of the people of Arizona to defend, in lieu of public officials, the constitutionality of initiatives made law of the State." The Court did use the word "agents"; but, read in context, it is evident that the Court's intention was not to demand a formal agency relationship in compliance with the Restatement. Rather, the Court used the term as shorthand for a party whom "state law authorizes" to "represent the State's interests" in court. * * *

There is much irony in the Court's approach to justiciability in this case. A prime purpose of justiciability is to ensure vigorous advocacy, yet the Court insists upon litigation conducted by state officials whose preference is to lose the case. The doctrine is meant to ensure that courts are responsible and constrained in their power, but the Court's opinion today means that a single district court can make a decision with far-reaching effects that cannot be reviewed. And rather than honor the principle that justiciability exists to allow disputes of public policy to be resolved by the political process rather than the courts, here the Court refuses to allow a State's authorized representatives to defend the outcome of a democratic election. * * *

In the end, what the Court fails to grasp or accept is the basic premise of the initiative process. And it is this. The essence of democracy is that the right to make law rests in the people and flows to the government, not the other way around. Freedom resides first in the people without need of a grant from government. The California initiative process embodies these principles and has done so for over a century. "Through the structure of its government, and the character of those who exercise government authority, a State defines itself as sovereign." *Gregory* v. *Ashcroft*, 501 U.S. 452, 460 (1991). In California and the 26 other States that permit initiatives and popular referendums, the people have exercised their own inherent sovereign right to govern themselves. The Court today frustrates that choice by nullifying, for failure to comply with the Restatement of Agency, a State Supreme Court decision holding that state law authorizes an enacted initiative's proponents to defend the law if and when the State's usual legal advocates decline to do so. The Court's opinion fails to abide by precedent and misapplies basic principles of justiciability. Those errors necessitate this respectful dissent.

UNITED STATES v. WINDSOR

570 U.S. 744, 133 S.Ct. 2675, 186 L.Ed.2d 808 (2013)

JUSTICE KENNEDY delivered the opinion of the Court.

Two women then resident in New York were married in a lawful ceremony in Ontario, Canada, in 2007. Edith Windsor and Thea Spyer returned to their home in New York City. When Spyer died in 2009, she left her entire estate to Windsor. Windsor sought to claim the estate tax exemption for surviving spouses. She was barred from doing so, however, by a federal law, the Defense of Marriage Act, which excludes a same-sex partner from the definition of "spouse" as that term is used in federal statutes. Windsor paid the taxes but filed suit to challenge the constitutionality of this provision. The United States District Court and the Court of Appeals ruled that this portion of the statute is unconstitutional and ordered the United States to pay Windsor a refund. [The United States took the position that DOMA was unconstitutional, but at the same time it continued to enforce the law pending judicial resolution of the issue. The Bipartisan Legal Advisory Group (BLAG) of the House of Representatives voted to intervene in the litigation to defend the constitutionality of § 3 of DOMA. The Court also appointed a law professor to act as amicus on the jurisdictional issue, since all the parties agreed the Court had jurisdiction.]

There is no dispute that when this case was in the District Court it presented a concrete disagreement between opposing parties, a dispute suitable for judicial resolution. "[A] taxpayer has standing to challenge the collection of a specific tax assessment as unconstitutional; being forced to pay such a tax causes a real and immediate economic injury to the individual taxpayer." Windsor suffered a redressable injury when she was required to pay estate taxes from which, in her view, she was exempt but for the alleged invalidity of § 3 of DOMA.

The decision of the Executive not to defend the constitutionality of § 3 in court while continuing to deny refunds and to assess deficiencies does introduce a complication. Even though the Executive's current position was announced before the District Court entered its judgment, the Government's agreement with Windsor's position would not have deprived the District Court of jurisdiction to entertain and resolve the refund suit; for her injury (failure to obtain a refund allegedly required by law) was concrete, persisting, and unredressed. The Government's position— agreeing with Windsor's legal contention but refusing to give it effect— meant that there was a justiciable controversy between the parties, despite what the claimant would find to be an inconsistency in that stance. Windsor, the Government, BLAG, and the *amicus* appear to agree upon that point. The disagreement is over the standing of the parties, or aspiring parties, to take an appeal in the Court of Appeals and to appear as parties in further proceedings in this Court.

The *amicus'* position is that, given the Government's concession that § 3 is unconstitutional, once the District Court ordered the refund the case should have ended; and the *amicus* argues the Court of Appeals should have dismissed the appeal. The *amicus* submits that once the President agreed with Windsor's legal position and the District Court issued its judgment, the parties were no longer adverse. From this standpoint the United States was a prevailing party below, just as Windsor was. Accordingly, the *amicus* reasons, it is inappropriate for this Court to grant certiorari and proceed to rule on the merits; for the United States seeks no redress from the judgment entered against it.

This position, however, elides the distinction between two principles: the jurisdictional requirements of Article III and the prudential limits on its exercise. The latter are "essentially matters of judicial self-governance." The Court has kept these two strands separate: "Article III standing, which enforces the Constitution's case-or-controversy requirement, see *Lujan* v. *Defenders of Wildlife,* 504 U.S. 555, 559–562 (1992); and prudential standing, which embodies 'judicially self-imposed limits on the exercise of federal jurisdiction,' *Allen* [v. *Wright,*] 468 U.S. [737,] 751 [(1984)]." *Elk Grove Unified School Dist.* v. *Newdow,* 542 U.S. 1, 11–12 (2004).

The requirements of Article III standing are familiar:

> "First, the plaintiff must have suffered an 'injury in fact'—an invasion of a legally protected interest which is (a) concrete and particularized, and (b) 'actual or imminent, not "conjectural or hypothetical." ' Second, there must be a causal connection between the injury and the conduct complained of—the injury has to be 'fairly . . . trace[able] to the challenged action of the defendant, and not . . . th[e] result [of] the independent action of some third party not before the court.' Third, it must be 'likely,' as opposed to merely 'speculative,' that the injury will be 'redressed by a favorable decision.' " *Lujan, supra,* at 560–561 (footnote and citations omitted).

Rules of prudential standing, by contrast, are more flexible "rule[s] . . . of federal appellate practice," designed to protect the courts from "decid[ing] abstract questions of wide public significance even [when] other governmental institutions may be more competent to address the questions and even though judicial intervention may be unnecessary to protect individual rights."

In this case the United States retains a stake sufficient to support Article III jurisdiction on appeal and in proceedings before this Court. The judgment in question orders the United States to pay Windsor the refund she seeks. An order directing the Treasury to pay money is "a real and immediate economic injury," indeed as real and immediate as an order directing an individual to pay a tax. That the Executive may welcome this order to pay the refund if it is accompanied by the constitutional ruling it wants does not eliminate the injury to the national Treasury if payment is made, or to the taxpayer if it is not. The judgment orders the United States to pay money that it would not disburse but for the court's order. The Government of the United States has a valid legal argument that it is injured even if the Executive disagrees with § 3 of DOMA, which results in Windsor's liability for the tax. Windsor's ongoing claim for funds that the United States refuses to pay thus establishes a controversy sufficient for Article III jurisdiction. It would be a different case if the Executive had taken the further step of paying Windsor the refund to which she was entitled under the District Court's ruling.

This Court confronted a comparable case in *INS* v. *Chadha*, 462 U.S. 919 (1983). A statute by its terms allowed one House of Congress to order the Immigration and Naturalization Service (INS) to deport the respondent Chadha. There, as here, the Executive determined that the statute was unconstitutional, and "the INS presented the Executive's views on the constitutionality of the House action to the Court of Appeals." The INS, however, continued to abide by the statute, and "the INS brief to the Court of Appeals did not alter the agency's decision to comply with the House action ordering deportation of Chadha." This Court held "that the INS was sufficiently aggrieved by the Court of Appeals decision prohibiting it from taking action it would otherwise take," regardless of whether the agency welcomed the judgment. The necessity of a "case or controversy" to satisfy Article III was defined as a requirement that the Court's " 'decision will have real meaning: if we rule for Chadha, he will not be deported; if we uphold [the statute], the INS will execute its order and deport him.' " This conclusion was not dictum. It was a necessary predicate to the Court's holding that "prior to Congress' intervention, there was adequate Art. III adverseness." The holdings of cases are instructive, and the words of *Chadha* make clear its holding that the refusal of the Executive to provide the relief sought suffices to preserve a justiciable dispute as required by Article III. In short, even where "the Government largely agree[s] with the opposing party on the merits of the controversy," there is sufficient adverseness and an "adequate basis for jurisdiction in the fact that the Government intended to enforce the challenged law against that party." * * *

While these principles suffice to show that this case presents a justiciable controversy under Article III, the prudential problems inherent in the Executive's unusual position require some further discussion. The Executive's agreement with Windsor's legal argument raises the risk that instead of a " 'real, earnest and vital controversy,' " the Court faces a "friendly, non-adversary, proceeding . . . [in which] 'a party beaten in the legislature [seeks to] transfer to the courts an inquiry as to the constitutionality of the legislative act.'" Even when Article III permits the exercise of federal jurisdiction, prudential considerations demand that the Court insist upon "that concrete adverseness which sharpens the presentation of issues upon which the court so largely depends for illumination of difficult constitutional questions." *Baker* v. *Carr*, 369 U.S. 186, 204 (1962).

There are, of course, reasons to hear a case and issue a ruling even when one party is reluctant to prevail in its position. Unlike Article III requirements—which must be satisfied by the parties before judicial consideration is appropriate—the relevant prudential factors that counsel against hearing this case are subject to "countervailing considerations [that] may outweigh the concerns underlying the usual reluctance to exert judicial power." One consideration is the extent to which adversarial presentation of the issues is assured by the participation of *amici curiae* prepared to defend with vigor the constitutionality of the legislative act. With respect to this prudential aspect of standing as well, the *Chadha* Court encountered a similar situation. It noted that "there may be prudential, as opposed to Art. III, concerns about sanctioning the adjudication of [this case] in the absence of any participant supporting the validity of [the statute]. The Court of Appeals properly dispelled any such concerns by inviting and accepting briefs from both Houses of Congress." *Chadha* was not an anomaly in this respect. The Court adopts the practice of entertaining arguments made by an *amicus* when the Solicitor General confesses error with respect to a judgment below, even if the confession is in effect an admission that an Act of Congress is unconstitutional.

In the case now before the Court the attorneys for BLAG present a substantial argument for the constitutionality of § 3 of DOMA. BLAG's sharp adversarial presentation of the issues satisfies the prudential concerns that otherwise might counsel against hearing an appeal from a decision with which the principal parties agree. Were this Court to hold that prudential rules require it to dismiss the case, and, in consequence, that the Court of Appeals erred in failing to dismiss it as well, extensive litigation would ensue. The district courts in 94 districts throughout the Nation would be without precedential guidance not only in tax refund suits but also in cases involving the whole of DOMA's sweep involving over 1,000 federal statutes and a myriad of federal regulations. * * * That numerical prediction may not be certain, but it is certain that the cost in judicial resources and expense of litigation for all persons adversely affected would be immense. True, the very extent of DOMA's mandate means that at some point a case likely would arise without the prudential concerns raised here; but the costs, uncertainties, and alleged harm and injuries likely would continue for a time measured in years before the issue is resolved. In these unusual and urgent circumstances, the very term "prudential" counsels that it is a proper exercise of the Court's responsibility to take jurisdiction. For these reasons, the prudential and Article III requirements are met here; and, as a consequence, the Court need not decide whether BLAG would have standing to challenge the District Court's ruling and its affirmance in the Court of Appeals on BLAG's own authority.

The Court's conclusion that this petition may be heard on the merits does not imply that no difficulties would ensue if this were a common practice in ordinary cases. The Executive's failure to defend the constitutionality of an Act of Congress based on a constitutional theory not yet established in judicial decisions has created a procedural dilemma. On the one hand, as noted, the Government's agreement with Windsor raises questions about the propriety of entertaining a suit in which it seeks affirmance of an order invalidating a federal law and ordering the United States to pay money. On the other hand, if the Executive's agreement with a plaintiff that a law is unconstitutional is enough to preclude judicial review, then the Supreme Court's primary role in determining the constitutionality of a law that has inflicted real injury on a plaintiff who has brought a justiciable legal claim would become only secondary to the President's. This would undermine the clear dictate of the separation-of-powers principle that "when an Act of Congress is alleged to conflict with the Constitution, '[i]t is emphatically the province and duty of the judicial department to say what the law is.'" Similarly, with respect to the legislative power, when Congress has passed a statute and a President has signed it, it poses grave challenges to the separation of powers for the Executive at a particular moment to be able to nullify Congress' enactment solely on its own initiative and without any determination from the Court.

The Court's jurisdictional holding, it must be underscored, does not mean the arguments for dismissing this dispute on prudential grounds lack substance. Yet the difficulty the Executive faces should be acknowledged. When the Executive makes a principled determination that a statute is unconstitutional, it faces a difficult choice. Still, there is no suggestion here that it is appropriate for the Executive as a matter of course to challenge statutes in the judicial forum rather than making the case to Congress for their amendment or repeal. The integrity of the political process would be at risk if difficult constitutional issues were simply referred to the Court as a routine exercise. But this case is not routine. And the capable defense of the law by BLAG ensures that these prudential issues do not cloud the merits question, which is one of immediate importance to the Federal Government and to hundreds of thousands of persons. These circumstances support the Court's decision to proceed to the merits.

JUSTICE SCALIA, with whom JUSTICE THOMAS joins, and with whom the CHIEF JUSTICE joins as to Part I [the discussion of standing excerpted below].

The Court is eager—*hungry*—to tell everyone its view of the legal question at the heart of this case. Standing in the way is an obstacle, a technicality of little interest to anyone but the people of We the People, who created it as a barrier against judges' intrusion into their lives. They gave judges, in Article III, only the "judicial Power," a power to decide not abstract questions but real, concrete "Cases" and "Controversies." Yet the plaintiff and the Government agree entirely on what should happen in this lawsuit. They agree that the court below got it right; and they agreed in the court below that the court below that one got it right as well. What, then, are we *doing* here?

The answer lies at the heart of the jurisdictional portion of today's opinion, where a single sentence lays bare the majority's vision of our role. The Court says that we have the power to decide this case because if we did not, then our "primary role in determining the constitutionality of a law" (at least one that "has inflicted real injury on a plaintiff") would "become only secondary to the President's." But wait, the reader wonders— Windsor won below, and so *cured* her injury, and the President was glad to see it. True, says the majority, but judicial review must march on regardless, lest we "undermine the clear dictate of the separation-of-powers principle that when an Act of Congress is alleged to conflict with the Constitution, it is emphatically the province and duty of the judicial department to say what the law is."

That is jaw-dropping. It is an assertion of judicial supremacy over the people's Representatives in Congress and the Executive. It envisions a Supreme Court standing (or rather enthroned) at the apex of government, empowered to decide all constitutional questions, always and everywhere "primary" in its role.

This image of the Court would have been unrecognizable to those who wrote and ratified our national charter. They knew well the dangers of "primary" power, and so created branches of government that would be "perfectly co-ordinate by the terms of their common commission," none of which branches could "pretend to an exclusive or superior right of settling the boundaries between their respective powers." [Federalist No. 49] (J. Madison). The people did this to protect themselves. They did it to guard their right to self-rule against the black-robed supremacy that today's majority finds so attractive. So it was that Madison could confidently state, with no fear of contradiction, that there was nothing of "greater intrinsic value" or "stamped with the authority of more enlightened patrons of liberty" than a government of separate and coordinate powers.

For this reason we are quite forbidden to say what the law is whenever (as today's opinion asserts) " 'an Act of Congress is alleged to conflict with the Constitution.' " We can do so only when that allegation will determine the outcome of a lawsuit, and is contradicted by the other party. The "judicial Power" is not, as the majority believes, the power " 'to say what the law is,' " giving the Supreme Court the "primary role in determining the constitutionality of laws." The majority must have in mind one of the foreign constitutions that pronounces such primacy for its constitutional court and allows that primacy to be exercised in contexts other than a lawsuit. See, *e.g.*, Basic Law for the Federal Republic of Germany, Art. 93. The judicial power as Americans have understood it (and their English ancestors before them) is the power to adjudicate, with conclusive effect, disputed government claims (civil or criminal) against private persons, and disputed claims by private persons against the government or other private persons. Sometimes (though not always) the parties before the court disagree not with regard to the facts of their case (or not *only* with regard to the facts) but with regard to the applicable law—in which event (and *only* in which event) it becomes the " 'province and duty of the judicial department to say what the law is.' "

In other words, declaring the compatibility of state or federal laws with the Constitution is not only not the "primary role" of this Court, it is not a separate, free-standing role *at all*. We perform that role incidentally—by accident, as it were—when that is necessary to resolve the dispute before us. Then, and only then, does it become " 'the province and duty of the judicial department to say what the law is.' " That is why, in 1793, we politely declined the Washington Administration's request to "say what the law is" on a particular treaty matter that was not the subject of a concrete legal controversy. And that is why, as our opinions have said, some questions of law will *never* be presented to this Court, because there will never be anyone with standing to bring a lawsuit. As Justice Brandeis put it, we cannot "pass upon the constitutionality of legislation in a friendly, non-adversary, proceeding"; absent a " 'real, earnest and vital controversy between individuals,' " we have neither any work to do nor any power to do it. Our authority begins and ends with the need to adjudge the rights of an injured party who stands before us seeking redress.

That is completely absent here. Windsor's injury was cured by the judgment in her favor. And while, in ordinary circumstances, the United States is injured by a directive to pay a tax refund, this suit is far from ordinary. Whatever injury the United States has suffered will surely not be redressed by the action that it, as a litigant, asks us to take. The final sentence of the Solicitor General's brief on the merits reads: "For the foregoing reasons, the judgment of the court of appeals *should be affirmed*." That will not cure the Government's injury, but carve it into stone. One could spend many fruitless afternoons ransacking our library for any other petitioner's brief seeking an affirmance of the judgment against it. What the petitioner United States asks us to do in the case before us is exactly what the respondent Windsor asks us to do: not to provide relief from the judgment below but to say that that judgment was correct. And the same was true in the Court of Appeals: Neither party sought to undo the judgment for Windsor, and so that court should have dismissed the appeal (just as we should dismiss) for lack of jurisdiction. Since both parties agreed with the judgment of the District Court for the Southern District of New York, the suit should have ended there. The further proceedings have been a contrivance, having no object in mind except to elevate a District Court judgment that has no precedential effect in other courts, to one that has precedential effect throughout the Second Circuit, and then (in this Court) precedential effect throughout the United States.

We have never before agreed to speak—to "say what the law is"—where there is no controversy before us. In the more than two centuries that this Court has existed as an institution, we have never suggested that we have the power to decide a question when every party agrees with both its nominal opponent *and the court below* on that question's answer. The United States reluctantly conceded that at oral argument.

The closest we have ever come to what the Court blesses today was our opinion in *INS* v. *Chadha*, 462 U.S. 919 (1983). But in that case, two parties to the litigation disagreed with the position of the United States and with the court below: the House and Senate, which had intervened in the case. Because *Chadha* concerned the validity of a mode of congressional action—the one-house legislative veto—the House and Senate were threatened with destruction of what they claimed to be one of their institutional powers. The Executive choosing not to defend that power, we permitted the House and Senate to intervene. Nothing like that is present here.

To be sure, the Court in *Chadha* said that statutory aggrieved-party status was "not altered by the fact that the Executive may agree with the holding that the statute in question is unconstitutional." But in a footnote to that statement, the Court acknowledged Article III's separate requirement of a "justiciable case or controversy," and stated that *this* requirement was satisfied "because of the presence of the two Houses of Congress as adverse parties." Later in its opinion, the *Chadha* Court remarked that the United States' announced intention to enforce the statute also sufficed to permit judicial review, even absent congressional participation. That remark is true, as a description of the judicial review conducted in the Court of Appeals, where the Houses of Congress had not intervened. There, absent a judgment setting aside the INS order, Chadha faced deportation. This passage of our opinion seems to be addressing that initial standing in the Court of Appeals, as indicated by its quotation from the lower court's opinion. But if it was addressing standing to pursue the appeal, the remark was both the purest dictum (as congressional intervention at that point made the required adverseness "beyond doubt"), and quite incorrect. When a private party has a judicial decree safely in hand to prevent his injury, additional judicial action requires that a party injured by the decree *seek to undo it*. In *Chadha*, the intervening House and Senate fulfilled that requirement. Here no one does.

The majority's discussion of the requirements of Article III bears no resemblance to our jurisprudence. It accuses the *amicus* (appointed to argue against our jurisdiction) of "elid[ing] the distinction between . . . the jurisdictional requirements of Article III and the prudential limits on its exercise." It then proceeds to call the requirement of adverseness a "prudential" aspect of standing. *Of standing.* That is incomprehensible. A plaintiff (or appellant) can have all the standing in the world—satisfying all three standing requirements of *Lujan* that the majority so carefully quotes—and yet no Article III controversy may be before the court. Article III requires not just a plaintiff (or appellant) who has standing to complain but *an opposing party* who denies the validity of the complaint. It is not the *amicus* that has done the eliding of distinctions, but the majority, calling the quite separate Article III requirement of adverseness between the parties an element (which it then pronounces a "prudential" element) of standing. The question here is not whether, as the majority puts it, "the United States retains a stake sufficient to support Article III jurisdiction," the question is whether there is any controversy (which requires *contradiction*) between the United States and Ms. Windsor. There is not.
* * *

A few words in response to the theory of jurisdiction set forth in Justice Alito's dissent: Though less far reaching in its consequences than the majority's conversion of constitutionally required adverseness into a discretionary element of standing, the theory of that dissent similarly elevates the Court to the "primary" determiner of constitutional questions involving the separation of powers, and, to boot, increases the power of the most dangerous branch: the "legislative department," which by its nature "draw[s] all power into its impetuous vortex." The Federalist, No. 48, at 309 (J. Madison). Heretofore in our national history, the President's failure to "take Care that the Laws be faithfully executed," U.S. Const., Art. II, § 3, could only be brought before a judicial tribunal by someone whose concrete interests were harmed by that alleged failure. Justice Alito would create a system in which Congress can hale the Executive before the courts not only to vindicate its own institutional powers to act, but to correct a perceived inadequacy in the execution of its laws.

JUSTICE ALITO, with whom **JUSTICE THOMAS** joins as to Parts II and III [but not as to the standing discussion excerpted below], dissenting.

The United States clearly is not a proper petitioner in this case. The United States does not ask us to overturn the judgment of the court below or to alter that judgment in any way. Quite to the contrary, the United States argues emphatically in favor of the correctness of that judgment. We have never before reviewed a decision at the sole behest of a party that took such a position, and to do so would be to render an advisory opinion, in violation of Article III's dictates. For the reasons given in Justice Scalia's dissent, I do not find the Court's arguments to the contrary to be persuasive.

Whether the Bipartisan Legal Advisory Group of the House of Representatives (BLAG) has standing to petition is a much more difficult question. It is also a significantly closer question than whether the interveners in *Hollingsworth* v. *Perry*—which the Court also decides today—have standing to appeal. It is remarkable that the Court has simultaneously decided that the United States, which "receive[d] all that [it] ha[d] sought" below, is a proper petitioner in this case but that the intervenors in *Hollingsworth*, who represent the party that lost in the lower court, are not. In my view, both the *Hollingsworth* interveners and BLAG have standing.

A party invoking the Court's authority has a sufficient stake to permit it to appeal when it has " 'suffered an injury in fact' that is caused by 'the conduct complained of' and that 'will be redressed by a favorable decision.' " In the present case, the House of Representatives, which has authorized BLAG to represent its interests in this matter, suffered just such an injury.

In *INS* v. *Chadha*, 462 U.S. 919 (1983), the Court held that the two Houses of Congress were "proper parties" to file a petition in defense of the constitutionality of the one-house veto statute, *id.*, at 930, n. 5 (internal quotation marks omitted). Accordingly, the Court granted and decided petitions by both the Senate and the House, in addition to the Executive's petition. That the two Houses had standing to petition is not surprising: The Court of Appeals' decision in *Chadha*, by holding the one-house veto to be unconstitutional, had limited Congress' power to legislate. In discussing Article III standing, the Court suggested that Congress suffered a similar injury whenever federal legislation it had passed was struck down, noting that it had "long held that Congress is the proper party to defend the validity of a statute when an agency of government, as a defendant charged with enforcing the statute, agrees with plaintiffs that the statute is inapplicable or unconstitutional."

The United States attempts to distinguish *Chadha* on the ground that it "involved an unusual statute that vested the House and the Senate themselves each with special procedural rights—namely, the right effectively to veto Executive action." But that is a distinction without a difference: just as the Court of Appeals decision that the *Chadha* Court affirmed impaired Congress' power by striking down the one-house veto, so the Second Circuit's decision here impairs Congress' legislative power by striking down an Act of Congress. The United States has not explained why the fact that the impairment at issue in *Chadha* was "special" or "procedural" has any relevance to whether Congress suffered an injury. Indeed, because legislating is Congress' central function, any impairment of that function is a more grievous injury than the impairment of a procedural add-on. * * *

Both the United States and the Court-appointed *amicus* err in arguing that *Raines* v. *Byrd*, 521 U.S. 811 (1997), is to the contrary. In that case, the Court held that Members of Congress who had voted "nay" to the Line Item Veto Act did not have standing to challenge that statute in federal court. *Raines* is inapposite for two reasons. First, *Raines* dealt with individual Members of Congress and specifically pointed to the individual Members' lack of institutional endorsement as a sign of their standing problem: "We attach some importance to the fact that appellees have not been authorized to represent their respective Houses of Congress in this action, and indeed both Houses actively oppose their suit."

Second, the Members in *Raines*—unlike the state senators in *Coleman*—were not the pivotal figures whose votes would have caused the Act to fail absent some challenged action. Indeed, it is telling that *Raines* characterized *Coleman* as standing "for the proposition that legislators whose votes would have been sufficient to defeat (or enact) a specific legislative Act have standing to sue if that legislative action goes into effect (or does not go into effect), on the ground that their votes have been completely nullified." Here, by contrast, passage by the House was needed for DOMA to become law. * * *

I appreciate the argument that the Constitution confers on the President alone the authority to defend federal law in litigation, but in my view, as I have explained, that argument is contrary to the Court's holding in *Chadha*, and it is certainly contrary to the *Chadha* Court's endorsement of the principle that "Congress is the proper party to defend the validity of a statute" when the Executive refuses to do so on constitutional grounds. Accordingly, in the narrow category of cases in which a court strikes down an Act of Congress and the Executive declines to defend the Act, Congress both has standing to defend the undefended statute and is a proper party to do so.

NOTES

1.   *Shifting Votes on Standing in* Hollingsworth *and* Windsor. The following table may help you track the different views of standing in these two cases:

Case	Justices Finding Standing	Justices Finding No Standing
Hollingsworth v. Perry	Kennedy, Thomas, Alito, Sotomayor	Roberts, Scalia, Ginsburg, Kagan, Breyer
United States v. Windsor	Kennedy, Breyer, Kagan, Ginsburg, Sotomayor, Alito (as to interveners)	Scalia, Thomas, Roberts, Alito (as to the government)

Thus, there are four groups of Justices:

1. *Finding standing in both cases*: Kennedy, Sotomayor, Alito (but only as to the interveners in *Windsor*, not the government).

2. *Finding standing in neither case*: Scalia and Roberts.

3. *Finding standing in* Windsor *but not in* Hollingsworth: Breyer, Kagan, and Ginsburg

4. *Finding standing in* Hollingsworth *but not in* Windsor: Thomas

The reasons why various Justices thought they called for different outcomes remains obscure. Yet both cases involve the continuing justiciability of a challenge to a law when the government's executive branch has failed to defend the law.

2. *Reconciling the Cases?* The main distinction between the cases seems to be that the executive branch officials representing the government wanted a judicial resolution in *Windsor* but not in *Hollingsworth*. This is reflected by the fact that the relevant officials continued to enforce the statute in the *Windsor* case but did not attempt to do so in *Hollingsworth*, and that they actually filed appeals (and a cert. petition) on behalf of the government in *Windsor* but did not file an appeal in *Hollingsworth*. Thus, in *Windsor*, the government as an entity was at least nominally before the Court and had a financial interest (since it would have to pay money if the case was affirmed). On the other hand, in *Hollingsworth*, the state was no longer a formal party, and its only continuing interest was the abstract one of having its laws upheld. Is this distinction a sufficient basis for distinguishing the cases?

An alternative but related perspective is that some of the Justices may have put the cases into two different legal frames. The California case fits into a string of cases in which legislators have tried to get standing, with the initiative proponents here having a similar position in the lawmaking process. In contrast, the DOMA case involves another recurrent situation in which the government is a party (not true in the California appeal) but chose not to defend a particular legal position. Given the different framing, it doesn't seem as much in tension with the DOMA ruling.

Or maybe the different treatment of the cases was strategic. Ginsburg, Breyer and Kagan may have felt that an incremental approach was better than deciding the constitutionality of state same-sex marriage restrictions immediately (or perhaps deciding it wrong, depending on Kennedy's view.) Perhaps Thomas wanted to reach the merits in *Hollingsworth* because the district court ruling had statewide effect, whereas in *Windsor* the district court ruling applied only to a single taxpayer.

3.   *The Development of Standing.* Historically, standing law was justified on the theory that a concrete stake in the dispute was needed in order to make the case truly adversarial. By *Windsor*, however, the need for an adversarial contest has faded only into an optional element of standing, which has been recast in separation of powers terms. Consider *Windsor* in this light. Clearly the Court isn't invading the executive's powers—after all, the executive has expressly invited the Court to decide the case. But is there a risk that the executive has too much ability to recruit the Court as an ally against Congress? Yet, wasn't that line crossed in *Chadha*?

4.   *An End-Run Around Hollingsworth.* If the challenge to Proposition 8 had been filed in state court, the state officials would not have been able to terminate the litigation by refusing to appeal. Because the case was filed in federal court, however, the state officials gained this extra control over the litigation, to the benefit of the plaintiffs. This seems anomalous. Future initiative proponents may want to avoid this situation. Could a future initiative appoint the initiative proponents as back-up representatives of the state, who could take over the litigation if the state failed to defend or file an appeal? Would the Supreme Court defer to this appointment as being a matter of state law, or would it still view this as merely a state effort to given the initiative sponsors "a ticket to federal court"?

5.   *Executive Options.* What should the executive branch do when it believes a statute is unconstitutional? Should it continue to enforce the statute, as the Obama Administration did with DOMA? Is it obligated to defend the statute in litigation? Was it appropriate for state officials to drop the case in *Hollingsworth*?

PROBLEM 9–4:
CAN CONGRESS SUE THE PRESIDENT?

The House of Representatives filed suit in late 2014 against President Obama, claiming that he unlawfully delayed implementation of part of the health care law and is also unlawfully funding part of the law in violation of the Appropriation Clause. (That clause provides: "No Money shall be drawn from the Treasury, but in Consequence of Appropriations made by Law.") Does the House have standing? In this connection, consider *Arizona State Legislature v. Arizona Independent Redistricting Comm'n*, ___ U.S. ___, 135 S.Ct. 2652 (2015), where the Court held that the state legislature had standing to challenge a popular initiative stripping it of its control over reapportionment. The legislature challenged the initiative, which transferred control over districting to an independent commission, as a violation of the Elections Clause. That clause grants control of federal election procedures in each state to the "Legislature thereof," subject to Congressional override. The Court rejected the constitutional claim on the merits, holding that the state initiative validly placed legislative control over redistricting in the commission. Justice Scalia argued in dissent that the legislature lacked standing. But according to the Court, the legislature did have standing because the effect of the initiative was to nullify any vote it might hold on districting, "now or in the future," depriving it of its preexisting legal powers. A footnote reserved the question of Congressional standing:

> The case before us does not touch or concern the question whether Congress has standing to bring a suit against the President. There is no federal analogue to Arizona's initiative power, and a suit between Congress and the President would raise separation-of-powers concerns absent here. The Court's standing analysis, we have noted, has been "especially rigorous when reaching the merits of the dispute would force [the Court] to decide whether an action taken by one of the other two branches of the Federal Government was unconstitutional." *Raines v. Byrd,* 521 U.S. 811, 819–820, 117 S.Ct. 2312, 138 L.Ed.2d 849 (1997).

In light of *Windsor* and *Arizona State Legislature*, should the House be granted standing against the President? Which of the House's legal claims has better prospects of surviving a standing challenge? Does the case present a political question?

Justice Kennedy's concurrence in *Lujan* indicated that Congress had some ability to expand the scope of standing, but left the extent of that power unclear, as did the Court's discussion of the *Lujan* concurrence in *Massachusetts v. EPA*. The following case sheds some additional light on that issue.

SPOKEO, INC. V. ROBINS
___ U.S. ___, 136 S.Ct. 1540, 194 L.Ed.2d 635 (2016)

JUSTICE ALITO delivered the opinion of the Court.

This case presents the question whether respondent Robins has standing to maintain an action in federal court against petitioner Spokeo under the Fair Credit Reporting Act of 1970 (FCRA or Act).

Spokeo operates a "people search engine." If an individual visits Spokeo's Web site and inputs a person's name, a phone number, or an e-mail address, Spokeo conducts a computerized search in a wide variety of databases and provides information about the subject of the search. Spokeo performed such a search for information about Robins, and some of the information it gathered and then disseminated was incorrect. When Robins learned of these inaccuracies, he filed a complaint on his own behalf and on behalf of a class of similarly situated individuals.

The District Court dismissed Robins' complaint for lack of standing, but a panel of the Ninth Circuit reversed. The Ninth Circuit noted, first, that Robins had alleged that "Spokeo violated *his* statutory rights, not just the statutory rights of other people," and, second, that "Robins's personal interests in the handling of his credit information are individualized rather than collective." Based on these two observations, the Ninth Circuit held that Robins had adequately alleged injury in fact, a requirement for standing under Article III of the Constitution.

This analysis was incomplete. As we have explained in our prior opinions, the injury-in-fact requirement requires a plaintiff to allege an injury that is both "concrete *and* particularized." The Ninth Circuit's analysis focused on the second characteristic (particularity), but it overlooked the first (concreteness). We therefore vacate the decision below and remand for the Ninth Circuit to consider *both* aspects of the injury-in-fact requirement.

The Constitution confers limited authority on each branch of the Federal Government. It vests Congress with enumerated "legislative Powers," Art. I, § 1; it confers upon the President "[t]he executive Power," Art. II, § 1, cl. 1; and it endows the federal courts with "[t]he judicial Power of the United States," Art. III, § 1. In order to remain faithful to this tripartite structure, the power of the Federal Judiciary may not be permitted to intrude upon the powers given to the other branches.

Although the Constitution does not fully explain what is meant by "[t]he judicial Power of the United States," Art. III, § 1, it does specify that this power extends only to "Cases" and "Controversies," Art. III, § 2. And " '[n]o principle is more fundamental to the judiciary's proper role in our system of government than the constitutional limitation of federal-court jurisdiction to actual cases or controversies.' "

Standing to sue is a doctrine rooted in the traditional understanding of a case or controversy. The doctrine developed in our case law to ensure that federal courts do not exceed their authority as it has been traditionally understood. The doctrine limits the category of litigants empowered to maintain a lawsuit in federal court to seek redress for a legal wrong. In this way, "[t]he law of Article III standing . . . serves to prevent the judicial process from being used to usurp the powers of the political branches," and confines the federal courts to a properly judicial role.

Our cases have established that the "irreducible constitutional minimum" of standing consists of three elements. The plaintiff must have (1) suffered an injury in fact, (2) that is fairly traceable to the challenged conduct of the defendant, and (3) that is likely to be redressed by a favorable judicial decision. The plaintiff, as the party invoking federal jurisdiction, bears the burden of establishing these elements. Where, as here, a case is at the pleading stage, the plaintiff must "clearly . . . allege facts demonstrating" each element.

This case primarily concerns injury in fact, the "[f]irst and foremost" of standing's three elements. Injury in fact is a constitutional requirement, and "[i]t is settled that Congress cannot erase Article III's standing requirements by statutorily granting the right to sue to a plaintiff who would not otherwise have standing."

To establish injury in fact, a plaintiff must show that he or she suffered "an invasion of a legally protected interest" that is "concrete and particularized" and "actual or imminent, not conjectural or hypothetical." We discuss the particularization and concreteness requirements below.

For an injury to be "particularized," it "must affect the plaintiff in a personal and individual way."

Particularization is necessary to establish injury in fact, but it is not sufficient. An injury in fact must also be "concrete." Under the Ninth Circuit's analysis, however, that independent requirement was elided. As previously noted, the Ninth Circuit concluded that Robins' complaint alleges "concrete, *de facto*" injuries for essentially two reasons. First, the court noted that Robins "alleges that Spokeo violated *his* statutory rights, not just the statutory rights of other people." Second, the court wrote that "Robins's personal interests in the handling of his credit information are *individualized rather than collective.*" Both of these observations concern particularization, not concreteness. We have made it clear time and time again that an injury in fact must be both concrete *and* particularized.

A "concrete" injury must be *"de facto"*; that is, it must actually exist. See Black's Law Dictionary 479 (9th ed. 2009). When we have used the adjective "concrete," we have meant to convey the usual meaning of the term—"real," and not "abstract." Webster's Third New International Dictionary 472 (1971); Random House Dictionary of the English Language 305 (1967). Concreteness, therefore, is quite different from particularization.

"Concrete" is not, however, necessarily synonymous with "tangible." Although tangible injuries are perhaps easier to recognize, we have confirmed in many of our previous cases that intangible injuries can nevertheless be concrete.

In determining whether an intangible harm constitutes injury in fact, both history and the judgment of Congress play important roles. Because the doctrine of standing derives from the case-or-controversy requirement, and because that requirement in turn is grounded in historical practice, it is instructive to consider whether an alleged intangible harm has a close relationship to a harm that has traditionally been regarded as providing a basis for a lawsuit in English or American courts. In addition, because

Congress is well positioned to identify intangible harms that meet minimum Article III requirements, its judgment is also instructive and important. Thus, we said in *Lujan* that Congress may "elevat[e] to the status of legally cognizable injuries concrete, *de facto* injuries that were previously inadequate in law." Similarly, Justice Kennedy's concurrence in that case explained that "Congress has the power to define injuries and articulate chains of causation that will give rise to a case or controversy where none existed before."

Congress' role in identifying and elevating intangible harms does not mean that a plaintiff automatically satisfies the injury-in-fact requirement whenever a statute grants a person a statutory right and purports to authorize that person to sue to vindicate that right. Article III standing requires a concrete injury even in the context of a statutory violation. For that reason, Robins could not, for example, allege a bare procedural violation, divorced from any concrete harm, and satisfy the injury-in-fact requirement of Article III.

This does not mean, however, that the risk of real harm cannot satisfy the requirement of concreteness. For example, the law has long permitted recovery by certain tort victims even if their harms may be difficult to prove or measure. See, *e.g.*, Restatement (First) of Torts §§ 569 (libel), 570 (slander *per se*) (1938). Just as the common law permitted suit in such instances, the violation of a procedural right granted by statute can be sufficient in some circumstances to constitute injury in fact. In other words, a plaintiff in such a case need not allege any *additional* harm beyond the one Congress has identified.

In the context of this particular case, these general principles tell us two things: On the one hand, Congress plainly sought to curb the dissemination of false information by adopting procedures designed to decrease that risk. On the other hand, Robins cannot satisfy the demands of Article III by alleging a bare procedural violation. A violation of one of the FCRA's procedural requirements may result in no harm. For example, even if a consumer reporting agency fails to provide the required notice to a user of the agency's consumer information, that information regardless may be entirely accurate. In addition, not all inaccuracies cause harm or present any material risk of harm. An example that comes readily to mind is an incorrect zip code. It is difficult to imagine how the dissemination of an incorrect zip code, without more, could work any concrete harm.

Because the Ninth Circuit failed to fully appreciate the distinction between concreteness and particularization, its standing analysis was incomplete. It did not address the question framed by our discussion, namely, whether the particular procedural violations alleged in this case entail a degree of risk sufficient to meet the concreteness requirement. We take no position as to whether the Ninth Circuit's ultimate conclusion—that Robins adequately alleged an injury in fact—was correct.

NOTES

1.   *What Decision on Remand?* In dissent, Justice Ginsburg argued that the complaint easily satisfied the concreteness requirement:

> In particular, Robins alleged that Spokeo posted "a picture . . . purport[ing] to be an image of Robins [that] was not in fact [of him]," and incorrectly reported that Robins "was in his 50s, . . . married, . . . employed in a professional or technical field, and . . . has children." Robins further alleged that Spokeo's profile of him continues to misrepresent "that he has a graduate degree, that his economic health is 'Very Strong[,]' and that his wealth level [is in] the 'Top 10%.' " Spokeo displayed that erroneous information, Robins asserts, when he was "out of work" and "actively seeking employment." Because of the misinformation, Robins stated, he encountered "[imminent and ongoing] actual harm to [his] employment prospects." As Robins elaborated on brief, Spokeo's report made him appear overqualified for jobs he might have gained, expectant of a higher salary than employers would be willing to pay, and less mobile because of family responsibilities.

As you read the Court's opinion, are these allegations sufficient?

2.   *How Far Can Congress Expand Standing After* Spokeo? The Court quotes with approval Justice Kennedy's language in *Lujan* to the effect that Congress can provide remedies for injuries that were previously unrecognized by the law and that it can also identify chains of causation that will then qualify legally as traceable. In terms of the concreteness requirement, the Court says, "[B]ecause Congress is well positioned to identify intangible harms that meet minimum Article III requirements, its judgment is also instructive and important." But how does Congress go about identifying such intangible harms? Is it sufficient if a statute grants standing for redress of a type of harm or does Congress have to make some specific finding about concreteness? What are the limits on the idea of concreteness? For instance, could Congress find that a reasonable fear of government surveillance is a concrete harm? Could it grant standing to challenge a threat to an endangered species to any scientist who studies the species or works professionally with members of the species? Recall that the Court had found neither type of injury sufficient to establish standing in the *Lujan* case.